CUMBRIA LIBRARIES
3800304700136 7

KT-568-542

In God's Hands

POPE ST JOHN PAUL II
KAROL WOJTYŁA

In God's Hands

The spiritual diaries
1962–2003

Translated by
JOANNA RZEPA

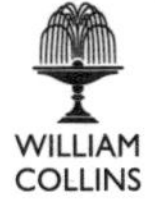

William Collins
An imprint of HarperCollins*Publishers*
1 London Bridge Street, London, SE1 9GF.

WilliamCollinsBooks.com
First published by William Collins in 2017

A catalogue record for this book is available from the British Library.

HB ISBN 978-0-00-810105-3
TPB ISBN 978-0-00-822557-5
eBook ISBN 978-0-00-810106-0

Typeset in Minion

Printed and bound in Great Britain by Clays Ltd, St Ives plc.

Contents

Introduction

Not since the publication of *Journal of a Soul*, the spiritual autobiography of Pope John XXIII, have we had such privileged access into the spirituality of a pope. This is what we have been given with the publication in English of the spiritual diaries of Pope John Paul II. *In God's Hands* has already been published in his native Poland and in Italy where it has been a phenomenal success. English-speaking readers will now benefit from the extraordinary insights of this spiritual journal.

The two notebooks from which it is drawn are not chronological. However, the first covers the years 1962–1984, whilst the second includes notes at retreats given to the Pope and Roman curia between the years 1985 and 2003. The electrifying element in this publication are the pages of handwritten reflections, explanations and prayers bearing characteristic insights of Pope John Paul II. There is an Ignatian structure to much of his response to the various presentations, homilies, feast days, Liturgy of the Hours and Mass celebrated during the retreats. This structure enables an amazing personal response to take place, with the unique ability to link such thoughts and texts to his own inner life as well as to the public ministry he was called to exercise in the Church and in the world.

In God's Hands is unusual in that the immediacy of the Pope's response is given, not just through his handwriting, but in the deepest thoughts elicited by the presentations of the retreat givers. This is not a sedate, refined or sanitised journal of devotion. It allows the reader to follow the different paths which lay before one who was sincerely discerning the will and plan of God unfolding in his own life.

In all this, the leitmotif of obedience to the will of God is obvious not least in his episcopal motto '*Totus Tuus*'. In his devotion to Mary, Pope John Paul II saw someone who was attentive to the will of God, the woman who listened, the woman who believed that God's plan could be fulfilled through her obedience. By the same token, that obedience, which is based on prayerful listening and the response which follows, was the foundation of the dynamism he was able to bring to the papal ministry.

'Prayer is the language of our hope' wrote Cardinal Ratzinger, quoted in one of the spiritual conferences eliciting a very full entry in the retreat notes. Herein lies another path to the heart of the love of God when 'Heart speaks to heart' (Cardinal Newman) but always in the silence of the heart. Of course intercession is part of the prayer of Pope John Paul II as he prays for the needs of the world and the Church and all people. But it is in his prayer of adoration and contemplation that he comes to know himself as he is known. This is the path of the mystic, recognising that heaven is '. . . a space that Christ made for man in God' (Ratzinger). This is also what allowed the Pope to spend time alone with God in prayer '. . . at the morning watch and even in the night' (*De profundis*). So often, such waiting on God is regarded as a waste of time. The act of faith that gives the time and space to such contemplation says that no time is wasted in which God is served. The service of God is the sanctification of time. No time is sanctified more than when it is a pure gift, given in faith with no other expectation than to 'be' in the presence of God. This is the prayer which permeates these diaries of Karol Wojtyła.

There is another language of prayer with which he was intimately familiar: the language of suffering. From the devastating attempt on his life in St Peter's Square on 13 May 1981, and the burden of ill health he subsequently bore, suffering was part of the reality of who he was. Old age and increasing infirmity limited his physical resources in ways which were surely both Calvary and cross to this once energetic man and skilled communicator. Even when he could no longer speak, he did not hide himself away from those who came to see and hear him. He had preached often on the meaning of the suffering of Jesus on Calvary and the significance of the cross in the suffering that each person has to bear. Now he was able to personify that teaching in his own weakness and vulnerability. The final pages of his diaries have lost the intensity and vigour of all that went before. It is significant that the last two entries touch closely the heart of his life and ministry: Mary, his patron and hope, standing at the foot of the cross followed by a meditation entitled, 'Jonah, or the fear of preaching the love of God'.

Having stood with Mary in her faithfulness throughout his life and having preached the love of God on the worldwide stage, now was the time to return to the Father. His final words on his deathbed were: 'Let me go to the house of the Lord' (Psalm 122). In the first chapter of the Gospel of John we read of the disciples of the Baptist asking Jesus, 'Master, where are you staying?' Jesus said to them, 'Come and see' (John 1:38). *In God's Hands* is a chronicle of one who responded to that invitation in prayer and in faith every day of his life.

+George Stack
Archbishop of Cardiff
Chair of the Department of Christian Life and Worship of the Bishops' Conference of England and Wales

Introduction to the Polish Edition

We present the reader with a book that covers the content of the two notebooks in which Bishop Karol Wojtyła, and later Pope John Paul II took personal notes and recorded his reflections, which related primarily to the retreats and reflection days which he attended between 1962 and 2003.

The text has not been abbreviated in any way. We have attempted to maintain the layout of the notebooks' pages, as well as any additional notation: underlining, textboxes, etc.; the marginalia are presented in the same way as in the original notebooks.

The words that were impossible to read are marked as [illegible].

The editorial interventions consisted in the following:

- restoration of the chronological order in the entries from the first notebook;
- translation of phrases and sentences recorded in foreign languages (mainly in Latin and Italian);
- correction of obvious spelling and punctuation mistakes;
- expansion of the abbreviations used in the reflections to facilitate reading; if these abbreviations were not easy to decipher, they were retained in their original form.

All editorial insertions are marked by square brackets.

Translator's Note

Pope John Paul II's notebooks were first published in Polish in 2014, and soon afterwards translated into several languages, including Italian, French, German, Romanian and Portuguese. It is a great joy to present the English-speaking reader with this translation. In order to help the reader fully to appreciate the richness of John Paul II's thought, the English edition provides notes with references to biblical quotations and other important sources used by John Paul II, as well as additional background information on people, places and events mentioned in particular entries. All biblical quotations are given according to the Revised Standard Version Catholic Edition. For other sources, wherever possible, full references are given to the editions used by John Paul II and to existing English translations. When citing from John Paul II's speeches and homilies delivered in Polish, I used the existing Vatican translations with minor adjustments where necessary. To make the edition more accessible, Latin names of regular prayers and services have been translated into English. The edition has greatly benefitted from Dr Mátê Vince's expertise in Latin and Greek, and Dr Andrea Selleri's assistance with Italian. I gratefully acknowledge their help.

Preface by the Metropolitan Archbishop of Kraków, Stanisław Cardinal Dziwisz

'I leave no possessions of which it will be necessary to dispose. As for the things I use every day, I ask that they be distributed as seems appropriate. Let my personal notes be burned. I ask that Fr Stanisław see to this, and I thank him for his kind help and collaboration over the years. I leave all my other "thank yous" in my heart before God Himself, because it is difficult to put them in words' (John Paul II, *Testament*, 6 March 1979).

This is the instruction that the Holy Father John Paul II left in his Testament. After his death in 2005, I faithfully fulfilled the Holy Father's will, giving away all his possessions, especially the personal memorabilia. I did not dare to burn the personal notes and notebooks that he had left behind because they contain significant information about his life. I saw them on the Holy Father's desk, but I never looked into them. When I saw his Testament, I was moved that John Paul II, whom I had accompanied for almost forty years, had entrusted me with his personal affairs.

I did not burn John Paul II's notes because they are a key to understanding his spirituality, that is, what is innermost in a person: his relationship to God, to other men and to himself. They reveal, so to speak, another side of the person whom we knew as the Bishop of Kraków and Rome, the Peter of our times, the Shepherd of the universal Church. They show his early life, in the years when he was ordained a bishop and installed in the Diocese of Kraków. They allow us to get a glimpse of the intimate, personal relationship of faith with

God the Creator, the Giver of life, the Master and Teacher. At the same time, they present the sources of his spirituality – his inner strength and his determined will to serve Christ until the last breath of life.

When I return to John Paul II's notes, I can see the figure of the Holy Father in the home chapel at Franciszkańska Street,[1] as he prays immersed in God, before the Blessed Sacrament, and I hear his sighs coming from the little chapel at the Apostolic Palace in the Vatican. His radiant face never revealed his inner experiences. He always looked at the cross and the icon of Our Lady of Częstochowa with courage. He learnt from her to surrender himself to God entirely, repeating the words of Louis-Marie Grignion de Montfort: *Totus Tuus ego sum, o Maria, et omnia mea Tua sunt* – 'I am entirely Yours, O Mary, and all that is mine is Yours'. Complete surrender to God in Mary's likeness and the fulfilling of God's will until the end were the characteristic traits of this man of prayer, who discovered the abundant world of the spirit in his relationship with God.

May reading the spiritual notebooks of John Paul II help everyone discover the spiritual depth of the people of the twenty-first century, and may it lead everyone to a greater love of God and other people.

Stanisław Cardinal Dziwisz,
Metropolitan Archbishop of Kraków
On the Feast of the Presentation of the Blessed Virgin Mary,
the Patron Saint of the Parish in Wadowice[2]
Kraków, 21 November 2013

1 The Bishop's Palace in Kraków, where Pope John Paul II resided as Bishop of Kraków (1958–78) and where he stayed during his papal visits to the city, is located at Franciszkańska Street.
2 Wadowice, a small city in southern Poland, was the birthplace of Pope John Paul II.

The Secret of Father Karol Wojtyła – Pope John Paul II's Spiritual Notes

Karol Wojtyła–John Paul II's personal notes already aroused interest at the time of his death. The Pope wrote in his Testament that Fr Stanisław Dziwisz, his personal secretary and closest collaborator, who had accompanied him for the nearly forty years of his episcopal service in Kraków and the Petrine ministry in Rome, should burn the notes. Fr Dziwisz, the current Metropolitan Archbishop of Kraków, did not burn them out of respect for their author, but presented them to the Congregation for the Causes of Saints, which examined the life of the Holy Father in the beatification process. A glimpse at the notes was enough to see that their author led a rich spiritual life that embraced all dimensions of his work.

The spiritual notes reveal the depth of Karol Wojtyła's life with God during the many years (1962–2003) when he served as Auxiliary Bishop, and then Archbishop of Kraków, Cardinal and Pope. They shed light on the secret of the heart of the Peter of our times, who was Bishop of Kraków in the difficult period of communism, and then for almost twenty-seven years led the Barque of St Peter through the turbulent waves of the twentieth and twenty-first centuries. The spiritual notes contain reflections on inner experiences, resolutions, prayers, meditations and remarks on spiritual progress. They express, above all, their author's relationship to God, who was the centre of his inner life.

1. Two notebooks

The spiritual notes were recorded in two notebooks: in the diaries 'Agenda 1962' and '1985'. Both diaries were printed in Italy by the Archdiocese of Milan.

In the first notebook, the author introduced his own page numbering, from 1 to 220. However, the notes are not ordered chronologically: the first entry is devoted to the retreat that Archbishop Karol Wojtyła attended with the Polish Bishops' Conference at Jasna Góra from 1 to 4 September 1971. In the following pages we find notes from earlier years – beginning with 1962 – which are interwoven with later retreats. The author recorded entries according to his own system and put together personal and spiritual experiences from various years.

The notes in this notebook cover the years when Karol Wojtyła was Auxiliary Bishop and Metropolitan Archbishop of Kraków, and include meditations from days of reflection and private retreats at Kalwaria Zebrzydowska; at the Benedictine Abbey in Tyniec; in Zakopane, at Jaszczurówka, at the Ursulines of the Agonizing Heart of Jesus; at the Bachledówka Pauline Monastery; in Kraków, in the district of Prądnik, at the Albertine Sisters', in the so-called 'cottage' (the house situated in the garden of the motherhouse of the Albertine Sisters' Convent at 10 Woronicza Street); at the Albertine Sisters' in Rząska; and the annual retreats of the Polish Bishops' Conference at Jasna Góra and in Gniezno. The first notebook also contains the notes from the first six years of John Paul II's pontificate. The notes end with the reflections on the retreat led by Cardinal Alexandre do Nascimento on 11–17 March 1984 in the Vatican.

The second notebook originally belonged to the Pope's Secretary, Monsignor Emery Kabongo, as witness the erased signature on the first page and the embossed paper seal. The centre of the seal contains the abbreviation 'EK' and the edge reads 'Library of Emery Kabongo'. These notes cover the years 1985–2003. They begin on the page dated 5 January and continue over the next 315 pages, not all of which have been written over.

Thus, the notes taken by Cardinal Wojtyła–Pope John Paul II can be organised in the following way:

The first notebook contains notes covering the years 1962–1984 and focuses on the following events:

- the retreat before leaving for Rome (8 July and 2 September 1962) [in this book p. 1]
- the retreat (*Dies recollectionis*) after the arrival in Rome for the first session of the Second Vatican Council (9 and 14 October 1962) [p. 2]
- the retreat on the anniversary of priestly ordination at the Felician Sisters' Convent in Rome (31 October–4 November 1962) [p. 5]
- the retreat at Kalwaria – The Shrine of Our Lady (6–7 July 1963?) [p. 12]
- the retreat in Tyniec (19–23 August 1963) [p. 13]
- the retreat before the installation ceremony in Wawel Cathedral (5–8 March 1964) [p. 20]
- the retreat at Jasna Góra led by Bishop Kazimierz Józef Kowalski (31 August–3 September 1964) [p. 23]
- the retreat in Tyniec (17–20 August 1965) [p. 30]
- the retreat at [?unknown] (7 November–2 December 1964?/1965?) [p. 36]
- the retreat at Kalwaria Zebrzydowska (31 October–1 November 1966) [p. 37]
- the retreat at the Albertine Sisters' Convent (19–21 December 1966) [p. 38]
- the retreat at [?unknown] (29 February 1968) [p. 44]
- the retreat in Tyniec (11–14 September 1968) [p. 45]
- the retreat at Bachledówka (9–13 August 1969) [p. 51]
- the retreat in Tyniec (4–7 November and 19 December 1970) [p. 60]
- the retreat at Jasna Góra led by Bishop Lech Kaczmarek (1–5 September 1971) [p. 67]
- the retreat at Kalwaria Zebrzydowska (5–6 July 1973) [p. 75]
- the retreat at Bachledówka (9–12 August 1973) [p. 76]
- the retreat at [?unknown] 4 July–24 August 1974 [p. 86]

- the retreat in Gniezno led by Bishop Jerzy Ablewicz (3–7 September 1974) [p. 87]
- the retreat at Bachledówka (4–8 July 1975) [p. 99]
- the retreat in Jaszczurówka (21–26 September 1976) [p. 107]
- the retreat at Kalwaria Zebrzydowska (5–9 July 1977) [p. 117]
- the retreat at Kalwaria Zebrzydowska (26–29 June 1978) [p. 126]
- election to papacy (October 1978) [p. 136]
- the Vatican retreats led by:
  - Father Faustino Ossanna OFM (4–10 March 1979) [p. 137]
  - Archbishop Lucas Moreira Neves OP (24 February–1 March 1980) [p. 149]
  - Bishop Jerzy Ablewicz (8–14 March 1981) [p. 168]
  - Father Stanislas Lyonnet SJ (28 February–6 March 1982) [p. 189]
  - Cardinal Joseph Ratzinger (20–26 February 1983) [p. 205]
  - Cardinal Alexandre do Nascimento (11–17 March 1984) [p. 221].

The second notebook covers the years 1985–2003 and the retreats led by:

- Archbishop Achille Glorieux (24 February–2 March 1985) [p. 235]
- Father Egidio Viganò SDB (16–22 February 1986) [p. 247]
- Father Peter-Hans Kolvenbach SJ (8–14 March 1987) [p. 265]
- Archbishop James Aloysius Hickey (21–27 February 1988) [p. 283]
- Cardinal Giacomo Biffi (12–18 February 1989) [p. 299]
- Father Georges Cottier OP (4–10 March 1990) [p. 316]
- Archbishop Ersilio Tonini (17–23 February 1991) [p. 333]
- Cardinal Ugo Poletti (8–14 March 1992) [p. 346]
- Bishop Jorge Arturo Agustín Medina Estévez (28 February–6 March 1993) [p. 363]

- Cardinal Giovanni Saldarini (20–26 February 1994) [p. 379]
- Father Tomáš Špidlík SJ (5–11 March 1995) [p. 395]
- Archbishop Christoph Schönborn (25 February–2 March 1996) [p. 400]
- Cardinal Roger Etchegaray (16–22 February 1997) [p. 419]
- Cardinal Ján Chryzostom Korec SJ (1–7 March 1998) [p. 433]
- Bishop André-Joseph Mutien Léonard (21–27 February 1999) [p. 448]
- Archbishop François Xavier Nguyễn Văn Thuận (12–18 March 2000) [p. 454]
- Cardinal Francis Eugene George OMI (4–10 March 2001) [p. 467]
- Cardinal Cláudio Hummes OFM (17–23 February 2002) [p. 475]
- Bishop Angelo Comastri (9–15 March 2003) [p. 479].

The entries in both notebooks were written in Polish. However, the author often introduced phrases in Latin and Italian, especially during the Vatican retreats. The Vatican retreats for the Holy Father and the Roman Curia were always preached in Italian.

2. The schedule of a retreat day

The daily schedule played an important role in the retreats and days of reflection. The order of the retreat that was developed in Kraków, when Bishop Karol Wojtyła began his ministry, included three talks; *Lectio spiritualis* – spiritual reading; *Corona Rosarii* – Rosary; *Via crucis* – the Way of the Cross; *Adoratio* – Adoration; *Matutinum* – Matins; *Lectio* – reading; *Sacrum* or *Officium Eucharisticum* – Holy Mass or Eucharist; *Vesperae* – Vespers; *Adoratio Sanctissimi Sacramenti* – Adoration of the Blessed Sacrament; *Completorium* – Compline.

During the retreats, Archbishop Karol Wojtyła followed the Ignatian method. He became familiar with this method in the seminary under the guidance of Fr Stanisław Smoleński, who was later made Auxiliary Bishop of Kraków. The method involved preparing a detailed outline of a topic for reflection and spiritual reading. During his episcopal ministry in Kraków, Archbishop Wojtyła led retreats and days of reflection himself, consulting Bishop Smoleński or Fr Aleksander Fedorowicz on spiritual topics. The latter was the spiritual father of the Lwów Seminary in Kalwaria Zebrzydowska in the 1960s, and then the spiritual director at the Laski Centre, near Warsaw. He would also come to Rome and offer counsel to the Holy Father.

This method of reflection allowed Fr Wojtyła to organise the whole retreat or reflection day according to a characteristic plan. The rhythm of the retreat day was set out by the breviary, which was recited according to the pre-conciliar method, with Matins, Lauds (laudatory prayers), Terce, Sext and Nones. Almost every day included:

- *Laudes* – Lauds
- *Meditatio ante Sacrum* – meditation before Holy Mass
- *Sacrum* – Holy Mass
- *Gratarium actio* – thanksgiving
- *Lectio S. Scripturae* – reading the Holy Scriptures
- *Meditatio* – meditation
- *Via crucis* – the Way of the Cross
- *Vesperae* – Vespers
- *Adoratio* – Adoration
- *Rosarium* – Rosary
- *Lectio spiritualis* – spiritual reading
- *Meditatio* – meditation
- *Matutinum anticipatum* – anticipated Matins
- *Lectio S. Scripturae* – reading the Holy Scriptures
- *Rosarium* – Rosary
- *Completa* – Compline
- *Hora Sancta* (*Sacra*) – Holy Hour
- *Lectio* – reading.

Bishop Wojtyła remained faithful to this order of reflection days and retreats throughout his life, which is evident in his later notes, in particular the notes from the period when he was pope.

3. The content of the notes

The notes taken during the retreats reflect the quality of Bishop Wojtyła's and Pope John Paul II's spirit. They show how spiritually sensitive he was to the problems that the Church in Poland and the Church in the world faced. He took the effort to prepare the topics of reflection days and private retreats by himself. At the retreat that he attended together with the Polish Bishops' Conference, he used the retreat leader's thoughts to develop his own reflection on his relationship with God and the ways in which he should fulfil his episcopal duties, which gave meaning to his life.

The author of the notes appears to be an extraordinarily regular and well-organised person, focused on spiritual topics. He refrains from describing his emotional states, current affairs and people involved in them. His entire focus is on the extent to which he can reflect Christ in his own life – Christ the Highest Priest. At the end of his entries, the Pope often adds the abbreviation: AMDG/UIOGD – *Ad maiorem Dei gloriam / Ut in omnibus glorificetur Deus* (For the greater glory of God / That in all things God may be glorified).

A characteristic feature of the notes is their Christocentrism. Fr Wojtyła related all his experiences to Christ, the Highest Priest. He sought to establish a personal contact with Him through regular prayer, meditation on the word of God and pastoral service. He related to Christ all his personal affairs and problems, which he had to face as diocesan bishop, cardinal and pope.

At the centre of all of Fr Wojtyła's days was the Holy Mass. He prepared for it through the morning meditation, thanksgiving after the Holy Mass and during the day, as well as the Holy Hour in the evening, before the Blessed Sacrament. For Fr Wojtyła, the Eucharist was the space where he could experience Christ's sacrifice and, at the same time, offer his own life as a sacrifice to God. It was his style of life, which consisted in the surrender of his own self, just as Christ gave up His life on the cross. Through the daily celebration of the Holy Mass, Fr Wojtyła was united with the unique sacrifice of Christ and entered into a personal relationship with the Triune God: Father, Son and Holy Spirit.

The Marian theme is another important feature of the notes. It is developed around the theology and spirituality of St Louis-Marie Grignion de Montfort (*Treatise on True Devotion to The Blessed Virgin Mary*). Mary appears in Fr Wojtyła's prayers and reflections as the One who received and fulfilled God's will in the most perfect way. Fr Wojtyła underlines Her greatness, which was expressed in the wonderful gift of divine grace that She received as the Mother of the incarnate Word. At the same time, the Holy Father considered Mary a person who was mature in faith and who, taking the decision to say '*fiat*' – let it be to me according to Your word – became a partaker in the divine plan of salvation.

4. Faithfulness until the end

In the last years of his life, John Paul II's notes became sparser. The Holy Father took note of the topic of the retreat and the order of the day. There is less of his own reflections. It is evident that he found writing more and more difficult. His handwriting also changed and became more irregular.

In 2005, the Vatican retreat was led by Bishop Renato Corti from Novara, who in accordance with the tradition gave talks in the Redemptoris Mater Chapel on 13–19 February. The topic of the retreat was: 'The Church in the service of the new and eternal covenant' ('*La Chiesa a servizio della nuova ed eterna alleanza*'). John Paul II took part in this retreat by listening to the radio broadcast from the chapel. He listened to all the talks and participated in the Spiritual Exercises, which he practised privately during retreats. He was accompanied by his personal secretary, Archbishop Stanisław Dziwisz, and other members of the household. The notebooks contained only the printed programme of this retreat, which the Holy Father held in his hand while listening to Bishop Corti's talks. John Paul II remained faithful to the tradition of annual retreats. His last retreat was made complete through his suffering, which became a special mark in his spiritual diary.

Fr Jan Machniak[1]

1 Father Jan Machniak (b. 1957) is a professor of spiritual theology at the Pontifical University of John Paul II in Kraków.

The Retreats

NOTE | NOTE

Recoll. (rocz.)

Praenotanda: 1962.

8.VII. ustawiono główne tematy rekol., które też zostały omówione z ojcem: 1) miłość
2) władza
3) twórczość
4) osoby

2.IX. przypomnienie tych 3 tematów i nowum (jakby wydobycie wspólnego mianownika wszystkich doświadczeń i przemyśleń): jestem bardzo w rękach Bożych – zawartość owego „Totus Tuus" otwarła się niejako w nowym miejscu. Gdy jakakolwiek sprawa staje się „moją" staje się w ten sposób własnością Maryi, można się jej podejmować, choćby nawet zawierała w sobie ryzyko. (chociaż nie wolno szafować: po ludzku tj. od strony wszystkich musi ona także być należycie opracowana. Od pewnego jednakże miejsca trzeba opuszczać rachuby ludzkie i jakoś chwytać Boże czynniki każdej trudnej sprawy. Zazębiają się tutaj dziwnie ściśle sprawy ze sprawami Bo

APPUNTAMENTI

Wszystko to także omówiłem z ojcem

18.IX.

1962
Recollectio (inter.) [Inner retreat]
Praenotanda [Introduction]

~

8 July The following key inner topics have been put together and discussed with the father:

1. death
2. power
3. creativity
4. people.

2 September The recollection of these topics and *novum* [novelty] (as if a common denominator was found for all the experiences and reflections): I am very much in God's hands – the content of this '*Totus Tuus*' ['Entirely Yours'][1] opened, so to speak, in a new place. When any concern 'of mine' becomes in this way Mary's, it can be undertaken, even if it involves an element of risk (though one must not overdo it: in human terms, i.e. on the human side, the issue needs to be dealt with thoroughly). At a certain point, however, one needs to abandon human calculations and somehow grasp the Godly dimensions of every difficult issue. A peculiar *iunctim* [junction] of issue 4 with issue 2 begins to emerge here.

I discussed all this with the father too.

---

1 The phrase '*Totus Tuus*' ('Entirely Yours'), which was John Paul II's apostolic motto, comes from a Marian prayer composed by St Louis-Marie Grignion de Montfort: '*Totus tuus ego sum, et omnia mea tua sunt. Accipio te in mea omnia. Praebe mihi cor tuum, Maria.*' ('I am entirely yours, and all that I have is yours. I take you for my all. O Mary, give me your heart.') In *Crossing the Threshold of Hope* (New York, 1994), John Paul II wrote: 'Totus Tuus. This phrase is not only an expression of piety, or simply an expression of devotion. It is more. During the Second World War, while I was employed as a factory worker, I came to be attracted to Marian devotion. At first, it had seemed to me that I should distance myself a bit from the Marian devotion of my childhood, in order to focus more on Christ. Thanks to Saint Louis de Montfort, I came to understand that true devotion to the Mother of God is actually Christocentric, indeed, it is very profoundly rooted in the Mystery of the Blessed Trinity, and the mysteries of the Incarnation and Redemption' (pp. 212–13).

1962
Dies recollectionis (sequ.) [Reflection days (continuation)] after the arrival in Rome for the first session of the Second Vatican Council

9 October Holy Mass; Lauds; Prime

I participated in the '*capella papalis*' ['solemn papal ceremonies'] on the fourth anniversary of the death of the late Pope Pius XII, thanks to whom I became a bishop. Thoughts: (a) moving from external to internal vision, I have realised that all those present are connected in one spirit and it is the Spirit of Christ, the Son of God. I experienced this unity in diversity very clearly, and with various degrees of participation taken into account. Not a gathering of many separate units, but the unity of substance. It is the substance of thought, doctrine – and it is attended to by the Pope and the Council. But it is also the substance of life, morals, which we realise within the one Church, through, above all, the *mysterium* (sacraments): the unity of our sacrificial posture with Christ's, sealed with the Communion; (b) a background thought that came to me was about the truth of priesthood and episcopacy, which was also given to me from within Christ's priesthood through His Vicar on earth (*Vicarius Christi*).[1]

Adoration: Christ is entirely within the Church and the Church is entirely within Christ. NB I constantly need to remind myself to wish for a good shepherd for the seat of St Stanislaus above all and fundamentally, without allowing for any '*mea*' ['mine'].[2]

---

1 *Vicarius Christi* (Vicar of Christ) is one of the titles held by the pope.

2 That is: 'my biases'. St Stanislaus (Stanisław) of Szczepanów (1030–79) was a bishop of Kraków who was martyred by King Bolesław II the Bold. The centre of worship of St Stanislaus is Wawel Cathedral in the

9 MARTEDI - s. Dionigio v. m. | s. Francesco Borgia - MERCOLEDI 10 OTTOBRE

Dies recoll. (segue) 1962. po przybyciu do Rzymu na I sesję Vat. II.

1. [Sacrum, Laudes Prima

2. Uczestniczyłem w capella papalis na 4. rocznicę śmierci Ojca Piusa XII, razem z [illegible] biskupami. Myśli: Apostolstwo od wczoraj [illegible] do wszystkich [illegible], uświadomiłem sobie, że wszystkich obecnych łączy jeden duch: to jest duch Chrystusa Syna Bożego. Z ogromną jasnością przeżywam tę jedność w Kościele i przy niezgłębionej różnicy stopnia partycypacji. Ale zebrani wiele odrębnych przesłanek, ale jedność Treści: jest to Treść myślowa, doktrynalna — i nad nią czuwa Papież wraz z [illegible]. Ale jest to również Treść życiowa, moralna, które w ramach jednego Kościoła realizujemy wszyscy przez misterium (sakramenta): jakoś postawy ofiarniczej z Chrystusem przypieczętowane Krzyżem. B) jako myśl drugiego planu była obecna prawda o kapłaństwie i biskupstwie, które niegdyś zostało wydzielone i dla mnie z Chrystusa Kapłana poprzez Jego zastępcę na ziemi (Vicarius Christi)

2. Ador. Chrystus jest cały w Kościele i Kościół jest cały w Chrystusie. M. [illegible] czuwać nad tym, abym był dobrego pasterza dla [illegible] św. Stanisława chodził przede wszystkim i zasadniczo, nie dopuszczając żadnych „mea".

3. Lektura schematu „De castitate, matrimonio, familia, virginitate"

4. Refleksja (meditatio): 1) quoad theoriam
2) quoad practicam

APPUNTAMENTI

(Problem jakiegoś [illegible] tej dziedziny / jeszcze raz [illegible] i „przypatrywanie" /

Reading the schema '*de castitate, matrimonio, familia, virginitate*' ['on chastity, marriage, family, virginity'].[1]

Reflection (meditation):

1. *quoad theoriam* [concerning theory]
2. *quoad practicam* [concerning practice].

(The problem of a general and 'perspectival' leadership in this area.)

14 October Meditation: Let us consider the most proper way for the human spirit to meet the Divine Spirit. Our Lord Christ laid the foundation for this meeting for every human being – and for the work of the Divine Spirit in the human spirit.

(The theological virtues: the means to adjust the human spirit to the Divine Spirit; the gifts of the Holy Spirit: the means, so to speak, of adjusting the Divine Spirit to the 'dimensions' of the human spirit.) A move towards the opening and submission of the human spirit to the Divine Spirit is necessary, particularly during the Council. The goal cannot be the expression or assertion of oneself, the human being, the human spirit alone – but above all the expression of that which comes from the Divine Spirit in the form of virtues and gifts. In this light, the fundamental attitude: (1) a permanent necessity to subordinate creativity to truth; (2) *experimentum divinum, non humanum* [the divine, not human, experience]; (3) humility.

Archdiocese of Kraków. Pope John Paul II was ordained to the priesthood there on 1 November 1946. On 28 September 1958, he was consecrated Auxiliary Bishop of Kraków.

1 *Schema constitutionis dogmaticae de castitate, matrimonio, familia, virginitate* [Draft of a dogmatic constitution on chastity, marriage, the family, and virginity] (Concilio Vaticano II, *Acta Synodalia*, vol. II, Periodus I, Pars IV, Congregationes generales XXXI–XXXVI, Vatican 1971, pp. 718–71) was prepared by the Theological Preparatory Commission in May 1962, and a revised version by Pope John XXIII was incorporated into the pastoral constitution *Gaudium et spes* (Joy and Hope).

[31 October – 4 November] 1962
Rome, at the Felician Sisters' Convent
Topic: The mystery of redemption

Deus, Redemisti nos Domine
in sanguine Tuo ex omni
tribu et populo et natione
et fecisti nos Deo nostro regnum
[God, by Thy blood, O Lord,
you didst ransom us from every
tribe and people and nation,
and hast made us a kingdom to our God][1]

31 October The retreat begins at 7.00 p.m.
Adoration; Matins

Introductory meditation: Sixteenth anniversary of [my] ordination to the priesthood – *recapitulatio, ut ita dicam, historica* [a historical recollection, so to speak][2]

Reading: Rahner K., *XX siècle – siècle de grâce?* [twentieth century – the century of grace?]. *Opus Creationis – opus Redemptionis* [the order of creation – the order of redemption].[3] (*La Rédemption au Coeur de Marie* [Redemption in Mary's Heart]).
Compline

1 November Rosary (petitionary); Lauds

Meditation: Memories from the ceremony of the sacrament of priesthood '*ut quidquid benedixerint, benedicatur, et quidquid consecraverint, consecretur et sanctificetur*' ['that whatever they

1 See Revelation 5:9–10.

2 John Paul II was ordained priest on 1 November 1946 by the Archbishop of Kraków, Cardinal Adam Stefan Sapieha.

3 A reference to the second chapter, entitled 'The order of redemption within the order of creation', of Karl Rahner's *Sendung und Gnade: Beiträge zur Pastoraltheologie* (originally published in 1959; the English translation by Cecily Hastings was published in 1963 as *The Christian Commitment: Essays in Pastoral Theology*).

-160-

31 MERCOLEDI - s. Quintino m.

Domine Redemisti nos Deo in sanguine Tuo ex omni tribu et lingua et populo et natione, et fecisti nos Deo nostro regnum

31.X.
H. 19 incipiunt Recoll.
Ador.
Mat.
Medit. wprowadzająca: 16. rocznica święceń kapłańskich — recapitulatio in sensum historicum
Lekt. Rahner K. XX siècle – siècle de grâce?
Knipl., opus creationis — opus Redemptionis (La Rédemption au cœur du monde)

1962 NOTE Roma, u s. Felicjanek
Temat: Tajemnica Odkupienia

1.XI
Ros. recitat.
Laudes
Medit. reminiscencje z ceremonii świec. kapł. „ut quidquid benedixerint benedicatur et quidquid consecraverint consecretur et sanctificetur" — o Dłoniach kapłańskich. — Wszystko jakoś było „nie tak", aż do momentu, bez momentu wielkiej uważności wobec Chrystusowego dzieła Odkupienia — o jego upodobnieniu Sacerdos cum grat. act. Prima
Medit. ulterius: Chrystus odkupuje Ojcu nas wszystkich tj. składa ofiarę zadośćuczyniącą (propitiatorium), w której jest całe Jego oddanie i zjednoczenie z Ojcem, tzn. Duch Ś. jako Tchnienie Obojga. Jesteśmy — my ludzie — poddani tym aktem Chrystusowego Odkupienia, wypowiedzieć możemy na zewnątrz tego, co zachodzi w porządku Osobowej Trójcy. Tajny, ale jednocześnie o nas ślady tej jedności Osobowej duchowej i [illegible]. W życiu odkupieńczym Chrystusa w swój sposób jest zawarte kapłaństwo jako kulminacja postawy ofiarniczej wobec jedności Stwórcy i jako stworzenia. W Odkupieniu (Redemptio) zawarta jest także jakaś zdolność do rewaloryzacji wszystkiego, co stworzone, a zwłaszcza co ludzkie — i to chyba także powinno udzielić kapłaństwo i jego ... w nim

APPUNTAMENTI

Via crucis
Lectio gr. (S. Paul et l'apostolat d'aujourd'hui) et alia
Ros (2)
Vesp.
Medit. (practica). Problemy

bless may be blessed, and whatever they consecrate may be consecrated and made holy'].[1]

– On the priest's hands – Nothing, however, was 'right', until the point when I felt great humility towards Christ's work of redemption – in this spirit, *Sacrum cum grat. act., Prima* [Holy Mass with thanksgiving, Prime].

Further meditation: Christ redeems us and all for the Father, i.e. offers an atoning sacrifice (*propitiatorium*), which consists in His complete devotion and union with the Father. Hence the Holy Spirit as the breath of both. We – people – are elevated by the act of Christ's redemption. Even though we remain outside of what 'happens' between the Persons of the Most Holy Trinity, we nevertheless experience the effects of this wonderful spiritual fertility and abundant love. The redemptive act of Christ the Lord embraces, in a special way, priesthood as the culmination of the sacrificial posture, which is, after all, not alien to man as part of the creation. Redemption (*Redemptio*) also involves a certain striving towards the re-evaluation of everything that is created, in particular everything that is human – and this, as well, should be shared by the priesthood and reflected in it.

The Way of the Cross
Spiritual reading (*S. Paul et l'apostolat d'aujourd'hui* [St Paul and Today's Apostolate] and others)
Rosary (II); Vespers

Meditation *practica* [concerning practical issues]: Problems: (a) Focusing on 'one's own' matters and the necessity to work on a wider range and broaden one's orientation in many disciplines; (b) certain conclusions on the issue of the 'priest–laypeople' balance, and further tasks; (a[1]) a search for concise and abstract formulae in relation to the human and priestly reality ('all' and 'different') esp. the needy.

Adoration: In the Eucharist, Christ the Lord allowed us to draw as close to Himself as possible – particularly through priesthood: the closest to who He is, [illegible] and what He fulfils.

1 A slightly altered quotation from the rite for ordination of priests from the *Pontificale Romanum* (the English translation is included in *The Roman Ritual: Complete Edition*, vol. 1, trans. Philip T. Weller, 1964).

Matins (for the dead); Litany of the Saints

Holy Hour: A personal moment with Christ, a personal wish – waiting for a response. *Propitiatio pro peccatis meis* [The atoning sacrifice for my sins].[1]

2 November Rosary; Petitionary prayers; Lauds

Meditation (a) Being much engaged in earthly tasks, in creative work, always to be ready: not to lose perspective. 'Re-evaluation' constitutes only one aspect of redemption, which in a sense is its least important aspect (when it comes to the values on 'this side'); (b) and with this understanding to comprehend the words of the liturgy '*quia in inferno nulla est redemptio*' ['for in hell there is no redemption'].[2]

Three Holy Masses; Thanksgiving
Reading (*L'Eglise dans le monde qui vient* [The Church in the modern world])
The Way of the Cross

Meditation: '*Copiosa apud Eum Redemptio*' ['with Him is plenteous redemption']:[3] Holiness is the source. In Christ the absolute holiness of God is united hypostatically with the holiness of man. God's holiness (as the love of good and the hatred of evil), but first and foremost as the love of good in everything, even the one who is evil (*per accidens* [contingently]). All good (the entire sum of values) outside God has its prototype in God Himself. God loves one in another – in this consists His holiness. This holiness is the basis for redemption – also understood as the 're-evaluation' of everything: God restores the value of everything in man, who is personally united with Him. He is Christ – *Redemptor* [Redeemer]: the holiness of man consists in receiving this good, which God loves – in this manner Christ becomes the model of holiness. In Him that holiness is in a way identical to redemption (*Redemptio*). In us it has to depend on, first, conversion to God, and second, re-evaluation of everything in accordance with the value that everything has in God, and which Christ the Lord has shown to us.

1 See 1 John 2:2.
2 A quotation from the Matins of the Dead, Third Nocturn.
3 See Psalm 129 (130):7.

Rosary; Adoration; Vespers

Meditation *super experimentum* [on experience]: (An element of risk.) Everything has to be permanently in God's hands and dependent on God's assistance. Hence no psychologisation, but moral and, first and foremost, religious orientation (i.e. in Mary's hands).

Conversation with M.W. (a) missionary–apostolic element; (b) God makes use of different people.

Penitential psalms

Meditation: Conversion *in actu quolibet* [in every action] has to consist in finding the will of Christ the Lord. There is no other method of opposing the various impulses of human vanity of life; the problem of power, criticism, envy, even together with a certain foundation of some 'transcendental' humility towards the Lord God.

Matins (at the Church of the Blessed Virgin Mary)

3 November Rosary; Petitionary prayers; Lauds
Meditation: Redemption began with '*Totus Tuus*';[1] Preparation for Holy Mass
Holy Mass; Thanksgiving
Spiritual reading (*L'individu dans l'Eglise* [The individual in the Church])

Meditation: Redemption began with '*Totus Tuus*': the one and only person, the new human being to whom God entrusted Himself. God–Son needed Her to fulfil His task. God–Son could entrust to Her His own being in this task, because it was first achieved in Her and He prepared Her for this *Totus Tuus*. Mary responded to this devotion of God in its entire redemptive sense, its entire dynamics. She drew from it and is still drawing that which is contained in it for each and every person: first, conversion, and second, re-evaluation. And in all who entrust themselves to Her, She performs both in due proportion.

My problem is solved here: recently I have felt I was very much in Mary's hands and close to God through two specific issues. Yet, has not the order been reversed? Am I not 'using'

1 See n. 1, p. 1 [2 September 1962].

it to do something that is 'very much mine'? The stance I am taking on these issues is total humility. Here is the solution: In Mary's hands, according to the '*Totus Tuus*' principle, the work of redemption must be realised also in me with the proportion between conversion and re-evaluation duly maintained.

The Way of the Cross (with Mary); Pastoral letter; Vespers; Rosary

Meditation: The most appropriate effects of redemption in the human being are deeds that stem from it – deeds that through Mary are rooted in Christ, through one's belonging to Her (*Tuus* [Yours]), and that are simultaneously in accordance with Christ's law, with His gospel – in the highest accordance. Here also, among other things, the issue of Father W. (Three possibilities: to simply remain humble and make use of what is at least partly true in there; to make light of it: he will improve as he is young; 'to keep watch' and make sure he has improved intellectually and also 'morally'. First and foremost, one needs to pray for him and for the right decision.)

Adoration; Final concluding meditation (the issue of envy); Matins (memorial of St Charles);[1] Rosary

4 November Holy Mass with the relic of St Charles's heart, celebrated by the Pope

Meditation: *ad instar s. Caroli afferre se ipsum ad bonum commune Ecclesiae et in domicilio et in Dioecesi, participans hoc modo in opere Redemptionis* [to work towards the common good of the Church both at home and in the diocese after the example of St Charles, thus participating in the work of salvation].

Adoration

[1 December 1962]

Missa ad intentionem satisfaciendi S. Cordi BMV [Mass offered in reparation to the Most Sacred Heart of Mary]

[2 December 1962]: First Sunday of Advent

There are, so to speak, two planes: the divine plane (the love of the Son–Word for the Father) and the human plane (people's

1 4 November marks the Feast of St Charles (Carlo) Borromeo.

yearning for the true God, for the revelation of God in the Son–Word). These two planes approach and come into contact with each other – this is the spirit of Advent.

My Advent (a reminder from last year): a strong wish for God–Christ to enter into every matter. In this context, there is the experimental meaning too: it is still *in fieri* [in the process of 'becoming'] in me, in others, in an objective way and regarding its future sense.

6–7 July 196? [probably 1963]
Kalwaria – The Shrine of Our Lady[1]

~

Aims:

1. To ask for peace and good for the Church of Kraków, efficacy of action, vocations.
2. To prepare the basis for the retreat.
3. To move forward certain tasks.

In general: preferably the form of reflection days (= meditation connected with other tasks).

Confession; Holy Mass; Meditation; The Way of the Cross; The Little Ways[2]

(a) Numerous threads, reflective and 'existential'. One needs to bring them all here and pass them into These Hands in accordance with the principle '*Totus Tuus*' ['Entirely Yours'].

(b) The main topic of the retreat emerges: 'between past and future'.

---

1 The Marian Shrine of Kalwaria Zebrzydowska, located near Kraków and designed to resemble the Way of the Cross in Jerusalem, is one of the most popular pilgrimage sites in Poland. In his apostolic address of 7 June 1979, Pope John Paul II reflected on the role the shrine played in his spiritual development: 'Kalwaria Zebrzydowska, the Shrine of the Mother of God, reproduces the holy places of Jerusalem connected with the life of Jesus and that of His Mother. They are called the "Little Ways". I visited them often as a boy and as a young man. I visited them as a priest. In particular, I often visited the Shrine of Kalwaria as the Archbishop of Kraków and Cardinal. We came here many times, the priests and I, to concelebrate before the Mother of God . . . More frequently, however, I came here alone and, walking along the Little Ways of Jesus Christ and His Mother, I meditated on Their holy mysteries and entrusted particularly difficult and uniquely significant issues of my ministry to Christ through Mary. I can say that almost none of these issues was successfully solved except here, through ardent prayer before the great mystery of faith that Kalwaria holds.'

2 The 'Little Ways' of Kalwaria are a set of pathways and chapels designed to inspire reflection and meditation on the passion of Christ and the life of Mary.

19–23 [August] 1963
Retreat in Tyniec[1]
Topic: Justification – grace

19 August Compline; Adoration; Meditation

20 August Lauds; Prime
Meditation before Holy Mass:

1. Holy Mass brings the rhythm of Christ, the rhythm of the Son of God into our lives.
2. (The integrating role of consciousness – the disintegrating role of sensuousness.)

Holy Mass; Thanksgiving; Reading the Holy Scripture; Reading the Council schema; Meditation; The Way of the Cross

A reference to the previous retreat held in Rome on 31 October – [4] November 1962. The dogmatic topic that requires a deeper spiritual reflection is the mystery of justification (*iustificatio*). Man cannot be 'just' before God; he can only be 'justified' before Him. The former is proved by the fact that man is not equal to God, his Creator, and the latter by Christ and the entire order of grace.

No creature can be in a position of justice before its Creator. Man is in a way a synthesis of creatures. As a creature in general, he and his existence are unconditionally dependent on his Creator; he is dependent also by virtue of his nature and, consequently, unequivocally subordinate. As a being endowed with vegetative (sensual) life, he is subject to the laws of life and death (*generatio et corruptio*) like other creatures. As a spiritual being – a person – he bears a more special resemblance to the Creator, which obligates him to maintain the order of justice, i.e. to give to everybody what rightly belongs to them

1 The Benedictine Abbey in Tyniec, a village on the Vistula River near Kraków, was founded in 1044. When Karol Wojtyła was a priest and Bishop of Kraków, he frequently visited the abbey.

-122-

19 DOMENICA s. Giovanni Eudes — s. Bernardo ab. dott. - LUNEDI 20 AGOSTO

1963

Rekolekcje. Tyniec. (19) 20, 21, 22 (23)

[temat: Usprawiedliwienie – Łaska]

19.8. Complet. Ador. Medit.

20.8 Laudes Prima

Meditatio ante Sacrum

1. Łaska w. nadaje życiu nowemu rytm Chrystusowy, rytm życia Bożego

2. [Integracyjna rola świadomości – decentralizacyjna zmysłowości]

Sacrum

Grat. actio

Lectio S. Script.: schematis Conc.

Medit.

Via Crucis

Nawiązanie do poprzednich rekolekcji 31 X.–3 XI 62 w Rzymie. Temat dogmatyczny, który wymaga rekolekcyjnego pogłębienia – to tajemnica usprawiedliwienia (iustificatio). Człowiek nie może być w stosunku do Boga „sprawiedliwy", może być wobec Niego tylko „usprawiedliwiony". Za pierwszym pojmujemy, iż człowiek nie jest równy Bogu swemu Stwórcy, za drugim Chrystus ono czyni poprzez Łaskę.

APPUNTAMENTI

Żadne stworzenie nie może być ~~sprawi~~ wobec swego Stwórcy w pozycji sprawiedliwości. Człowiek jest pod każdym względem stworzeniem. Jako stworzenie w ogóle jest bezwzględnie zależny od swego Stwórcy w istnieniu, zależny też w swej naturze i z tej racji jednoznacznie podporządkowany. Jako istota obdarzona życiem vegetatywnym (wegetatywnym)

(which also includes paying religious worship to God). The fact of personhood does not render invalid man's vegetativeness and *animalitas* [animal nature], which turns him into 'ash and nothing'[1] before his Creator. As a person, man can enter into personal contact with the Creator; this contact, however, has to be initiated by the Creator. When He initiates it, it consists (like the act of creation) in an act of mercy, because man as a creature is fully dependent and subordinate. In particular, he needs to be justified because of his sin, which, as an offence to God, does harm to the very essence of this personal contact understood in the way it is understood and intended by the Creator – and it is His prerogative to define the essence of the contact He establishes with His rational creature.

Justification comes through Christ, the Son of God, who initiates this essential contact and gives it, to a certain extent, the qualities of His contact with the Father. Therefore, justification is expressed in us as the new *esse* [being] – '*esse ad Patrem*' ['being towards the Father'] (i.e. sanctifying grace), and the continuation of this personal contact consists in faith, hope and love.

Vespers

Adoration: Lord Jesus hid in the womb of Mother Mary, which He left as a human being – and in the womb of Mother Church, so that it could give birth to sons of God.

Rosary; Spiritual reading (G. Vann)[2]

Meditation: I note down briefly: the (diocesan) bishop's authority and vocation require, on the one hand, generosity and courage, and on the other hand, service to everybody and universal charity, in particular charity for priests. Regarding all these points: reservations. '*Episcopatum desiderare*' ['To aspire to the office of bishop'][3] – but it cannot be '*propter se*' ['for oneself']. Many things have yet to 'burn out' and ripen.

1 The quotation comes from the drama *Dziady* (*Forefathers' Eve*) by the acclaimed Polish Romantic poet Adam Mickiewicz.

2 Gerald Vann OP (1906–63) was a British theologian and philosopher. He wrote on faith, mysticism, war and St Thomas Aquinas.

3 See 1 Timothy 3:1.

Providence is sweet. Very useful reflections, and thereby quieting down.

Anticipated Matins

One more thing: what has a particular value is suffering for the sake of the matter – it brings more benefit than all the efforts. (Fr Pr.).

Reading; Rosary; Compline; Reading

21 August Lauds; Prime; Rosary; Reflection; Holy Mass; Meditation

It happened that today I celebrated Holy Mass to mark the reception of the habit and profession at the Daughters of Divine Charity. It allowed me to bring yesterday's topic – the mystery of justification – closer to the mystery of the Church. The Church – the mystical body of Christ – is, so to speak, '*esse ad Patrem*' ['being towards the Father']. The sisters, who through their vows choose Christ for their bridegroom, in a special way enter into this '*esse ad Patrem*' not only personally, but they also impress the sign of this '*esse*' ['being'] on the life of our entire society. Hence they are much needed by the Church and in the Church. In a way, they constitute its vertical core. At the same time, it needs to be observed that their special vocation and involvement stems from the mystery of justification. It is simultaneously the fruit and the realisation of this justification.

The Way of the Cross

Meditation: Although yesterday it was said that man – a creature – cannot be *stricto sensu* [in the strict sense] 'just' before God, but needs to be justified by Him, this justification nevertheless aims to create the type of relationship between man and God that consists in justice; in any case, it builds its elements and conditions. God wants man to be 'just' intrinsically (*intrinsece*) and not only 'justified' (extrinsically – *extrinsece*). This is indicated by a contrast with the reality of sin, which is an 'offence to God'. If the Creator had placed his rational creature, man, entirely beyond the relationship of justice, sin would be impossible: An offence is to some extent a violation of justice with regard to a person (and also charity). The Creator gave primary justice to man through grace, and after the sin, He did not deprive him of the possibility of such a relationship. This possibility gestures towards the supernatural order, the order of grace, but it is grounded in the natural order: in the fact that man is a person.

Christ the Lord justified man, that is, helped and has been helping man to be just before God. Man is 'just' before God through '*esse ad Patrem*', which is grace. The Church as the mystical Christ helps man achieve the same, because its task is to be the continuation of Christ and His work. Doing this, Christ and the Church simultaneously contribute to the fulfilment of human personhood. Man is fully a person when he is 'justified', that is 'just' before God. Without this – one could say – his personhood remains incomplete, it is unfulfilled.

Man was justified, because he could be (can be) and was (is) unjust before God. Whereas God wants – and He wants it through Christ – man to be just before Him, so indirectly He also wants him to be 'made equal' with regard to God – of course through grace. It seems to be the most essentially revealed (genuinely revealed) part of the entire ethics, and simultaneously the most essentially ethical (genuinely ethical) part of the entire revelation (theology!).

Vespers

Adoration: Christ hidden in the womb of the Church, so that He can reveal Himself to humankind. The grace of maturation.

Rosary; Meditation: *casus* [the case of] W. (T., I.) separately
Reading: *De statibus perf.* [On the stages of perfection]; Holy Scripture; G. Vann
Matins; Matins (II) for the Feast of the Immaculate Heart of the Blessed Virgin Mary; Compline
Moreover: thoughts of death!

22 August: Feast of the Immaculate Heart of the Blessed Virgin Mary

Lauds; Prime; Meditation; Holy Mass; Thanksgiving; Rosary; Conversation with Sister Aug.
Reading: Holy Scripture; schema *De clericis* [Concerning the clergy]

Meditation:

1. The mystery of justification evokes the awareness of the human creature's unjustness to God–Creator. This

awareness grows bigger and brings out the need of restitution: to make amends to Christ – Him, who has atoned for us all and 'justifies' all.

2. Furthermore: justice has followed from justification, which points to the primacy of grace, as it puts us in the position of justice before God: it is this justice that the Lord God wants from us and that He wants in us.
3. The primacy of grace in being – and as a consequence the primacy of grace in action. In the past year it became very clear to me in a well-known context. It undoubtedly means reliance on God. Example: St Peter on the lake – if I look at the man, I am overwhelmed by pessimism; when I look at Christ, trust returns. However, this trust and reliance cannot be presumptuous. Even here some measure of justice should be considered.
4. Justice in relation to one's position. A bishop bears a particular responsibility for the Church – and this responsibility should be contained in his justification and justice before the Highest and Only Shepherd of souls. One needs both generosity and humility, in fact, a supernatural courage, not only a 'drive for importance'.

The Way of the Cross: Station XII: the courageous is the one who is ready for the cross!
Vespers

Adoration: Lord Jesus gathered His apostles in the Upper Room and instituted the Eucharist in front of them. He took with Him perfectly ordinary people.

Rosary

Meditation: Problem of '*successio*' ['succession'] – separately. The grace of humiliation. Other concerns: priests, family (W. and others), earlier ones.

Matins; Conversation with Br Michael – v. helpful; Compline

Holy Hour: Our justification follows in a way from our very injustice, because the Lord Jesus accomplished it through His death, which He suffered most unjustly. Justification was then decided solely through the Redeemer's inner act, the act of love and atoning and justifying sacrifice.

23 August The Way of the Cross; Lauds; Holy Mass with a homily; Thanksgiving (Rosary); Prime

Meditation: All the thoughts from the retreat somehow come together in this week's prayer (*11 Post Pent.* [Eleventh (Sunday) after Pentecost]).

Omnipotens sempiterne Deus,
qui abundantia pietatis Tuae
et merita supplicum excedis et vota –
effunde super nos misericordiam Tuam,
ut dimittas quae conscientia metuit
et adiicias quod oratio non praesumit
Per Dominum . . .[1]
[Almighty ever-living God,
who in the abundance of Your kindness surpass the merits
and the desires of those who entreat You,
pour out Your mercy upon us
to pardon what conscience dreads
and to give what prayer does not dare to ask.
Through our Lord . . .]

1 See the Collect for the 27th Week in Ordinary Time.

[5–8] March 1964
Before the installation ceremony[1]

~

5 March Funeral of Fr Dean J. Śliwa RIP in Wieliczka[2]

Meditation on death: The reality of Christ's priesthood emerges out of death in a special way: He stands before the Father as the eternal priest, and we stand before the Father with what we share in Christ's priesthood.

Conversation at the Visitation Sisters'
Conclusion at the Abbey in Tyniec[3]

6 March Holy Hour; Lauds; Holy Mass; Prime

Meditation: On the relation 'priest–shepherd' in Christ the Lord and in each of us.

Reading: 'Der Bischof als Priester und Hirt seiner Diözese' [The Bishop as the Priest and Shepherd of His Diocese];[4] Daniélou: Temple [illegible];[5] Estreicher: [illegible]; [Zarewicz]: *Biskupstwo Krakowskie* [The Bishopric of Kraków].[6]

Meditation: On the ways in which my actions are 'rooted' in God's mysteries (preparation for confession).

The Way of the Cross; Adoration; Office

7 March Holy Mass

Meditation: '*Domine Deus, in simplicitate cordis mei laetus obtuli universa; et populum tuum, qui repertus est, vidi cum ingenti gaudio: Deus Israel, custodi hanc voluntatem*' ['Lord God . . .

---

1 John Paul II was appointed Archbishop of Kraków by Pope Paul VI on 13 January 1964. The installation ceremony took place in Wawel Cathedral on 8 March 1964.

2 Wieliczka is a town in southern Poland, in the administrative district of Kraków.

3 See the previous chapter '19–23 [August] 1963: Retreat in Tyniec'.

4 Paul Heinrich Nordhues, 'Der Bischof als Priester und Hirt seiner Diözese' [The Bishop as the Priest and Shepherd of His Diocese], *Theologisches Jahrbuch* [Theological Yearbook] (1961), pp. 126–140.

5 Jean Daniélou, *Le signe du temple ou la présence de Dieu* (Paris, 1942); published in English as *The Presence of God*, trans. Walter Roberts (London, 1958).

6 Ludwik Zarewicz, *Biskupstwo Krakowskie z Pocztem Swych Pasterzy* [The Bishopric of Kraków and its Clergy], (Kraków, 1880).

Przed wyjazdem

5 LUNEDI - s. Virginio — ss. Perpetua e Felicita vv. - MARTEDI **6** MARZO

5/III 1964 (czwartek)

a) pogrzeb śp. x Dziekana J. Kluzy w Kozielicach

medytacja o śmierci. Ze śmierci i pogrzebu [illegible] wyrasta się uczestnictwo kapłaństwa Chrystusa: przed ojcem staje On jako kapłan wieczny, a my z Nim, co mamy udział w Jego kapłaństwie

b) rozmowa u ks. [illegible]

c) zakończenie w opactwie Tynieckim

6/III piątek

a) godzina [illegible]

b) Laudes, Sacrum, Prima

c) medytacja o wzorku ~~[illegible]~~ „Kapłan – pasterz" w Chrystusie Panu i w każdym z nas

d) lektury

„Der Bischof als Priester und Hirt seiner Diözese"

Danielou: ~~Eglise~~ Temple ecclésial

Estreicher: o katedrze

Zamorski: Biskupstwo w Krakowie

e) medytacja: o korzeniach moich grzechów w tajemnicach Bożych (praepar. ad confess.)

f) via crucis

g) adoratio

h) officium

40. Via Crucis [illegible] super quaedam verba exercitiorum spir.

41. VIII konf. (De Beata)

a) s. Bernardus: Totus mundus exspectat responsum Mariae – ecce ancilla Domini. Przez te słowa Maryja stała się Matką naszego pojednania z Bogiem – przez te słowa wypowiedziane w Nazarecie, powtórzone pod krzyżem. // Bóg pojednał się z ludźmi w Chrystusie za pośrednictwem Maryi.

b) Maryja objawia swoje Niepokalane Poczęcie, gdy rodzić ma nowy świat – wszystkich powołanych synami przyjmuje, aby jednać ludzi z Bogiem

Musimy Jej w tym dopomagać, i trzeba współpracować (co by się stało, gdyby Maryja odpowiedziała „nie"? co by się stało, gdyby o. Maksymilian odpowiedział „nie"?)

APPUNTAMENTI

c) Trzy „apres" u s. Bernarda

przed: odpowiedź nasza oświetlona na czasy – czasy Maryi, była one wpisana ofiara. Ofiara jest implikacją czasu (cfr. ~~obraz~~ analiza obrazu MB Nieust. Pomocy – na lichtarzu „Stanie ostatnie") – przez takie tylko czasy można się ponownie oddać Maryi, jak o. Kolbe. Czasy takie zdobywa się

in the uprightness of my heart I have freely offered all these things, and now I have seen your people, who are present here, offering freely and joyously to you. O Lord, the God of . . . Israel, keep forever such purposes'].[1]

The Way of the Cross; Meditation: Priest and shepherd; Confession; Vespers
Pilgrimage to the tomb of Bl. Wincenty Kadłubek, Bishop of Kraków

8 March Installation

1 See 1 Chronicles 29:17–18.

31 August – 3 September 1964 Retreat led by Bishop K[azimierz] J[ózef] Kowalski[1]

31 August Talk: The retreat moves on to focus on the most sacred humanity of Christ (*ergo: Mater Eius* [that is: His Mother]) = *sileant doctores . . . unus est magister: Christ . . . recedant creaturae . . . Tu mihi loquere solus* [let the scholars be silent . . . there is one teacher: Christ . . . let the creatures depart . . . Let only You speak to me]. Indeed, I wish for and fervently beg for answers on various matters. Finally: for a '*kenosis*', that is, for the destruction of self-love as a condition for listening to (in a way, a participatory dialogue in) this retreat.

1 September Matins; Lauds; Prime

Participation in Holy Mass: with a meditation on the topic of '*humilis Tuae Crucis Sequela*' ['humble imitation of Your Cross'] (Bl. Bronisława).[2]

Talk: Mission and adoration, or rather the mission to adore God. The foundation for this adoration [is] in the order of creation (creation *ex nihilo* [out of nothing] and creation *ad Deum* [towards God]): 'You are she who is not';[3] and furthermore: the foundation in the order of grace, which is entirely and exclusively *ex benevolentia et misericordia Divina* [out of God's benevolence and mercy]. Therefore, man, and even more so the priest/bishop, is '*doulos*', God's slave.

An analysis of the attitude to atheism: Cardinal Mercier's suggestive statement on Kant: '*le plus grand malfaiteur du*

---

1 Kazimierz Józef Kowalski (1896–1972) was a Polish priest, theologian and philosopher. He served as Bishop of Chełm (1946–72).

2 Blessed Bronisława (*c.*1203–59) was a Polish nun of the Order of Canons Regular of Prémontré.

3 This is a quotation from one of St Catherine of Siena's visions in which Christ addressed her with the following words: 'Do you know, daughter, who you are and who I am? If you know these two things you have beatitude in your grasp. You are she who is not, and I am he who is.' Raymond of Capua, *The Life of Catherine of Siena*, trans. Conleth Kearns (Dublin, 1980), 1, X, 92, p. 85.

monde contemporain' ['the greatest malefactor of the contemporary world'] (since he maintains that the phenomena and noumena do not tell us anything about God). The attitude grounded in Pope Paul VI's encyclical *Ecclesiam suam*[1] (a dialogue with atheism) = atheism and its alternations: statolatry, materialism and the worship of one's self (idols).

Talk: The retreat leader called the moment when Plato formulated the term '*participatio*' (participation) one of the happiest moments of the human mind. With the help of this term, human thought, inspired by the revelation, could reach the reality of God and the mystery of God. For God is the One who gives Himself (the antithesis of the 'clenched fist'). The retreat leader speaks beautifully about all the material creatures' participation in being, and how their wealth becomes more and more visible to man – next, the living creatures' participation in being: vegetation, sensual–affective life, spiritual life – stages, or rather incomparable domains. Even higher there is the supernatural life: grace.

Now we will move on to the participation that we, priests, have in what is most personal to Christ: in His priesthood. And in an even more complete way in episcopacy: we offer all natural and supernatural concerns of all the members of our dioceses. The retreat leader speaks in an especially beautiful way of how episcopacy should bring about the union of fatherhood and motherhood: the participation of the Divine Heart of Jesus and the Heart of Mary. It finds expression in the care for those who are in the greatest spiritual and corporal need.

Spiritual reading: (the encyclical *Ecclesiam suam*)

The Way of the Cross
Rosary
Vespers } *communis* [together]

Talk: The bishop participates in Christ's authority. What is at stake is how to use this authority. There is a way of using authority that the Master describes as appropriate for the

1 The encyclical *Ecclesiam suam* (His Church) was promulgated by Pope Paul VI on 6 August 1964.

'kings of this world': they rule in such a way that their subjects can feel their authority and, what is more, they have to consider such rulers their benefactors.[1] 'But not so with you' says Christ.[2] The proper mode of wielding authority in the Church must be pastoral, which was emphasised so much by John XXIII. '*Caritatem facientes in veritate*' ['Enacting love in truth'].[3] There must be a close relation between truth and love, just like between the Persons of the Most Holy Trinity *veritas praecedit* [the truth comes first].

V. interesting sentence: atheism gives birth to satellites. God's love seeks brotherhood.

On the topic of the importance of truth in the life and work of the bishop: the truth of the spoken word, the truth of judgements made about others: *audiatur et altera pars* [let the other side be heard as well]. The issue of advisors.

On the topic of charity: it has to be universal, it cannot be particular and it cannot create divisions. Next: it has to be servile; servitude perhaps best expresses love. Finally: it has to be forgiving. All this needs to be learnt beside the Heart of Jesus through the Heart of Mary.

Anticipated Matins (memorial of St Stephen); Adoration; (Evening) Mass, 7.00 p.m.; Litany of the Saints; Benediction; Compline

2 September Rosary; Meditation; Morning Mass, 7.30 a.m.; Lauds; Prime

Talk: On sanctity and love, based on the calling and life of St John the Evangelist. The exegesis of some passages in his Gospel, in particular the reassurance given by the Redeemer (love opens itself up, and this opening inspires others). It is this fire, this apostolic zeal, that it is mostly about. Have I inspired anybody?

Much on the attitude to the Eucharist: to protect it with utmost care (it was also mentioned in yesterday's Benediction), but also to make it accessible as widely as possible.

Love is kindled by the Heart of the Lord Jesus and enters it together with others. The sanctity of an open heart.

(The Little Hours)

1 See Mark 10:42–45.
2 See Luke 22:25.
3 See Ephesians 4:15.

Now the example of St Peter, who both was v. imperfect and considered himself such, 'for I am a sinful man'.[1] Each of us is a sinful man too, but also bishops as a group (the times of Arianism, the French Revolution, d'Herbigny).[2] To dispose of the '*acceptatio personae propriae*' ['acceptance of oneself'] and then to stand before Christ the Lord. Since we are called to greater love, sin becomes a greater burden for us, and it can, above all, 'break' the entire Church, particularly one's own diocese. Therefore *odium peccati* [the hatred of sin] is necessary. This is also fire: and here one needs to call good what is good, and evil what is evil. When it comes to one's own and others' struggle against sin, it is not enough to reproach and destroy, but one has to always introduce positive ideals.

Question: How do we benefit from our own confession? The choice of the right confessor, not necessarily one, who is our forgiving Christ. In addition to that, to value those who reproach us. Away with flatterers. And not to break down in the face of persecution: because sin enters this way. To avoid occasions for sin. Not to undertake to solve 'satanic' problems (the temptation of the Lord Jesus: *apage satanas* [go away, Satan]). A discussion with Satan is possible only when we are very much united with Christ and 'deep in the Mother of God'. Each victory over Satan should be a stimulus for even greater humility and alertness.

The attitude of the bishop to the sinner: an open heart, to accept humiliation even from the mouths of sinners, and when the time comes – *fortiter agere* [to act firmly]. And, finally, to believe in the victory of grace over sin (*ubi abundavit delictum, superabundavit gratia* [where sin grew bigger, grace was even more abundant]). Our task is to bring down grace. Not to surrender before any sin (*delictum*). *Misericordia = summa christianitas* [Mercy = the highest form of Christianity].

The Way of the Cross [illegible]; Rosary (together); Vespers

---

1 See Luke 5:8.

2 Michel-Joseph Bourguignon d'Herbigny (1880–1957) was a French bishop who was involved in a failed attempt to establish a Catholic hierarchy in the Soviet Union in the 1920s. In 1937, he was forced to abdicate and banned from any public role.

Talk: We follow St Paul, '*douloi Jesu Christi*':[1] Christ's slaves – not to weaken it! The retreat leader speaks about the rhythm of inner life: between the periods of dullness, when one needs to keep the lamp of faith and love always burning, and the periods of growth. It is about constant obedience to Jesus and Mary. It should move forward in uniform acceleration. Growth in wisdom and charity, which is related to the cross (*stultitia crucis* [the foolishness of the cross]).[2] Not to be discouraged by crosses. The cross is our dowry – above all, it was Mary's dowry. The Lord Jesus underwent passion three times: in the sacramental, spiritual and bloody ways (the first holy hour of Christ's Mother during the agony and in Gethsemane), and then Her presence under the cross. When we celebrate the Holy Mass, we are '*en Christo*' ['in Christ'] – and at the same time we receive the Mother from Christ – 'this is your Mother' . . . The influence of Mary's motherhood through the Holy Mass. Celebrating the Holy Mass, we can be '*en Christo*', enter into Him together with the Mother of God as His slaves. The happiness derived from celebrating the Holy Mass: here we are at the roots of the priestly vocation. Jesus never denies the sufficient number of priestly vocations to the Church. If this number falters, the cause must lie within us – not Christ. Our death is the completion of our sacrifice '*en Christo*', a participation in the Lord Jesus' resurrection along the entire path of our inner life. We have to change in the hands of the Mother of God in such a way as to raise the level of the Church in Poland for ages to come.

We follow Our Lady of the Rosary. Joyful Mysteries.

Sorrowful Mysteries.

Glorious Mysteries.

Adoration; Matins; Benediction [illegible]; Penitential psalms; Compline

3 September Laudes (St Pius X); Rosary; The Way of the Cross; Prime; Holy Mass

Meditation: '*instaurare omnia in Christo*' ['to unite all things in Christ'].[3] '*Terrena non metuit*' ['He feared no earthly powers'] (St Pius).

Talk: Faith. Jesus demands faith in Him, in His person (*in Me*

1 See Romans 1:1.
2 See 1 Corinthians 1:23–25.
3 See Ephesians 1:10.

veritas [truth is in Me]). He demands strong faith (resilient and exultant), unconditional faith (*modicae fidei* [of little faith]). Faith comes from the Father (*Pater revelavit* [the Father revealed]), it is the divine light and divine truth instilled in our minds. An example of faith: the annunciation to Zechariah versus the annunciation to the Blessed Virgin Mary (a very beautiful analysis). How much of the 'flesh and blood'[1] is still in our theological virtue of faith? The example of the Mother of God. St Louis-Marie Grignion de Montfort says the Mother of God's faith is preserved in the holy Church. Participation in Mary's faith is the only way against perils and threats to faith.

Faith makes use and should make use of reason 'to ponder and treasure God's truth in one's heart'.[2] It is the function of the depth: '*ancilla*' ['servant'].[3] The greatness of Mary's faith throughout Her entire life (thirty years, Calvary, Pentecost). The apostles were sustained by Mary's faith. Let us be so too – in order to provide sustenance to others. To do so, we need to be '*douloi*' ['slaves'].

Does everything in me 'live out of faith'? One needs to believe in an episcopal way. The example of the Holy Father Paul VI: the way he speaks about the Mother of God! Building the Church through universal faith, but at the same time with our own local contribution.

Talk (final): St Paul as the model of Christian hope, though he was a Roman citizen. It was different with '*Ancilla*' (*Virgo Marya* [Virgin Mary]), no human connections, no human support. And therefore Her hope is the greatest. At all stages of Her life. Under the cross, and especially later: She supported the early Church with this hope of Hers. And Her hope is kept within the holy Church. To what extent do we participate in Mary's hope? The Church in Poland is in the position of '*ancilla*', that is a servant.[4] The Lord God allows for this in order to make our hope grow. *Stabat Mater – stabat episcopus sub Cruce*

1 See Matthew 16:17.

2 See Luke 2:19.

3 See Luke 1:38.

4 During the years of communist rule in Poland (1945–1989), the Catholic clergy were often subject to oppression and invigilation by the authorities and their secret service.

Christi [the Mother stood – the bishop stood under Christ's cross].[1] Do we live with hope? Do we find support essentially and exclusively in God's grace? In what mood do people go back after meeting us? If they stand, inspired by the bishop's optimism, we have fulfilled our service to hope. 'Grant me, Mother, Your hope, and fill my heart with Your hope' (*nostra conversatio in coelis est* [our citizenship is in heaven]).[2] Nothing can threaten us, neither Satan, nor the world, nor sin – if there is Christ's power in us in the same way it is in Mary.

And during this retreat God's love has been poured into our hearts, as it was into Mary's, by the Holy Spirit.

1–3 November [probably 1964]

Visiting the shrines: Montèvergine – S. Giovanni Rotondo – S. Michele in Gargano – Lanciano (!)

4 November: Memorial of St Charles Borromeo

At the Felician Sisters' – *quaedam reasumptio* [a certain conclusion]

1 *Stabat Mater Dolorosa* [The Sorrowful Mother Stood] is a thirteenth-century Marian hymn attributed to Jacopone da Todi.

2 See Philippians 3:20.

17–20 [August] 1965
Retreat in Tyniec
Topic: Justification, theological virtues

17 August Holy Mass read on the Memorial of St Hyacinth of Poland (OP). After the arrival in Tyniec: Vespers; Adoration; Compline

18 August Morning prayers [illegible]; (Rosary); Lauds; Holy Mass; Thanksgiving; Matins; Prime; Act of Consecration to the Blessed Virgin Mary

Meditation: Referring back to the retreat of 1963, I wish to expand on the topic of 'justification'. I find this topic academically (theologically) appealing and at the same time internally, personally important. The topic develops into a reflection on theological virtues, i.e. divine virtues.

Faith. The catechism's definition: 'to accept as true all that God has revealed to us and that holy Church proposes for our belief'[1] can be interpreted and even experienced in different ways. The intellectualist (ideological) interpretation is different from the personalist (charitological) interpretation. It is not only about the sum of truths (propositions) which the mind accepts through the authority of 'God who reveals them' – and more directly: Christ, the Church (cf. *motiva credibilitatis* [compare motives of credibility]).[2] It is about the specific supernatural relationship of man – a person – with the personal God (*Trinitas SS* [the Holy Trinity]). The nearer foundation of this relationship is the mind (reason). The proper subject matter of this human faculty is truth. Faith is a readiness, indeed, it is an act of reason which is ready to accept God's truth as its own truth. *Communicatio in veritate cum Deo* [Communion with God in truth]. It is probably the highest act – one of the highest acts – in a relationship of a person to a person. This readiness to communicate in truth

---

1 See the *Catechism of the Catholic Church*, 1842.
2 See the *Catechism of the Catholic Church*, 156.

becomes, in a particular way, renewed through revelation, and in general with its help (in its extension lies theology). Faith consists in the acceptance of revelation, but it is possible thanks to the readiness of the mind mentioned above, which revelation takes for granted and simultaneously makes fully possible.

The Way of the Cross: main theme '*viator* – *comprehensor*' ['wayfarer – comprehensor'];[1] The Little Hours; Reading the schemas; Vespers for Wednesday
Adoration: it somehow provides me with topics for the afternoon meditation
Meditation on practical issues: dialogue, the Church of dialogue, others separately
Matins; Spiritual reading; Compline

19 August

Lauds; Prime (communal); Holy Mass with petitionary prayers before and after; Writing pastoral texts

Meditation: To continue yesterday's topic, it must be first observed that faith would require a much broader analysis, including the issue of atheism (unbelief) and the attitude to it. (The Church of dialogue is in fact the object of the virtue of hope.) Hope itself is a very rich and complex virtue. It is not possible to conduct its multidimensional analysis right now. Just some dimensions. In hope there is something of faith and something of charity. Fundamentally, it is the wish for what God offers us in revelation, which we mentally accept through faith. It is then our wish for and choice of God and the entire world of supernatural goods. There is a certain personalist dimension in this; hope turns us towards God as the aim, hope is the wish for or even the desire of 'the everlasting hills'.[2] But it is here that its second dimension is revealed, and it could be called the 'dimension of strength'. Will I manage? A certain evaluation of one's own strength in relation to the aim. And after this evaluation, trust: God Himself will give me strength for that. '*Deus adiuvabit*' ['God will help']. So the relationship of a person to the Person in hope has two dimensions: first, the readiness to wish for that which God wishes for (through this dimension hope frees us from ideological negativism and the senselessness of life), and, second, trust (through this

Here also '*timor*' ['fear'].

1 See Thomas Aquinas, *Summa Theologica*, trans. Fathers of the English Dominican Province (London, 1947–48), vol. 2, part III, question 15, article 10.
2 See 'The Litany of the Sacred Heart of Jesus'.

dimension hope frees us from despair). The first dimension takes place thanks to the second, and vice versa. And an essential and indispensable element of the justification of man before God is realised through the entire virtue of hope in both its dimensions. Hope is an attitude of the human being towards God (a person towards the Person) in which one is 'just', i.e. in the right position towards the one who is God. This attitude results from grace and simultaneously leads to it. (NB personalist and revealed morality in some way consists of analysing such attitudes.)

The virtue of hope turns towards eternity and temporality at the same time. God, helping us reach eternity in temporality, simultaneously helps us fulfil His plan, which is focused on eternity, in temporality. It is all about making this plan of His ours. Hope does not accept fiction nor 'substitutes'. However, it permeates our various temporal tasks, which we undertake through God's will. Without hope – without putting trust in Him and having confidence that He will help – it would definitely be impossible.

The Way of the Cross: Main theme: salvation is linked to hardship – hope takes this into account too.

The Little Hours; Reading schema XIII;[1] Vespers for Thursday; Rosary continued
Adoratio SS-mi, ubi Xristus tamquam fons et stabilis mensura vitae humanae praesens adest [Adoration of the Holy Sacrament, in which Christ is present as the fount and permanent measure of human life]
Afternoon meditation on practical issues, on these separately; Anticipated Matins
Reading (on the priesthood of laity by Father Przybylski)
Compline; Holy Hour – priesthood as the main topic – for priests and vocations

20 August: Memorial of St Bernard

Lauds; Prime; Rosary; Prayers (preparation for Holy Mass); Holy Mass; Thanksgiving; Writing texts related to 5 September and the following days

Meditation: Love, the virtue of charity, is an even broader topic than the previous one. First of all, the fact that God is love puts it above everything, and makes it the centre towards which all participation gravitates. Charity is the 'fulfilment of

1 Schema XIII was eventually developed into *Gaudium et spes* (Joy and Hope), the Pastoral Constitution on the Church in the Modern World, promulgated by Pope Paul VI on 7 December 1965.

Bóg pomaga nam osiągać dojrzałość w doczesności, pozwala nam równocześnie realizować w doczesności swój plan nastawiony na wieczność. Chodzi tylko o to, aby ten Jego plan stał się naszym. Naturalnie nie przyjmuje jakiejś nowej „postaci". Wnika ona natomiast w różne nasze zadania doczesne, jakie podejmujemy z woli Boga. Bez nadziei – bez zawierzenia Jemu i ufności, że On dopomoże – byłoby to stanowczo niemożliwe.

Via Crucis: 3 Główny wątek: ~~nadzieja wszystkiego także i to, że~~ zbawienie przychodzi z trudem – nadzieja wszystkiego także i to.

Horae min.

Lectio schema XIII.

Vesp. f. V.

Ros. in continuo

Adoratio SS-mi, ubi Christus ~~tamquam~~ fons et stabilis mensura vitae humanae praesens adest

Meditatio postmeridiana de practicis, de quibus reparatum

Matutinum anticipatum

APPUNTAMENTI

Lectio (o kapłaństwie wszystkich i ścisłym)

Complet.

Godzina św. – jako główny temat kapłaństwo: za kapłanów i o kapłanów.

20. VIII. S. Bernardi

Laudes, Prima

Ros. prec. (praeparatio ad sacrum)

justification'. It is even more than '*plenitudo legis*' ['the fulfilling of the law'].[1] Through love the fullest and the most mature contact of a person with the Person can be established – the contact that faith and hope have already foregrounded. It seems that both these virtues share something with charity, they prepare one for it and lead one towards it. It is not surprising that charity cannot exist without them (though they can exist without charity). At the same time, the essence of charity exceeds what faith and hope are by themselves. There is more in charity – and through this 'more' it remains incomparable to the other two. It is difficult to grasp this 'more'. It seems that charity is always responsible for the union with a person that takes place within that which is good, and the union with that which is good that takes place in a person. Its nature is, in a sense, bipolar, being simultaneously 'personalist' and 'axiological'. It has to be love 'above all' for God, who is the fullness of good – and for creatures, specifically people, according to the measure of good they represent. Love is not bound to a person in a way that would make it impossible for it to go beyond that person (where it is possible) towards good. At the same time, a proper relation between good and charity makes it always possible to turn love towards other people – not only one specific person, but people in general. Love is characterised by the properties which St Paul wrote about (1 Cor. 13). Its essence is beyond properties and it is such a participation in God that it fills all eternity.

The Way of the Cross: Expanding on these reflections, e.g. Station II: '*ubi amatur, iam non laboratur, et si laboratur, etiam labor amatur*' ['in love, there is no hardship; even in hardship, the hardship is loved']; Station VIII: the strength of love lies also in the identification of that which is not love – even though it appears to be – for what it is.

The Little Hours; Adoration (Words of Our Lord Jesus Christ on the cross); Rosary; Vespers; Afternoon meditation on practical issues (separately)

1 See Romans 13:10.

Continuation: 26 September, 28 September [probably 1965]

7/8 November: *Dies recol.* [Reflection days]

Main thoughts: (a) *participatio in sacerdotio Christi - in summo sacerdotio* [participation in Christ's priesthood - in the highest priesthood]; (b) priesthood and the days of death (1–2 November) coincide in my life in a significant way; (c) then thoughts '*de redemptione*' ['of redemption'] come back (*redemptio* - redemption = the restoration of full worth to man and creatures in general); (d) a supplement to the meditation on theological virtues: charity is a participation in the very person, and differs from faith and hope in that it leads to a participation in a person, thus, a union; (e) just like at the retreat, also here one feels an eagerness to complete tasks (which at this stage I have put in some order).

[19]64 (65?)

7/8 November This day was a kind of anticipation of the retreat day (intertwined with other activities). The key thoughts of the day: (1) the reality of the Most Holy Trinity (preface); (2) the issue of 'meaning – service'.

2 December Matins; Holy Mass; Lauds; Prime

Meditation 1: The Church as the means to the end, which is God Himself: the union of persons–souls with Him. Simultaneously, the same Church as *Sponsa* [Bride]: the divine order is the order of love.

Meditation 2: God Himself gives 'meaning' to man and his actions. At the same time, there is a drive towards this 'meaning' in man. This drive is turned into service when man accepts the meaning given to it by God. This 'meaning' is always larger than man. It overwhelms him.

Vespers; The Way of the Cross (associations with Genesis)

Meditation 3: A timely one on the topic of '*pastor – auctor*' ['shepherd – creator']

Conclusion: to order things according to the meaning given to them by God, though the question remains.

Meditation 4: Litany of the Saints. *Modus procedendi* [how to proceed] in case 1.

Adoration; (Talk for the Felician Sisters)
Spiritual reading (F. Wulf SJ, *La vie spirituelle dans le monde d'aujourd'hui*)[1]
Matins; Rosary; Penitential psalms; Compline

1 Friedrich Wulf SJ (1908–90) was a German priest, editor of the journal *Geist und Leben* (Spirit and Life), and a theological consultant at the Second Vatican Council. This is a reference to his *Geistliches Leben in der heutigen Welt* [Spiritual Life in Today's World] (Freiburg, 1960), published in French as *La vie spirituelle dans le monde d'aujourd'hui* (Mulhouse, 1964).

31 October – 1 November 1966 [Kalwaria] (Twentieth anniversary of priestly ordination)

The Little Ways:[1] An extraordinary theological fusion of Christ's way of the cross and His Mother's way. Christ's priesthood was planted, sown and deposited in the people of God as their permanent inheritance. My own priesthood was also born out of the people of God's inheritance.

Holy Mass at the altar of the Blessed Virgin Mary; Talk on current issues; (1 November) the ordination of subdeacons in the cathedral; The Way of the Cross; Prayers for the dead

Meditation 1 } On the course of my priesthood
Meditation 2 }

1 See n. 2, p. 12 [6–7 July 1963].

19–21 December 1966
Retreat at the Albertine Sisters' Convent
Topic: *iustificatio – restitutio – (vocatio)* [justification – restitution – (vocation)]

~

19 December Preparation for Holy Mass: 'Order – grace' (Meditation 1); Holy Mass, Thanksgiving; Lauds, Prime

Meditation 2: Vocation and eschatology. Having to consider some more specific issues related to my vocation, I am looking for the broadest background possible. The human vocation is eschatological, directed at God Himself through participation in His life and eternity. Recently I have connected this eschatological vocation with the idea of '*restitutio*': the creation's return to the Creator. Such a return is, so to speak, the primary function of the Son–Word: Christ. At this point the earthly Advent exceeds its historical boundaries. Everything in Christ aims for '*restitutio*' [a return to the original condition] – for a return to the Father. Man participates in this in a conscious way through faith. Conscious participation in Christ's '*restitutio*' coincides with human justification (*iustificatio*) as the basic conception of being in grace.

The second eschatological element is judgement. We also await Christ from this angle: first, historically, as Word made flesh – Word that is truth: the truth-norm expressed in the Gospels. Then as Word–Judgement ('The Father judges no one but has given all judgement to the Son').[1] As the consequence of incarnation and redemption, the Word's judgement will be as if a special 'self-judgement' of humankind: a judgement in the light of the Word.

Thus, eschatology takes shape as a particular connection between these two elements: '*restitutio*' and '*Verbum*–

1 See John 5:22.

Iudicium' ['Word–Judgement']. Death is a border only from the human perspective.

The Way of the Cross (text by E. Krajewska written in the Pawiak prison);[1] The Little Hours
Spiritual reading (Fr Granat, dogmatics: The ultimate destiny of man and the world),[2] Steinmann: Paul of Tarsus,[3] Burke: on St Paul of the Cross ('Hunter of Souls'), Rosary (III)

Meditation 3: *De quibusdam particularibus in vocatione mea* [On particular aspects of my vocation]: a continuation of the topic of 'meaning given to man by God' – the grace of state[4] is contained within these boundaries, to cooperate with it, to be faithful to it.

Meditation 4: *De apostolatu laicorum* [On the apostolate of the laity]

Vespers; Adoration of the Blessed Sacrament; Matins of the following day; Litany of the Saints; Compline

20 December Preparation for Holy Mass

Meditation 1 (short): *recapitulatio* [summary]; Petition for the development of what was outlined on the first day

Lauds; Holy Mass; Thanksgiving; Prime; Spiritual reading

Meditation 2: Our (all people's) vocation in Christ. Christ is, above all, a great calling which permeates temporality, but gestures towards eternity. It permeates temporality and attempts to organise it from the angle of '*restitutio*', that is a return to the Father. The double meaning of the cross is connected to this – and the double '*elevatio*' ['elevation'] during the Holy Mass. The cross as the victim – the expiatory destruction. And the cross as the labour of constant search for the correct value

1 Elżbieta Krajewska (1923–44) was a member of the Polish anti-Nazi resistance movement (the Home Army). She was arrested in 1943, tortured in the notorious Pawiak prison in Warsaw and sent to Auschwitz concentration camp, where she died in 1944.

2 Wicenty Granat (1900–79) was a Polish priest and theologian who served as the rector of the Catholic University of Lublin (1965–70). He published extensively on dogmatic theology and Christian humanism. The reference here might be to his book *Eschatologia: Rzeczy ostateczne człowieka i Świata* [Eschatology: The Ultimate Destiny of Man and the World] (Lublin, 1962).

3 This may be a reference to Alphons Steinmann's book *Zum Werdegang des Paulus – die Jugendzeit in Tarsus* [Towards the Development of Paul – His Youth in Tarsus] (Freiburg, 1928).

4 See the *Catechism of the Catholic Church*, 2004.

(re-evaluation) of everything – the values which were intended and established by the Creator–Father. Jesus is our guide in this search and His cross is the sign of labour connected to it. (This is a side-reflection on St Paul of the Cross – and the constitution *Gaudium et spes*.)

The vocation is the consequence of the calling, God's voice in Christ. It has consequences for all people, but for every person [they are] different – special. A glance at my vocation. It has (like every vocation) a social and charismatic sense.

The Way of the Cross according to Bishop Wł. Bandurski;[1] The Little Hours; Spiritual reading

Meditation 3 *de particularibus* [on particular issues]: In relation to the Church, I must strictly follow my own vocation – the vocation which the Lord God gave to me. Not to go beyond this vocation, because the grace of state is strictly linked to it. In such a following of one's vocation, its proper meaning and boundaries, one finds strength for various 'inner reactions'. Cooperation with the grace of state will form the basis of the fulfilment of the vocation with love and faithfulness.

Vespers; Adoration of the Blessed Sacrament; Matins for the Feast of St Thomas the Apostle;

Meditation 4: *de apostolatu laicorum* [on the apostolate of the laity] (hereafter in writing);

Rosary (II); Reading the Holy Scripture (Letter to the Romans)

Meditation 5 *ubi quaedam alia particularia assumuntur* [where other specific issues are addressed]: 'The line of fatherhood' – dialogue – TP – synod – *ad ulteriorem considerationem* [for further consideration].

Penitential psalms; Compline

21 December: Feast of St Thomas the Apostle

Preparation for Holy Mass

Meditation 1: Yesterday, an accumulation of problems – today, judgement.

1 Władysław Bandurski (1865–1932) was a Polish priest and honorary chaplain of the Polish Legions in the First World War.

21 VENERDI - s. Tommaso Ap. | s. Demetrio m. - SABATO **22**

DICEMBRE

mocą [illegible] „wszystko i wielkości z [illegible] w ręku Boga.

Tak oto eschatologia zarysowuje się jako szczególne uwypuklenie tych dwu elementów „restitutio" i „Verbum-Judicium". Śmierć jest tylko granicą od strony stworzenia.

Via Crucis (tekst E. Kasperskiej z [illegible])

Horae min.

Lectio spir. (x Granat, Dogm.: Krąg oświecenia chrześcijańskiego i [illegible])
Steinmann: Paweł z Tarsu
Bourke: o. Paweł od Krzyża (Pasjonista)

3. coronae Rosarii BMV.

Medit. 3 De quibusdam particularibus in vocatione mea i ciąg dalszy na temat „znaczenie", jakie nadaje wszystkiemu śmierć — w tych granicach zawiera się także stanie, z nich wypływa [illegible], jej [illegible]

Medit. 4. De apostolatu laicorum

Vesp. Adorat. SS-mi

Matut. Dici sequ. Lit. sanct.

Compl.

20.XII. Laudes. Praepar. ad Sacrum. Sacrum. Grat. act. Lectio spir.

Medit. 3. Oratio: recapitulatio. Prima: prośba o zrozumienie tego, co się zarysowało w dniu pierwszym.

Medit. 1 Powołanie nasze (wszystkich ludzi) w Chrystusie. Chrystus

APPUNTAMENTI

jest naprzód wszelkim Stworzeniem, które pragnie ~~i organizuje~~ doskonałości, ale wskazuje na ostateczność. Pragnienie doskonałości i staje się już zorganizowanie pod kątem „restitutio" czyli oddania Ojcu. Z tym się wiąże podwójne znaczenie Krzyża – i podwójne „elevatio" we Mszy św. Krzyż jako ofiara – wyniszczenie zadośćuczynienie. I Krzyż jako trud ciągłego szukania

Petition for the grace of judgement; Lauds; Holy Mass; Thanksgiving; Prime; Spiritual reading

Meditation 2: A reflection on my own vocation. Its elements (constitution *Lumen gentium*[1]): the Father, the shepherd, the teacher–'sanctifier' – deserve a separate, contemplative study. The concept of the 'father' contains the beginning, the begetting of life and constant care for its maintenance in one's own children. It is about life in its material and spiritual sense. The latter refers to spiritual fatherhood. The 'shepherd' is also the father when it comes to the concern for maintaining life (this is a narrower concept), and he is simultaneously the 'leader of the sheepfold' – the one who manages and governs. Teaching (the teacher) and sanctification are contained in the function of the father and shepherd.

We are constantly and repeatedly asked to grow gradually ever deeper roots in our people (*crescere in plebem suam* [to increase among one's people]).[2] At the same time, this growing of roots offers a fuller entrance into the elements of vocation mentioned above. Their verification. A vocation also points to certain inner and outer forms of life.

The Little Hours; The Way of the Cross according to Fr W. Smereka's commentary; Spiritual reading

Meditation 3: Thinking of people: 'W.' – this relationship is above all religious. This is its specificity. The sense of belonging governs the relation to God: First, it removed the most fundamental obstacle, and then, it has maintained and supported this relationship. (Conclusion: this form of belonging should probably not be done away with or fundamentally changed.) 'T.' and 'M.': the sense of belonging has above all a moral meaning, it helps to put one's moral life in order – in a way, on two different poles of life. 'T.': it is more of an attachment than belonging; a certain struggle for belonging is taking place, especially for its moral consequences.

Vespers; Adoration of the Blessed Sacrament; Matins of the following day

1 *Lumen gentium* (Light of the Nations), the Dogmatic Constitution on the Church, was promulgated by Pope Paul VI on 21 November 1964. It was one of the key documents of the Second Vatican Council.
2 See the antiphon and responsory '*Ecce sacerdos magnus*'.

Meditation 4: *De apostolatu laicorum* [On the apostolate of the laity]

Afterwards: reading three texts related to the Act of Consecration to the Mother of God[1]
A visit to the exhibition on Brother Albert[2]

Meditation 5: Three themes merge into one. The theme of 'dialogue' and the theme of 'TP' together with the consecration to the Mother of God. This year in a special way 'I renew and ratify in Thy hands the vows of my Baptism'.[3] After all, my vocation and mission of today is contained within these vows. It is a mission of labour, because it has to integrate both defence and dialogue properly. That is why it needs to be – as the consequence of my baptism – entrusted to Mary in the spirit of holy slavery.[4] The completion of a difficult mission, which humanly nobody knows how to complete, through this consecration becomes an object of hope.

Rosary (III); Compline; Reading the Holy Scripture

---

1 Cardinal Stefan Wyszyński, Primate of Poland, made an act of consecration of the Polish Church to the Mother of God on 3 May 1966 at the Shrine of Our Lady of Częstochowa, during the celebration of the millennial anniversary of Poland's Christianisation. During his first visit to Poland, Pope John Paul II referred to this event in the homily he gave on 4 June 1979: 'I wish to confirm and renew the act of consecration pronounced at Jasna Góra on 3 May 1966, on the occasion of the Millennium of Poland. With this act the Polish Bishops wished, by giving themselves to you, Mother of God, "in your maternal slavery of love", to serve the great cause of the freedom of the Church not only in their own homeland but in the whole world.'

2 St Albert Chmielowski (1845–1916), also known as Brother Albert, was the founder of the Albertine Brothers and Sisters. He devoted his life to charity work, helping the homeless and the underprivileged. He was canonised by Pope John Paul II on 12 November 1989.

3 See St Louis-Marie Grignion de Montfort's 'Prayer of Consecration' in *God Alone: The Collected Writings of S. Louis-Marie de Montfort* (Liverpool, 1967).

4 On the idea of 'holy slavery' as total devotion to Mary, see St Louis-Marie Grignion de Montfort's *The Secret of Mary* (Charlotte, NC, 1947).

29 February 1968
(*in via* [on the way])

~

Day of reflection

Meditation 1 on the topic: (a) '*dinumerare nos doce dies nostros, ut perveniamus ad sapientiam cordis*' ['teach us to count our days that we may gain a wise heart'][1] (Ps. 89); (b) *nos confitentes poscimus Te, iuste Iudex cordium* [in confession we plead with You, righteous Judge of hearts].[2]

Meditation 2 on the overall picture of the 'Roman' matters
Penitential psalms; Litany of the Saints; Holy Hour; (Yesterday: the Way of the Cross)

---

1 See Psalm 89 (90):12.
2 See the hymn '*Nox atra rerum contegit*' ('The Dusky Veil of Night').

11–14 September 1968
Retreat in Tyniec
Topic: Union and rejection

Further preparation: Kalwaria Zebrzydowska: 9 and 10 July:

(a) (The question of how to put the Council into practice in Poland.)
(b) The Little Ways, petition for God's blessing, 'not to do harm'.

11 September The end of the visit of the icon of the Mother of God to the Myślenice Deanery (Głogoczów) and the beginning of the visit to the Bolechowice Deanery (Zielonki): presence, the Word of God.[1]

Studying notes from previous retreats – preparing the subject matter

12 September: Feast of the Most Holy Name of Mary

Lauds; Prime; Private Mass; Thanksgiving; '*In me omnis spes vitae et virtutis*' ['In me is all hope of life and of virtue'][2] – as a Marian motto for the retreat

Meditation 1: Ten years have passed since my episcopal ordination and the retreat in Tyniec that preceded it. Time draws me away from this central fact in my life very quickly. The fact that will be of decisive significance for my death and for eternity.

Time and eternity – not as an abstract idea, but as a share of one and the same person. The perspective of participation in eternity, that is in God. This perspective is grounded in the

---

1 The icon of Our Lady of Częstochowa, also known as the Black Madonna of Częstochowa, has been closely linked with Polish history. In 1953–56, during the anti-religious campaign by the communist government of Poland, Cardinal Stefan Wyszyński, Primate of Poland, ordered that the icon travel around the country and visit a number of deaneries. John Paul II visited the image of Our Lady of Częstochowa four times during his pontificate.

2 See Sirach 24:18.

reality of the Person – 'on the side' of God and on the human side.

The reality of the human person as a unity endowed with a certain transcendence and immortality of the soul (this matter awaits an in-depth consideration): Experience reveals to me not only the unity of existence, but also its complexity. Transcendent = spiritual; the basis of transcendence is the spirit. An awareness of the essential indestructibility of that which is spiritual and transcendent in a person (= its essence is such that it cannot be destroyed), e.g. moral or intellectual value. Hence the conclusion about the existence of an immanent cause in the human being, which is also indestructible. At the same time, the obvious evidence for the destructibility of the body: our 'I' as the body – destructible; as the spirit – indestructible.

The Little Hours; Conversation with Br Aug. on the matters of governance in the Church; Vespers

Adoration: The notion of *transsignificatio* [a change of meaning] and *transfinalisatio* [a change of aim] are not enough in themselves – *trans-substantiatio* [transubstantiation] reflects the depth of the mystery. 'Beyond' the reality of the Eucharist is the reality of God–Man, who 'gives Himself entirely' to us.

Rosary (III)

Meditation 2: On the matters which play a considerable role in my moral consciousness and conscience. First, their nature '*in se*' ['in themselves']: diversity, the good – does it not include any subjectivity? – then '*per accidens*' ['contingently']: the confessional – similar, but different – a 'new stage'. A passionate petition for divine grace to help me carry out these matters well.

Matins; Holy Hour: Christ face to face with the Father: Your will – call for vigilance (*Humanae vitae*) – betrayal or weakness? (of priests).

Compline

13 September Lauds (communal); Concelebrated Mass; Thanksgiving; Prime (private)

Meditation 1 (*potius consideratio* [rather a consideration]): On my role in the Council of Bishops; on 'complementarity' – which is important now because of the preparation for the implementation of the Council in Poland. Also here, at the retreat, I collect and put in order my thoughts which relate to this and I begin writing.

Rosary (I); Prayer for the gifts of the Holy Spirit; Rosary (II)

Meditation 2: Further reflection on the last things. Man is called to a union with God. This final union is a mystery of faith: heaven as well as hell and purgatory. *Excedit intelligentiam* [it exceeds our understanding]. If an analogy of any kind can be evoked here, it is the relationship of persons. In this light, the union is, firstly, 'personal', which means that it is a union in truth and love founded in mutual knowledge (seeing) and will; and it is, secondly, a union of persons: the union of the human person with the Persons of the Most Holy Trinity: with the Father through the Son in the Holy Spirit.

Rejection, that is, a non-union due to the lack of 'personal' foundation in truth and love, may be followed by a rejection of a person.

Finally: reaching maturity necessary for the union in contrast to the lack of maturity.

The Way of the Cross: The reflections on the Stations of the Cross partly followed the previous theme. The cross is, on the one hand, a tragedy of the rejection of God by the chosen people, yet at the same time, the cross rises above the tragedy of this rejection through the power of the redemptive, atoning and uplifting sacrifice – cf. the triple fall and the rising from weakness and mistake – from error and fault – from lies and hatred. Mary takes part in this, and She also helps us overcome that which causes our downfall.

The Little Hours; Conversation with Br Michaële (as if [illegible] an ascetic talk) on the topic: 'the apostolate fundamentally grounded in prayer and sacrifice'; Vespers

Adoration of the Blessed Sacrament: Marked by the revival of faith in the presence of the very same Christ who suffered on the cross: 'transubstantiation' – the beginning of this presence and its permanent foundation. He is present to give Himself to people. Here again the understanding of the 'personal' order helps a lot.

względu można tutaj zaczerpnąć analogii – to z relacji osób. ~~Zjednoczenie~~ W tym dziele zjednoczenie 1° jest „osobowe" – to znaczy jest zjednoczeniem w prawdzie i miłości opartym na poznaniu (widzeniu) i woli – oraz 2° zjednoczeniem osób: zjednoczenie osoby ludzkiej z osobami Bożymi Trójcy Przenajśw.: z Ojcem przez Syna w Duchu Św.

Odrzucenie czyli nie-zjednoczenie z braku ~~gruntu~~ podstawy „osobowych" w prawdzie i miłości – w ślad za tym dopiero może iść odrzucenie osoby.

Wniosek: dojrzewanie do zjednoczenia wobec braku dojrzałości

Via Crucis: rozważanie przy stacjach przy upadkach za wszystkim upadkiem. Krzyż jest z jednej strony dramatem ~~[illegible]~~ jakiegoś odrzucenia Boga przez lud wybrany, a równocześnie ponad dramat tego odrzucenia ~~[illegible]~~ ten sam Krzyż wyrasta mocą ofiary odkupicielskiej: zadość-czyniącej i dźwigającej (cf. potrójny upadek i powstanie z pokusy i słabości – z błędu i wady – z kłamstwa i niemocy). Uczestniczy w tym Maryja, która zarazem pomaga nam przezwyciężać to, ~~czego~~ co jest naszym upadkiem.

Horae m.

APPUNTAMENTI

Colloquium cum f. Michaele (quasi miesięczna konferencja asc.) na temat: apostolstwo gruntowne podbudowane modlitwą i ofiarą

Vesp.

Ador. SS-mi pod znakiem odczuwania w Obecności tej samej Chrystusa, który konał na krzyżu: i przetworzenie – pomiędzy tej

Meditation (consideration): A continuation of the morning's questions. Then the topic of the love of the enemy. Testimony to the truth given in a courageous and tenacious way is necessary. Defence of the Church and righteousness is necessary. What remains is the attitude to people: one needs to pray all the more.

Message du S. Père aux prêtres [The Holy Father's letter to all priests] (to mark the end of the year of faith).

Other signs of the 'negative attitude': When I greatly desire the good of e.g. my community, I need to be careful that this 'great desire' does not turn into a kind of hostility towards others.

Rosary (III); Penitential psalms; Litany of the Saints; Office prayers; Compline

14 September: Feast of the Exaltation of the Holy Cross

Lauds; Participation in the concelebrated Mass, and simultaneously:

Meditation 1: (Consideration): A continuation of yesterday evening's meditation. One needs to be vigilant because even here I have heard of some breakdowns. There needs to be a deep wish for the good, and a courageous defence of the Church, righteousness and truth – but one needs to be vigilant so that it does not become an ordinary 'vehemence'. This difficult aspect of self-improvement should be entrusted in particular to the Mother of God (Saturday!).

Prime; Participation in the Low Mass, and simultaneously: Rosary (I), Rosary (II)

Meditation 2: In a sense a continuation of yesterday morning's reflection on the topic of union with God. Today I consider the 'structure of condemnation'. Condemnation, just like salvation, the union with God, is a mystery of faith. However, if one can *per analogiam* [by analogy] use personalist structures, various stages are, so to speak, revealed. A failure to meet in truth and love caused by some weakness or mistake is something other than the rejection of God – because He upsets e.g. one's vanity.

Actually, we only know the figure of the condemned angel ('. . . prepared for the devil and his angels').[1]

And Christ says: 'the one who does not believe will be con-

1 See Matthew 25:41.

demned'[1] and 'depart from me into the eternal fire . . . truly I tell you, just as you did not do it to one of the least of these, you did not do it to me.'[2] One needs to consider these mysteries further:

The structure of rejection is closely linked to the structure of conscience (*quod non est ex fide, peccatum est* [whatever does not proceed from faith is sin]):[3] the question of good and bad faith (*bonae et malae fidei*). The rejected angel is certainly of bad faith; he hates God, even though he knows that He is the fullness of good, and he does not want to serve Him, even though he knows he ought to.

The problem of 'conviction': certain conscience – and doubtful conscience (one must not act in accordance with the latter). The problems '*ad cautelam*' ['for caution'].

The Way of the Cross (in unity with the Mother of God); The Little Hours; Conversation with Br Ludwik (and Marian) – about vocation; Vespers

Adoration of the Blessed Sacrament: Thanksgiving for the wonderful reality of the Eucharist, in which I have been participating for so many years as a priest, and for ten years as a bishop!

Consideratio super sacerdotio et de sacerdotibus [Reflection on priesthood and priests]: During the retreat I read a report on the debates of priests from the Kraków Archdiocese on this topic during deanery and inter-deanery conferences. Regarding the need to appoint a council of priests and clergymen.

I concluded the retreat by taking part in the closing day of the visit of the icon of the Mother of God to Giebułtów and the beginning of its visit to Modlnica. I constantly, and specially, consecrate my ten years of episcopacy and further service, as long as divine providence allows, to the Mother of God. I entrust to Her the matter of the renewal of *presbyterium* [priesthood] in particular.

Evening Mass for Monika and Jacek on the tenth anniversary of their marriage
UIOGD

1 See Mark 16:16.
2 See Matthew 25:41, 45.
3 See Romans 14:23.

9–13 August 1969
Retreat at Bachledówka[1]
Topic: 'Good in its divine source and its human verification'

~

9 August In the afternoon: preparation for the retreat: (a) Holy Mass, penitential psalms; (b) reading notes from previous retreats; (c) searching for the topic (*Myst. SS Trinit., myst. Ecclesiae: sacerd. populi regal., mysterium iniquitatis: triplex concupisc.* [The mystery of the Holy Trinity, the mystery of the Church: the priesthood of a royal people,[2] the mystery of evil: the triple concupiscence[3]]); (d) apart from that – a glance at the Church that the Holy Spirit has entrusted to me.

10 August Intentions; Preparation for Holy Mass; Lauds; Holy Mass; Thanksgiving and prayers; Prayer for the gifts of the Holy Spirit

Meditation 1: Vatican II and, in particular, the Constitution on the Church, takes for its starting point God's eternal love for man ('*philantropia divina*'). The mystery of the Most Holy Trinity is seen from the perspective of this love (*missiones Div. Person.* [the divine Persons' mission]). This starting point, which reveals above all God's immanence ('God for man, for the creation') needs to be considered in more depth, in the direction of God's transcendence. God's eternal love 'for man' is explained by and stems from the fact that 'God is love'.[4]

(Contemplation of the mystery of deity.) We think of God through creatures and on the basis of creatures. Although we ascribe to Him to an infinite degree (*per viam eminentiae* [by way of eminence]) all types of perfection that we find in the created world, deity, God's nature – which the Father, the Word and the Holy Spirit possess – is not only a summation of these

---

1 Bachledówka is a retreat centre in the village of Czerwienne, in southern Poland, run by the Pauline Fathers. When Karol Wojtyła lived in Kraków, he often visited Bachledówka. He led retreats there in 1969 and 1975.

2 See 1 Peter 2:9.

3 See 1 John 2:16.

4 See 1 John 4:8.

perfections inferred from the world. Deity is transcendent in relation to everything that is created. Despite the similarity and '*per viam eminentiae*', God is 'completely different' from the world.

A special point of this contemplation of deity – 'God in Himself' – is the mystery of good. It seems that within the world good is always connected to some need, it responds to some need – and this is how one can discover and verify it. Human thought and human sensitivity to values move towards '*bonum in se*' ['good in itself'] with much difficulty. However, the contemplation of good beyond the structure of our needs, longings and desires is the deepest need and yearning of the human soul, which reflects the trait of divine likeness, characteristic of the human soul.

God Himself as good is – if one may say so – beyond any need. He is the Absolute, or the fullness of good, and also the fullness of glory. He does not need any of the creatures nor man to add anything to His divine perfection, happiness and glory. And this is why God's '*philantropia*', the love of man and creatures in general – beyond any need or usefulness – introduces us into the correct order of good. And it alone constitutes and guarantees this order.

If we were left with the worldly dimension, where good is to a large extent explained by need, benefit and usefulness – and this interpretation is the main trait of the materialistic axiology – man would be doomed to an almost hopeless search for '*bonum in se*'. And by the same token he would be doomed to dampen the deepest desire that lives in his soul, the desire for selfless good – and the selfless desire for good.

God determines and at the same time releases this desire – and through this He creates the foundations for love in the human world. 'I came to bring fire to the earth.'[1] For love presupposes good in itself, '*bonum in se*'.

Adoration: Glorification of God coming out of the depth of my heart, God as the good which exceeds everything else and which came close to man – and through the sacrament of its

1 See Luke 12:49.

prandium [lunch]

presence – the Eucharist – is still among us. Sacramentally, but in a way personally.

Reading: Fr Jaworski, 'On the philosophical and pre-philosophical knowledge of God'
Reading: Fr Macharski, 'Remarks on the organisation of pastoral units' – and a reflection on the tasks of the diocese

At the same time, the retreat is to help me deepen my love for the Church, which the Eternal Bridegroom has entrusted to me. In the margin of these reflections I make notes on the topic of the implementation of the Council and the diocesan structures.

Rosary; Vespers

Meditation 2: 'The Church has been seen as "a people made one with the unity of the Father, the Son and the Holy Spirit"' (*L[umen] G[entium]* 4).

A continuation of the meditation on the mystery of God oriented towards the reality of the Church (*Myst. Ecclesiae* [The mystery of the Church]) in accordance with my own plan for the retreat ('*philantropia*'). The Father, the Son and the Holy Spirit in the unity of the Godhead and the inexpressible mystery of the personal union in the Trinity simultaneously carry out this wonderful mission which shapes the divine reality of the Church. The Church is born and lives by the principle of this mission; it is the Church's foundation, so to speak. Through this mission and in this mission humankind partakes in the divine unity, which brings about the unity of people in the Church and through the Church. First, it is an inner unity of man established by truth and love, and then the principle of communality among people.

The entire Church – and its every part – receives this unity from the mission of the divine Persons. The mystery of the universal Church and the particular Church.[1]

The divine mission is shared by people in the Church in various ways.

Matins of the following day; The Way of the Cross; Rosary; Compline; Examination of conscience

1 See the *Catechism of the Catholic Church*, 832–5.

11 August Morning intentions; Lauds; Prime; Holy Mass; Thanksgiving (and Rosary)
Reading: (Catechism); (*Congr. pro Clericis* [Congregation for the Clergy])
Prayer for the gifts of the Holy Spirit

Meditation 3: 'If anyone loves the world, love for the Father is not in him. For all that is in the world, the lust of the flesh and the lust of the eyes and the pride of life, is not of the Father but is of the world. And the world passes away, and the lust of it; but he who does the will of God abides for ever.'[1]

The human 'I'– the dignity of the person, and the human body, and all flesh, and all material goods are from the Father, from God. And the entire order of ends and needs to which these goods correspond is also from God. The triple concupiscence, however, comes from the world. Father–God guarantees (as was said yesterday) good, the value of every creature (*bonum in se* [good in itself]). The creature which follows the proper needs assigned to it does not lose its proper value. The three forms of concupiscence – each of them differently – lose sight of this value (e.g. the value of the human 'I' or the body or other visible creatures). At the same time, they lose the correspondence of values to real needs; they lose the order of ends. The tragedy of concupiscence (including the pride of life) lies in the very fact that – when losing this order – it diminishes the value of creatures for whom it strives blindly.

This is fostered by the human sensual energy (disordered) and the limitation of the thought horizon, which has something in common with the 'fallen spirit' when it comes to the pride of life. However, it (pride) is also 'of this world'. In summary: the lack of possibility to see creatures and oneself, the body, material goods from God's perspective. Seeing them from this perspective enhances their value and ennobles the striving for them; it balances the needs and desires for created goods.

The analysis has proved that the 'triple concupiscence' constitutes a strictly theological category characteristic of revelation. It cannot be equated with psychological or other similar categories, e.g. 'the lust of the flesh' cannot be identi-

1 See 1 John 2:15–17.

ową więź i o niej udziela się ludzkości ta Boska jedność, która w Kościele i przez Kościół stanowi o zjednoczeniu ludzi. Jest to naprzód zjednoczenie wewnętrzne wokół prawdy i miłości, a z kolei zasada wspólnoty pomiędzy ludźmi.

Kościół cały przyjmuje z posłannictwa osób Bożych tę jedność – i każda jego część. Tajemnica Kościoła powszechnego i Kościoła partykularnego.

Posłannictwo Boże staje się w Kościele na różny sposób udziałem ludzi.

Matut. Dici segn.

Via Crucis

Corona B. Ros.

~~Examinl.~~ Exam. cons.

11. VIII. Int. mat.

Laudes Prima

Sacrum

Grat. act. (+ Cor. m.)

Lektura / Kazan.

(Congr. pro Clericis)

APPUNTAMENTI

Implorando Dona Spiritus S.

Medit. III.

„ jeśli kto miłuje świat, nie ma w nim miłości Ojca. Albowiem wszystko, co jest na świecie: pożądliwość ciała, pożądliwość oczu i pycha żywota nie pochodzi od Ojca, ale ze świata. A prze-

fied with 'sex appeal' nor the pride of life with the drive for importance.

Adoration: The glorification of the One who is '*Primogenitus omnis creaturae . . . in Quo omnia constant . . .*' ['the First-born of all creation . . . in Him all things hold together . . .'].[1] The fixing of our eyes on Him will entirely revise our attitude to creatures and help us leave the limiting perspectives of the triple concupiscence, and enter into God's perspective.

Prandium [lunch] Reading: Gilson, 'The concept of God in the philosophy of St Thomas Aquinas';[2] 'The Implementation of the Council and the diocesan structures' (cont.)
The Way of the Cross (according to the psalms); Rosary

Meditation 4: In the light of the reflection on the triple concupiscence – self-reflection and inner judgement.

(a) 'the meaning that the Lord God will give to me' – trust, a desire to serve, but . . . restlessness
(b) once again the judgement of conduct *(experimentum) in se* and *quoad alios* [in oneself and in relation to others]
(c) the implementation of the 'Church of the poor', how to work for it?

(By the way, matters such as the evaluation of character: reflexivity, complementarity, the question of 'personality', etc.)

Matins of the following day (memorial of St Clare); Rosary (of the day); Penitential psalms
Imploratur sinceritas conscientiae et rectum de omnibus iudicium (de Dom. XI: . . . ut dimittas, quae conscientia metuit, et adicias, quod oratio non praesumit) [Prayer for honest conscience and right judgement on everything (from the eleventh Sunday: . . . pour forth your mercy upon us, so that you set aside those things which our conscience fears, and apply what our prayer dares not)][3]
Veni S. Spiritus [Come, Holy Spirit]; Compline

12 August: Memorial of St Clare

Morning intentions; Lauds; Prime; Holy Mass; Thanksgiving (Rosary)
Reading: (*S. Congr. pro Clericis respons.* [Response from the Congregation for the Clergy])

1 See Colossians 1:15–17.
2 This might be a reference to Etienne Gilson, *The Christian Philosophy of St Thomas Aquinas* (New York, 1956).
3 See the Collect for the 27th Sunday in Ordinary Time.

Meditation 5: God – the world. Love is of God; lust is of the 'world'. Love refers to the relation with '*bonum in se*' [good in itself] of every single thing, and the situating of it in its true order of ends and needs. Lust changes this order into an order of pure 'usefulness' (utility) and in this way diminishes '*bonum in se*' (value) of the human being and every created thing. It is against this background that the work of salvation undertaken by the Church as the work of God can be explained. Salvation consists in the bringing of love into the 'world'. Because, if only lust remained in the world and in the creation, then the world, and man in it, would be doomed to a kind of 'self-destruction' of value – their own value, the value of all creatures.

This tension on the one hand, and the work of salvation on the other, constitute the deepest principle of conjunction: the Church and the world.

Salvation is the work of God carried out by the Man who was the Son of God, that is, by Christ. The fact that Christ was a prophet, priest and king is not only a historical accumulation of attributes and functions, but it also points to the relevant aspects and characteristics of the work of salvation. And this is why these characteristics still have to abide in the Church as the people of God, since it is the sign and the sacrament of the salvation of the 'world' (above all, the salvation of humankind).

Prophecy is the expression of God's truth. It is the truth about God Himself and about creation. The 'axiological' truth which defines values. The work of salvation is based on this truth; thanks to it, the work of salvation can introduce love and overcome lust in the world.

Priesthood is the returning (the offering in sacrifice) of all that is created to the Creator. It also involves a double 'prophetic' function – revealing the relationship of values: God – creation, and bringing all the passing values closer to the eternal value, and all creation, above all man, to God. Priesthood has an eschatological sense.

Kingship comes from this service to God, and it is the inner order in man, that is, self-control; and it is the reign over the world of creatures through man.

These three features of the work of salvation are at the same time – in man – the features of the living faith.

(Prophecy = knowledge; priesthood = the consecration of oneself to God; kingship = deeds that follow from this.)

The work of salvation has its meaning and 'eschatological' direction: It consists in the final union with God, but it also has a 'cosmological' meaning and direction, since it is the 'salvation of the world'. Besides, the former meaning and direction is realised through the latter.

Adoration: All this predisposes one to glorify the Eucharistic Saviour ever more passionately, and this glorification is connected to a petition to take part in His work in as fruitful a way as possible.

lunch

Reading: Fr Kamiński, Methodological questions relating to the philosophy of God;[1] 'The Implementation of the Council and the diocesan structures' cont.
Rosary

Meditation 6: (Re-evaluation of all the recent and, in a way, all previous retreats.)

I see my task as participating in the work of salvation, and this task consists in the implementation of aspects of this work both in myself and in other people. In other people – in a different way than I used to, when I could do it in a direct way (direct priesthood). Today it needs to be done in a more indirect way (with exceptions), but also with a broader scope. Here a reference to certain specific matters ('community'). One needs to take care and learn to do it effectively, and to act in the right direction, to work together with others who do it in the best spirit.

And here my thoughts turn to Mary. 'The Work of redemption' began with '*Totus Tuus*' ['Entirely Yours'] – from the 1962 retreat.[2] At this stage of my participation in the work of salvation, and in these circumstances and in the face of these tasks, I need to repeat this. To find the way, solutions, patience, resilience, courage and unity in the principle of '*Totus Tuus*'.

1 Reference to Stanisław Kamiński, 'Zagadnienia metodologiczne związane z filozofią Boga' [Methodological questions relating to the philosophy of God], in: *Studia z filozofii Boga* [Studies in the Philosophy of God], vol. 1 (Warsaw, 1968), pp. 380–403.
2 See n. 1, p. 1 [2 September 1962].

The Lord Jesus hid His Mother in His work – but He hid Her in such a way that everyone who really wishes to take part in it can find Her.

The Way of the Cross (prayer of the heart); Matins of the following day

Rosary Litany of the Saints Compline	many matters which are constantly in my prayers at present and will still be in the future: the retreat turned to the Church which the Lord has entrusted to me.

13 August Holy Mass; Thanksgiving

4–7 November 1970
Retreat in Tyniec
Topic: 'The threefold meaning of episcopacy'

Further preparation: 18 May (fiftieth birthday); 2 July: Kalwaria Zebrzydowska – meditation along the Little Ways

4 November In the evening: The Little Hours; Vespers

Meditation 1: An outline of the topic: episcopacy: rootedness – (*episkopein* [to view, to consider]) = an all-embracing view. Leadership; (Rosary).

Meditation 2: The outline of the topic cont.: 'matters'.

Matins; Adoration of the Blessed Sacrament; Compline
Reading: Fr Stefan Schudy, 'The Priesthood of Jesus Christ' (*Coll. Theol.*)[1]

5 November Lauds; (Prime); Mass – concelebration (conversation with Fr Augustyn); Thanksgiving; The Joyful Mysteries of the Rosary
Reading: Fr H. de Lubac, *La foi chrétienne. Essai sur la structure du Symbole des Apôtres*[2]
The Way of the Cross: association with the Gospel of Cana of Galilee

Meditation: On rootedness. The fundamental reality of revelation and faith is the Son of God's 'rootedness' in human nature, in humankind, in the human family, in every human being. This rootedness takes place through the Church, which is the Bride and the 'Lamb's Spouse'. In this relationship the Church 'enables' her Bridegroom to take root in humankind ever anew, in the course of generations – and in this way she constantly 'gives birth' to new people for God by way of the supernatural likeness to Christ. This fundamental process of Christ's taking root in people through the Church is fulfilled by the power of the Holy Spirit, who acts in the human soul

---

1 Stefan Schudy, 'Kapłaństwo Jezusa Chrystusa w nauce Vaticanum II' ['The Priesthood of Jesus Christ in the Doctrine of the Second Vatican Council'], *Collectanea Theologica*, vol. 39, no. 4, 1969.
2 Henri de Lubac, *The Christian Faith: An Essay on the Structure of the Apostles' Creed*, trans. Richard Arnandez (San Francisco, 1986).

in His own particular way. The holy sacraments serve to signify and realise simultaneously Christ's rootedness in man. In the sacraments Christ receives us – it happens so even in the Eucharist, when we receive Him, and in baptism, when Christ receives us for the first time. Christ's 'taking root' in man constitutes the ground for the justification and the union. Christ is '*Consubstantialis*' ['consubstantial'] and '*Missus*' ['sent'] at the same time: remaining consubstantial with the Father in accordance with His deity, He is simultaneously sent: the Father 'gave' Him. His mission is still ongoing: He continues it, taking root in humankind and in every human being. This rootedness constitutes the 'ontological' ground for man's justification before God and the union with God for every human being. It is also the primary reality; whenever we think of our rootedness in Christ. Because the latter is only secondary and derivative. We take root in Christ according to the principle of His 'taking of root' in human nature, in humankind, in the human family and in every human being.

Our rootedness in Him takes place *ex opere operato* [by the work performed] (that is, by the power of His actions in the Church, outside the Church and through the Church).[1] At the same time, however, a broad perspective for '*opus operantis*' ['the efficacy of the agent'] opens up. One needs to 'carry out' thoroughly one's rootedness in Christ through one's entire consciousness and attitude. Rootedness through baptism, through priesthood and episcopacy. It is simultaneously a participation in Christ's vocation, in His mission. Because Christ is '*Consubstantialis*' and '*Missus*'.

The Little Hours; 'Matters'; Vespers

Meditation: *Lumen gentium* emphatically teaches how Christ, glorified in heaven, is simultaneously present in the bishops of His Church and acts through them to lead people to truth and salvation. Christ's 'rootedness' needs to be conceived through all forms and levels of the Church community, including the bishops' community: '*communio Ecclesiarum – communio episcoporum*' ['the communion of Churches – the

1 See the *Catechism of the Catholic Church*, 1128.

communion of bishops'], as last year's Council reminded us. While acting towards this end, forming the right attitude, becoming involved and accepting involvement – one needs to take care of:

1. The intention with which one undertakes tasks (*Cons. de Laicis, Congr. pro clero, Congr. pro Eccles. Orient., Congr. Pro Cultu Div. – Synod* [the Pontifical Council for the Laity, Congregation for the Clergy, Congregation for the Oriental Churches, Congregation for Divine Worship – the Synod])
2. The Bishops' Conference, Province: complementarity which is being thoroughly and laboriously developed – the Synod: the preparation of the subject matter, the attitude to D. K. (H. B.). The Commission of the Bishops' Conference
3. The Chapter: The Commission of the Bishops' Conference
4. Diocese: the steps taken are probably right and necessary: thoroughness and gradation.

Adoration of the Blessed Sacrament: 'apart from me you can do nothing';[1] Eucharist = 'With Me'; 'Matters'; Fr Augustyn's talk on the topic of 'immersion in Christ's death' according to St Paul; Rosary; Matins; Holy Hour as a 'priestly hour'; Compline
Reading: Fr H. de Lubac (cont.)

6 November Lauds (Prime); Holy Mass – concelebration; Thanksgiving; 'Matters'
Reading: Fr H. de Lubac (cont.)

Meditation: 'Seeing – *episkopein*'.

The basis for this is faith in its supernatural essence: participation in the knowledge which God Himself has. One must ask to partake in this, since it is a gift given by the Person to a person.

One must ask for it and deepen it by oneself (the issue of the increase of faith) in two directions: (1) in the direction of eschatological fulfilment, so that this perspective never gets weaker (different current events point to it). Faith is the primary result of Christ's rootedness in us – and the expression of our rootedness in Him. Hence the relationship:

1 See John 15:5.

rootedness–seeing. (2) One must ask to see the universal Church and its issues and the 'local' Church through the lens of faith. This is a special meaning of *'episkopein'*, the seeing in faith of the universal–local Church as that part of the people of God whom Christ leads to the Father through the bishop. This in turn results in seeing individual people from this perspective.

The Way of the Cross: Reference to yesterday's talk: participation in Christ's death and resurrection: only Christ's resurrection has an eschatological meaning – 'Christ, being raised from the dead, will never die again.'[1] The death of Adam's descendant; the birth in Christ.

The Little Hours; Rosary

(During the morning Mass I was nourished by the spirit of trust in God's work during the retreat, despite all human shortcomings and obstacles.)

Vespers; Adoration of the Blessed Sacrament (following the Friday custom)

Meditation (pract.):

(a) 'Experience' has a certain communal sense: there is a force in man that directs his feelings in a given domain. The matter at stake is man's ability to control his feelings by himself and by virtue of this force. This is also a type of a 'test of grace', because it is only with the help of grace that man can achieve that. At the same time, it is about the correct interpretation of values: the objective side of 'experience'. The margin of error or fault? imperfection? *peccatum leve* [venial sin]?
(b) Question: Can the misfortunes that recently befell people close to me be considered a punishment? (marginal thoughts) May they be considered a sign? What are they supposed to signify?
(c) Multidirectional work, in particular creative work: intensive, the issue of necessity.

Many thoughts on the topic of grace and its proper meaning and interpretation.

1 See Romans 6:9.

With reference to (a), (b), (c) it is important that grace is included in it:

1. grace in its objective meaning = the good willed by God
2. grace as help.

Reading: Fr de Lubac (cont.)
Litany of the Saints; Penitential psalms

Consideration: (a) *occasione anniv.* [illegible] [on the occasion of the anniversary [. . .]]
= *Episcopus debet esse 'homo videns'*? [The bishop should be the 'man who sees'?]
(b) *videns in multis* [who sees in many matters] ('matters')
(c) the need for increased eschatological awareness – in the course of years – with the simultaneous growth of the involvement in the Church.

Rosary; Anticipated Matins; Compline

7 November (From the Saturday office of the Blessed Virgin Mary: Holy Mass in the afternoon); Lauds; Adoration of the Blessed Sacrament

Meditation: during the concelebrated Holy Mass in which I participated. Topic: the Mother of God: *quem totus non capit orbis, in Tua se clausit viscera, factus homo – lumen aeternum mundo effudit* [He, whom the whole world cannot hold, enclosed Himself in Thy womb, being made man – gave forth to the world the everlasting light].[1]

The Holy Mass revealed itself to me as *Sacramentum Messiae* [the sacrament of the Messiah], an act of redemption, in which He is alone with the Father and before the Father. At the same time, the Mother makes this act possible – She, so to speak, creates a space in which this act is fulfilled. She also participates in it most completely from the first '*fiat*' ['let it be']. She complements it to the fullest and draws from it to the utmost. *Totus Tuus* [Entirely Yours]. Mary can lead us into participation in the act of redemption, *Sacramentum Messiae*, in the simplest and most mature way.

Totus Tuus.

1 See the Gradual in *Missa Salve Sancta Parens.*

Rosary; Petitionary prayers; Conversation with the Prior
Two Letters – two problems: (a) to W.; (b) for the Solemnity of Christ the King as a celebration of social charity
Rosary

Meditation: Leadership. The bishop has to lead his Church. This is a separate task which cannot be undertaken without 'rootedness' and 'seeing'. The completion of this task enters the dimension in which Christ – the Good Shepherd – is the foundation, the beginning and the end. In this meditation the question is only briefly raised and outlined. I will have to return to it. The bishop's leadership over the Church needs to be embedded in Christ as the Good 'Shepherd'.

This is not an easy task. It rests on the office and spiritual gifts of episcopacy. This issue will have to be elaborated on too. The following profiles can be outlined: leadership through thought; leadership through example – role model; leadership through heart – and the humble pursuit of all matters with prayer.

The Little Hours; The Way of the Cross: following Marian themes and the text of the Magnificat; Rosary, until Vespers

Completion: 19 December [probably 1970]

In the morning: Matins; Lauds; Prime

Meditation: Reflection on the entire topic of rootedness – seeing – leadership: esp. that last topic. The leadership of thought, example, command and above all the leading of matters and people with prayer.

Reflections on 'borderline' matters
Rosary; The Way of the Cross (Advent); Reading

Adoration: The need for a more complete expression of my consecration to God has grown over the last few months, which were full of human experiences.*

* response (T. to (b)) only as a sign that one must always be ready.

The framework for this consecration has been formed by the consecration to the Sacred Heart of Jesus and the act of 'holy slavery': '. . . my body and soul, my goods, both interior and exterior, and even the value of all my good actions, past, present and future; leaving to Thee (Mother) the entire and full right of disposing of me, and all that belongs to me, without exception, for the greater glory of God, in time and in eternity . . .'[1]

Within this fundamental act of consecration and the entrusting of myself, I wish: (1) to be at Lord Jesus' complete disposal when it comes to the service and ways of serving the people of God in the Church; (2) to accept all experiences, which according to His thought and will belong to the entirety of my earthly path; (3) asking only for grace, so that I could always live up to the task: so that I could accept, undertake, serve.

1 See the Act of Consecration to the Immaculate Heart of Mary in Louis-Marie Grignion de Montfort, *The Secret of the Rosary*, trans. Mary Barbour (Bay Shore, NY, 1954).

1–5 September 1971
The Bishops' Conference Retreat at Jasna Góra
Led by Bishop L[ech] Kaczmarek[1]

~

1 September Introductory [meditation]:

1. *Dinumerare nos doce dies nostros, ut perveniamus ad sapientiam cordis* [So teach us to number our days, that we may get a heart of wisdom] (Ps.).[2]
2. *Voluntas Tua – pax mea* [Your will – my peace] (St Gregory of Nazianzus).
3. God is omnipotent – man is impotent? (Primate).

2 September Rosary; Petitionary prayers; Prayer to the Holy Spirit; Participation in the Mass celebrated by His Excellency Primate Stefan Wyszyński[3]

Meditation: I turn to the Mother of souls, of my soul! The Mother of conscience, the Mother of divine grace, the Mother of the inner man, the Mother of the inner mysterium – at the start of the retreat that is to shed new light on the way of the soul. I entrust to Her all (theological, diocesan Synod's, personal) concerns.

Talk: *Episcopus – imago Patris* [Bishop – image of the Father]. How to act on this 'image'? (*paura* [fear], *prudenza* [prudence], *pazienza* [patience]). Not to take any decision without prayer. The proper meaning of the dialogue with priests. Goodness and firmness.

---

1 Lech Kaczmarek (1909–84) was a Polish priest and theologian. He served as Auxiliary Bishop of Gdańsk (1959–71) and Bishop of Gdańsk (1971–84).

2 See Psalm 89 (90):12.

3 Stefan Wyszyński (1901–81) was a Polish prelate who served as Bishop of Lublin (1946–48) and Archbishop of Warsaw and Archbishop of Gniezno (1948–81). In 1948 he assumed the title of the Primate of Poland. He was made cardinal on 12 January 1953 by Pope Pius XII. He was imprisoned and placed under house arrest in 1953–56 for his opposition to the communist regime in Poland.

Ancillary reflection: Confrontation of fatherhood as a value which comes from above, from the Father, with the contemporary idea of social life, which comes from below, and which, in a way, does not leave any place for the father. A fervent prayer for fatherhood to be fulfilled in the Church despite these unfavourable circumstances – although, as the retreat leader said, 'priesthood (and so also episcopacy) will be ever more difficult' (Malraux).

The Little Hours (word for the Week of Mercy)

Talk: 'Blessed is he whom thou dost choose and bring near' (Ps.)[1] – the problem of emptiness as the cause of priests' resignations. Priest, bishop: *forma gregis* [example to the flock].[2]

Conversations with priests who are going down a path with no way out – formational conversations aimed at renewing priesthood in individual priests. Care for priests and their pastoral duties. The bishop knows what threatens contemporary priests (neomodernism, Bultmann, Küng) – practical materialism, pessimism ('earthly life is not the highest value' – Fr Kolbe's words).[3] The lack of prayer, routine, lack of love for learning – the bishop knows that priests need unity, mutual love, openness to the world (*Ecclesia semper reformanda* [the Church always being reformed]).[4]

Reflection: (a) petition for the ability to turn to the value that lies beyond the value of earthly life; (b) ([illegible] – the witness [illegible] of my devotion to God); (c) on the topic of what serves the unity among bishops and what impedes that unity (*de affectu collegialitatis* [on the feeling of collegiality]).

('The bishop is the parish priest of parish priests and the father of the fathers of families' – St Francis de Sales.)

---

1 See Psalm 64 (65):4.

2 See 1 Peter 5:3.

3 St Maksymilian Maria Kolbe OFM (1894–1941) was a Polish Conventual Franciscan friar who volunteered to die in place of a stranger in the Nazi death camp of Auschwitz. He was canonised by Pope John Paul II on 10 October 1982.

4 The precise origin of this phrase is obscure although the sentiment behind it can be traced back at least to St Augustine. It has widely been seen as a slogan of both the Protestant Reformation and the Counter-Reformation. In the twentieth century, it was popularised by the Swiss theologian Karl Barth and subsequently picked up by Hans Küng. A similar idea, that of *Ecclesia semper purificanda*, is to be found in the writings of Vatican II (e.g. *Lumen gentium* 8).

Spiritual reading: (1) Sacraments of the post-Concilliar Church; (2) *Znak*;[1] (3) on Fr M. Kolbe
Rosary (longer); The Way of the Cross (shorter)

Talk: *Episcopus – homo doloris* [Bishop – man of suffering]. Longing for heaven, thoughts about death and eternity; let us not be afraid of death, but let us be afraid of the responsibility for life; responsibility for 'our sheep'.

Suffering in the bishop's life: *falsi fratres* [false brothers] and others – one needs deep trust in Christ. Suffering is marked by a particular kind of consecration, hence our eyes are turned upwards, 'beyond the crossbeam of the cross'. The philosophy of suffering is best understood when one becomes humble and aware of the frailty of life. One needs to prepare oneself for suffering without becoming immersed in suffering. To be a Christian and not to want to suffer is a blasphemy (Tertullian). Suffering brings us closer to God in a fuller, faster and firmer way. It is a condition of spiritual maturity.

Petition to Mother Church to stand in suffering (*Stabat Mater*) and not to fall, and to maintain '*Magnificat*'.

Adoration (thoughts on the fourth talk); (Anticipated) Matins; Holy Mass concelebrated in the Chapel of the Blessed Virgin Mary; Reading (afterwards)
Eucharistic service (Primate: topics: for authentic priesthood at the Synod, consecration of the entire Church to the Mother of the Church, beatification of Fr Kolbe, collegial unity of the Bishops' Conference)
Holy Hour (evening); Compline

3 September Holy Hour (morning); Rosary; Petitionary prayers; Lauds; Prime; Concelebrated Mass

Talk: *Episcopus – custos fidei – custos morum* [Bishop – custodian of faith – custodian of morals]. A description of the situation in Poland and around the world (theocentrism – communocentrism – anthropocentrism – anthropotheism). Novelties, progressivism (*effrenata novitas* [unbridled striving for novelty]). The attitude to theologians – with a simultaneous sense of the bishop's responsibility, his special responsibility for faith, 'strengthen your brethren in faith'! (Gospel).[2] To defend law and truth until death! (Bishop Fischer). At the same time,

1 *Znak* (Sign) is a Polish Catholic journal founded in 1946.
2 See Luke 22:32.

it is necessary to renew theology and *kerygma*, to change the language while maintaining the identity of the content.

> Contemporary man finds himself in a crisis which is directly proportional to the difficulty of issues he needs to solve and to the price he pays for his mistakes.

The Church abides in divine truth by the power of Christ's guarantee – this is the special mission and responsibility of the bishops.

The question of preaching the word of God in a way that speaks to everyone (*pateat* [so that it becomes accessible], *placeat* [so that it pleases], *moveat* [so that it moves]). The danger of certain truths of faith being marginalised.

Reflection: Am I to blame for anything in this area? Petition for light (*opus fac evangelistae, ministerium tuum imple* [do the work of an evangelist, fulfil your ministry]).[1]

The Little Hours; Writing a letter to the youth on Fr Maksymilian Kolbe

Talk: *Episcopus – vir orationis* [Bishop – man of prayer].

St Francis de Sales: The salvation of your neighbour is also your own salvation. The best means to achieving perfection is preaching the Gospel/(evangelical). *Delectatio contemplationis* [delight of contemplation] has to be accompanied by pastoral zeal:

sacrificare [to offer sacrifice] *orare* [to pray] *docere* [to teach] *visitare* [to pay visits]	Bishops' tasks are all dependent on prayer.

Eucharistic and Marian piety. Enduring and faithful piety, despite many tasks and fatigue. To the latter two '*non est applicandum totum cor*' ['one cannot devote one's whole heart']. To draw energy for work, for tasks from prayer. To be Mary and Martha at the same time.

(The prayer of Copernicus; the prayer of van Beethoven.)

1 See 2 Timothy 4:5.

-5- 16

9 MARTEDI - s. Giuliano | s. Aldo erem. - MERCOLEDI **10**

GENNAIO

Pobożność eucharystyczna i maryjna. Pobożność [illegible] [illegible], zwłaszcza wśród [illegible] zajęć i zmęczenia. Do takich „non est applicandum [illegible]". Z modlitwy czerpać siłę do pracy, do zadań. Być [illegible] [illegible] [illegible].

[modlitwa [illegible] w Betlejem]

Poczucie bliskości Pana Boga

Trzeba [illegible] modlitwę, [illegible]. [illegible] na modlitwę [illegible]. Modlitwa jest to dialog z Bogiem, [illegible] [illegible]. Kierkegaard [illegible] [illegible] – [illegible] modlitwa [illegible] [illegible] [illegible] do [illegible].

Matce Bożej polecamy naszą [illegible] modlitwę, [illegible] na modlitwie [illegible] z Apostołami

Lectio spirit. (Augustinus)

Via Crucis na [illegible] (kaplicy [illegible])

Corona Rosa (na [illegible])

Vesp.

J. Kraj.

Episcopus – vir praedicationis. W [illegible] słowa [illegible] się prawdą, nulla acceptio personarum [illegible] [illegible] [illegible] (liturgia, [illegible]), ale [illegible] [illegible] [illegible]. Być [illegible] [illegible] [illegible] – [illegible] [illegible] [illegible] [illegible] [illegible] [illegible] [illegible] [illegible] do życia [illegible] [illegible], ale [illegible] od bliźnich. [illegible] [illegible] [illegible] [illegible] [illegible] do bliźnich.

APPUNTAMENTI

Refleksja: quomodo munus praedicationis adimpleam?

Matut.

Adorat. – 11 [illegible]

The feeling of God's closeness.

One needs to promote the prayer of adoration, thanksgiving. To submit all in prayer. 'Prayer is a dialogue with God, even though we often turn it into a monologue.' Kierkegaard: To pray means to listen – the more internal prayer becomes, the less I want to say in it.

Let us entrust our ability to pray to the Mother of the Church – the one who prayed with the apostles in the Upper Room.

Spiritual reading (afterwards); The Way of the Cross along the defensive walls of the Jasna Góra Monastery (a different bishop led the prayer at each Station); Rosary (on the walls); Vespers

Talk: *Episcopus – vir predicationis* [Bishop – man of preaching]. He always has to follow the truth in his use of the word, *nulla acceptio personarum* [regardless of the person]. At the same time, he should show understanding (humanism, moralism). But first and foremost, Christ has to be the central point of his life (re-evaluation).

marriage ⟷ celibacy
horizontalism ⟷ verticalism

(what to preach on selectively?)

The proper vision of the human being and their happiness, the disappearance of inner life – the cardinal virtues. The principle of 'the cult of man' – in addition to that, propensity for inner life led in isolation from others. Meanwhile the true Christian is the one who has supernatural love for their neighbours.

Reflection: *quando munus praedicationis adimpleam?* [when do I fulfil the task of preaching?].

Matins; Adoration of the Blessed Sacrament; (Film about the Jasna Góra Monastery); The Jasna Góra Appeal; Litany of the Saints; Compline

4 September

Meditation on the Act of Consecration to the Mother of God: (The fact that Jesus Christ gives us His Mother for ours – this is an important element of the order of grace and the entire givenness.)

Concelebrated Mass; Thanksgiving; Rosary; Petitionary prayers; Prayer to the Holy Spirit; Lauds; Prime

Talk: (On liturgy; bishop – liturgy.) The bishop must be the preacher of truth in adverse times (love in opposition to hatred). One has to pay much attention to liturgy. The bishop should turn his face to everyone. The implementation of the Council: the putting into practice of *mysterium salutis* [the mystery of salvation], understood better than ever before. This all (even ecumenism and dialogue) takes place through the liturgy. 'My task is to serve Christ the Lord' – this is the basis of the liturgical attitude. The Church is never more true to itself than in the liturgy celebrated by bishops. The Mother of God, who looked after, took care of and revealed Jesus, is the role model.

The Little Hours; Writing a note on sacred architecture

Talk: (On striving for happiness.) The law of harmony; the law of struggle; the law of development – these three laws govern our striving for happiness. In all this, one has to constantly rely on God's mercy, so that God's grace in me is not fruitless. Ferrari (Italian mathematician) – one understands Christianity better while on one's knees. Zeal and great devotion to the Mother of God. To trust especially in moments of sadness and dejection. (There is not and cannot be a bishop who is entirely calm about everything.) *Mihi vivere Xristos est et mori lucrum* [For to me to live is Christ, and to die is gain].[1] Through all these paths described here, the bishop wins salvation. He walks towards it, leading others to it.

The only joy that can fill the human soul fully is God. *Solus Deus* [Only God]. Mary's example comes from this.

In the afternoon: Conclusion; Confession; Chapter 15 of St John; Reflection in the chapel; The Way of the Cross; Reading
Ultimum autem officium coram SS. in capella BMV: ubi festivitas diei sequentis ferventer praeparata est [The last service before the Blessed Sacrament in the Chapel of the Blessed Virgin Mary: where tomorrow's festivity was being fervently prepared]
Vespers; Compline; Matins; Penitential psalms; Rosary

On this last day I experienced a particular awareness of God in His personal transcendence in relation to the created world: the awareness of the Creator and Father, who is one God with the Son and the Holy Spirit. At the same time, an awareness of the extraordinary immanence of this God in the world, above all in humankind, by the power of redemption performed by

1 See Philippians 1:21.

the Son, from where sanctification in the Holy Spirit comes. The awareness of God who holds the world and permeates the world.

Mary is present in this mystery in a special way, She is particularly closely united with redemption and sanctification, and through these with the Church.

Evening adoration in the Chapel of Jasna Góra: Preparation for the Act of Consecration of the World to the Mother of the Church (Primate: 'being led by almost foolish faith')

5 September The Act of Consecration of the World to the Mother of the Church: concelebrated High Mass at 11.00 a.m. In the afternoon: the coronation of the image of Our Lady of Solace in Wieluń (5.00 p.m.)

5–6 July 1973
Kalwaria Zebrzydowska

Dies recollectionis [Reflection days] of double nature: thanksgiving and petition; the day's aim was to bring together different matters as well as to prepare us for holiday.

5 July

Meditation: reference to last year's retreat; Adoration; Liturgy of the Hours

Holy Hour: Priesthood and sacrifice are inscribed very deeply into the reality of creation: of the world and of the human being. While this reality, on the one hand, shows the dependence of everything that is created on the Creator, on the other hand, it in a particular way expresses and actualises the relationship of the gift, the giving of oneself, which is special to the human being as a person. This relation is 'introduced' by Christ into the Trinitarian, that is ultimate, dimension.

6 July

Lauds; Holy Mass; Daytime prayers; Rosary

Meditation: The Little Ways of Jesus[1] – in relation to yesterday's primary reflection, a meditation on the matters *pro praeteritio et pro futuro* [relating to the past and future] connected to the petitionary prayer for these issues.

The Way of the Cross; Litany of the Saints; Penitential psalms; Adoration (Reading: Prof. G. Labuda, 'Factum Św. Stanisława' [The Factum of St Stanislaus][2] – remarks)

---

1 See n. 2, p. 12 [6–7 July 1963].

2 Gerard Labuda's paper was delivered at a conference devoted to St Stanislaus held in Kraków on 25 May 1973. A revised and expanded version of the paper was published as *Św. Stanisław: Biskup Krakowski, Patron Polski* [St Stanislaus: Bishop of Kraków, Patron Saint of Poland] (Poznań, 2000).

9–12 August 1973
Retreat at Bachledówka[1]
Topic: *SS-ma Trinitas* [The Holy Trinity]

9 August Vespers from 3.00 p.m.

Adoration of the Blessed Sacrament: *Xtus praesens nobis in Patre, Xtus dans nobis cum Patre Spiritum SS-um. – Homo – ager expectans* [Christ is present for us in the Father, Christ together with the Father gives us the Holy Spirit – Man – an expectant field].

Rosary (III); Petitionary prayer

Reading various texts: the Letter of the Bishops' Conference for 26 August; Information on the Holy Year: Reconciliation.[2]
Inde post Viam Crucis, in qua mysterium Cordis Xti praecipue contemplabatur, fit [Then, the Way of the Cross, in which the mystery of Christ's Heart was contemplated, was followed by]:

Evening meditation: Retreats grow out of the entire network of problems and tasks of the universal Church and the Polish Church. Retreats also have to be somehow rooted in these matters. They cannot lead away from the episcopal mission, but have to lead ever deeper into it. Among those tasks the one that has priority in our region is Catholic upbringing. Due to the present threats, one needs a stronger affirmation (statement). This affirmation takes shape in both the Holy Year's theme, '*Reconciliatio*' ['Reconciliation'], announced by Pope Paul VI, and even more in the upcoming Synod of Bishops on the theme of '*Evangelisatio*' ['Evangelisation']. These topics mutually explain and direct each other. A plan outlining them for the Church in Poland and in the Archdiocese needs to be prepared.

This matter has to be connected with the general issue of Catholic culture in Poland, especially the contribution of

---

1 See n. 1, p. 51 [9 August 1969].

2 On 9 May 1973, Paul VI announced the Holy Year (Jubilee) for 1975. Its two main themes were: Renewal and Reconciliation.

Catholic scholarship (and church scholarship: theology) to Polish scholarship (the feast day of St John Cantius: 500th anniversary of his death).

Rosary (I)
(Reading a chapter from the book): *Maryja nasz wzór* [Mary: Our Role Model] by Fr F. Ziebura[1]
Supper, followed by: Matins for the Feast of St Lawrence
Holy Hour: *contemplatio Xti in Monte Oliveti sec. misteria ros. cor. II: ubi veritas iustificationis invenitur sub diversis aspectibus* [contemplation of Christ on the Mount of Olives according to the Sorrowful Mysteries: where the truth of justification is revealed in diverse ways]
Compline
Finally, reading the article: 'Sumienie a autorytet' [Conscience and Authority] by Fr Dr S. Rosik (*Studia theol. varsav.*)[2]

10 August: Feast of St Lawrence, deacon and martyr

Getting up about 6.00 a.m. and first prayers according to the morning intention; (Short) meditation before the Holy Mass on the readings on St Lawrence from the breviary and preparation for the Mass; Holy Mass for the Feast of St Lawrence (*ad peccata remittenda et conversionem semper pleniorem obtinendam infra haec exercitia* [for the forgiveness of sins and for an experience of an ever-fuller conversion during this retreat]); Afterwards: thanksgiving; Lauds; Rosary (I) (petitionary prayers); Prayer to the Holy Spirit

Reading: 'Die Mitte der Botschaft. Jesu Tod und Auferstehung' [The Centre of the Good News: Jesus' Death and Resurrection] by Jacques Guillet *in ephem.* [in the journal] *Communio* (*Inter. Theol. Zeitschrift*).[3]

Meditation: *De mysterio Patris* [On the mystery of the Father]: (cf. *Mystère du Père* [The mystery of the Father] by Fr Guillou read over the holiday).[4] The analogy of fatherhood/father that is given to us in the created world is simultaneously rich and multidimensional, and limited and disproportionate in relation to the reality of the 'Father' in God. God to some extent identifies with the Father, but at the same time He exceeds everything that we can conceive of 'fatherhood' in created reality, especially in human reality. The father is the one who gives life, who passes on humanity and allows it to develop,

1 Franciszek Ziebura, *Maryja nasz wzór* [Mary: Our Role Model] (Paris, 1973).

2 Seweryn Rosik, 'Sumienie a autorytet' [Conscience and Authority], *Studia Theologica Varsaviensia* [Warsaw Theological Studies], vol. 11, no. 1 (1973), pp. 161–85.

3 Jacques Guillet, 'Die Mitte der Botschaft. Jesu Tod und Auferstehung' [The Centre of the Good News: Jesus' Death and Resurrection], *Die Internationale katholische Zeitschrift Communio* [The International Catholic Journal *Communio*], vol. 2 (1973), pp. 225–8.

4 Marie-Joseph Le Guillou, *Le Mystère du Père. Foi des Apôtres, gnoses actuelles* [The Mystery of the Father: The Faith of the Apostles and Modern Gnosis] (Paris, 1973).

And yet Jesus did not hesitate to speak of God as the 'Father'

the one who is the point of reference for the child, the equivalent of the certainty of existence and goodness.

Father–God is essentially impermeable in terms of the world and creation. He is the mystery that lies beyond everything and that determines everything. This mystery is illuminated in relation to one point of reference: This point of reference is Christ – 'no one knows the Father except the Son and anyone to whom the Son chooses to reveal Him'.[1] Thanks to Christ, we also 'know' the Father to some extent and have access to Him. In Christ's consciousness, as well as in His mission and words, the Father completely overshadows the 'Absolute', even though at the same time He in a sense absorbs it. The Father is also the Creator and the Lord ('I thank Thee, Father, Lord of heaven and earth, that . . .').[2] He is the fullness of existence and goodness, the beginning, the ultimate support, the certainty and fulfilment of all fulfilments. If man can think of Him in any meaningful way, it can be only on the condition that, following Christ, he accepts the truth about love. The Father is the fullness of being, truth and good, who in His own special way accepts the world – from the very reality of creation, the giving of life, to the human being, whom He creates 'in His image, after His likeness' to let him partake in His own divinity.[3] In all this, He is constantly – being at the very heart of the created world, especially the human being – beyond the reach of our created imagination and thoughts. Yet at the same time

He is the only anchor of certainty and the condition of the development of everything, especially the human being (cf. upbringing). Outside 'the mystery of the Father' there is no evolution of man in truth and love (cf. Guillou's thesis).

The Way of the Cross (Friday) which develops the contemplation of the Passion of Christ: He is constantly turned towards the Father and the basis of this relationship informs the diverse ways in which He relates to different people and groups He meets on His way.

1 See Matthew 11:27.
2 See Matthew 11:25.
3 See Genesis 1:26.

Daytime prayers; After lunch – a break; Reading; Rosary (II); Rosary *ad Vulnera Redemptoris* [to the Wounds of the Redeemer]; Adoration in the spirit of Christ's final words; Vespers
Reading the decree of the Synod of Bishops: '*De evangelizatione in mundo hodierno*' [On Evangelisation in the Contemporary World]

Evening meditation: *Super munera mea episcopalia* [On my episcopal tasks]. This is a continuation of yesterday's afternoon meditation. There is a need for undertaking tasks and putting them in order, to organise them according to their merit. Each of these tasks includes many smaller tasks, more detailed and specific (e.g. the attitude to brother priests, to laypeople, to individual departments of the Curia, TP, etc.). The bishop's work has to be concrete, pastoral; it cannot remain only general, theoretical (unproductive talk, even though one undoubtedly needs councils, conferences and meetings).

Above all, the entire style of episcopal activity has to be governed by the following premises:

1. 'My Father is working still, and I am working' ( ).[1]
2. 'Apart from me you can do nothing' (Christ).[2]
3. 'Do whatever he tells you' (Mary).[3]

It is about allowing God–Father, Christ the Lord and His Mother to work through me at all times. Hence the entire activity of the bishop is contained in prayer and devotion (sacrifice).

Rosary (III); (Beginning to write the Declaration on Christian education); Finally:

Concluding meditation *intra devotionem Eucharist.* [during the Eucharistic service]: Rosary, litanies etc. This meditation, on the one hand, brought together the fruits of yesterday's reflections, and, on the other hand, expanded on the Marian theme. The Mother of God remains in a special relationship to the 'mystery of the Father'. She receives into Herself His participation in the world, in the human being – grace, to the fullest among all created beings. Hence the first words spoken to Mary: 'full of grace'.[4] She also adds to this participation, to grace, a human shape. In

1 See John 5:17. Empty brackets in the original.
2 See John 15:5.
3 See John 2:5.
4 See Luke 1:28.

[illegible]

Legitur S. Sergii (Paralipom. I).

Matutinum anticipatum (BMV in Sab)

Legitur Directorium de pastorali ministerio episcoporum

Dominum Psalmi poenit. - secundum intentionem diei, qui dies fuit paenitentiae (cf. Sacram.)

Completorium.

Legitur adhuc de [illegible]. „Vana [illegible]", „Responsum [illegible] card. [illegible]" auct. [illegible].

11. VIII. de BMV in Sab.

in h. 6 mysteria et primae fiunt orationes intentionem diurnam sequentes.

7. Ante Sacrum meditatio brevior super lectiones Breviarii (de Malach. Proph. i Dies Domini - et de Lumen Gentium VIII: Mariae figura Ecclesiae). Tunc sequitur

APPUNTAMENTI

Sacrum (ad int. memoriam Episcoporum et presbyteratus fratrum atque filiorum, etiam eorum qui defecerunt). Postea gratiarum actio (cum Missa Patris Generalis ord. [illegible]) et

Laudes matutinae

this mission of Hers, She constantly becomes and still is the Mother of the Church. But a reflection on these mysteries has to be preceded by a meditation on the Son of God according to the words 'He who has seen me has seen the Father' (J).[1]

Reading the Holy Scripture (2 Chronicles); Anticipated Matins (Saturday office of the Blessed Virgin Mary)
Reading the Directory for the Pastoral Ministry of Bishops
Praying the penitential psalms in accordance with the intention for the day, which was a penitential day (cf. Holy Mass); Compline
Until now: reading the journal *Nasza Przeszłość* [Our Past], 'Wspomnienie o kard. A. Sapieże' [Remembering Cardinal A. Sapieha] by P. Żółtowski

11 August Saturday office of the Blessed Virgin Mary; Getting up at about 6.00 a.m. and first prayers in accordance with the intention for the day
Shorter meditation on the readings from the breviary before the Holy Mass (from Prophet Malachi: The day of the Lord – and from *Lumen gentium* VIII: Mary as the figure of the Church)
Then follows the Holy Mass (offered for my brothers and sons in episcopacy and in priesthood, and also for those who resigned from priesthood); Afterwards: thanksgiving (a thanksgiving prayer for the Father General of the Order of Saint Paul the First Hermit during the Holy Mass); and Lauds
After breakfast: Rosary (I); Petitions and prayers to the Holy Spirit; Then, writing the Declaration on Christian education (cont.). After some time:

Morning meditation (longer): *De mysterio Filii* [On the mystery of the Son]: The Lord Jesus said, 'he who has seen me has seen the Father', and at another time, 'I and the Father are one'.[2] These words are the main theme of the meditation. The Son is, so to speak, the 'visibility' of the Father; the Son is not only the Father's invisible image, which is the consubstantial Word, but also His 'visualisation' in the history of humankind, which He enters by becoming Man. God–Man: The God of history simultaneously circumscribes the entire history of salvation and centres it around Himself. In this utmost closeness – to man, to humankind, to history – Jesus–Son-of-God acts, above all, as consubstantial with the Father (*Consubstantialis*). At the same time, He prepares the ground for further such work in the Church. This divine action coming from His Person enters deeply into human history from Bethlehem to Calvary. Above all, it enters into the event of the cross, the atoning sacrifice, which has a redeeming power.

1 See John 14:9.
2 See John 14:9 and John 10:30.

The entire canvas of human history, life and death, does not overshadow Son–God. This meditation powerfully revealed to me His reality, in which the Father became (and is still becoming) particularly visible. The mystery of the Son–Word's birth is unfathomable. The analogy of human birth 'through the body' fails here. The Son is eternally consubstantial – and, as the Son, is eternally being born by the Father. There is no dependence here, the birth is an expression of the Son's consubstantiality with the Father – as well as with the Holy Spirit in the unity of the Godhead.

The Way of the Cross: new thoughts, new associations with the words of the Holy Scripture – based on the previous meditations

Reading at lunch: *Maria nasz wzór* [Mary: Our Role Model], and in particular 'Zbiór dokumentów katedry i diecezji krakowskiej' [Collected Documents on the Cathedral and Diocese of Kraków] (St. Kuraś)[1]

Daytime prayer (Terce)

At around 3.00 p.m., reading in the chapel: 'Die Christuserfahrung des Ignatius von Loyola' [Ignatius Loyola's Experience of Christ] by Robert Stalder (journal *Communio*)[2]

Adoration of the Blessed Sacrament; Rosary (II); Daytime prayers (Sext, None)

Then reading a passage from the 'Declaration in defence of the Catholic doctrine of the Church against certain errors of the present day' by the Congregation for the Doctrine of the Faith (*Mysterium Ecclesiae* [The mystery of the Church])

Meditatio postmeridiana circa aliquos aspectus personales (uti adhuc: methodus procedendi in oratione fundetur). Praecipue commendantur [illegible] *successivi cum sacerdotibus* [Afternoon meditation about certain personal questions (like previously: let the method of proceeding be based on prayer). Particularly advisable are [. . .] with priests] (!)

Rosary (III); First Vespers for Sunday

Evening meditation: *Recapitulatio diei totius* [Summing up the whole day]: *mysterium* [mystery] of the Son, the 'visibility' of God, His 'historicity' is connected to the Mother, Mary, in a special way. She is the first one, in a way, to determine this visibility and historicity. And this is why our entire relation with the visible God, with the Son – and through Him with the invisible Father – takes place through Mary. In any case, the relation cannot exclude Her, and it is well known that it is thanks to Her that this relation is the most complete and most potent.

1 Stanisław Kuraś, *Zbiór dokumentów katedry i diecezji krakowskiej* [Collected Documents on the Cathedral and Diocese of Kraków] (Lublin, 1973).

2 Robert Stalder, 'Die Christuserfahrung des Ignatius von Loyola' [Ignatius Loyola's Experience of Christ], *Communio*, vol. 2 (1973), pp. 239–50.

At the same time, one thought kept returning to me in the meditation: how Mary, experiencing God's 'visibility' and 'historicity' every day in Her Son–Man, simultaneously had to experience His divine transcendence. Amazing and unfathomable life.

(Meditation throughout the Eucharistic service and Rosary); Anticipated Matins for Sunday
Reading the 'Directory for the Pastoral Ministry of Bishops'
Litany of the Saints and others; Compline
Finally, reading the book *Polacy w Australii [i Oceanii] 1790–1940* by L. Paszkowski (in the context of my recent participation in the Eucharistic Congress in Melbourne)[1]

12 August

Getting up at 6.00 a.m.; Intention; Daily prayers; Lauds in the chapel
Meditation before Holy Mass, with the preparation of the Liturgy of the Word and the homily, was from the beginning directed at the mystery of the Holy Spirit
Adoration of the Blessed Sacrament; 8.00 a.m., Holy Mass with a congregation, homily; Reading from the Divine Office

Meditation (longer): *De mysterio SS-mi Spiritus* [On the mystery of the Holy Spirit]: 'God is spirit, and those who worship Him must worship in spirit and truthy' (J).[2] Our conception of God's spirituality is based on our meagre experiences of our own human spirituality. The 'purely' spiritual and 'purely' personal reality at the same time. The Father, the Son and the Holy Spirit are the Spirit. 'The Spirit searches everything, even the depths of God.'[3] We know that He is holy and that He is a Person, like the Father and the Son. We know that He 'proceeds' from the Father and the Son as love. God is love. The Holy Spirit is the love of the Father and the Son. He is 'holy' because holiness consists in love. His 'proceeding' from the Father and the Son is simultaneously His being in unity with the Father and the Son and – in a way – constituting that unity (*communio*). Beyond this, however, the mutual givenness of the Son with the Father and the Father with the Son in the Holy Spirit – and the mutual 'breathing' of the Spirit – is an absolute mystery of faith. The Holy Spirit is the 'hidden God'

1 Lech Paszkowski, *Polacy w Australii i Oceanii 1790–1940* (London, 1962). A revised and expanded version of the book was published in English as *Poles in Australia and Oceania 1790–1940* (Sydney, 1987). The 40th International Eucharistic Congress took place in Melbourne on 18–25 February 1973.

2 See John 4:24.

3 See 1 Corinthians 2:10.

(*Deus absconditus*). If He is an inner gift with whom the Father and the Son are united, then He was revealed to people as, above all, the Gift. He was revealed by Christ, who described His passion and death as the price of that Gift for man: 'for if I do not go away, the Counsellor will not come to you; but if I go, I will send him to you' (J).[1]

Here we already pass from '*Trinitas theologica*' ['theological Trinity'] to '*Trinitas oeconomica*' ['economic Trinity']: the Persons' actions in the work of human salvation. The Holy Spirit – for the price of the Son's passion and death – becomes the gift for souls: 'He will guide you into all the truth', 'God's love has been poured into our hearts through the Holy Spirit who has been given to us': the Holy Spirit is the source of human holiness, and holiness consists in truth and love.[2] They express the very essence of 'spirituality' and holiness, also on the human level. In a sense, revelation tells us more about the Holy Spirit in the 'economic' than in the 'theological' order. But He is also '*Deus absconditus*' [the 'hidden God'] in the economic order. While the Son–Christ is God's 'visibility' and 'historicity' – the Holy Spirit introduces us back into His 'invisibility'. And yet the Holy Spirit is, above all, action, He is efficacy and fruitfulness – without entering into our sphere of vision. His work in the soul, which is very efficacious and fundamental indeed, is always the work of the Invisible in the invisible.

Lunch at 1.00 p.m. and thanksgiving at Bachledówka
Reading on the way to Kraków: Holy Scripture (the end of 2 Chronicles); Directory for the Pastoral Ministry of Bishops; Fr Wciórka – the end of the book on Teilhard de Chardin[3]
Sunday Vespers; 4.00 p.m., Bachledówka, participation in the visit of the icon of Our Lady of Częstochowa;[4] Holy Mass; Sermon
In the evening: Rosary (II), (III); Anticipated Matins; Compline
Deo Gratias! [Thanks be to God]
De Maria numquam satis [One cannot say too much about Mary]

1 See John 16:7.
2 See John 16:13 and Romans 5:5.
3 Ludwik Wciórka, *Szkice o Teilhardzie* [Studies on Teilhard] (Poznań, 1973).
4 See n. 1, p. 45 [11 September 1968].

7/8 November [probably 1973]

In the afternoon – Tyniec, *recapitulatio* [summary]:

1. Trinitarian
2. The Good Shepherd.

Thanksgiving; The Way of the Cross; Litany of the Saints; Penitential psalms

1974
Ante exerc. spir. [Before the Spiritual Exercises]

4/5 July Kalwaria[1]

23/24 August Rząska (at the Albertine Sisters')

(Fr Granat: *Ku człowiekowi i Bogu w Chrystusie*)[2]
Remembering previous retreats, especially the retreat of 1973; Office for the Feast of St Bartholomew (the Way of the Cross; Adoration)
Topic: 'evangelisation' (Synod; CRIS);[3] Reading texts; Participation in Holy Mass; Rosary

Reflections lead to a re-evaluation – based on previous reflections – of the main problems and tasks of spiritual life (1) personal, (2) in the archdiocese and in Poland, (3) in the universal Church (Synod), in order to understand God's thoughts and submit to the actions of the Holy Spirit through the mediation of the Mother of God. Only in this way can one maintain the balance in one's soul, retaining it in love, purity and humility in the face of all these problems and tasks.

---

1 See n. 1, p. 12 [6–7 July 1963].
2 Wincenty Granat, *Ku człowiekowi i Bogu w Chrystusie* [Towards Man and God in Christ] (Lublin, 1972).
3 CRIS might refer to Sacra Congregatio pro Religiosis et Institutis Saecularibus (Sacred Congregation for Religious and for Secular Institutes).

[3–7 September] 1974, The Holy Year Retreat in Gniezno Topic: God was in Christ reconciling the world to Himself. We beseech you on behalf of Christ, be reconciled to God. (St Paul)[1] Led by Bishop J[erzy] Ablewicz[2]

3 September Wrocław

Funeral of Bishop A. Wronka. Concelebration and the Word of God were a kind of 'memento' on the way to Gniezno.

Gniezno

8.00 p.m. The opening of the retreat/(absent)/separately: *Veni Creator* [Come, Creator]

And I will pray the Father, and He will give you another Counsellor, to be with you for ever – the Spirit of truth. He will guide you into all the truth, for He will take what is mine and declare it to you.[3]

Evening reading

4 September Morning intentions; Rosary; Petitionary prayer; Lauds; Mass concelebrated at the altar of St Adalbert; Thanksgiving

9.00 a.m. Talk 1:

Reference to Ephesians

(a) Christ is the sign of the invisible God, His visible image (God's portrait painted on Man's face). Example: Panin, Solzhenitsyn.[4]

---

1 See 2 Corinthians 5:19–20.

2 Jerzy Ablewicz (1919–90) was a Polish priest and theologian. He served as Bishop of Tarnów (1962–90).

3 See John 14:16 and 16:13–14.

4 Aleksandr Solzhenitsyn (1918–2008) and Dimitri Panin (1911–87) were Russian writers imprisoned in the Soviet gulag camps. They subsequently described their experiences in *The Gulag Archipelago* and *The First Circle* (Solzhenitsyn) and *The Notebooks of Sologdin* (Panin).

(b) Christian – priest – bishop as a sign of Christ.
(c) The bishop is a sign of Christ because he proclaims the glory of the Father. Do I proclaim God, who is love; or love, which 'is God'? – verticalism ⟷ horizontalism.
(d) The bishop is a sign of Christ – the Good Shepherd. Hence the priority of pastoral work in a bishop's life. Does anything overshadow this single work or distract me from it?
(e) The shepherd knows his sheep (do I know my priests? my alumni? my congregation?). Do I do everything I can to win those who are far away? New initiatives – *creativitas* [creativity] in the good sense of the word.
(f) Bishop – a living sign of Christ. His heart, his blood (the example of St Januarius), his hands (the example of the priest from Brzozów) are always ready to give, never to receive nor take away.

Meditation

Talk 2: On the breviary.
'*Jesus Christus orat pro nobis ut Sacerdos noster, orat in nobis ut caput nostrum, oratur a nobis ut Deus noster*' *(s. Aug.)* ['Jesus Christ prays for us, as our priest; He prays in us, as our head; He is prayed to by us, as our God' (St Augustine)].[1]

(a) On Christ's prayer, which He said so often, at so many places and times.
(b) On the breviary: the hymn of God's glory transplanted into the earthly life of the Church.
(c) Since Christ prays for us in the breviary, we need to have hearts as wide open as He has.
(d) A communal psalm of the bishops (cf. Acts of the Apostles) bears the stigma of the Holy Spirit. His power. Vespers should be separated and communal Lauds introduced.
(e) Collective prayer and constant prayer. We need to have faith in the power of constant prayer. *Status orationis* [the state of prayer], existential prayer.
(f) This is what the breviary is for: the liturgy of hours. The truth of hours.

1 Augustine, *Ennarationes in Psalmos* [Expositions of the Psalms] 85.1, Patrologia Latina vol. 36.

NOTE NOTE

14. Complet.
Benedictio St-mi: reassumptio totius diei. / Spiritus S. - calor verbi [a vehiculum Spiritus S. — bene elegantiam]
15. Lectura, Dormitio

5. IX
16. Surgere
Orationes matutinae
Laudes
17. Sacrum concelebratum
ad alt. S. Adalberti
grat. actio
18. IV. Konf.
Ecclesia non est relinquenda, sed regenda.

29. VI. 68. (rano)
Dr. Skup.
Medyt. I na temat „Dinumerare nos doce dies nostros, ut perveniamus ad sapientiam cordis" (Ps. 89) b) nos confitentes poscimus Te, iuste Iudex cordium
Medyt. II na temat [illegible] „[illegible]"
[illegible] / Lit. SS.
Grat. ac.
[illegible]: Via Cassia]

a) (Przywał „war ber Klucza") kościół — władza kluczy, władza Piotra, władza Biskupa (Mat. 16) Vat. II. LG, III. Które Piotr nie ma Kościoła z kluczami Biskupów, które Piotr przekazuje władzy Biskupów i wspomina (zakończenie) // Vat I.: znamienna reakcja Bismarcka, wypowiedź Biskupów niemieckich, którą Pius IX nam potwierdził.
b) „Przestań się lękać — ja mam klucze" (Apokalipsa) „Klucze Piotra — klucze do naszego wnętrza z depozytem wiary i łaski. Klucze, które tak otwierają, że nikt nie zamknie, i tak zamykają, że nikt nie otworzy" (Izaj.). Kościół jest tęsknotą za takimi kluczami, za pewnością, za opoką
c) Władza biskupów łączy się z krzyżem (cfr. Porównanie ś. Pawła [illegible]): Każdy kościół w opozycji o całą wolę Boga — to musi się łączyć z dźwiganiem krzyża. (Dowodem: pontyfikat Pawła VI) Jest to prawie [illegible] wtajemniczone starcie z szatanem (Il Papa e il diavolo)
d) — I dlatego może się zdarzyć w biskupie pokusa ucieczki od władzy (ś. Bonifacy: Ecclesia non est relinquenda sed regenda / veritas [illegible] potest, sed vinci et falli non potest). Ducha Ś. nam dał, abyśmy pokonali szatana w trudzie, choć czasem może się zdawać, że on wygrywa. „Otrzymaliśmy namaszczenie od Świętego" (I Jana)

APPUNTAMENTI

(g) The pinnacle of pastoral work – and at the same time, its source, because this is when Christ prays in us.
(h) Further discussion of the new breviary.
(i) How is it with my breviary? Do I, despite many tasks, try to retain the truth of hours?
(j) Prayer – the breath of the mystical body (Paul VI) is not only the fruit of every man's religious sense, but above all, the fruit of the Holy Spirit's work in us '*qui orat in nobis gemitibus inenarrabilibus*' ['who prays for us with sighs too deep for words'] (St Paul)[1] – so 'we pray in the Spirit' (St Paul).[2]
(k) And then the liturgy of hours will lead us to the heavenly liturgy (cf. Isaiah, Revelation).

Shorter meditation; Angelus; Examination of conscience (in relation to preaching)
(After lunch) reading: Fr Granat, *Ku człowiekowi i Bogu w Chrystusie* [Towards Man and God in Christ] and others

The Way of the Cross: An amazing text, the prayer to the Holy Spirit, who is the 'maker of the Eucharist'. The entire Way of the Cross is a reference to the Holy Mass; each Station refers to a different word, a different meaning, a different problem, e.g.

I: to the words of greeting
III: to *confiteor* [I confess . . .]. On the sins of neglect in the lives of priests and bishops
IX: on celibacy
XII: on the entire celebration of the Most Holy Sacrifice.

It would be worthwhile to have the entire text!

Letter to the youth

Talk 3: On death as *exspectatio* [expectation].

(a) *sit mors pro doctore* [let death be our teacher] (St Augustine).
(b) (Lack of work on the future of humankind (Prof. Rzepecki) interview in *Kultura*).[3]

1 See Romans 8:26.
2 See Ephesians 6:18.
3 *Kultura* [Culture] was a leading Polish émigré literary and political magazine. It was published from 1947 to 2000 by the Literary Institute in Rome and then in Paris. It was edited and produced by Jerzy Giedroyć.

(c) *theologia expectationis* [theology of expectation] and the spirituality of our waiting for the Lord:

according to St John/according to St Paul, Romans 8; Philip.
'we await His coming in glory'
waiting for the Lord – and readiness for death

The example of Pius XI.

(d) *Christus – metuendus Pastor* [Christ – fearsome Shepherd]. Waiting for the Lord fills our consciousness and tries each of us especially in difficult moments: 'tell me what you are waiting for?'

(e) Eschatological testimony. Our waiting for Christ is such a testimony – and this testimony is given by celibacy '*propter regnum coelorum*' ['for the sake of the kingdom of heaven'][1] for ourselves and for others.

(f) It is about chastity that is not limited to sexual matters. All our sacrifices as well as all our work etc. testify to our waiting for the Lord.

(g) The theology and spirituality of expectation give us the skill of dying, the ability to die by submitting everything to God and the Church. Bishop Łoziński: 'Do not pray for my healing, pray for me not to waste the grace of suffering.'

(h) *Maranatha!* [Our Lord, come!][2]

(i) '. . . and He will serve them!'[3] . . . The eternal life consists in Christ serving us: *Auctor et consummator fidei nostrae* [The pioneer and perfecter of our faith].[4]

(j) *Re-capitulatio in Xto* [Conclusion in Christ]: everything will come back to Christ, everything will be at His feet, everything will be concluded in Him, 'that God may be everything to every one'[5] . . . – And it is there that Christ 'will serve us' . . . with truth (!) and fatherly love (!). *Pater futuri saeculi* [Everlasting Father];[6] the joy of seeing the Father's face.

1 See Matthew 19:12.
2 See 1 Corinthians 16:22.
3 See Luke 12:37.
4 See Hebrews 12:2.
5 See 1 Corinthians 15:28.
6 See Isaiah 9:6.

(k) 'No longer do I call you servants, but friends'[1] – this is what *Xtus* [Christ] said at the first consecration – so He shall serve the bishops with truth and brotherly, friendly love.

(l) 'I consider that the sufferings of this present time are not worth comparing with the glory that is to be revealed to us' (Romans 8).[2]

(m) Therefore it is worth it to follow Christ, it is worth it to consider everything 'refuse'.[3]

Vespers; Adoration; (Anticipated) Matins; Rosary (I), (II), (III); Compline; Benediction with the Blessed Sacrament: conclusion of the whole day (the Holy Spirit – the Fire of the Word; the vehicle of the Holy Spirit – the Blood of Christ); Reading; Sleep

5 September Getting up; Morning prayers; Lauds; Holy Mass concelebrated at St Adalbert's altar; Thanksgiving

Talk 4: *Ecclesia non est relinquenda, sed regenda* [The Church is not to be abandoned but to be controlled].[4]

(a) (Example: 'the world without the key'.)
The Church – the authority of the keys, the authority of Peter, the authority of the bishops (Matthew 16). Vatican II, *L[umen] G[entium]* III. Peter's keys are not in conflict with the bishops' keys; Peter's keys confirm the bishops' authority and strengthen it. Vatican I: the significance of Bismarck's reaction, the significance of the German bishops' response, which was immediately approved by Pius IX.

(b) 'Fear not – I have the keys' (Revelation).[5] Peter's keys – the keys to happiness related to the deposit of faith and grace. 'The keys that will open so that none shall shut and that will shut so that none shall open' (Isaiah).[6] There is a longing for such keys, for a bedrock, in the world.

---

1 See John 15:15.

2 See Romans 8:18.

3 See Philippians 3:8.

4 See 'Letter of Saint Boniface to Archbishop Cuthbert of Canterbury' in *The Letters of Saint Boniface*, trans. Ephraim Emerton (New York, 1940), pp. 136–41 (138).

5 See Revelation 1:17–18.

6 See Isaiah 22:22.

(c) Bishops' authority is connected with the cross (cf. St Paul's speech in Miletus).[1] To lead the Church in accordance with God's will – this must be connected with the carrying of the cross. (Evidence: Paul VI's pontificate.) It is, above all, the inevitable struggle with Satan (*Il Papa e il diavolo* [The Pope and the devil]).

(d) And therefore the bishop might experience a temptation to flee from authority (St Boniface:
Ecclesia non est relinquenda sed regenda
Veritas fatigari potest, sed vinci et falli non potest.
[The Church is not to be abandoned but to be controlled
The truth can be impeded, but it cannot be conquered nor deceived]).
The Holy Spirit has anointed us so that we can conquer satan in difficulties, even though sometimes it might seem that he is winning. 'You have been anointed by the Holy One' (1 John).[2]

(e) The crosier (*Baculum* from *battero* = to strike) should bear two marks: the mark of fatherhood and the mark of the Eucharist. (The Church, through the will of God, is a monarchy, it will never be a democracy), but it is a fatherly monarchy. Paternalism is a mistake, fatherhood is the truth (1 Cor. 15: For though you have countless guides in Christ, you do not have many fathers . . . I became your father in Christ Jesus through the gospel).[3]

(f) What contradicts the bishop's fatherhood? Permissivism, protectionism, parochialism, indecisiveness, verbosity (empty talk), overproduction of dialogue. The bishop's fatherhood has to be full of love and prudence.

(g) The mark of the Eucharist: one needs to follow the Eucharistic Christ – for God, one needs to be the host, and for people, the bread (*imitamini quod tractatis* [imitate what you practise]): Theology of bread.

During the retreat one should see that which should be placed on the paten, but which we do not place there. (Could we not

1 See Acts 20:17–35.
2 See 1 John 2:20.
3 See 1 Corinthians 4:15.

give more to people?) Brother Albert's theology of bread: One has to imitate the Eucharistic communion.

Meditation

Talk 5: On the retreat confession, on the sacrament of penance. The grace of our Lord Jesus Christ, and the love of God, and the communion of the Holy Spirit.

(a) The Father's love is forgiving – Luke 15 – on the prodigal son. The way to happiness leads through the confessional – each Lord's Prayer is an amazing psychotherapy – the sacrament of penance: to rebuild our love of God completely (not 'almost' completely).
(b) The grace of our Lord Jesus Christ is with us in the sacrament of penance. *In amplexu Crucis* [Embracing the Cross], we can receive all graces and cleanse ourselves from all sins. The Catechism of the Catholic Church: 'through the sacraments we celebrate our existence'.[1] Through the sacrament of penance a personal intervention of the merciful Christ takes place in my soul.

Example: Servants of God, Brother Balicki and Cardinal Mercier. *Bene, Domine quia humiliasti me* [Lord, it is good that you made me humble].[2]

- Contrition for God's graces which I have wasted, in the confession.
- Confession always has to be connected with work on oneself, constant rebuilding, since the bishop '*positus in Ecclesia quasi in statu perfectionis acquisitae*' *(S. Th.)* ['is placed in the Church as if in acquired perfection' (St Thomas Aquinas)].

(c) The communion of the Holy Spirit; in confession the Holy Spirit is certainly with us (Seraphim of [Sarov]: the aim of Christian life is to acquire the Holy Spirit) – 'peace be with you' – rebuilding the communion with the Holy

1 See the *Catechism of the Catholic Church*, 1210–11.
2 See Psalm 118 (119):71.

Spirit, we are rebuilding the communion with the Church, with our neighbours.

All this is the aim of our retreat confession.

Short meditation; Rosary; Examination of conscience; After lunch – reading; Confession; Adoration; Vespers; Rosary
The Holy Year's pilgrimage to St Adalbert's tomb: enriched by the jubilee indulgence
Concelebration; Introduction by His Eminence Cardinal Primate

[Talk] 6: *Contio* [Sermon]: on the words from St John's Gospel on the grain of wheat which falls into the earth . . . and bears fruit. Three grains – the first is Jesus Christ, the second – St Adalbert, the third – we. The entire theology of the Holy Year indulgence was developed on this basis.[1]

Procession and benediction with the Blessed Sacrament, including: Holy Hour in the spirit of satisfaction; Penitential psalms; Litany of the Saints; Compline; Reading

6 September Getting up; Morning prayers; Lauds; Prime; Concelebration at the tomb of St Adalbert; Thanksgiving

Talk 7: Glory to you, Word of God.

(a) The beauty of the Word of God; reflection on the first human word; Modrzejewska;[2] [illegible] (cf. Parandowski, *Alchemia słowa*).[3]
(b) The word of God is the power of God to save man (*per Evangelica dicta deleantur nostra delicta* . . . [let the words of the Gospel erase our sins . . .]). Lord, only say the word and my soul shall be healed . . . The word of God has an amazing therapeutic power. From the Synod of Bishops' *instrumentum laboris* [working paper]: *vi Spiritus Sancti praedicatio Verbi Dei semper efficax est* [by the power of the Holy Spirit, the preaching of the Word of God is always effective]. Although sometimes we cannot see the effects clearly. – *Verbum – Sacramentum* [Word – Sacrament].
(c) *Rex regum – metuendus Censor* [The King of kings – fearsome Judge] (!) demands of us to preach the entire

1 See John 12:24.
2 Helena Modrzejewska (1840–1909) was a Polish actress famous for her tragic and Shakespearian roles.
3 Jan Parandowski, *Alchemia słowa* [The Alchemy of the Word] (Warsaw, 1950).

word of God; Acts of the Apostles – St Paul's speech in Miletus: the entire will of God. According to St Paul, the violation of this entirety resembles murder. (Paul says: I am innocent of the blood of all of you . . . for I did not shrink from declaring to you the whole counsel of God.)[1] The doctrine of faith is complete or it does not exist at all (*bonum ex integra causa, malum ex quovis defectu* [a thing is good when good in every respect; it is wrong when wrong in any respect]). The bishop needs to have '*sensum limitis*' ['a sense of his limitations'].

[What is the situation in Poland? It is better than in the West, but certain books and journals which should not have been granted an imprimatur have been published – How about me? –]

(d) The aim of preaching the word of God, evangelisation, is salvation. The usual path to salvation is through Christ present in the Church. Involvement in the world (pre-evangelisation) cannot be an anti-testimony, i.e. an end in itself. It also has to be a testimony given to God and the eschatological reality.
(e) *Metuende Censor* [O fearsome Judge]: Christ is also *metuendus Censor* [fearsome Judge] of our language. The language that does not grow old is the language of the Gospels. It is a language that calls us to follow Christ. One needs to take the effort to find the appropriate contemporary language, but also not to lose the biblical language.

[What is the language that I use to speak to people like? Do I preach the Gospel with full conviction, with full feeling? (Eat this scroll.)[2] Do I preach it to please God, not people? The enemy of evangelisation is hidden in the small word 'almost'.]

(idol – a sin, idol – an error)

1 See Acts 20:26–27.
2 See Ezekiel 3:1.

Meditation: a general description of the retreat – examination of the (bishops') spirit; The Way of the Cross considered individually in relation to certain words of the retreat.

Talk 8: (*De Beata* [On the Blessed One])

(a) *s. Bernardus: totus mundus exspectat responsum Mariae – ecce ancilla Domini* [St Bernard: the whole world expects Mary's response – She is the handmaid of the Lord]:[1] Through these words Mary became the Mother of our reconciliation with God – through these words uttered in Nazareth, and repeated under the cross. God reconciled the world in Christ through the mediation of Mary.

(b) Mary reveals Her Immaculate Conception when – while a new world is being born, a new world full of wars – She comes to reconcile people with God.
We must help Her with this, work with Her. What would have happened if Mary had said 'no'? What would have happened if Fr Maksymilian had said 'no'?[2]

crede! [believe!]

(c) The three '*aperi*' ['open!'] of St Bernard.[3] The response of the heart open to faith – Mary's faith was paid for dearly with Her sacrifice. Sacrifice is the implication of faith (cf. the analysis of the icon of Our Lady of Perpetual Help – in the East, 'a terrible vision') – only through this kind of faith can we become Mary's assistants, like Fr Kolbe. Such faith reaches prophetic dimensions.

> Is this the answer of faith that I give to God every day, together with Mary?

(d) St Bernard: Mary's lips are open to adore God: *confitere!*

---

1 See Luke 1:38.

2 See n. 3, p. 68 [2 September 1971].

3 '*Aperi, Virgo beata, cor fidei, labia confessioni, viscera Creatori*' ['Open, Blessed Virgin, your heart to faith, your lips to confession, your womb to your Creator']. See St Bernard, 'Homilia IV' in *Sancti Bernardi Opera Omnia* IV, vol. 4, Sermones I, ed. J. Leclerq and H. Rochais (Rome, 1966), pp. 53–4. For the English translation see St Bernard, 'Homily IV: The Annunciation and the Blessed Virgin's Consent' in *Sermons of St Bernard on Advent and Christmas*, ed. J. C. Hedley (New York, 1909), pp. 59–70.

confess! The Mother of God is the Mother of brave confession. Evidence: Fr Kolbe.

> Is the answer that I give to God every day an answer of faith, notwithstanding the circumstances, together with Mary?

(e) St Bernard: *Suscipe!* [Receive!]. Mary taught Fr Kolbe how to accept God through love. Mary heals us from our coldness (satan's name – 'coldness') so that we can work with Her to reconcile people with God. An amazing 'thank you' of St Bernadette Soubirous.

(f) The nation, world, Church and heaven await our – Polish bishops' – constant answer, 'yes' uttered with Mary. The future depends on this and nothing else. Amen.

Magnificat; Act of Consecration to Our Lady (Primate); Benediction with the Blessed Sacrament
Major Council of the Bishops' Conference in the afternoon
Breviary; Adoration; Rosary

7 September Concluding meditation: In order to respond 'yes' to God with the Most Holy Mother, one has to be a sign of Christ through prayer (breviary), celebrating the Eucharist, the spirituality of expectation, solemnity of authority, verbal service, the spirit of penance . . .

Deo gratias! [Thanks be to God!]

4–8 July 1975
Retreat at Bachledówka[1]

~

4 July: Anniversary of the Cathedral's Consecration

(First Friday): preparation of the 'material', arrival at Bachledówka about 9.00 p.m.
Adoration of the Blessed Sacrament; Compline

5 July

Morning prayers; (First Saturday) Introductory meditation 1, in which the following topic emerges: Creator – Judge – God and Father of our Lord Jesus Christ
First reading; Lauds; Holy Mass; Thanksgiving
Reading: *Analecta Cracov*. 1975: 'Nowa interpretacja dogmatów'[2]
Rosary (petitions); Prayer to the Holy Spirit

Morning meditation 2: 'I thank Thee, Father, Creator (Lord) of heaven and earth, that Thou hast hidden these things from the great and revealed them to babes'[3] – The truth about creation and the truth about God as the Creator is the first step the human mind takes towards God. This first step seems very difficult to many people today due to certain cognitive assumptions that have developed in the modern understanding of the world. This understanding is devoid of transcendence. 'The great' in a way become the slaves of such an understanding. In the same reality, 'babes' discover being, beauty, goodness, coincidence, creativeness – all that St Thomas so successfully described in an objective way. Man indispensably needs this first step through the visible creation (the world) towards the invisible Creator (compare Wisdom, Romans).

The discovery of the Creator is not only the belief in the First Cause, which is *Esse Subsistens* [Being Itself]. It is also – and first and foremost – the discovery of love. To create means not only to reveal power, omnipotence that surpasses all, but also it means: to give being, existence and goodness, therefore – to love!

---

1 See n. 1, p. 51 [9 August 1969].
2 Ignacy Różycki, 'Nowa interpretacja dogmatów' [New Interpretation of the Dogmas], *Analecta Cracoviensia*, vol. 5–6 (1973–74), pp. 303–27.
3 See Matthew 11:25.

The Way of the Cross: *In quam verba Mariae vel de Maria introducuntur (XII: Misit Deus Filium suum natum ex Muliere . . . Signum magnum apparuit . . . et verba e Magnificat, ex Annuntiatione)* [In which Mary's words or words about Mary are introduced (Station XII: God sent forth His Son, born of woman . . . And a great portent appeared . . . and Mary's words from the Magnificat, from the Annunciation)].[1]
Meanwhile: Terce; Sext; None; Reading (as above)

Adoration: The Eucharist makes it possible for our life still to revolve around 'the dimension of the living God'.

Vespers; Rosary; Petitionary prayer

Meditation 3: According to St John, man turns away from God, the Creator and Father, through concupiscence, which is not 'of the Father', but 'of the world'.[2] It deprives us of true and full joy of creation and joy derived from creation. It diminishes the perspectives of experience.

I considered the entire issue of A.T.[3] against this background, trying thoroughly to understand it, and above all begging for the right steps. (To some extent also A.P.) and others, considered previously.

(Anticipated) Matins for Sunday after Holy Mass; Paul VI's encyclical on joy[4]

Concluding meditation of the day [Meditation 4]: Mary as the fullness of the Creator's experience, the fullness of creation and one's own creativeness: *fecit mihi magna* . . . [has done great things for me].[5] Because the fullness of creation is grace: God wishes to create, but He even more wishes to create 'things', to give Himself personally. Mary is the one who is the most open to it. Mary teaches us openness to God's work. Let us imitate her without failure!

The Jasna Góra Appeal; Compline (after reading)

6 July

Morning prayers; Intention; In relation to the Divine Presence (the beginning of the meditation): God and Father of Our Lord Jesus Christ
Lauds; Holy Mass; Thanksgiving; Rosary
Reading: the journal *Analecta Cracoviensia*
Prayer to the Holy Spirit

1 See Galatians 4:4 and Revelation 12:1.
2 See 1 John 2:16.
3 This might be a reference to Anna-Teresa Tymieniecka (1923–2014), a lifelong friend of Karol Wojtyła–John Paul II.
4 Reference to Pope Paul VI's apostolic exhortation *Gaudete in domino* (On Christian Joy) issued on 9 May 1975.
5 See Luke 1:49.

Meditation 5: Further contemplation of the Creator's mystery concentrates on the creation of the human being, who is made in the image and likeness of God. Awareness and freedom, hence also conscience, enter the world of visible creatures. God–Creator reveals Himself as God–Judge through conscience. We will discuss this theme of the retreat later. One needs to enter more deeply into the dynamism of creation, which is revealed together with the creation of man. Protoevangelium (Genesis 1–3) has to be interpreted more fully.

The essence of the mystery of creation does not consist only in creation out of nothing. It is present more fully in givenness: Existence is a gift – it becomes a gift in creation. And it reaches man as a gift. In him the act of creation signifies such dynamism of givenness on the part of the Creator that cannot be exhausted in existence, life or even spiritual likeness. Through all this and beside all this, God gives Himself to man in such a way that is possible only in friendship. The dynamism of creation leads to grace. At the same time, friendship attains the features of a covenant: There cannot be any friendship without certain expectations. Nevertheless, the created man remains in the fullness of the dynamism of givenness and enters the communion (*communio*) with God–man (Adam–Eve), and the communion entails a gift and mutual givenness. Sin – the breaking of the covenant – destroys this order. Concupiscence is in a way a renunciation of the gift.

The structure of creation as free givenness (out of nothing) and the dynamism which follows from this allow us to introduce an evolutionary theme (creation is immanently directed towards fullness) into our considerations of the mystery.

First and foremost, however, the entire dynamism of creation (cf. Genesis 1–3) allows us to see in it a kind of pouring out of the love with which the Father has eternally embraced the Son–Word. 'Without Him was not anything made that was made.'[1] The mystery of creation has a Trinitarian character and, in a further perspective, a Christological character: 'the God and Father of our Lord Jesus Christ'.[2] The omnipotent

1 See John 1:3.
2 See Ephesians 1:3.

Father creates 'through Him and with Him and in Him' – in order to make the entire creation, above all man, 'through Him and with Him and in Him' – 'return' to the Father.

The Way of the Cross – the Trinitarian and Christological dimensions
Terce; Sext; None; Reading etc., Rosary; Vespers
Adoration of the Blessed Sacrament: Jesus is present and acts: let me not waste any word nor any inspiration of the Holy Spirit

Meditation 6: The pride of life is not of the Father, but of the world (BT translation),[1] and the world passes away, and the lust of it; but he who does the will of God abides for ever.[2]

Reflection: (a) petition for a proper discernment of specific problems in the spirit of humility, i.e. the spirit of truth and generosity; (b) petition for fidelity to an established formula (in relation to the so-called drive for importance): to desire only the significance which will be given to me by God Himself – and work with Him; and finally (c) not to resign from the highest 'ambition', which is the desire for sanctity.

Reading; Anticipated Matins of the following day (Feast of Ss Cyril and Methodius); Rosary

Concluding meditation of the day [Meditation 7]: Mary stands in the middle of the dynamism of creation: full of grace. Together with Her I try to resolve issues like (a) and (b). My 'ambition' of sanctity is also connected to Her: *Totus Tuus*.[3]

Reading (the encyclical on joy); Compline

7 July: Feast of Ss Cyril and Methodius

Morning prayers
The beginning of the daily meditation: before the face of God Himself, creation – fulfilment
Lauds; Holy Mass (Eucharistic prayer 4); Thanksgiving
Reading: *Kim jest dla mnie Jezus Chrystus*[4] – *Analecta Cracoviensia*

Meditation 8: The dynamism of creation leads to fulfilment.

1 Reference to *Biblia Tysiąclecia* (the Millennium Bible), one of the most important twentieth-century Polish translations of the Bible. The first edition of this translation was published in 1965 on the millennial anniversary of the Christianisation of Poland.

2 See 1 John 2:17.

3 See n. 1, p. 1 [2 September 1962].

4 *Kim jest dla mnie Jezus Chrystus: wypowiedzi w ankiecie 'Tygodnika Powszechnego'* [Who Is Jesus Christ for Me: Responses to the Survey Conducted by 'Tygodnik Powszechny' (*The Catholic Weekly*)], ed. Józefa Hennelowa (Kraków, 1975).

25. Meditatio conclusiva diei (VII)
Maryja stoi u progu dynamizmu zbawienia: łaski pełna. Jej z Nim zjednoczenie rozstrzyga sprawy typu a/ i b/. Z Nim też wiąże „anielskość" rzeczy: razem nas

26 Lectura (enc. o [illegible])
Complet.

7.VII. — S. Cyrilli et Methodii

27. Preces matut. coram Ipso
Inchoatio Meditationis diei: spełnienie
stworzenie – spełnienie

28 Laudes

29 Sacrum (can. IV) Grat. actio

30 Lektura (~~[illegible]~~ Kim jest dla mnie Jezus Chrystus – teol. [illegible])

31. Meditatio (VIII)
Dynamizm stworzenia zmierza do spełnienia. Wcześniej mówiliśmy, że stworzenie jest obdarowaniem ze strony Stwórcy, mimo to o jego granicach płaskie (ograniczoność) ostateczny sens. Zwiąże się to z celowością. Stworzenie spełnia się niewątpliwie na poziomie „natury", gdy działa o istocie pozbawionej transcendencji. Spełnienie polega na tym, że ta rzecz żyje, że trwa jako gatunek, że podlega ewolucji. Ich spełnienie natury do świata; a od strony Stwórcy polega na tym, że wszystkie te rzeczy [illegible] cały świat wyraża Jego Istnienie i Jego Mądrość, Jego Moc, „na zewnątrz" i nie

APPUNTAMENTI

Precisely because creation is the gift of the Creator, it has to have a final sense in His own plan (providence). It is related to purposefulness. Creation is fulfilled constantly on the level of 'nature' among creatures deprived of transcendence. Fulfilment consists in them being alive, their existence as species, their evolution. Their fulfilment belongs to the 'world'; and from the Creator's perspective, this fulfilment consists in the fact that all those creatures, and through them the entire world, express His presence, His wisdom and His power 'externally', in a way outside of God.

The relationship between creation and fulfilment is different for beings endowed with transcendence. This is man in the visible world (and, apart from it, the world of pure spirits). The fulfilment of man is immanently linked to judgement. For judgement is an act of transcendence. It is realised in the voices of conscience, and there has to be finally a kind of synthesising judgement. In this judgement, man–conscience meets God–Just Judge. The judgement equates transcendence 'towards truth'. However, it consists in arriving at the truth about love ('in the evening of your life you will be judged by your love') and the truth for love.

For man is called to fulfilment through participation in God, who is love. God–Trinity is the self-contained fullness, above all fulfilment of the world and the human heart. At the same time, this fullness outlines the horizon of fulfilment for all creation in the human being. At the end of his life, man will be judged by the ways in which he served the fulfilment of the world, whose transcendent end is God as fullness. This fulfilment finds its realisation in the partaking of God, which will lead to God being all in everything. The foundation of this fulfilment is not personal transcendence, but grace, which ingrains the participation in God's life, which is fullness, in this transcendence.

(Many themes are still to be developed here).

The Way of the Cross; Terce; Sext; None
In the afternoon we enter the final stage of the retreat (rest, reading)

Adoration of the Blessed Sacrament: Joyful conviction that Christ is, and giving thanks for that, and a fervent petition for Him to be with me in everything that I wish to root in Him and develop with Him – despite all my weakness and even though '*conscientia metuit*' ['the conscience is anxious']: so that He Himself develops properly good things beyond my weakness and clumsiness.

Meditation 9: Reference to specific issues – and once again to 1 John on the triple concupiscence, which is 'of the world'. The lust of the eyes may take the form of not only desire for material goods, but also for any visible success achieved to fulfil one's self-love in any area. Hence, one needs to look at facts critically.

The triple concupiscence impedes creation's way to fulfilment. If we follow different impulses, reactions, feelings, sometimes it is difficult to discern and draw boundaries. Christ the Lord gave us one method and taught us one attitude, which seems to constitute the simplest remedy for the triple concupiscence. It is the attitude and method of service. One has to follow it, cutting across the entire complicated field of inner tensions, which are born of the lust of the eyes, the flesh and the pride of life.

Anticipated Matins of the following day (Feast of St Elisabeth); Reading and letters; Penitential psalms; Litany of the Saints; Rosary

Concluding meditation [Meditation 10]: Mary took the path from creation to fulfilment in the simplest and quickest way. This is how Her response at the Annunciation can be translated: I am the handmaid of the Lord. The attitude of service emerges spontaneously, surpassing the area of the triple concupiscence so common to man. Therefore She is – as Vatican II reminds us – the fulfilment of what the entire people of God in the Church strive for. One needs to learn from her the simplest – and at the same time most deeply grounded – resolution.

Compline; Reading

8 July The conclusion of the retreat takes place at Kalwaria Zebrzydowska.[1]

1 See n. 1, p. 12 [6–7 July 1963].

The Little Ways of Our Lady;[1] Rosary

Meditation 11: On these paths the people of God often reflect on the mystery of the creation and fulfilment, bringing together Christ and Mary in their hearts.

I also come here to bring my retreat intentions to their hearts and ask for the grace of little fulfilments on the way to the highest fulfilment.

Holy Mass in the Sacred Chapel before the Miraculous Image
(In the afternoon: the funeral of Prelate Stanisław Słonka in Żywiec-Zabłocie)

---

1 See n. 2, p. 12 [6–7 July 1963].

21–26 September 1976
Retreat in Zakopane–Jaszczurówka at the Grey Ursulines'
Topic: *Sacerdos – Propheta – Rex* [Priest – Prophet – King]

~

21 September: Feast of St Matthew

Vespers at 4.30 p.m.

Introductory meditation: Fr W. spoke in the morning about 'the vocation of the sinner' – this is what he said about today's patron saint. Every vocation is threefold and consists of the dimensions of the priest, the prophet and the king. Matthew's calling to join the twelve apostles was also like that. We will try to follow this threefold nature of vocation during the retreat. And every vocation through Christ–Just Lamb is the calling of a 'sinner'. It contains an inner dimension of 'justification' proportionate to the dimension of sinfulness. We will also try to follow up on this during the retreat. The first light.

Anticipated Matins; Eucharistic devotion
Reading (*Znak*),[1] and others: D. M. Stanley SJ, *A Modern Scriptural Approach to the Spiritual Exercises*, chapter 2.[2]
Compline

22 September Prayers; Preparation for Holy Mass
Meditation (short):

'*o pia Deitas, o tremenda Maiestas,*
ego miser, inter angustias deprehensus,
ad Te, fontem misericordiae, recurro . . .' (*S. Ambrosius*)

---

1 See n. 1, p. 69 [2 September 1971].

2 David M. Stanley, *A Modern Scriptural Approach to the Spiritual Exercises* (Chicago, 1967). John Paul II read this book in Polish translation: *Słowo Boże światłością i drogą: Pismo Św. u źródeł rekolekcyjnej odnowy*, trans. Jan Korewa and Felicja Zielińska (Kraków, 1975).

['God of loving kindness and awesome majesty, I, a sinner caught by many snares, seek safe refuge in you. For you are the fountain of mercy . . .' (St Ambrose)].

Holy Mass; Thanksgiving; Lauds
Reading: (a) *Ateneum Kapłańskie* [Priestly Atheneum] (on the spirituality of priests);[1] (b) 'Sign of Contradiction' (Vatican retreat)[2]
Rosary; Prayer to the Holy Spirit; The Way of the Cross; The Little Hours; (Letter to the priests and an invitation to a pilgrimage to Kalwaria)

Meditation (long): Priesthood. Christ the great priest. St Paul (Hebrews) gives a 'priestly' interpretation of Christ's mission, and above all His passion and death. Although Christ did not call Himself a priest, He ultimately revealed the sense of priesthood, above all the 'priestly' profile of human existence.

Priesthood is inscribed in the world and in the human being as two deeply interconnected poles of existence. Priesthood expresses creativeness as a dependence on the Creator and, at the same time, as a relatedness and directionality towards the Creator. Man is capable of, indeed, called to this relatedness and directionality, since he has been appointed the 'ruler' of creation. He was also endowed with self-control. Therefore, as the ruler of creation and the ruler of himself he can make offerings – that is, give an active gift to God: the gift of all creation and, above all, the gift of himself. In this sense, priesthood is a special synthesis of created existence which finds the fullest and deepest expression in man and through man. From this perspective, priesthood is born out of love and it highlights love as the communion of creatures and the communion of creatures with the Creator.

Jesus Christ revealed this priestly sense of creation and human existence through all His words and deeds. Above all, through His passion and death, which was a sacrificial deed. We find this strictly priestly sense of existence in the Eucharist as the sacrament of death and resurrection celebrated under the forms of bread and wine, which express the synthesis of creation and at the same time constitute food. Christ–high Priest. His priesthood is for all people who accept that which

1 *Ateneum Kapłańskie* [Priestly Atheneum] is a Polish journal of theology founded in 1909.
2 Karol Wojtyła, *Sign of Contradiction* (New York, 1979). This is the published version of the retreat talk that Karol Wojtyła delivered at the Lenten retreat for Pope Paul VI and the Roman Curia in 1976.

defines it. All the baptised participate in it, as in baptism, the first sacrament, they received an ability to offer 'spiritual sacrifices', to bring to God – Creator and Father – the gift of all creation and the gift of themselves by the power and in the name of Christ. Those who receive the sacrament of priesthood have the power to celebrate the Eucharist, that is, to renew that in which Christ's priesthood has found expression and has been preserved. They have this power for the sake of others, for the sake of the building of the Church.

The high Priest . . . is found to be just. Not only does Christ's priesthood express the sense of human and creation's existence, it also actualises the justice towards the Creator.

Adoration of the Blessed Sacrament (thanksgiving for the Eucharist and for the grace of priesthood); Vespers; Rosary (II), (III)

Meditation: I became a priest of Jesus Christ in the Church of Kraków (it has been almost thirty-one years), of which I am now the bishop. Episcopacy also means a marriage with the Church of Kraków: a certain participation in the marriage and bridal love which binds Christ to the entire Church, so that the Church is 'without spot or wrinkle'.[1] The bridal love of the Church of Kraków is my vocation: Bridal means full of total devotion.

It is from this perspective that I consider different issues, various aspects of my episcopal work in the Archdiocese of Kraków, pastoral work with youth, families, vocations – the seminary, the Faculty of Theology, the synod, my attitude to priests. On the latter issue '*numquam satis*' ['never enough']. Having undertaken different tasks outside of my Church (altogether about three months), I wish to return to its issues with much zeal. It is part of my inheritance from the Lord, from Christ–Good Shepherd.

Matins (anticipated)

Meditation (short): Mary is the Mother of the Church; She is also the Mother of priests. She bears in Herself a unique fullness and unique maturity of 'royal priesthood'.[2] What is relevant

1 See Ephesians 5:27.
2 See 1 Peter 2:9.

to it can be found in Her in plenitude. Thus She is also the Mother of priests and the Mother of the bridal love to the Church, by which every bishop should live, following Christ.

Note: 1. special illumination during the reflection on the glorious mysteries (divine–human mystery [illegible]).

2. First outline (but quite detailed) of my thoughts on the topic: what does 'salvation' mean?

Litany of the Saints
A Modern Scriptural Approach to the Spiritual Exercises, chapter 3.[1]
Compline; (Reading)

23 September Morning prayers; Preparation for Holy Mass

Meditation (short): '*Deus cui omne cor patet et omnis voluntas loquitur, et quem nullum latet secretum – purifica per infusionem Sancti Spiritus cogitationes cordis nostri . . .*' ['Almighty God, to whom all hearts are open, all desires known, and from whom no secrets are hidden: cleanse the thoughts of our hearts by the inspiration of your Holy Spirit . . .']

Holy Mass; Thanksgiving; Lauds
Reading: (a) Vatican retreat;[2] (b) *Ateneum Kapłańskie* (as above)
Rosary (III); Petitionary prayer for the seven gifts of the Holy Spirit; Daytime prayers; The Way of the Cross
Writing to WP[3]

Meditation (*longa in deambulando* [long, while walking]): Prophetism. *Christus profeta magnus* [Christ the Great Prophet]. In a sense, one can speak of the 'prophetic' structure of our reality, just like yesterday we spoke of the 'priestly' one. God is the fullness of being, but also the fullness of truth. Man naturally tends to truth – and towards God as the fullness of truth. This configuration constitutes the basis of the 'prophetic' structure of reality, in which we live and act. God as the fullness of truth gives Himself to man. Not only in His inner mystery is He the Word, but in the Word He establishes contact with man. This is an entirely free initiative of His. At the same time, it

1 See n. 2, p. 105 [21 September 1976].
2 See n. 2, p. 108 [22 September 1976].
3 This might be a reference to Wanda Półtawska (b. 1921), who was a lifelong friend of Karol Wojtyła–John Paul II.

corresponds to the tendency to truth which is natural to man, to his spirituality.

A prophet is one who speaks on behalf of God; he expresses God's truth, with certain limitations, in a human language. Therefore prophetism is connected to revelation and faith. '*Multifarie multisque modis loquens Deus olim in Profetis, novissime locutus est nobis in Filio*' ['In many and various ways God spoke of old to our fathers by the prophets; but in these last days He has spoken to us by a Son'].[1] Christ is the fullness of revelation, 'the final word' of the Word. In Him and His apostles it is 'completed'. At the same time Christ shares His 'prophetism' (*munus profeticum* [prophetic mission]) with those who receive His word. One of the primary attributes of the people of God is their participation '*in munere profetico*' ['in the prophetic mission'] of Christ.

Thus prophetism is an attribute of faith which is professed and, what is more, faith which is preached through teaching, but also through practice, which testifies to the faith. The Second Vatican Council revealed the amazing size and scope of this participation. Preaching the gospel is particularly important for bishops, and it is the task of priests, orders and laypeople. Faith, teaching, knowledge (theology) and conscience need to be coordinated in the prophetic structure of the Church. For there exists a special prophetism of conscience – and it is important for everyone, including those who do not believe, but 'seek truth with a sincere heart'.

For the entire prophetic structure of the people of God finds its support not only in the word of God, but also in the human tendency to truth. The former and the latter shape the *munus profeticum* [prophetic mission] in its real dimension through one another. The key problem that remains is that of how man understands reality – how man understands the word of God in reality, so that he can testify to it.

Adoration of the Blessed Sacrament: (This is the place in which I find myself in the fullness of truth and love. Here I seek support for my petitions and actions. Grace comes from here.)

1 See Hebrews 1:1–2.

Vespers; Rosary (I), (II)

Meditation on the topic of (T.C.): I thought about these issues previously, wondering what the vocation and what the temptation is here. I consider these things in the context of the gifts of the Holy Spirit. The gift of fear of the Lord is definitely the basis. It is the fear of sin (as far as the thing itself can offend God) as well as the fear of scandal. I undertake action on the basis of this fear and following prayer, counsel and obedience, and with a conviction that this action involves a special good, which cannot be seen or understood. The gift of piety (*donum pietatis*) is doing its work here. This good is expressed by the words of Cor. [Corinthians] 'do you not know that your body is a temple of the Holy Spirit within you'[1] (the spirituality of the flesh and all that is related to the flesh).

This is the state of conscience before action and during an action. And conscience after the action? It orders one to remain in prayer for a constant identification of the good, which was intended, and for fortitude in the current circumstances. Here, again, the gift of counsel. To differentiate between the proper and improper consequences (the situation of WP: certain suggestions). The scapular.

A Modern Scriptural Approach to the Spiritual Exercises (chapter 6)[2]
Anticipated Matins (after the Mass); Reading
Holy Hour, in the context of the Vatican retreat: contemplation; Mary – Reparatrix
Compline; (Reading)

24 September Morning prayers

Meditation (short): '*Ure igne Sancti Spiritus renes nostros et cor nostrum, Domine, ut Tibi casto corpore serviamus et mundo corde placeamus.*' ['Grant, O Lord, we pray Thee, that the fire of Thy Holy Ghost may in such wise cleanse our reins and our hearts: that we serving Thee in pureness both of body and soul may be found an acceptable people in Thy sight.'][3]

Holy Mass with thanksgiving; Lauds
Reading: (a) *Ateneum Kapłańskie*; (b) Vatican retreat: writing the introduction[4]

1 See 1 Corinthians 6:19.
2 See n. 2, p. 105 [21 September 1976].
3 See the Litany of the Saints.
4 See n. 2, p. 108 [22 September 1976].

Rosary (I); Prayer for the seven gifts of the Holy Spirit; The Way of the Cross (Vatican); Terce; Sext; None

Meditation (*longa in deambulando* [long, while walking]): *Munus regale* [Royal mission]. Kingship as a rule is inscribed in the act of creation. The Creator is the Lord. And the Creator–Lord tells people: 'rule'. This configuration has lasted incorrupt throughout human history. Dominion over nature is, however, connected to work (compare Marxist conceptions) in which man not only 'takes rule' over the material and makes use of it, but also 'integrates' it into himself. Ruling does not mean only 'superiority', it means the right to give orders and administer. In this sense, reign has become a standard of social life (authority and different social systems). First and foremost, however, it is inscribed into human nature so that man's task is to rule over himself. His proper 'kingship' is expressed precisely in this act, even though *G[audium et] S[pes]* introduces in this context the dominion over nature, which is imbued with moral rules too.

Historical experience teaches us that social and economic structures of power in different ways shape 'the kingdom of this world'.

Christ the Lord said before Pilate: 'my kingship is not of this world'.[1] What is the nature of the 'kingship' that He preached and that we should realise, taking part *'in munere regali' Christi* ['in the royal mission' of Christ]? It is erected on the foundation of love. Christ, the Son of God, came to fulfil in the world a different order of reign than that which is based on the natural 'kingship' of man (even though Christ also embraces this order and includes it '*in munere regali*' ['in His royal mission']). This order is realised when the Son gives to the Father all and everything so that the Father was 'everything to every one'.[2] This is the 'kingship' of submission and love, the kingship of service, thanks to which God, being the Lord of everything, can reveal Himself as love in everything and everyone.

1 See John 18:36.
2 See 1 Corinthians 15:28.

– Tu nie mówi Chrystus o panowaniu. Tu uświadamia ten niezmierzony zapas dobra człowieka. Panowanie nad przyrodą tkwi się z porządku (cfr. koncepcja marx.), w której człowiek nie tylko „opanowuje" twórczo i posługuje się nią, ale także „tworzy" nie siebie". Panowanie nie oznacza tylko „używania", oznacza prawo rozkazywania i jej kierowania. W tym znaczeniu panowanie wiąże się z prawidłowością życia społecznego (władza i różne ustroje). ~~tu;~~ Środek wszelkiego jednak tkwi ono w strukturze samego człowieka, który jest zadany sobie, aby (nad sobą) sobie panować. I w tym się wyraża jego najbardziej własna „królewskość", która ? gł zawiera taki całokształt panowania nad przyrodą, przedstawiając zasadniczo moralność.

Doświadczenie historyczne uczy, że pozorne i ekonomiczne struktury panowania ludzkiego różnią znaczenie „królestwa z tego świata".

Chrystus raz przed Piłatem powiedział: „Królestwo moje nie jest z tego świata". Jaka jest specyfika owego „królestwa", które głosił i które mamy urzeczywistniać „uczestnicząc w munus regale" Chrystusa? Jest ono zbudowane na fundamencie miłości. Chrystus tym Bożym przynosił, aby doprowadzić do społeczności w świecie nowy porządek pano-

APPUNTAMENTI

Thus Christ–King changes – or rather completes – the primary sense of kingship. It does not consist in reigning (even reigning over oneself), but in submission. In this sense, 'to serve' – means 'to reign'.

Adoration of the Blessed Sacrament (Lord Jesus' words on the cross); Vespers; Reading and writing texts; Rosary (II)

Meditation (long): On death. This is a meditation on the future, which is unknown. And it should stay so. For it should remain the proportion of grace, trust. It will certainly be a task, a trial. One should not stop praying for the strength to face it.

Death itself is a 'liminal situation'. Man experiences dying. This experience should be related to the experience of 'now' ('now' is analysed together with some of its themes, e.g. the theme of 'friendship' – and an attempt to understand the current situation). Dying will also be a kind of 'now' at some point – the final of such moments in life. Much depends on that moment. But that moment also depends on the entire life. We do not choose the time and kind of death. It is chosen for us. God chooses it. Could not one say that God chose the time and kind of death for Fr Józef RIP?

Let us pray for that final 'now'.

Anticipated Matins (Feast of Bl. Ladislas of Gielniów). After Mass:

Meditation (short): On the Heart of Jesus through the Heart of His Mother. This year is the twenty-fifth anniversary of the consecration of Poland to Her Heart. Consecration always takes place in the heart – and through the heart.

Reading and writing texts: *A Modern Scriptural Approach to the Spiritual Exercises* (chapter 5)[1]
Penitential psalms; Litanies; Compline

25 September: Feast of Blessed Ladislas of Gielniów[2]

Prayers; Lauds; Adoration (Christ is the life of the soul – especially during a retreat); Holy Mass; Thanksgiving

1 See n. 2, p. 105 [21 September 1976].

2 Bl. Ladislas of Gielniów (c.1440–1505) was a Polish priest and a member of the Order of Friars Minor. He served as the Order's provincial in 1487–90 and 1496–99. He was beatified on 11 February 1750 by Pope Benedict XIV.

26 September Morning meditation: Philippians 1:9, 10; cf. 6: *Caritas vestra magis ac magis abundet in omni scientia et in omni sensu. Ut probetis potiora, ut sitis sinceri et sine offensa* [(That) your love may abound more and more, with knowledge and all discernment, so that you may approve what is excellent, and may be pure and blameless].[1] *Confido quia, qui coepit in vobis opus bonum, perficiet usque in diem Christi Jesu* [And I am sure that he who began a good work in you will bring it to completion at the day of Jesus Christ].[2]

1 See Philippians 1:9–10.
2 See Philippians 1:6.

5–9 July 1977
Retreat at Kalwaria Zebrzydowska[1]

5 July

(After 8.00 p.m.): Vespers; Rosary; Anticipated Matins (Feast of Bl. M. T. Ledóchowska);[2] Adoration of the Blessed Sacrament; Compline; Reading
Searching for the topic: Sin

6 July

(From 6.00 a.m.): Morning prayers; Petitionary prayers

Meditation 1 (short): *De profundis* = from the depths I have cried out to you: from the depths of creativeness – sinfulness – responsibility, but also from the depths of trustfulness, whose sign is the Immaculate One.

Holy Mass with thanksgiving; Morning Lauds
Reading: (a) Card. Garrone, *Marie hier et aujourd'hui*;[3] (b) Fr Teofil Wilski, 'Zagadnienie osobowego "zróżnicowania" w Jedności stwórczego i zbawczego działania Trójcy Św.' (*Collectanea Theologica*)[4]
Rosary (I); Prayers to the Holy Spirit; Terce

Meditation 2: *De peccato originali* [On original sin]: An attempt to look at the entire mystery.

(a) As an event that took place between God and man (more broadly: creation). Original sin consists in man's 'breaking away', just like the angel did before, from the fullness of givenness, which is contained in the work of creation. It is not possible to understand original sin without reference to the fullness of givenness – that is, love. Original sin is a refusal to partake in love, in the good of all creation coming from love, and above all, in the good of love itself. In this sense, it is the loss of grace.

---

1 See n. 1, p. 12 [6–7 July 1963].

2 Bl. Maria Teresa Ledóchowska (1863–1922) was a Polish missionary and founder of the Missionary Sisters of St Peter Claver, dedicated to service in Africa. She was beatified by Pope Paul VI on 19 October 1975.

3 Gabriel-Marie Garrone, *Marie hier et aujourd'hui* [Mary Yesterday and Today] (Paris, 1977).

4 Teofil Wilski, 'Zagadnienie osobowego "zróżnicowania" w Jedności stwórczego i zbawczego działania Trójcy Św.' [The Question of Personal 'Differentiation' in Unity of the Holy Trinity's Work of Creation and Salvation], *Collectanea Theologica* 45/3 (1975), pp. 31–48.

(b) As an inner fact (*actus humanus* [human act]), the sinfulness of original sin can be explained through its motives. The motives were suggested externally. It is the temptation: a promise that is not fulfilled. The evil spirit says 'you will be like God, knowing good and evil'.[1] Such an understanding means leaving behind the 'pure good' (that is the original gift), yet it does not give man (as it did not give satan) the power to determine what is good and what is evil.
(c) As an inner fact (*actus hum.* [human act]), original sin is disobedience, which St Paul clearly proved. Not only does it put human will in opposition to God's will, but it also leads to man's rejection of 'God's righteousness': the world of values willed by the Creator.
(d) In this context, original sin is the loss of the highest gift – that is, participation in the nature and life of God Himself.
(e) Drawn into the life of the 'world' itself, man begins to be subjected to the triple concupiscence.
(f) The original sin is the moment from which God's 'economy' of creation gives way to the economy of salvation. A return of the dimension and meaning of the gift to man takes a different, more difficult way: the way of the cross.

The Way of the Cross: The cross means that the world is undertaken by God at the point to which it was brought by man.

Sext; None
(After lunch and rest, reading '*Relatio quinquennalis*' [Five-year report])
Vespers; Adoration of the Blessed Sacrament before the image of the Blessed Virgin Mary: the divine direction of communion becomes particularly clear in this adoration.

At the Little Ways of Our Lady

Meditation 3: Based on the *Relatio 5-alis* [Five-year report] on the Church:

- which has grown out of the Eucharistic communion of the Upper Room in the Holy Spirit
- which has a hierarchical structure

1 See Genesis 3:5.

Chodzi nie tylko o przeciwstawienie woli ludzkiej woli Boga, ale zarazem o odrzucenie
przez człowieka „Bożej [illegible]" i rzuta
wartości chcianej przez Stwórcę.
d) w tym bowiem grzech pierworodny oznacza utratę największego Daru – tj. mamy
udziału w ~~życiu~~ naturze i życiu samego
Boga.
e) odzyskujemy w życiu samego świata człowiek zaczyna podlegać trojakiej pożądli-
wości
f) grzech pierworodny jest momentem, w którym „Bożemu" Słowu ustępuje przed
ekonomią Odkupienia – Przypomnieć wynie-
sienie i zranienie daru człowieka i rzuta
później imię, tradycję Boga i Boga łaski
8. Via Crucis: księgi oznacza, że wszystko zostało
przyjęte przez Boga w tym wszystkim, do której doprowadził go człowiek. / Sexta, Nona,
9. (Po obiedzie i spacerze lektura o Relatio
quinquennalis) Vesp.
10. Ador. SS.mi coram imagine BMV.:
najpilniej wpatrywać się w Nią Boleś-
[illegible] Kościoła
11. Medit VI.

APPUNTAMENTI

na bazie Relatio 5-alis o Kościele, który wyrósł ze wspólnoty chrześcijań-
[illegible] [illegible] i [illegible]
— który ma swą strukturę [illegible]
— Rel. 5-alis jako akt poznania,
wierności i solidarności – postawy z Naszą ...
Piotra / Con. Ros. II

– *Relatio 5-alis* [Five-year report] as an act of obedience, faithfulness and solidarity–unity with St Peter's successor.

Rosary (II)

At the Little Ways of Our Lady

Meditation 4: Question about intention. Intention versus action. The possibility of reworking the intention. Transparency in relation to God Himself. In relation to people. Petition for grace and illumination for the 'theology of the body'.

Rosary (III); Anticipated Matins for the Feast of Ss Cyril and Methodius in the chapel of the 'Little Tomb of Our Lady'
After supper – Introduction and comments on *Relatio quinquennalis* [Five-year report] (writing)

Meditation 5 (short): On the Immaculate One – in the context of Meditation 1 – as *Origo mundi melioris* [the Beginning of a better world].

Compline

7 July: Feast of Ss Cyril and Methodius

Getting up; Morning activities; Daily prayers

Meditation 6 (short): On the spirit of the fear of God:
'lest after preaching to others,
I myself should be disqualified'[1]

Preparation for Holy Mass; Holy Mass in the chapel before the image of the Blessed Virgin Mary; Thankgiving; Lauds; Prime
Reading: continuation: (a) Cardinal Garrone; (b) Fr T. Wilski
Rosary (III); Prayers to the Holy Spirit; Terce

Meditation 7 (longer) *in deambulando* [while walking]: Cont. *de peccato originali – postea: de peccato personali* [On original sin – then: on personal sin].

(a) *Invenitur mysterium* [Discovering the mystery]. When we meet with a mystery, we ought to predict different human reactions. And hence one needs properly to differentiate between a mystery (that which surpasses our understanding) and difficulties or contradictions. The former cannot be reduced to the latter. A mystery is something which lies beyond the barrier of our

1 See 1 Corinthians 9:27.

understanding, but towards which our understanding can be directed; understanding or at least questioning.

What will always remain a mystery in original sin is the relationship of free will to grace, which is the same as the relationship of God's everlasting wisdom and love to creation's resistance.

Through this mystery one can 'see' ever more clearly that God intended to give man life on the super-human level. The incarnation and redemption throw light on this matter. The original and primary (and so also final) measure of man's deed is outlined by his participation in wisdom and love, which come from God.

Video meliora . . . etc. [I see what is better . . . etc.]

(b) Turning to man's personal sins, we have to assume the *status naturae lapsae* [state of lapsed nature], i.e. original sin with its consequences. In a way, this 'reduces' human ability to sin (in relation to the prelapsarian state), but does not cancel it. If will is more inclined to evil than to good, it does not mean that it is not 'inclined' to good at all. Therefore man may commit sins, including mortal sins. One's lifespan is the time in which one works for salvation or damnation. Nevertheless, the actual proportion of grace, good or evil will, discernment, clarity of conscience, different atavisms, etc. given to a certain person makes the judgement of guilt pass into the sphere of mystery. God alone can be the Judge of man.

(c) Nevertheless, one has to live in fear of God, work on the delicacy of conscience. One needs to keep God's law, commandments and the mystery of justification always before one's eyes. God threw the light of the Decalogue on the soil of human conscience *in statu naturae lapsae* [in the state of lapsed nature], and Christ in turn said that love is the final answer. As Psalm 118 teaches us, one has to reflect constantly on moral law, analysing every commandment and counsel in the light of the Great Commandment.

Sext; None
The Way of the Cross; in the Marian spirit: reflection on particular Stations through Mary's words, in a way, in Her heart
After meal and rest, working on the letter to the Holy Father (writing)
Examination of conscience ([illegible]); Vespers

Adoration of the Blessed Sacrament: The whole Church, with all its matters, has grown and is still growing out of the Eucharist.

Meditation 8: On the topic of the Holy See and the Catholic Bishops' Conference of Poland: to address this topic in the spirit of living faith, love, obedience and full responsibility.

At the Little Ways of Jesus

Rosary (I), (II); Anticipated Matins in the chapel of 'The Little Tomb of Our Lady'

Holy Hour (meditation 9):

At the Little Ways of Jesus

(a) *invenitur Cor* [discovering the Heart]: One has to establish a living contact with this Heart, to feel His loneliness in the Garden of Gethsemane, the inner torment He experiences due to the particular injustice 'from His arrest until His death' before Annas, Caiaphas, Pilate and Herod – and in the unfathomable mystery of redemption of all sins: the original and the personal.
(b) To feel the passion of His torment during the Way of the Cross, the whipping and the crowning with thorns, in a special way – and to profess what these mysteries mean to me.

Seven penitential psalms; Litany of the Blessed Virgin Mary; Litany of St Joseph; Writing continued after supper

Meditation 10 (short) *post. Lit. ad Christum Sacerdotem et Victimam* [after the Litany of Jesus Christ, Priest and Victim] on the Mother of the Eternal Priest, my priesthood, all my priests (Maksymilian!), all vocations to the priesthood.

Compline

8 July: Feast of St Elizabeth of Portugal

Getting up; Intentions; Daily prayers

Meditation 11 (very short): '*Tempus recollectionis mane instat*' ['The time of the retreat comes in the morning'] – this is always true; '*quam mercedem reddet mihi Justus Iudex?*' ['what payment will the Righteous Judge award to me?'].[1]

Preparation for Holy Mass; Holy Mass before the Image of the Blessed Virgin Mary; Thanksgiving; Lauds

1 See 2 Timothy 4:8.

Reading after meal: (a) Card. Garrone (like before); (b) Fr T. Wilski (like before); And some writing
Rosary (I); Prayers to the Holy Spirit; Terce; Preparing the meditation

Meditation 12 (long): (*De peccato et scandalo* [On sin and scandal]):

(a) The Creator, bringing man (a person and a community) into life, showed him the way to salvation, that is, to full good and to the shaping of the ever more mature 'world of good'. This way leads, at the same time, through man's heart (conscience) and through the community. Good has its social dimension, and this dimension is revealed when 'people as the children of God unite in truth and love in the likeness of the Most Holy Trinity'. Such unity serves good, it multiplies and spreads it in an amazing way.
(b) In opposition to good, there is also a social dimension of evil. It is connected to what we call the other's sin. The first (original) sin was in fact the other's sin: it began with a temptation of the evil spirit, and in turn passed from a human being (woman) to a human being (man). The other's sin consists in different forms of scandal.
(c) Christ said 'woe to the world for temptations to sin'[1] and cursed those who cause scandal. The contemporary world is full of diverse forms of scandal. Scandal has, in a way, become the programme of social life. At the same time, an important moral significance of scandal is renounced: Evil is not called evil. Thus the triumph of evil is even greater. The contemporary world needs Christian communities – children of God – united in truth and love very much, to 'detoxify the atmosphere' (such a thought occurred to me in relation to the meeting with the Catholic youth group). The task of the bishop-shepherd is to create such communities, to renew the existing ones. To oppose evil, to deprive it, as far as it is possible, of its social dimension.
(d) Today the social dimension of every sin is underlined: not only does it destroy good in a given person, but also in the community of the Church. The primary dimension

1 See Matthew 18:7.

of evil and sin is and always will be the 'offence to God'. Nevertheless, it is true that it destroys the spirit and causes moral death not only of an individual, but also of entire societies. Sin – and death!

(e) The diverse forms of scandal as the other's sin require one to feel increasing responsibility for good and for one's brothers.

At the Little Ways of Our Lady

The Way of the Cross; *Crux fidelis* [Faithful cross]; *Popule meus* [My people]; Mystery of redemption
After meal and rest, writing (the letter to the Holy See) and reading
About 3.00 p.m., Adoration of the Blessed Sacrament (meditation on the seven words spoken by Jesus on the cross)

Meditation 13 on the topic of: the Catholic Bishops' Conference of Poland and the Holy See. The topic follows from the entire reality of Christian life. It is also the fruit of the redemption, which we remember at the Little Ways of Kalwaria[1] – this faith and this life.

Vespers; Litany of the Saints (by the chapel of 'Herod's Palace')

Meditation 14: At the beginning of my holidays I come to the Mother of God, as I do every year, to entrust Her with the archdiocese for the time of my absence – and to entrust Her with my rest. I think about all I will do and the people I will meet. I analyse the motives, attitudes and behaviour. '*Dabitur vobis in illa hora*' ['It will be given to you in that hour'].[2]

Apart from this, I consider the issue of 'TP'.

Rosary (II); Prayer to the Five Wounds; Rosary (III); Anticipated Matins (Saturday office of the Blessed Virgin Mary)
After meal: writing, reading
Litany of the Sacred Heart of Jesus, Blessed Virgin Mary, St Joseph

Meditation 15 (short): *Recapitulatio* [Conclusion] of all the themes taken up at the retreat, the most valuable: that it was possible to reflect on them in the vicinity of the image of Our Lady of Kalwaria – the sign of Mary's presence in the life of the people of God, in my own life – to which I always gladly return.

Compline

1 See n. 1 & n. 2, p. 12 [6–7 July 1963].
2 See Matthew 10:19.

9 July (Saturday office of the Blessed Virgin Mary)

Meditation 16: *Maria – Origo mundi melioris* [Mary – the Beginning of a better world]: This great new world, which God created in Her, in the Immaculate One, which lasts and shines, into which we enter to become new people. This is also the aim of a retreat.

Concelebration for the Oasis;[1] The word of God; Thanksgiving

1 The Oasis Movement (also known as the Light–Life Movement) is an international Catholic movement that promotes and supports the spiritual formation of Christians. It was founded in Poland by Fr Franciszek Blachnicki.

26–29 June 1978
Retreat at Kalwaria Zebrzydowska
Topic: *martyria – diakonia – koinonia* [witness – service – community][1]

26 June

(*Mane Cracoviae visitatio ecclesiae s. Joseph – uti praeparatio remota* [In the morning, a visit to the Church of St Joseph in Kraków – as an early preparation].)
About 5.00 p.m., arrival at Kalwaria and the beginning of the retreat meditation. (Before the Blessed Sacrament and the Mother of God): the retreat allows us to approach truth and love more closely.
Vespers for Monday; Rosary (I)
Meditation (longer):

three main dimensions of Christian existence

(a) The main topic of the retreat is set out: '*martyria – diakonia – koinonia*' (witness – service – community).
(b) The retreat has to involve special obedience to the Holy Spirit (listening to the word in the Spirit).
(c) The retreat has to enliven our love for Christ – the Lord and the Master, the Redeemer and the Bridegroom.
(d) The retreat has to unfold in a special unity with Mary (the shrine! personal and communal tradition).
(e) The retreat – as *scrutinium cordis (reple cordis intima!)* [examination of the heart (fill the innermost heart!)].
(f) The retreat – in anticipation of the jubilee of St Stanislaus (1979).[2]

Holy Mass (in the chapel of the Blessed Virgin Mary); Thanksgiving; Litany of the Blessed Virgin Mary; Rosary (II), (III); Litany of the Sacred Heart of Jesus; Reading some texts

---

1 The primary meaning of *martyrium* (pl. *martyria*) is witness, but in a Christian context it also refers to martyrdom as the ultimate form of Christian testimony.

2 1979 marked the ninth centenary of the martyrdom of St Stanislaus, the patron saint of Poland. In his apostolic letter *Rutilans agmen* (The Glowing Band) issued on 8 May 1979, Pope John Paul II emphasised the importance of this anniversary for the Church of Poland: 'This jubilee is of supreme importance and is very closely connected with the history of the Church in Poland and of the Polish nation. For more than a thousand years this nation has enjoyed a very special relationship with the Church, which she has valued highly. We repeat that that voice cannot remain silent, the more so because, by the inscrutable designs of God, he, who a short while before had been the successor of St Stanislaus in the episcopal see of Kraków, has been elected to the see of Peter as Supreme Pastor of the Church.'

27 June (*Peri martyrias* – on witness.)

Getting up; Preparation; Intentions and daily prayers

Morning meditation: 'In Him is everything' (Romans)[1] – and 'everything' refers to God Himself in His invisible reality and 'everything' refers also to Christ, God–Man, who has united and is uniting all creation in Himself and leads to the summit. The 'world of values' in its greatest fullness is revealed through Him. It is, so to say, another dimension of theology.

Lauds and other prayers; Holy Mass in the chapel of the Blessed Virgin Mary; Thanksgiving; Terce
Reading some texts (*Jesus*, *Handbook of the Oasis Movement*) and writing

Midday meditation (longer): Christ stands in the centre as '*testis fidelis*' ['faithful witness'][2] – He who bears witness to the truth. He bears witness to the Invisible in the visible and audible; He bears witness with His words and deeds; He bears witness with His very self!

This is an entirely different dimension of knowing God and knowing God's world. It is different from any human 'examination', which is bound to experience and the principles of reason. Bearing witness is very closely connected to experience. The witness is he who experienced (and experiences). Therefore Christ 'the only Son, who is in the bosom of the Father' (John) remains at the heart of bearing witness.[3] The world 'leads' to God (the Absolute). He bears witness.

Christ, in turn, calls witnesses; He looks for those who 'will be His witnesses'. Their witness is the undertaking of the prediction-promise. It is the continuation of the prophecy. The Church is erected on the foundation of the apostles and prophets (so to speak, on the two dimensions of bearing witness).

Witnesses are called (1) to bear witness about Christ (Christ crucified and risen from the dead, Christ teaching and performing miracles); (2) to participate in Christ's witness – the witness He bears to the Father, the Son, the Holy Spirit, the Church and the world.

---

1 See Romans 11:36.
2 See Revelation 1:5.
3 See John 1:18.

In the centre of '*martyria*' ['witness'] – as one of the primary dimensions of Christian existence – one finds these words: 'and He (i.e. the Holy Spirit, the Spirit of truth) will bear witness to me – and you also are witnesses, because you have been with me from the beginning.'[1] Our witness has its origin in His witness and it owes its divine nature to Him only.

Witness can be borne (1) by words (these words are not only information, but also annunciation and prophecy); (2) by actions that come from the words (actions bear witness by themselves – they in turn provide support and confirmation for the witness of words). Through words and actions our witness embraces (3) the entire existence of the human witness; therefore, it is the witness to life; if the witness to death is added to this, then death is – in this very context – the fulfilment of life, its seal of credibility.

The Way of the Cross: Further development of the main reflection on witness. Christ, who bore witness to the truth (Station I), also proved that there is no greater love than to give one's life for one's brothers (Station II and following). During His way of the cross, He witnessed different weaknesses (failures) of the human heart (Stations V, VI). Through His destruction, kenosis (Stations IX, X, XI, XII), He became a particularly significant and 'faithful' witness to God's holiness. In the end, He gave the final witness to human existence through His death and resurrection (Stations XIII, XIV). All this was kept in a special way in the Mother's Heart (Stations IV, XIII) – Her Marian witness is at the beginning of the Church.

(3.00 p.m.) Adoration of the Blessed Sacrament: (The sacrament, which is the permanent witness to the Lord's love for us, is still celebrated, still exists, so that we can receive Him, and He is in everyone who receives Him: the dimensions of the Eucharist.)

(meal)

Vespers
Reading continued: *Handbook of the Oasis Movement* (A)
Rosary (II)

1 See John 15:26–27.

Meditation (longer):

At the Little Ways

1. St Stanislaus: bishop – martyr – patron saint (Christ's witness, a bishop of the Church, patron saint of Poland: the dimensions of the jubilee).
2. *Martyria – diakonia – koinonia* are bound together and enrich each other in the episcopal service; the Church and the world expect witness from the bishop and that witness is the primary ministry and condition for all other ministry; episcopal ministry finds its special expression in the community (many different communities whom I serve): 'community': unity is in a way a test of his ministry.

   The bishop's witness is a witness coming 'from the office', but the 'office' is also the source of his charismatic gift.
3. In accordance with these premises – an attempt to look at different actions and tasks, especially those which are related to the heritage and jubilee of St Stanislaus.
4. Petition for a proper 'spirit' for these actions: they have to be measured by the measure of witness, service and community (unity) – one has to be cautious not to resort to other measures!

Rosary (III); Penitential psalms; Anticipated Matins in the Little Tomb of Our Lady; Litany of the Blessed Virgin Mary; Litany of St Joseph; Litany of the Sacred Heart of Jesus; Prolonged reading

Meditation (short):

'For in Him are all things.'[1]

From Him and through Him I relate my little 'everything' to Christ's 'all things', when I say to His Mother '*omnia mea Tua sunt*' ['everything that is mine belongs to You']. I entrust everything to Her – and thank Her for everything; for God's grace.

Compline

28 June (*Peri diakonias* – on service.)

Getting up; Intention; Daily prayers; Preparation for celebrating Holy Mass

1 See Romans 11:36.

Morning meditation (short): 'In my Father's house are many rooms – I go and prepare a place for you . . .'[1] This 'preparation' in a way becomes a synonym of '*diakonia*', the service which Christ gives to everyone and to all. Let us not interfere with His service – but assist Him.

Eucharist before the image of the Blessed Virgin Mary; Thanksgiving; Lauds
Reading: (Martelet: '*16 theses de christologie sur le sacrement du mariage*' [Sixteen Christological Theses on the Sacrament of Marriage] and others). And writing: (regarding the visit to the West German Bishops' Conference)
Rosary (I); Terce; Sext; None

Meditation (longer): We begin with the words 'I came not to be served but to serve'[2] – for they are at the centre of this dimension of Christian existence which is called '*diakonia*'. This dimension comes directly from Christ, it is in Him and from Him. In this dimension God enters the world: by becoming man. As man–creature He becomes a servant, for each man is God's servant. This is the order of creation, the order of justice. Christ comes to renew this service (since man had rejected it), and therefore He undertakes this service Himself.

At the same time, He reveals a different dimension of service hidden in God's Fatherhood. In Him, in Christ, God in a way serves man, serves his salvation. He serves and does not stop serving: Christ's 'service to human salvation' continues in the Church, in the sacraments and above all in the Eucharist. This, in a way, reversed order of service and rule (of the Lord – and the Servant), however, has its deep justification. For service out of justice is different from service out of love. Christ reveals the latter meaning of service and introduces it into the life of the Church and the history of humankind.

In the dimension of justice, service means only dependence and subordination, and it is subjected to the measure of things which can be deserved. Service out of love shows the sovereignty of the person, his 'kingship': to serve God means to 'reign'.

The dimension of Christian existence called '*diakonia*' is formed in accordance with these premises. It is an

1 See John 14:2–3.
2 See Matthew 20:28.

important dimension because it is founded on Christ. '*Metanoia*' ['a change of mind'], a breakthrough in humanity and turn to Christianity, takes place through this dimension. The scope of this breakthrough is as broad as possible, it reaches the sphere of politics ('I rule here' . . . 'I serve here'), social life, human relations. It has a great, fundamental meaning for the community, in particular the community of the Church. For as much as the only proper, personal point of reference in the attitude of service is God, in a different sense it can also be a community as a place of many types of service, the place of human fulfilment in diverse kinds of service. Charismatic gifts point to the meaning of this service; they shape its theology.

Thus '*diakonia*' as a dimension of the entire Christian existence must be the topic and goal of the formation of every Christian, in particular the priest, the bishop. The theology of service is of primary importance for this formation, as well as the psychology of service (the attitude of service – versus the drive for importance: you mean as much as you serve), characterology, the ascesis of service linked to the love for the community.

Christ's Mother, the handmaid of the Lord, leads us to Christ–Servant.

The Way of the Cross: Continued meditation going back to the same source. Yahweh's servant before Pilate (you would have no power . . .), under the cross (greater love has no man than this . . .), falling (learn from me) – 'bear one another's burdens' (Simon of Cyrene, Veronica) – 'obedient unto death . . . even death on a cross . . .' and all these things in order to 'prepare a place for you in my Father's house (heart)'[1] – among all this there is also the following supplication: Teach me the obedience which is the heart and power of being a superior.

(meal)

Adoration of the Blessed Sacrament: The mystery of the Eucharistic ministry – the sacrament of permanent service – the sacramental continuation of Yahweh's Servant: 'take and eat . . .'[2] As if it was a constant self-emptying congruent with the nature

1 See John 19:11, John 15:13, Matthew 11:29, Galatians 6:2, John 14:2.

2 See Matthew 26:26.

of the food – and simultaneously the sign of a personal communion.

Vespers; Rosary (II); Litany of the Saints

Meditation (longer):

(a) I wish for certain questions that are important to my service to begin and germinate here (for instance, my visit to the German Bishops' Conference) and, of course, the entire year of St Stanislaus above all.

(b) I wish for other issues, which I consider my '*diakonia*', to be illuminated and put in order in here. It is good if the Lord Himself brings about cleansing moments. One needs to see them with the eyes of faith, the eyes of the spirit. One has to exercise patience and forbearance.

Above all, such moments have to be deeply and constantly endorsed and rooted in prayer.

Devotion to the Sacred Heart of Jesus; Rosary (III); Litany of the Blessed Virgin Mary; Litany of St Joseph

Conclusion (examination of previous retreats) and (short) meditation:

Christ says: I go to prepare a place for you in my Father's house. Mary: I go to prepare a place for you in my Son's Heart.

And this is the most important thing among all other important things: *mysterium solius Christi – mysterium totius Christi – culmen caritatis* [the mystery of Christ Himself – the mystery of the whole Christ – the culmination of love].

Compline

29 June: Feast of Ss Peter and Paul

(1) [illegible]
(2) report from the visit
(3) letter [illegible]
(4) official letter regarding [illegible]

(*Peri koinonias* – on 'community'.)

Getting up; Intention and daily prayers; Prayer for the gifts of the Holy Spirit

Meditation (short): '*Communio Sanctorum*' as *terminus ad quem* [The 'communion of saints' as the end point]. On the way to this goal, Christ calls Peter (and Paul) '. . . depart from me, for I am a sinful man, O Lord . . .'; '*sufficit tibi gratia mea* . . .' ['my grace is sufficient for you . . .']; and, on this rock I will build my Church and I will give you the keys.[1]

1 See Luke 5:8, 2 Corinthians 12:9, Matthew 16:18–19.

-80-

31 GIOVEDI - Ascensione | **N O T E**

Wielu, także przynajmniej zapoczątkowanych się i załatwionych (tak np. sprawa Episkopatu [illegible]) i uzyskanie przedtem urzędowe całego roku w Krakowie

b) proszę, aby mnie sprawy, które także uważam za moje „osobiste", dorzucały też pewnej przesileniu, uporządkowaniu. Dobrze, gdy Pan mnie oprzątnął mocniej oczyszczając. Trzeba je wciąż oczyszczać ciała, oczyszczać ducha. Trzeba zachować czystość i dziewiczość.

Każde uczucie trzeba je głęboko i wewnętrznie [illegible] i zakorzeniać w modlitwie

Dies. 11 – Cordis Iesu

Cor. ros. (III). Lit. BMV. Lit. S. Joseph

27. Recapitulatio (przemówienie rekolekcyjne)
et meditatio (brevis)

Chrystus mówi: Idę przygotować wam miejsce u Domu Ojca

Maryja: idę przygotować wam miejsce w Sercu Syna.

I to jest ośrodek wszystkich owych spraw najważniejszych: mysterium solius Christi – mysterium totius Christi – culmen caritatis

APPUNTAMENTI

28 – Complet.

1) [illegible]
2) [illegible]
3) [illegible]
4) [illegible]

29. VI

uroczystość ss. Piotra i Pawła
(peri koinonias – o „wspólnocie")

Lauds for the Feast [of Ss Peter and Paul]

Adoration of the Blessed Sacrament: Christ is 'communion'. He established the sacrament of His body and blood to introduce us into the communion which He is Himself.

Reading and writing some texts: *Handbook of the Oasis Movement* and others
Rosary (III); Terce; Sext; None for the Feast [of Ss Peter and Paul] (on the way)

Meditation (longer): '*Koinonia*', the community, is the third principal dimension of Christian existence. The word 'community' is, above all, ambiguous and not entirely adequate. It is often used interchangeably with words such as 'society' or 'population'. As for Christian existence, it begins with Jesus Christ, who Himself constitutes a 'communion'. First and foremost, He alone is the unity of God and man, having in Himself full grace, that is, full power to reconcile man with God. For in Him God gives Himself to man, both in the personal and the communal manner. In this sense, Christ is the 'communion' – He alone is the communion. And He alone creates the communion with the Father in the Holy Spirit. The dimension of 'communion' is a kind of transfer of the Trinitarian mystery into the diverse human reality.

For man is a social creature and he lives in society; he also forms different communities – nevertheless, human societies and communities lack the depth of truth and love that characterise the reality of divine '*Communio*' ['community']: divine life. A need emerges at this point to analyse all that is endorsed by the human notion of the 'social', the 'communal' (and also in the term 'communism', which on the surface is so close to '*Communio*'). All these things are subjected to human limitations in different ways – and at the same time they also limit man. In various circumstances social life is reduced to the existence of a disciplined mass. Man has difficulties in reconciling individuality with diversity in his heart. He misses that which is contained in '*communio*'.

Let us put aside this philosophico-sociological analysis. Further meditation concentrates on the prayer for that which should be called the 'charisma of communion' (community). This charisma is particularly important for the bishop: the man who in a way has to be the headstone of the community

– and has to build this community with his whole self. What is meant here is not only the 'internal-ecclesiastical' sense of such an act of building, but also its 'external' sense: building the community with the nation, with society, with different groups, to some extent also with the enemies . . . Prayer for the charisma of 'communion'.

The Way of the Cross: The prayer continues during the Way of the Cross, since it was on that way that Jesus undertook 'reconciliation', established the deepest communion through His redemption. There are many issues that one should pray and petition for at particular Stations of this way, taking into account all the experiences of life and death itself at the end.

(At 1.30 p.m.) Holy Mass in the chapel of Our Lady with a short talk to the candidates for the first year of the Seminary (and the handing out of enrolment documents)
(meal) Reading: *Handbook of the Oasis Movement* (A)
Rosary (I)

Holy Hour before the image of the Blessed Virgin Mary:
(a) Reference to Gethsemane – call for reparation.
(b) Reparation through Our Lady, who knows best Her Son's Heart and my heart.
(c) Reparation in proportion to the failures in a given area: witness – service – community.
(d) Reparation in relation to: the triple concupiscence.
(e) Our Lady knows best when and how this reparatory prayer may turn into thanksgiving and a petitionary prayer.
(f) Litany of our Lord Jesus Christ, Priest and Victim; Litany of the Sacred Heart of Jesus; Litany to the Blessed Virgin Mary.

Conclusion; (Rosary (II)); (Anticipated) Matins of the following day (on the way to Kraków)
Kraków: the Church of Ss Peter [and Paul]: concelebration and prayer for the Holy Father Paul VI
Te Deum

[October 1978]

On 13 October 1978 my dear friend, Bishop Andrzej Deskur[1] suffered from an unexpected stroke, which left him partially paralysed. Despite the treatment at the Gemelli Hospital, and then in Switzerland, the paralysis has not receded.

On 14 October, on my way to the conclave that was to elect the successor after John Paul I's death (26 August – 28 September 1978), I visited Andrzej in hospital.

It is difficult for me not to link the fact that I was elected that successor on 16 October with the event that preceded the election by three days. The sacrifice of Andrzej, my brother in episcopacy, seems to me to have been a preparation for this event. Through his suffering everything has been inscribed into the mystery of the cross and redemption accomplished by Christ.

I can see a certain analogy with an event from eleven years ago, when – while I participated in a consistory in Rome and I was appointed to the College of Cardinals – my friend, Fr Marian Jaworski[2] lost his arm in a train accident near Nidzica.

Andrzej, who has worked at the Pontifical Council for Social Communications (recently as its president) since the fifties, introduced me to many important matters of the Apostolic See. His cross became the last word of my initiation.

Debitor factus sum . . . [I have become a debtor . . .]

---

1 Andrzej Maria Deskur (1924–2011) was a Polish priest and theologian. He served as secretary of the Preparatory Secretariat for the Press and Entertainment, member of the Conciliar Commissions for Bishops, for the Clergy, for the Laity, and for the Press and Entertainment, president of the Pontifical Commission for Social Communications, and president of the Pontifical Academy of the Immaculate Conception. In 1985, John Paul II made him a cardinal.

2 Marian Jaworski (b. 1926) is a Polish-Ukrainian priest, theologian and philosopher. He has served as the rector of the Academy of Theology in Kraków, established by John Paul II in 1981, the Metropolitan Archbishop of Lviv, and president of the Ukrainian Bishops' Conference. In 1998, John Paul II appointed him a cardinal *in pectore*.

4–10 March 1979
Retreat in Rome, Chapel of St Matilda[1]
[Led by Fr Faustino Ossanna OFM][2]

~

4 March: First Sunday of Lent

6.30 p.m.: Vespers

Talk 1:

(a) Reference to *Angelus*.
(b) Announcement of the topic: 'To open oneself to Jesus'.
(c) Need for prayer.

Morning meditation; Compline

5 March

Getting up; Morning prayers

Morning meditation: *Sacrificium Deo spiritus contribulatus. Cor contritum et humiliatum, Deus, non despicies* [The sacrifice acceptable to God is a broken spirit. A broken and contrite heart, O God, Thou wilt not despise].[3]
Holy Mass; Thanksgiving; Lauds

Talk 2: Christ lives in us (*cur Deus homo?* [why did God become man?]):

(a) Testimonies (St Paul – Augustine – others).
(b) Experience is more important than dogmatic formulae; communion with Him who lives in us in the most real of ways.
(c) His life in us, His presence and the communion with Him is power: It is the source of witness, which speaks against all sorts of atheisms, secularism and the 'death of God'.

---

1 St Matilda's Chapel, now called the Redemptoris Mater (Mother of the Redeemer) Chapel, is located in the Apostolic Palace in Vatican City and reserved for the exclusive use of the pope. It was renamed in 1987 at the request of Pope John Paul II.

2 Faustino Ossanna OFM (b. 1920) is an Italian priest and theologian. He has served as the vice-rector of the Theological Seminary in Padua, professor of moral theology at the Pontifical University of St Bonaventure and professor of moral ethics at the Catholic University of the Sacred Heart in Rome. He was appointed Apostolic Examiner of the Roman Clergy by John Paul II in 1989.

3 See Psalm 50 (51):17.

homo homini deus ⟷ *homo factus est Deus*
[man is god to man ⟷ God became man]

(d) Each of us needs to seek this power constantly! This is the most important thing.

Prayer to the Holy Spirit; Meditation; Terce

Talk 3: Christ lives in us – and we live in Him:

(a) prayer
(b) ascesis
(c) action.

These are the means which gradually make everything an expression of Christ who lives in us (St Francis).

Meditation; Sext; None; (Prayer); Rosary (I), (II), (III); The Way of the Cross (shorter); Vespers

Talk 4: Call to sanctity – this is the fundamental answer to the question '*cur Deus Homo?*' ['why did God become man?']. So that He can work towards sanctity in everyone.

Individual sanctity.

Sanctity to which a specific person is called in a specific situation and circumstances – '*nonostante tutto*' ['despite everything'] (from a youth survey).

This is a call that one needs to take 'personally' (I am called, Christ wants to work on this particular and unique sanctity in me and with me).

The characteristics of sanctity according to contemporary needs: (1) the 'human'; (2) the 'personal'; (3) the 'ecclesial'.

The call to sanctity can be clearly heard now, just as it could after the Council of Trent.

Ministry aligned with 'mediocrity' is not enough.

Adoration of the Blessed Sacrament

Talk 5: Vocation to the apostolate:

– '*messis multa*' ['plentiful harvest']:[1] The situation in the world is disconcerting for many reasons, the situation of the Church: Evil has entered the temples.

1 See Matthew 9:37.

16. V Konf.

Powołanie do apostolstwa

– „messis multa", ~~apo~~: sytuacja nasza wielce zróżnicowana, sytuacja Kościoła: do wewnątrz [illegible]

– ~~apo~~ potrzeba apostołów: seminaria! ale seminaria nie wystarczają; rodzina i parafia i środowisko

apostolstwo świeckich ~~wspo~~-dopełnia całe kapłaństwo (communauté de base)

– Kościół i [illegible] [illegible] jedynie [illegible]

17. Ros. Benedictio eucharistica

18. Missa (anticipanda)

19. Medit. (reassumptio totius diei) [Lectura: „Poenitemini" adh. P. Pauli VI de I. Stanisl. – et alia]

20. Complet. (Letto)

6. III.

1. Surrexit. Preces mat.
2. Meditatio de Testamento
   conficiendo (ut 1) vera ut vivat iudicii Tua
   bonum 1) ut manus nostra Tuo desiderio fulgeant)
3. Sacrum concel.
   gratiarum actio
4. Laudes
5. VI Konf. Chrystus i nasz wkład: Eucharystia

a) Mysterium fidei
– jak [illegible] i wyznanie Kościoła
w Marka, Mateusza, Łukasza, Jana, Pawła
poprzez Tomasza i Akwinatu
do Pawła VI (wiara żywa)

APPUNTAMENTI

b) Jest to [illegible] wiara w kapłaństwo
wiary w siebie – kapłana

c) ta wiara wyraża się całym osobistym i społ.
przez Apostol.

Trzeba [illegible] bogato opracowane
w przeglądzie i życiu

Taccuino:
n. Jan – Evangelista

- The need for apostles: seminaries! But family, parish and community should also become seminaries.
  The apostolate of the laity compensates for the lack of the priest (*communauté de base* [basic ecclesial community]).
- The root and the branches live one life.

Rosary; Eucharistic Benediction; Matins (anticipated); Meditation (conclusion of the whole day); Compline
Reading: *Paenitemini*;[1] Pope Paul VI's Testament; on St Stanislaus; and others

6 March

Getting up; Morning prayers
Meditation *de testamento conficiendo* [on writing the Testament]:
(1) *vera et iusta iudicia Tua, Domine* [true and just are Thy judgements, O Lord];[2] (2) *ut mens nostra Tuo desiderio fulgeat* [so that our souls light up with longing for You].
Concelebrated Mass; Thanksgiving; Lauds

Talk 6: Christ in our hands: The Eucharist

(a) *Mysterium fidei* [The mystery of faith].
  – As the Church has taught and preached since Mark, Matthew, Luke, John, Paul through Thomas Aquinas to Paul VI (living faith).
(b) This is also the faith in the priesthood. I have faith in myself – a priest.
(c) This faith is expressed in personal and social, private and public cult.

The talk is enriched by examples from real life.
Our guide: St John the Evangelist.

Eucharistic Adoration; Prayer to the Holy Spirit; Terce

Talk 7: *Cur Deus – Panis?* [Why did God become bread?]

Answer:

1. *ad instituendam communionem* [to institute the communion]
   He in me – He for me.
   I in Him – I for Him.
2. *ad instituendam 'communitatem'* [to institute the 'community']
   (*comunità* – community).

---

1 The apostolic constitution *Paenitemini* (Be Converted) was issued by Pope Paul VI on 17 February 1966.
2 See Revelation 16:7.

Strict link between the Eucharist and the community. The Eucharist is in the hands of priests!

Meditation; Sext; None; *Angelus*; (Then: fasting); Rosary (I); The Way of the Cross; (John 6); Vespers

Talk 8: '*Mia Messa*' ['My Mass']

(a) The meaning of the entire '*ordo Missae*' ['the order of the Mass']
(b) On the present situation (disconcerting symptoms)
(c) How do priests celebrate the Mass?
How do I celebrate it?

Claudel's remark: 'Christians do not leave the Mass as if they had met the Risen One, but as if they had been at a funeral . . .'[1]

Matins (anticipated)

Talk 9: '*Fons et culmen*' ['Source and summit']
The Eucharist as '*fons et culmen*':

1. of ministry
2. of pedagogy
3. of the priest's spiritual life.

Rosary (II); Eucharistic Benediction; Rosary (III); Concluding meditation; Compline
Reading: on St Stanislaus; [illegible]; documents on Lefebvre

7 March Getting up; Morning prayers

Meditation: On the law that God wants to record not with ink on paper, but with the Holy Spirit in living people's hearts.

Holy Mass with thanksgiving; Lauds

Talk 10: Christ lives in the Church
'*Sacramentum vel signum Christi operantis ad salutem humani generis.*' ['The sacrament or sign of Christ acting to save humankind.']

(a) *signum* [sign]: the topicality of this concept in contemporary thought.
(b) *sacramentum: non tantum signum sed donum* [sacrament: it is not just a sign, but a gift].

1 Paul Claudel (1868–1955) was a French poet and playwright. Many of his works focus on Catholic topics.

The Church is a gift. The Church reveals the gifts (of the world and of man).
The Church makes everything a gift. The meaning of service! (*servitium – dona* [service – gift]).

(c) Christ acting through the Church as a sign that is a sacrament. We are all this reality, we are to constitute it and to keep it alive. (Very beautiful talk.)

Adoration of the Blessed Sacrament; Prayers to the Holy Spirit; Terce

Talk 11: Christ lives in the Church through His word:

(a) through the word of the Scriptures, which is not a literary relic – but through which Christ speaks all the time.
(b) through the word of the Church, that is Tradition and Magisterium, through the entirety of preaching and teaching.
(c) through the prophetic consciousness of the entire people of God.
(Many very important statements by many Bishops' Conferences, by many bishops.)

Meditation on all those points and the following matters: Lefebvre, St Stanislaus, Poland
Sext; None; Rosary (I), (II); The Way of the Cross; Vespers
(Reading and writing texts for the second Sunday of Lent)

Talk 12: Jesus Christ acts in the Church through the sacraments:

(a) Magisterium, in particular Vatican II.
(b) Each of us is the subject of the sacrament (minister of Holy Communion).
(c) Sacraments to which we should pay special attention:
  (i) *Penitentia* [penitence]
  (ii) Sacrament of family (matrimony)
  (iii) Sacrament of priesthood.
  (All this is illustrated with examples and quotations.)

Matins (anticipated)

Talk 13:

(a) (ἐγώ) *aedificabo Ecclesiam* [(I) will build my Church][1] – analysis of the sentence.

1 See Matthew 16:18.

(b) Everyone has their place in the Church, their vocation.
(c) The special place of Peter.
(d) The Mother's place: the Mother's space! The whole Church, and the whole world, is such a space: The Mother of the Church is there for the whole world, for all people – the retreat leader illustrates this truth beautifully through the analogy with the word '*Niepokalanów*'[1] [City of the Immaculate Mother of God]. The Church is the *Niepokalanów* on earth – and so will it be in heaven.

Rosary (III); Eucharistic Benediction; Meditation (synthesis of the day); Compline

8 March

Getting up; Prayers

Meditation: (a) *redemptio pretioso Sanguine* [redemption through the precious Blood]; (b) *iudicium verum iudicate* [render true judgements][2] – *at dimiseritis (casus Hol.)* [but you shall forgive (the case of the Holocaust)].

Holy Mass with thanksgiving; Lauds

Talk 14: Christ and the world:
→ the world created in Christ
1. Texts by Ss John and Paul:
→ Christ comes into the world
→ to 'reconcile' all creation in Himself
2. Attitudes:
the world – the topic of knowledge
the world – creatures and products that I am to use for the glory of God and for the work of salvation (Fr Kolbe)
3. Conclusions:
(a) not to 'throw' material things out of the Church – this great amazing reality moved by the power of the Spirit
(b) to affirm man
(c) to search for places where knowledge and faith meet.

Adoration of the Blessed Sacrament; Prayer to the Holy Spirit

1 Niepokalanów (literally: *City of the Immaculate Mother of God*) is a Polish community of Franciscan friars based in Teresin, near Warsaw. It was founded in 1927 by Father Maksymilian Kolbe, who was imprisoned in the Nazi concentration camp of Auschwitz and volunteered to die in place of a stranger. He was canonised as a saint-martyr by Pope John Paul II on 10 October 1982.

2 See Zechariah 7:9.

Talk 15: Christ and man:

1. Different attitudes to people from indifference to various shades of utilitarianism.
2. Christ's attitude:
   (a) As you did it to one of the least of these my brethren, you did it to Me.[1]
   (b) The commandment of love. This attitude expresses freedom from any form of utilitarianism; it reaches the human being because they are a human being, it embraces the poorest and the disinherited.
3. One needs to control oneself constantly in close and more distant, small and great dimensions to make sure one is faithful to this attitude.

Meditation: (*Eleemosyna* – alms)
(Visiting the Cardinal Secretary of State in hospital)
Sext; None; Angelus; Rosary (II), (III); Vespers

Talk 16: Jesus Christ and history:

(a) history as the presence of evil
(b) history as the presence of good
(c) history as the 'relation' of good and evil.

To be able to reconcile? To be able to extract good from evil! (on the wolf of Gubbio).

I arrive at a conclusion . . . will I manage? I can do all things in Him who strengthens me.[2]

(When we give, we are given.)

Matins (anticipated)

Talk 17: Christ of our hope:

1. To change the world – waiting for Christ.
2. Joyfully to await meeting Christ in the mystery of death – versus the fear of death (contemporary man 'excluded' death from his life).
3. *Maranatha!* [Our Lord, come!][3]
   It brings hope to this world and for this world.

1 See Matthew 25:40.
2 See Philippians 4:13.
3 See 1 Corinthians 16:22.

10. Medit. [Eleemosyna - jałmużna]

11. Sexta, Nona, Ang. [Todosłowny kazn. Sekr. Stanu o szpitalu]

12.

Cor. Ros. (II/III)

13- Vesp.

14- XVI konf. Jezus ~~historia~~ historii (Chrystus)

a) historia jako obecność zła

b) historia jako obecność dobra

c) historia jako „zmaganie się" dobra i zła

Umieć zgubić? Umieć wydobywać dobro z zła! (o [illegible])

+ [illegible] [illegible] [illegible] wszystko [illegible], który [illegible] [illegible]

15. Matins (ancilla.) [dzień, pierwszy obchodzony]

16 XVII konf. Chrystus naszej walki:

1. zmienić świat — oczekuje Chrystusa

2. wychodzić z radością na spotkanie Chrystusa w tajemnicy śmierci — a strach przed śmiercią (wszak wspólnymi „wychodząc" śmierci w naszym życiu)

3. Maranatha — znów nadzieja w tym świecie i dla tego świata

4. Sytuacja walki — pozostać wiernym!

17. Cor. Ros. I

18. Benedictio euch. [Lekt.

19. Litania Sanctorum a. Stan.

20. Godzina święta — Monte Cassino [illegible]]

Kompleta

APPUNTAMENTI

9. III 1. Surgite, Ps. Preces

2. Medit. [Baranek Boży!]

— niewinność, którą Chrystus nosi sobie od początku (w łonie Matki Chrystusa), która wypełnia się przede wszystkim, co składa się na jego życie, która spełnia się po wszystkim: wszystko [illegible]

4. The situation of the youth – to remain young!

Rosary (I); Eucharistic Benediction; Litany of the Saints; Holy Hour; Compline
Reading: St Stanislaus; *Morale et ancien Test.* [Morality and the Old Testament]

9 March

Getting up; Intentions; Prayers

Meditation on the **Lamb of God**

The reality that Christ carries in Himself from the beginning (John the Baptist's words), which is fulfilled through everything that becomes part of His life, which is fulfilled after everything: which surpasses everything.

Holy Mass with thanksgiving; Lauds

Talk 18: Mother of God:

1. *Est hora nostra – nos sumus Evangelium – Concilium in manibus nostris* [This is our hour – we are the Gospel – the Council is in our hands].
2. Christ – the central topic.
   The contemporary world is, above all, searching for Him. He enters into the middle of contemporary man's anxieties.
3. Christ stands at the door and knocks[1] – do not be afraid! We, above all, should not be afraid of Christ. This is only about our 'credibility', our evangelical authenticity – because the world needs Christ.
4. Let Christ's Mother help us with this.

Adoration of the Blessed Sacrament; Prayer to the Holy Spirit

Talk 19: To show Christ's true face to the world:
How? The language of ministry, the language of culture.

1. First and foremost, people want Christ as a living person, close to man, a friend.
   A 'school of love' rather than a 'school of theology'?
2. In order to bring Christ closer in this way, one needs to show a lot of selfless love.

1 See Revelation 3:20.

3. Christ – Lord – nowadays man often finds himself in bad hands – he seeks good hands.

The Way of the Cross; Sext; None; Angelus; Rosary (I), (III); Prayers for Friday; Penitential psalms; Vespers

Talk 20: The Cross:

1. Paschal theology is linked to passion theology.
2. We crucify God in our times: in how many forms? Military atheism, secularism, immorality, the 'trading' of religion in politics and beyond.
3. Suffering, diseases, unjust distribution of goods, enslavement of man, loneliness, wars.
4. The 'crucified' apostle – repentance (St John Vianney).
   (a) The apostle has to show clearly that he has chosen God and His plan.
   (b) He has to know and take into account his own limits.
   (c) He has to serve and give.
   'In my flesh I complete what is lacking in Christ's afflictions.'[1]

Matins (anticipated)

Talk 21: Mary:

1. Christ became man through the Virgin, and so salvation has come to people.
2. *L[umen] G[entium]* VIII and *Mater Ecclesiae* [Mother of the Church] (Paul VI).[2]
3. The Church is being born out of the Lord's pierced side in order to be born on the day of Annunciation. Mary is present at the first and second birth. She is there waiting for the Holy Spirit (Mary and the choice of the new apostle; Mary and Peter).
4. Mary in today's Church: As the Mother, She helps us to create a brotherly community. As the handmaid, She helps us to serve everyone. As the Mother, She stands at the threshold of the Church; She keeps watch over its openness and closure.

1 See Colossians 1:24.

2 The Mother of the Church (in Latin, *Mater Ecclesiae*) is a title that was officially given to the Virgin Mary during the Second Vatican Council by Pope Paul VI.

5. Mary and we. '*Cultus marialis*' ['Marian cult']. Our work with Mary, so that She can be the Mother of the Church and the world. Mary is the role model for the Church. She is a special role model for women (the place of women in the Church) – to give women Mary's face: this is the new contemporary cult of Mary.

7.30 p.m. Cardinal J. Villot, Secretary of State, passed away.

Rosary (II); Eucharistic Benediction; Meditation (synthesis); Compline
Reading: (St Stanislaus; *Morale et ancien Test.* [Morality and the Old Testament])

10 March

Getting up; Morning prayers

Meditation: *Ubi est, mors, victoria tua?* [O death, where is thy victory?][1] – let the people of our times discover anew Christ, who is the conqueror of sin and death.

Lauds

Talk 22: Magnificat.

1. Human vocation to the joy coming from the communion with God – the only certain source of happiness.
2. (Analysis of selected lines). Exegesis.
3. God wants me to be faithful. Let us work for eternity.
4. Through the Magnificat we renew the hope of the Churches every day. Our Lady of the Cenacle.

Concluding words

1 See 1 Corinthians 15:55.

24 February – 1 March [1980] Retreat in Rome, St Matilda's Chapel Led by Archbishop L[ucas] Moreira Neves [OP][1]

24 February 6.00 p.m.: Vespers

Introduction (Talk 1):

Retreat:
- loneliness
- under God's eyes
- communing with Him
- in the fullest depth of one's 'self'.

Topic: Priesthood

Reasons:
- a fundamental topic
- common
- very topical.

May Christ come to the participants in the retreat as He did to the disciples on their way to Emmaus.

Eucharistic Adoration; Anticipated Matins; Rosary; Compline

25 February Act of Consecration; Prayers
Meditation: *Dominum Deum tuum adorabis et Illi soli servies* [You shall worship the Lord your God and Him only shall you serve].[2]
Holy Mass; Thanksgiving; The Way of the Cross (Genesis 1–3); Lauds

Meditation (Talk 2): Vocation to the priesthood:

(a) *momentum aeternitatis* [a moment of eternity] in getting to know and choosing God Himself (compare texts by Isaiah, Jeremiah, the calling of Nathanael: *Ego Te cognovi* [I knew You][3]).

---

1 Lucas Moreira Neves OP (1925–2002) served as the Auxiliary Bishop of São Paulo, Secretary and Prefect of the Congregation for Bishops, and Archbishop of São Salvador da Bahia. He was appointed a cardinal by John Paul II in 1988.

2 See Matthew 4:10.

3 See John 1:48.

(b) The moment (or rather the inner process) – between man and God – numerous biblical and contemporary testimonies.
(c) The process of grace: the awareness of the gift that is an expression of love – undeserved good.
(d) The process (moment) of the identification with the priesthood: 'I could not be anyone else but a priest . . .'
(e) All this – requires faithfulness and prayer (Lord, who called me on that day – call me today).
(*Domine, qui me vocasti illa die – voca me hac die.*)

Reflection; Act of Consecration to the Blessed Virgin Mary; Prayer for the gifts of the Holy Spirit; Terce

Meditation (Talk 3):

(a) 'the gift of God that is within you through the laying on of my hands.'[1] This gift (grace) is '*charisma*', which is contained in the vocation, and which is a good gift for the community of the Church. The essence of the gift is participation in the priesthood of Christ Himself.
(b) Together with this gift, one receives special power in relation to the Eucharist, sacraments, word of God, people of God.
(c) A special grace of state corresponds to this power; the grace of ordination also brings the 'character', through the sacrament of holy orders, a man–priest becomes someone 'else'.

To be faithful to the grace of priesthood, to one's priesthood, means to have trust, to trust the grace that we have received from God together with the priesthood. We are called to renew this grace (Letter to Timothy),[2] especially on the anniversaries of our ordination.

Reflection; Sext; None
Text on Divine Mercy (*Dives in Misericordia Deus*)[3] – read out

1 See 2 Timothy 1:6.
2 Compare 2 Timothy 1:6: 'Hence I remind you to rekindle the gift of God that is within you through the laying on of my hands.'
3 The encyclical *Dives in misericordia* (Rich in Mercy) was promulgated by John Paul II on 30 November 1980.

Reflection: The priest is also a person who certainly experiences mercy in a special way.

Adoration of the Blessed Sacrament; Rosary (I)
Reading (on the persecution of the Church in Albania)[1]
Vespers

Meditation (Talk 4):

- The primary aim of priesthood and the priest's life is the glory of God. The idea of God's glory permeates the entire Old Testament.
- The inner splendour of divine majesty.
- God's pure perfection.

In the New Testament, the glory of God is the subject of Christ's life and actions. The high priestly prayer of Jesus. Then – the eschatological meaning (compare Revelation) (*s. Aug.: Gloria Dei erit sine fine, ubi cognitio Dei erit sine confine* [St Augustine: God's glory will be infinite when our knowledge of God becomes unlimited]).

- For the priest is called to glorify God in everything: liturgy: the Eucharist (*minist. presbyt.* [priestly ministry]); *ministerium pastorale* [pastoral ministry] (to help the faithful live the mystery of salvation).
- The priest has to be the witness of that which the world often ignores (Example: St .... of the Holy Trinity).[2]

Mistica della gloria di Dio [Mystery of God's glory]

(UIOGD – AMDG).[3]

1 The persecution of the Church in Albania began in 1945, when churches and religious institutions had their property confiscated. Many priests and religious leaders were imprisoned, sentenced to hard labour or executed. In 1967, Enver Hoxha, the First Secretary of the Party of Labour of Albania, declared the state atheist. He carried out a violent antireligious campaign to extinguish all forms of religion in Albania. Most religious buildings were closed, destroyed or converted to other uses. The law against public religious practice was rescinded only in December 1990.

2 This may be a reference to St Elizabeth of the Holy Trinity (1880–1906) who was a French Discalced Carmelite, mystic and spiritual writer. She was beatified by Pope John Paul II on 25 November 1984 and canonised by Pope Francis on 16 October 2016.

3 See p. xxi.

Modlitwa arcykapłańska (ś. Jana)

przyjścia Chrystusa w chwale – oznaczenie eschatologiczne (Apostoł.) [S. Aug.: gloria Dei erit sine fine, ubi cognitio Dei erit sine confine.]

– Otóż kapłan jest powołany do tego, aby we mysteria dawał chwałę Boga: Liturgia & Eucharystia (uczestn. presbyt.)

ministerium pastorale = przyczyniać się do tego, by [illegible] tajemnica zbawienia.

– Musi kapłan być świadkiem tego, do czego świat przywiązuje często małą wagę. (Przykład: ś. .... w Trojej [?] Łaty)

Mistica della gloria di Dio / UIOGD – AMDG /

non nobis Domine, non nobis, sed nomini Tuo da gloriam / od pierwszej do ostatniej kartki życia. / Refleksja /

12. Matut. (anticipatum)

13. Medit. (Konf. V)

„Homo Dei" (od Tim.)

(z tradycji St. Testam.) Sacerdos – homo Dei

a) ten, który szuka Boga: z historii, ewangelizowaniem, wierząc w cierpieniu – quaerere Deum (cysterci u Benedykt. [?])

– quaerere faciem Dei (w Psalmach, w Ewang.)

[Panie, który dałeś mi łaskę, że Cię znalazłem, pozwól mi szukać Cię, abym Cię nie stracił]

– quaerite regnum Dei

reguła ś. Bened.: – si revera Deum quaerit

b) ten, który jest świadkiem Boga / doświadczenia Boga /

– świadkiem może być tylko ten, kto poznał

– świat współczesny b. potrzebuje takiego świadectwa. (świat zsekularyzowany)

c) ten, który jest znakiem Boga

– kapłan powinien być znakiem ojcowskiej dobroci Boga dla ludzi [Kościół jest znakiem i sakramentem w Kościele wszyscy jesteśmy powołani znakiem i sakram.]

– zwłaszcza musi być takim znakiem sprzeciwu. [Graham Greene: ostatni kapłan / Tojuba [?]]

[S. Aug.: da mihi vim, ut semper Te quaeram / quaerendo Te]

APPUNTAMENTI

14. Nov. [II] / Benedykcja Euch.

15 Nov. III · Sygnum [?] Compl.

26.II

1. Obl. Medit. „faciem Tuam Domine requiram"

2 Sacrum / Grać [?] act.

'*Non nobis, Domine, non nobis, sed Nomini Tuo da gloriam*' ['Not to us, O Lord, not to us, but to Thy name give glory'].[1] From the first to the last page of life.

Reflection; Matins (anticipated)

Meditation (Talk 5):

'*Homo Dei*' (*ad Tim.*) ['Man of God' (Letter to Timothy)][2]
(from the Old Testament tradition)
Sacerdos – homo Dei [Priest – man of God]

- *quaerere Deum* – [to seek God]
  (frequent in the Prophetic Books, in the Psalms)
- *quaerere faciem Dei* [to seek God's face] in the Gospel
- *quaerite regnum Dei* [seek the kingdom of God]
  the Rule of St Benedict
- *si revera Deum quaerit* [if he truly seeks God].

(a) He who seeks God with love, involvement and at times suffering.
(Lord, You gave me the grace of finding You, let me be afraid of losing You.)

(b) He who is God's witness, who bears witness to God:
- Only he who knows can be a witness.
- The contemporary world needs such witness v. much (secularised world).

(c) He who is the sign of God:
- The priest should be a sign of God's fatherly goodness to people.
- Sometimes he has to be a sign of contradiction too.

The Church is the sign and sacrament. In the Church we are all in a way a sign and sacrament.

(Graham Greene – The last priest)[3]

(Toynbee)

(*s. Aug.: da mihi vim, ut semper Te quaeram/quaerendi Te* [St Augustine: give me strength so that I always seek You/ to seek You]).

1 See Psalm 113:9 (115:1).
2 See 1 Timothy 6:11.
3 Probably a reference to Graham Greene, *The Power and the Glory* (London, 1940).

Rosary (II); Eucharistic Benediction; Rosary (III); Synthesis; Compline

26 February Act of Consecration
Meditation: '*faciem Tuam Domine requiram*' ['Thy face, Lord, do I seek'].[1]
Holy Mass; Thanksgiving; The Way of the Cross; Lauds

Meditation (Talk 6):

- *Ricordati di Gesù Cristo* [Remember Jesus Christ][2]
- *Ricordati del carisma . . . per imposizione delle mie mani* [Remember the charisma . . . through the laying on of my hands][3]

Relationship:
Jesus Christ – Priest (priesthood)
Legame esistenziale [Existential bond]
Bond that shapes the being itself.

- *ministro di Gesù Cristo (Jesu Christi)* [minister of Jesus Christ] in the likeness of the apostles. This '*ministerium*' ['ministry'] forms a special '*communio*' ['communion'] between the priest and Christ: *comunione in passione* [communion in suffering].
  The more he is a 'servant' (minister) to Christ, the more he is one to the people.
- '*in persona Xristi*' ['in the person of Christ'] – (St Paul: *in presenza* [in the presence]). St Thomas gave new meaning to this formula – and the Council follows that, above all, when it speaks of *actio liturgiae sacerdotis* [the liturgical action of the priest] (*Eucharistia, Poenitentia* [sacrament of the Eucharist, sacrament of penance]) – but also in the entire pastoral ministry.

s Pauli [St Paul's] [illegible].

Vivo ego, iam non ego, vivit tamen in me Christus [It is no longer I who live, but Christ who lives in me].[4]

Reflection; Passion according to St Matthew; Terce

1 See Psalm 26 (27):8.
2 See 2 Timothy 2:8.
3 See 2 Timothy 1:6.
4 See Galatians 2:20.

Meditation (Talk 7):

What is the priesthood of Jesus Christ?

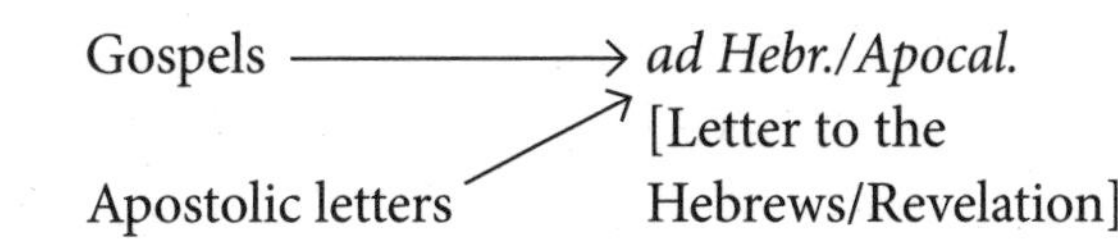

Although this does not refer to Christ as a priest, it shows priesthood in Him in a totally new and original sense.

ad Hebr. [The letter to the Hebrews] synthesises all this, referring to Christ directly as a priest.

(a) The priest has to be particularly close to God – no one is as close to God as Christ.
(b) The priest has to be close to the people to mediate between them and God – no one is as close to the people as Christ.
(c) The priest – offering, sacrifice. Christ was the priest of His own offering–sacrifice.
(d) The most original: Christ is a merciful priest who has experienced suffering and stands in solidarity with all those who suffer.
(e) Christ's priesthood is fulfilled in all acts of His life, but above all, in the cross – and then in the resurrection and ascension to the right side of the Father *ad interpellandum pro nobis* [to intercede for us].[1]

ad Hebr. [The letter to the Hebrews] emphasises that the priesthood of Christ is different from the priesthood of the Old Testament:

- *s. Thom.* [St Thomas Aquinas]
- *ratione Unionis hypost.* [because of the hypostatic union]
- *ratione gratiae Capitis* [because of the grace of the Head].

Reflection; Mercy – Justice; Sext; None; Adoration of the Blessed Sacrament; Rosary (I)
Reading: as yesterday (Albania)
Vespers

1 See Hebrews 7:25.

Meditation (Talk 8):

The Good Shepherd (John 10)
Psalms – Ezekiel – Zechariah
Shepherd – a messianic title
Analysis of selected elements of the parable:

- The sheep know his voice and follow him.
- The good shepherd knows his sheep and calls them by their names.
- The good shepherd lays down his life.
- He does not flee from the wolf (he is faithful).
- He seeks 'other' sheep.
- The ideal of unity: 'one flock and one shepherd'.[1]

Revelation. The Lamb – is the shepherd.

Ricordati di Gesù Cristo – buon pastore [Remember Jesus Christ – the good shepherd].

Matins (anticipated)

Meditation (Talk 9):

Jesus forms the apostles – He wishes to reveal Himself to them in different situations – the response should be 'to follow Him'.

To follow Him one has to get to know Him – believe in Him – love Him – St Augustine: '*amando habitamus corde*' ['we live with a loving heart'][2] – to love the Father and people; neighbours in Jesus.

Jesus leads the apostles *ad veram experientiam Sui – cfr. Joannes, cfr. Paulus* [to the real experience of Himself – cf. John, cf. Paul].

Christ wants to form His priests like He formed the apostles.

(It is also a sign of friendship that they speak of the Friend; compare the disciples in Emmaus.) The priest needs to have a personal experience of Christ – which one arrives at, like the apostles, after a long and enduring journey – this experience becomes a testimony – this experience is a grace that one needs to ask for.

1 See John 10:16.
2 See Augustine, *Commentary on the First Epistle of St John* II.12, *Patrologia Latina* vol. 35.

Rosary (II); Eucharistic Benediction; Rosary (III); Compline

27 February Act of Consecration; Visit to the Blessed Sacrament; Meditation on the theme of talks 7 and 9; Lauds

Meditation (Talk 10): *Sacerdotium Ecclesiae*: the priesthood of the Church itself.

(a) Peter: (*gens electa, populus sacerdotalis* [a chosen race, a priestly people])[1]
Revelation
Luther: negation of the ministerial priesthood, in favour of the priesthood of all believers
Trent: emphasises the hierarchical priesthood
Twentieth century – considering the fact that hierarchical priesthood took precedence over the priesthood of all believers – theology has begun to return to '*sacerdotium commune*' ['universal priesthood'] culminating in Vatican II.

(b) How is the priesthood of all believers expressed? Exegesis of *L[umen] G[entium]* and other documents of Vatican II – witness of the Absolute – all action in the spirit of '*sacrificii spirit.*' (spiritual sacrifice) – but above all through '*consecratio mundi*' ['consecration of the world'] (T. de Chardin: Mass on the altar of the world)[2] (Cardinal Journet).
- This means that the entire Church is priestly (the Church in its entirety is a priest).
- A wealth of quotations from Vatican II, *L[umen] G[entium]*, *Sacr[osanctum] Conc[ilium]*[3] and others.

(c) The Church constantly learns from Christ how to be a priest/priestly. This is a somewhat forgotten topic; one has to pay more attention to it.

The priesthood of the Church finds expression in, above all, the Eucharistic sacrifice and prayer.

1 See 1 Peter 2:9.
2 See Pierre Teilhard de Chardin, *Hymn of the Universe*, trans. Gerald Vann (London, 1969), chapter 1.
3 *Sacrosanctum Concilium* (This Sacred Council), the Second Vatican Council's Constitution on the Sacred Liturgy, was promulgated by Pope Paul VI on 4 December 1963.

Reading: St Augustine; P. Claudel
Reflection; Adoration of the Blessed Sacrament; Prayer for the gifts of the Holy Spirit

Meditation (Talk 11):

Sacerdotium ministeriale [Ministerial priesthood]:

(a) Some members of the Church receive priesthood (i.e. participation in the priesthood of Christ and the Church) in a particularly intense way.
(b) They receive it always from God through the mediation of the Church. They receive it in the form defined by the Church, on the conditions set by the Church – and not according to their personal project.
(c) The hierarchical (ministerial) priesthood is closely linked to the universal priesthood: it serves the universal priesthood, draws attention to it (comparison: not single peaks, but peaks among mountain chains).

s. Paul ad Col: 'factus sum minister Ecclesiae' [Letter of St Paul to the Colossians: 'I became a minister of the Church'].[1]

Reflection; Holy Mass; Thanksgiving; The Way of the Cross; Sext; None; (Reflection: the case of Lefebvre); Rosary (I), (II); Passion according to St Luke; Vespers
Spiritual reading: on the persecution of the Church in Albania; Fr J. Woroniecki: On Divine Mercy (every day)[2]

Meditation (Talk 12):

(a) It is the priest who gathers the people of God – he is the one who forms the community.
St John the Baptist gathered the people of God – and above all Christ Himself (St John, '*ut dispersos filios Dei congregaret in unum*' ['to gather into one the children of God who are scattered abroad'])[3] – in turn, the apostles.
This remains the task of bishops and priests: they gather people by the power of the word and sacrament, but also by the power of their own service.
(b) And this service is not easy. The service of unity is not an easy service. It began with the community of the apostles,

1 See Colossians 1:25.
2 Possibly a reference to Jacek Woroniecki, *Tajemnica miłosierdzia Bożego* [The Mystery of Divine Mercy] (Poznań, 1945).
3 See John 11:52.

which one theologian called an 'impossible community' (it became possible thanks to Jesus) (cf. Matthew and Simon the Zealot).

There are many factors that make this community 'impossible' at different times. Personal, subjective factors, but also social and, to a larger extent, ideological differences.

(c) The priest has to be beyond all that can divide – he has to be a man who connects people.

This is a great and difficult task, which requires working together with grace. The Eucharist builds the Church. The priest builds the Church.

Rosary (III)

Meditation (Talk 13):

Priest – *Ecclesiastico* – Man of the Church (John Paul I's words on Paul VI).

Eph. Christus dilexit Ecclesiam [Ephesians: Christ loved the Church]; this love of Christ for the Church creates the Church.

et donavit Semetipsum pro Ea [and gave Himself up for Her].[1]

(a) He who loves the Church and gives himself and his strength up for it – this is filial love: the Church–Mother, but also paternal love: (*'generat' Ecclesiam* ['begets' the Church]), full of adoration for the Church with which he fully identifies himself.
(b) He who serves the Church: the greater the love for the Church, the more complete the service. The more he identifies with his priestly vocation, the better he serves the Church (St Polycarp's words).
(c) He who works for the Church: the type of work is not important, what is important is an awareness of the mission one is carrying out (on the work in the Curia, which is often almost invisible).
(d) He who suffers for the Church in the image of Christ: '*passione della Chiesa*' ['the passion of the Church']; different kinds of suffering linked to pastoral work –

1 See Ephesians 5:25.

persecutions – experiencing one's limits; being disappointed by the people of the Church.

May everyone see true people of the Church in us.

28 February Act of Consecration to the Blessed Virgin Mary; Prayer to the Holy Spirit; Meditation; Lauds

Meditation (Talk 14): Priest – and people.

(a) Older literature – contemporary literature – Vatican II. The priest is a man consecrated to God, 'among people' (*Presbyterorum ordinis*[1]): *pater* [father] – *mater* [mother] – *pastor* [shepherd] – *magister fidei* [teacher of faith] – *frater* [brother] (human brotherhood in the spirit of faith: the brotherhood of priests themselves).
(b) In relation to lay people (*fratelli nella fede* [brothers in faith]): he tries to be close to them in the manner outlined so well by Vatican II. The Church cannot be built through the opposition of clergy and laity nor through the mixing of charismata.
(c) Lay people do not expect their priest to do their work in the world for them, to become a 'lay person', but they expect him to be with them in a priestly manner, to illuminate them and to support them spiritually.
(d) *'Optio praeferentialis' pro pauperibus* ['the preferential option' for the poor] (Vatican II, Puebla[2]) – in a purely evangelical, not political way.
(e) (Objective) loneliness that opens man to God. (Psychological) loneliness: the feeling of loneliness. (Claudel's letter) ought to be overcome with love for people.

Non sum solus: Pater, familia humana: Ecclesia [I am not alone: Father, human family: the Church].

Holy Mass; Thanksgiving; Prayers; Terce; Sext; None; Prayer for the gifts of the Holy Spirit

1 The decree *Presbyterorum ordinis* (The Order of Priests) on the ministry and life of priests was promulgated by Pope Paul VI on 7 December 1965.

2 John Paul II opened the Third General Conference of the Latin American Episcopate in Puebla, Mexico, on 28 January 1979.

Meditation (Talk 15):

(a) *Sacerdos – educator in fide* [Priest – educator in faith] (*Presb[yterorum] Ord[inis]*).

evolutio textus conciliaris [the evolution of the conciliar text].

verba perpulchra s. Gregorii [St Gregory's most beautiful words].

s. Pauli [St Paul's]: For though you have countless guides in Christ, you have only one father in faith (educator).[1]

People expect the priest to educate them in the fullness of faith.

(b) Hence the first duty: preaching, evangelisation. The Council of Trent speaks of the priest above all in relation to the altar; Vatican II: above all in relation to preaching the faith – of course with regard to the *Sacramenta Fidei* [mysteries of faith]. This is a difficult task and it is often bound to suffering: the priest has to communicate the realities of faith more with his life than his words.

(c) He who does not have faith can communicate concepts, but only a person of faith can communicate faith. Those who are to lead the people of God have to walk in faith, act in faith.

In order to be a person of faith, the priest has to be faithful to the Magisterium of the Church, devoted to learning. But above all, he has to seek Christ with all his strength.

(Reflection: Pope Paul VI's Testament); Rosary (I); The Way of the Cross (with meditation); Adoration of the Blessed Sacrament (meditation); Vespers; (Rosary (III))
Spiritual reading: Fr J. Woroniecki, on Divine Mercy; on the persecution of the Church in Albania

Meditation (Talk 16):

(a) Shepherding – pastoral work – from the apostolic times to our times. Reference to the analysis of the Good Shepherd – St Augustine (the quotation in which the line '*non intravit per portam – non est bonus pastor*' [he who

1 See 1 Corinthians 4:15.

does not enter by the door – is not a good shepherd][1] is repeated).

(b) Thus the first quality: a true shepherd, having received power from Christ, remains bound to Him, the only Shepherd of souls. The second quality: the knowledge of the sheepfold and sheep, which is also translated into structures – dioceses, parishes, *communità di base* [basic ecclesial communities]. The third quality: the shepherd has to be a true guide (he cannot walk too fast nor too slowly), knowing that others are following him. The fourth quality: readiness to seek the lost sheep. The fifth quality: to be available.

(c) To match these qualities, one has to have numerous traits. Above all: care (*sollicitudo*); sympathy – alertness; goodness: infinite understanding, and an open but at the same time demanding heart; courage.

(d) To be a shepherd is an important part of the priestly vocation and the brotherhood with people, which corresponds to the vocation.

s. Bened. Labre [St Benedict Labre]: less;
s. Vinc. a Paulo [St Vincent de Paul]: more.

Matins (anticipated); Passion according to St Luke

Meditation (Talk 17):

(a) *S. Liturgia (Const. Sacrosanctum concilium)* [Holy Liturgy (Constitution on the Sacred Liturgy)] – the summit of Christian life. Sacraments – the summit of the liturgy. The Eucharist – the summit of the sacraments. Infinite richness of the liturgy (a) (b) (c) (d).

(b) The priest is a liturgist: *minister et dispensator mysteriorum Dei* [servant and steward of the mysteries of God].[2] He is a brother to people through a proper celebration of the liturgy too. Believers have the right to it. They also have a right to prepare well for it.

(c) The most important moment in the life of the Church is when the Eucharist is celebrated. The priest is there

1 See John 10:1–2.
2 See 1 Corinthians 4:1.

entirely for the Eucharist. It is by celebrating the Eucharist that the priest becomes most similar to Christ. The most '*incommunicabile*' ['incommunicable'] act of the priest, and at the same time, the most social act. (*s. Pietro Damiani: Dominus vobiscum* [St Peter Damian: the Lord be with you]).

Penitential psalms; Holy Hour; (Rosary (II); Litany of Our Lord Jesus Christ, Priest and Victim); Compline

29 February Act of Consecration; Prayers
Morning meditation: (*erit vobis sanguis agni in signum* [the blood of the lamb shall be a sign for you])[1]
Lauds

Meditation (Talk 18):

Vocation to holiness – the central chapter of *L[umen] G[entium]*

(a) It is first and foremost the saint who builds the Church.
The priest has a special vocation to holiness. The saint–priest undertakes the tasks of his vocation more properly, more deeply and more fruitfully. This depends on one's spiritual life. Therefore, spiritual life will be the topic of today's reflection.
(b) Priesthood, priestly sanctity, requires a thorough Christian formation: One needs to be a mature Christian. It simultaneously requires mature humanity.
Presb[yterorum] Ord[inis] includes the evangelical counsels in the spirituality of priests – but from the perspective of service proper to the priestly vocation: analysis of the council texts – focused on detail.
(c) The sanctity of the priest's life: testimony. The contemporary world listens to testimony more than to priests and bishops.

The Way of the Cross; Terce

Meditation (Talk 19):

(a) How to reconcile the duties of priestly service with the need to strive for sanctity? *Presb[yterorum] Ord[inis]*

1 See Exodus 12:13.

A-105

29. II
– 1. Obl. Orn.
Medit. mat. (erit vobis sanguis aqua in signum)

2. Laudes

3. Medit. (Konf. XXIX)

Powołanie do świętości – centralny wątek LG

a) najbardziej budujemy Kościół – świętością.
Kapłan ma szczególne powołanie do świętości. Święty kapłan o wiele ~~skuteczniej pełni~~ owocniej, głębiej, owocniej, pełniej spełnia zadanie swego powołania. Zależy to od życia duchowego. Stąd życie duchowe – bardzo zaniedbane dziś. Zwracać

b) Kapłaństwo, świętość kapłańska zakłada gruntowną formację chrześcijańską: musi być dojrzały w chrześcijaństwie. Zakłada równocześnie dojrzałe człowieczeństwo.
Presb. Ord. ustala rady wskazujące do duchowości kapłańskiej – jednakże pod kątem służby [illegible] powołania kapł.: analiza tekstów sob. – uwzględniająca.

c) Świętość życia kapł.: świadectwo. [illegible] bardzo świadectwo niż kapłana i biskupa.

4. Via Crucis   Tertia

5. Medit. (Konf. XXX)

a) Jak pogodzić obowiązki służby kapłańskiej z wymogami dążenia do świętości? P.O. (Presb. Ord.) daje na to odpowiedź zasadniczą. Kapłan uświęca się przez swą posługę, służbę. Jakże mogłoby być inaczej, jeśli w zjednoczeniu z Chrystusem [illegible] Jego sługą, w duchu Jego [illegible] odpuszcza grzechy i tp.

b) A jednak wspomniany [illegible] tryb życia nie omija, nie oszczędza kapłana. Abstrakcyjne sposoby, uchować [illegible] styl służby kapł. – trzeba nade wszystko modlitwy, medytacji słowa Bożego. – Trzeba utrafić w ową chrześcijańską [illegible] simplicitatis: ~~[illegible]~~ zasada życia [illegible]

c) [illegible] APPUNTAMENTI Zadanie Chrystusa (PO)
Elementy tego naśladowania: [illegible] woli Bożej – [illegible] posłuszeństwa
Oto też trzeba ~~szczególnie~~ prosić P. Jezusa

6. Sacrum
grat. actio. [illegible]

7. Lectura spir.: O. J. Woroniecki: O [illegible] Bożym; O prześladowaniu Kościoła w Albanii   Pasja wg z. Jana

8. Sexta hora

gives a fundamental answer. The priest becomes a saint through his service, thanks to it. How could it be otherwise if – in the unity with Christ – he preaches His word, in the spirit of His mercy he forgives sins, etc.

(b) Yet the contemporary stressful lifestyle does not exclude and spare the priest. In order to face it and maintain the sanctifying style of priestly service, one needs, above all, prayer and meditation on the word of God . . .

(c) One needs to find the Christian *misterium simplicitatis* [mystery of simplicity]: the principle of inner life that is the fruit of the imitation of Christ (*P[resbyterorum] O[rdinis]*).

Elements of this imitation: seeking the will of God – pastoral love.

This is what one has to ask the Lord Jesus for in particular.

Holy Mass; Thanksgiving; Prayers; Passion according to St John
Spiritual reading: Fr J. Woroniecki: on Divine Mercy; on the persecution of the Church in Albania
Sext; None; Reflection on the entire Testament of Paul VI; Rosary (I), (II) Chaplet of the Holy Wounds of Christ;[1] Vespers

Meditation (Talk 20):

(a) The priest's prayer: prayer is an inner matter – and an expression of the inside. The priest, praying, ought to act in unity with the Highest Priest – Christ. To join Him in His prayers. To connect Him to our petitions. To use His words. To learn how to pray from those who have learnt it from Christ.

(b) The priest – the liturgist: the liturgist's prayer in unity with the Church.

Personal prayer: the prayer of silence, in which we try to open ourselves to God's eyes (*communio* [communion]).

Examples . . . Carrel: prayer does not change external reality – but it changes me so that I can change that reality.

1 The Chaplet of the Holy Wounds of Christ (also known as the Rosary of the Holy Wounds) is a Rosary-based prayer inspired by the visions of Bl. Marie Martha Chambon (1841–1907).

(c) The priest who prays becomes a living witness to what prayer is. Apart from this, the priest's prayer should be an intercessory prayer, like Abraham's or Moses's prayers, St John Vianney – such prayer is particularly important for the man who is responsible for society, for a community. People expect this from a priest. They want him to be a 'master' of prayer, a man of prayer.

Adoration of the Blessed Sacrament
Litany of the Sacred Heart of Jesus, Blessed Virgin Mary, St Joseph (also on other days)

Meditation (Talk 21):

(a) Priesthood (the priest) – and devotion to the Blessed Virgin Mary.
    Devotion – similar to all Christians. Above all – full of great simplicity.
    Examples: full of trust and full of love (*magis Mater quam Regina* [more a Mother than a Queen]).
(b) This devotion should be grounded in the word of God, in theology.
    Characteristic traits of the priest's devotion to Our Lady – the Mother of the Highest Priest, the Mother of the Saviour; *associata al Sacerdozio di Suo Figlio* [associated with the priesthood of Her Son].
    P[resbyterorum] O[rdinis] underscores Mary's '*docilitas*' ['docility'] to Christ's work and Christ's mystery – and this is an example for the priest.
(c) It is difficult to speak of the entire issue: the priest's Marian spirituality. Just a few elements:
    - prayer to Mary; Marian contemplation (Claudel, Bernanos)
    - to serve Mary by bringing others to Her
    - to enter the 'school' of Our Lady (Pius XII's words): to learn from Her
    - to consecrate (to offer) oneself to Our Lady – to offer Her our problems, and above all, to entrust ourselves to Her. *Totus Tuus.*[1]

1 See n. 1, p. 1 [2 September 1962].

Matins (anticipated); Talk; Litany of the Saints; Rosary (III); Compline

1 March

Act of Consecration; Prayers
Morning meditation (*Totus Tuus*)
Holy Mass; Thanksgiving; Lauds

Concluding meditation (Talk 22): Paschal joy – the joy of the priesthood

The joy of the priesthood is, in a way, the primary condition for fulfilling the priestly vocation and awakening other vocations. Spiritual zeal (*fervor*) is related to this – brotherly *communio* (community) is a condition for joy.

The joy of the priesthood is a point of support in difficult experiences and persecutions – it overcomes them. It disappears, however, when there is not enough living contact with Christ, with the Eucharist, with the word of God.

This joy is a gift from God – one has to ask for it, keeping one's heart always ready. Your joy is perfect in heaven. The Church and the world need priests of such perfect joy very much.

Final words; Meeting with the retreat leader

AMDG UIOGD[1]

1 See p. xxi.

8–14 March 1981
Retreat at St Matilda's Chapel
Led by Bishop J[erzy] Ablewicz[1]

~

8 March 6.00 p.m.: Vespers

Introduction (Talk 1): 'Will you be my witnesses?'[2]
What does contemporary man need?

(a) Reflection – entrance into oneself (conscience):
   – decisions of Pius XI and Pius XII with regard to the Vatican retreats.
(b) You shall be my witnesses – this is the most important:
   – Man is by nature a 'witness'.
   – Christ wants man to be a witness of God.
   – To be Christ's witness means to receive Christ – the witness (revelation): to receive His revelation.
   – To be a witness means to 'respond': *populi meus, responde mihi!* [my people, answer me!].[3]
   – Only through such witness can we change the world!
(c) The basic problem of the retreat has to be related to
   'you shall be my witnesses'! Until the last breath (the example of Pius XI).
   ↓

Am I a witness of Christ?

(W. Kasper, *Jésus le Christ* [Jesus the Christ][4] and others)
Concluding meditation
Anticipated Matins; Compline

---

1 See n. 2, p. 87 [3 September 1974].
2 See Acts 1:8.
3 See Micah 6:3.
4 The original was published in German as Walter Kasper, *Jesus der Christus* (Mainz, 1974). It appeared in English as *Jesus the Christ*, trans. V. Green (London, 1976).

9 March

Intentions

Morning meditation: '*Ipsi vidistis quomodo portaverim vos super alas aquilarum et assumpserim mihi*' ['You have seen how I bore you on eagles' wings and brought you to myself'] (Exodus 19:4)

Holy Mass; Thanksgiving; Lauds (memorial of St Frances of Rome); Prayer to the Holy Spirit

(Iwaszkiewicz, The Russian woman)

Talk 2: *Spiritus Sanctus super me* [The Holy Spirit is upon me].[1]

- Christ acts by the power of the Holy Spirit.
- *Sanguis Christi – Vehiculum Spiritus Sancti* [the Blood of Christ – the Vehicle of the Holy Spirit].
- *Spiritus S. est Spiritus Christi* [the Holy Spirit is Christ's Spirit] (*pneumatologia – Cristologia* [pneumatology – Christology]).
- *Calor Verbi: Spiritus S.* [the Fire of the Word: the Holy Spirit].
  → He is also the source and foundation of our witness.
  → He is the source of our prayer (prayer is a mystery).
  Augustine: *quasi 'docta ignorantia'* [as if 'learned ignorance'].

(Archbishop Baziak)

- Prayer is an act of opening to the Holy Spirit (*Veni!* [Come!]).
  (*Apertura* [aperture]); this 'aperture' = habitual, existential prayer.
- The Holy Spirit constantly rejuvenates the Church; becoming older, we can maintain spiritual youth in the Holy Spirit: *Calor Verbi Aeterni* [the Fire of the Eternal Word].

Reflection: Main conclusion: constant opening (aperture) to the Holy Spirit is a constitutive condition for 'you shall be my witnesses'.

Passion according to Matthew

Talk 3: Christ: the visible image (ontologically) of the invisible God.

- Hence: when Christ calls Himself the Light, when He says 'follow me' – He points to the fact that we should become 'followers of God' and, in this sense: His witnesses.

1 See Luke 4:18.

(Dostoyevsky, Kołakowski)

- To be a witness – to imitate! – as if to recreate Christ's traits in oneself.
  (A retreat question: Do I imitate? Do I recreate?)
  Because: people want to 'see Christ' in us.
- We should be a letter from Christ, written . . .[1]
  (A retreat question: Am I a letter from Christ?)

Reflection; The Way of the Cross
Reading: *Unitatis redintegratio*[2]
Rosary (II), (III); Vespers

Talk 4: Bearing witness through the priesthood.
Every Christian is a witness of Christ, a letter from Christ. The priest is such a witness in a special way, by the power of the character of holy orders. The meaning of the words: *hoc facite in meam commemorationem* [do this in remembrance of me].[3] '*Memoria*' in the Aramaic language means 'repetition'.

(Hess, P. Lohn)

- *Credo in caracterem sacerdotalem* [I believe in the priestly character]: as the basis of my identity, my 'I' was permeated with Christ's priesthood, it was in a way absorbed in His priesthood.
  (A great passage on the nature of the sacrament of holy orders)
  '*sigillo*' ['seal']
  (Guitton: '*Montini non esiste*' ['Montini does not exist'])[4]
- One has to defend the priestly character against three dangers:

  (1) *sacrilegium* [sacrilege], . . ., . . . (we will be held responsible before Christ the Judge for His priesthood in us)
  (2) *hypocrysia* [hypocrisy]: agreement in the heart, not only on the lips
  (3) *egoismo* [egoism]: unity in the priesthood of Christ, the meaning of Peter: the verification of character

1 See 2 Corinthians 3:3.
2 *Unitatis redintegratio* (Restoration of Unity) is the Second Vatican Council's decree on ecumenism. It was promulgated by Pope Paul VI on 21 November 1964.
3 See Luke 22:19.
4 Jean Guitton (1901–99) was a friend of Pope Paul VI (born Giovanni Battista Montini).

(Paul: *videre Petrum* [to visit Peter]).[1]
(A great talk in its entirety, full of faith, persuasion, theological coherence.)

Reflection; Anticipated Matins

Talk 5: Mary – the most perfect witness of Christ. *Vergine del silenzio* [the Virgin of Silence]. The Gospels record only seven utterances by Mary. We will analyse them to confirm her witness.

- 'How can this be, since I have no husband' . . .[2] Virginity as witness borne to God.

(Hemingway, J. Balicki, Daszyński)

- 'Behold, I am the handmaid of the Lord; let it be to me according to Your word'.[3] The witness of service for which the whole creation, the whole world is waiting (St Bernard: the contemporary world needs the authority of service).
- *Autorità del servizio* [the authority of service]: The world needs such priestly service.
- On the beauty of service.
- The attitude of service can best overcome sadness and the greatest suffering.
  Beata! [Blessed!]
  The greatest paradox of Christianity.
- *Felicità. Servizio* [Happiness. Service]: The world expects the Church to bear the witness of service in the likeness of Mary.

Dante

Reflection: The witness of service in the likeness of Mary.

Rosary (I)
[Reading:] Kasper, *Jesus le Christ* and others
Eucharistic Adoration; Concluding meditation; Compline

10 March

Intentions
Morning meditation: '*intra in cubiculum tuum et, clauso ostio, ora Patrem*' ['go into your room and shut the door and pray to your Father'][4]
Holy Mass with prayers; Lauds

Parandowski

Talk 6: Witness – of the Word of God – the human word.

1 See Galatians 1:18.
2 See Luke 1:34.
3 See Luke 1:38.
4 See Matthew 6:6.

La filosofia cerca
la teologia trova
la religione possiede Dio.
[Philosophy seeks,
theology finds,
religion possesses God.]
The Word of God creates, constitutes 'religion'.
↓

Brandstaetter

A spring that is inexhaustible

Am I a religious person?
The most important progress: religious progress.

St John Chrysostom

Reading of Holy Scripture, whose light is inexhaustible.
Holy Scripture: '*La spada del verbo di Dio*' [the sword of the word of God]: it is also the power of:

- cleansing
- sanctifying
- conquering Satan (cf. the temptation of Jesus)
- victory of 'pure religion'.[1]

'The library of the heart': Holy Scripture should fill the libraries of hearts.
Paradiso della Parola di Dio . . . [Paradise of the Word of God].
Gloria Tibi Verbum Dei! [Glory to You, Word of God!].

Reflection: Yes: the heart is to be a library of the Word of God, uttered in Scripture. This library has to be constantly open to important questions, needs, situations . . .

(Passion according to St Mark); Terce

Auschwitz

Talk 7: Witness borne to the Father.

- 'Father . . . Abba'[2] – the greatest witness, the most uplifting one, the witness borne by Christ.

Clemenceau

  St Theresa: I build everything on *Pater Noster* [Our Father].
- 'Abba' – in Gethsemane: In the Gethsemane of our lives 'Abba' remains a source of strength.

1 See Hebrews 4:12.
2 See Mark 14:36.

10. VII

1. Akt. necess. Meditatio mane.
{ „intra in cubiculum tuum, et clauso ostio, ora Patrem!"

2. Sacrum cum meditatione

3. Laudes

4. Konf. VI

— Świadectwo — Słowa Bożego —
słowo ludzkie —
słowo Boże —
tworzy, konstytuuje „religię"!

Źródło, które się nie wyczerpuje
{ czy jestem człowiekiem religijnym!
najważniejszy postęp: postęp religijny

lektura Pisma ś., którego światło jest niewyczerpalne

Pismo ś.: to równocześnie miecz (!) „la spada del verbo di Dio".
— oczyszczania
— rozcinania — zwyciężania nad szatanem. (por. kuszenie P. Jezusa)
— zwycięstwo „czystej religii"

— „biblioteka serca":
Pismo ś. winno wypełniać bibliotekę serc

— „Paradiso della Parola di Dio ..
gloria tibi Verbum Dei!

Ta filosofia cerca —
Ta teologia trova —
La religione possiede Dio

4a Refl Tak: serce ma być biblioteką Słowa Bożego, wypowiedzianego w Piśmie. Chodzi o to, aby ta biblioteka była stale otwarta na wszelkie pytania, potrzeby, sytuacje ..

(Passio sec. S. Marcum)

5. Tertia.

6. Konf. VII, Królestwo darowane Ojca

APPUNTAMENTI

— „Ojcze .." Abba
najwspanialsze świadectwo, najbardziej pewne na chwilę, synostwo, które dał Chrystus
Św. Teresa: wszystko buduje na Ojcze nasz

— „Abba" — w Getsemani: w Getsemani naszego życia „Abba" pozostaje źródłem mocy

— Ojcostwo duchowe kapłanów
polega na dawaniu światła: Ewang. (wiara)
na zbliżaniu do sakramentów
[Słowo Słowa Bożego - Eucharystii!]

Spiritual fatherhood of priests

consists in giving light: the Gospel (faith), in bringing closer to the sacraments (the table of the Word of God – Eucharist).

- The contemporary world is an 'orphan'. It lacks fathers and those who give witness to Fatherhood. There is no true brotherhood without the Father.
- The Church is not an 'orphan' as long as it does not lack those who bear witness to the Father, who call 'Father! Abba!'

P. Leiber SJ
T. Breza: *Porta di bronzo* [Bronze gate]

[the special meaning of the Holy See
the service of 'fatherhood']

Meditation; Reflection; Sext; None; The Way of the Cross ('*miserere*' ['have mercy']); Adoration of the Blessed Sacrament; Litany of the Saints and others; Rosary (III), (I); Vespers

Talk 8: Bearing witness to Christ's resurrection.

- Women, apostles, forty-day paschal pedagogy.
- The fruits of the retreat should consist in bearing special witness to the resurrection: not only as faith, but as '*vivere pascha*' ['the living out of Easter'].
- The witnesses of Christ's resurrection are not politicians: Politicians want to resolve all matters in the dimension of temporal life; they do not want to enter into the glory with Christ.
- Resurrection: The witness of resurrection responds to the questions of chastity – celibacy – marital honesty.
- Is my way of thinking 'paschal'? (graphologist on saints)
- 'Paschal' work on oneself: work on oneself is of paschal nature . . . with the help of the grace of Christ: '*pascha nostrum*' ['our Passover']. (Congar)
- *attesa pascuale* [paschal waiting]: The witness to the resurrection is a man who lives in paschal expectation. The day of this expectation is above all Sunday. **Lack of Sunday**.
  (The value of man depends on what he expects.)
  A retreat question: what do I expect?

- Contemporary humankind needs paschal witness in particular!
  The witness of Christ risen from the dead.

A. Manzoni

Reflection
Anticipated Matins

Talk 9: *Maria, testimonianza della cultura* [Mary, the testimony of culture].

St Louis M. de Montfort

(Revealed – the Visitation and greeting of Elizabeth.)

- Nature and culture become bound together in Mary, considering Her Immaculate Conception and constant cooperation with grace: She is the Mother of true culture and true humanity, especially true priestly culture.
  (Do I surrender my nature to grace to reach such culture?)
- *Regina urbanissima* [the most cultivated Queen]: Culture is revealed in service.
- *Pneumatophora* [the Carrier of the Holy Spirit]: Culture is born out of the covenant of nature with the Holy Spirit.
  Our Lady did more for the good of human culture than . . . ?
  Contemporary man has a special need of true humanity: the Immaculate Mother of Christ is its fullness.

Tatarkiewicz

St Francis – St Francis de Sales.
(Mary greets Elizabeth – do I greet others?)

Rosary (II); Eucharistic devotion (adoration); Concluding meditation; Compline
[Reading:] Kasper, *Jésus le Christ*, and others

11 March

Intentions
Morning meditation: '*in corde eorum scribam eas (leges), non atramento, sed Spiritu Dei vivi*' ['I will write it (my law) upon their heart, not with ink but with the Spirit of the living God'][1]
Holy Mass; Prayers; Lauds

Talk 10: Witness through the Eucharist: '*imitamini, quod agitis (tractatis)*' ['imitate what you do (administer)'].[2]

Celebrating the Eucharist, the Lord's sacrifice in which

1 See Jeremiah 31:33 and 2 Corinthians 3:3.

2 The words '*Agnoscite quod agitis: imitamini quod tractatis*' ('Understand what you do, imitate what you administer') used to be uttered by a bishop ordaining new priests.

Christ is both the priest and the victim (*victima*), the priest himself has to become '*victima*'. (Example from Dachau: Fr Bednarski.) This refers to '*martirio bianco*' ['white martyrdom'], which may prepare us for '*martirio rosso*' ['red martyrdom'].

Fr Bednarski
Br Albert
Nowaczyński
[illegible]
Cardinal.

(St Ignatius: *martirio* – in Eucharistic categories.)

(*Martirio bianco* – to overcome desires and faults.)

Witness through the Eucharist – Do I bear such witness?

Br Albert: to become bread for others.

Not only is the Eucharist a sign, but also the efficient cause of life to others: the efficient cause of social virtues. Paul VI, JP II.

Mother Teresa
of Calcutta

The priesthood of Christ is 'always' (*semper*) fulfilled, the meaning of Christ's presence in the tabernacle: the prisoner of His love to all people. He calls us all to go to everyone with love (the meaning of papal visits).

(The Holy Mass is a gathering and sending out!)

The Eucharist should define the Apostolic See's style of work.

Reflection; Passion according to Luke
Terce

Talk 11: Bearing witness . . . with an undivided heart.[1]

- Chastity. Body from God – and redeemed: 'You are not your own' (1 Cor. 6:19).
- Christ is pure chastity and pure virginity!

  Clerical celibacy is a supernatural mystery (cf. Christ's words: not all men can understand),[2] and at the same time a gift from God, *carisma* [charisma], to devote oneself to the kingdom with an 'undivided heart'. This gift is made real in a given person despite their weaknesses.

  Do I think of this in such a way?
- Moreover, the truth (of perfect chastity) ought to be read in the wider context of '*nexus virtutum*' ['network of virtues'] and Christ's call to take up Christ's cross. The '*indivisum cor*' ['undivided heart'] can be explained in this context. The greater the ideal, the greater the sin.

Heidegger

Golubev

(Hitler)

1 See Psalm 85 (86):11.
2 See Matthew 19:11.

- '*Propter regnum coelorum*' ['for the sake of the kingdom of heaven'] . . .[1] '*per Me e per il Vangelo*' ['for My sake and the Gospel's'] . . .[2] Priesthood cannot be identified with celibacy, but celibacy supports priesthood and gives it special efficacy.
- Celibacy: making a commitment 'for ever' – in this is the greatness of man. *Testimonianza escatologica* [eschatological testimony]. The contemporary world needs such testimony. This world is the world of 'divided hearts'.
  How do I live out my celibacy?

Concluding meditation; The Way of the Cross (Lenten songs); Sext; None; *Angelus*; Adoration of the Blessed Sacrament; Rosary (I), (II); Penitential psalms; Vespers [Reading:] *Marialis cultus*[3]

Tolstoy

Talk 12: The witness of death

- Death is a mystery. Christ turns the mystery of death into the witness of death, the Gospel.
- Death is a necessary part of life. It deprives man of all the goods of this world. (The form of this world passes away.)

Sartre

- Is death absurd? Life is only a pilgrimage, after which we are going to meet Christ in eternal bliss. Therefore: not absurd, but divine (logic) of the divine plan.
  '*Maranatha*' ['Our Lord, come!'][4]
  Question: do I live in the spirit of '*Maranatha*'?

German philosophy?

(– Theory of a definitive decision (?))
- Christ turned the mystery of death into the witness of final responsibility. Christ's 'I am' at the particular judgement will conquer evil and the sinner.

Mercier

- Responsibility before God and 'for God' (Matthew 25).
  Question: Do I live with such responsibility?

J. Szczepański, Marx

- Death is a liberation, not because it frees us from systems and 'ideologies', but because it leads to a meeting with Christ who has conquered death.

Bonhoeffer

St Thomas Aquinas

- This freedom, liberation: It is Christ the Lord who serves His servants at the table of truth – 'Heureka' di Parasso

1 See Matthew 19:12.

2 See Mark 8:35.

3 *Marialis cultus* [Devotion to Mary] is the title of Pope Paul VI's apostolic exhortation on the devotion to the Blessed Virgin Mary issued on 2 February 1974.

4 See 1 Corinthians 16:22.

– Truth will make us free![1] Truth in love. Christ will reveal the Father's love.

Little Sister: Death (St Francis)

Anticipated Matins

Talk 13: Mary – a special witness of the history of salvation – Magnificat.

Genesis 3: *Protoevangelium* – Revelation.

- That 'I will put enmity between you and the woman'[2] became the history of salvation in the history of Abraham's family (Abraham's progeny). Abraham began the procession to the Messiah.
- Mary had faith in the likeness of Abraham's faith (*figlia di Abramo* [Abraham's daughter]). Among many moments, in particular: Isaac – Jesus (the father's sacrifice, the mother's sacrifice).
- We are to be witnesses to the history of salvation in the image of Mary. Mary contributes to the history of salvation with her '*humilitas*' (humility, humiliation) in the image of Christ. It is this '*kenosis*' (humiliation) that moves the history of salvation forward – it is a difficult path. On the other hand, joy in God and adoration (even the Qur'an).

'Papa e il diavolo' (on Paul VI) Luther

'*Il Papa e il diavolo*' – *determina storia di salvezza* ['The Pope and the devil' – determines the history of salvation]. (Luther: The Commentary on the Magnificat.)
- Mary shows that true joy lies in that with which we contribute to the history of salvation.

[Reading:] (Kasper, *Jésus le Christ*, and others)
Rosary (III); Eucharistic Adoration and Benediction; Concluding meditation; Compline

12 March

Intentions
Morning meditation: '*Humiliamini Deo . . .*' ['Humble yourselves before the Lord . . .'].[3] '*Subditi estote Deo, resistite diabolo et fugiet a vobis*' ['Submit yourselves to God, resist the devil and he will flee from you'] (James 4).[4] (Cf. Talk 13.)

1 See John 8:32.
2 See Genesis 3:15.
3 See James 4:10.
4 See James 4:7.

Holy Mass; Prayers
[Reading:] *Regimini Ecclesiae universae*[1]
Lauds

Talk 14: *Anti-testimonianza*: Anti-testimony.
Sin is an anti-testimony!

- The tablets with the Ten Commandments (broken by Moses): the law bestowed on human nature. Then the law of the Gospel: 'I am the Lord your God, who brought you out of the land of Egypt, out of the house of bondage'.[2] The sin against truth and justice: God has fundamental rights in relation to the creation, to man: 'The Charter of God's Rights'! 'The sin of the world'.

Question: Do I understand my service at the Holy See as the defence of the divine law? The law of the Creator and Redeemer.

- If sin is an anti-testimony, then the sin of the priest – whom Christ calls to a special 'friendship' with Him – is such an anti-testimony in a particular way ('*abysso*' ['abyss']).
- Sin – an anti-testimony against life, the supernatural organism of grace. In particular, the sin of the priest who is supposed to serve this life!

St John Vianney
St John Bosco

- Sin violates the dignity of the human person. Through grace, man is the temple of the Holy Spirit. Sin destroys this temple. Through sin, man renounces the dignity of the Son of God. Sin 'diminishes' man.
- The social aspect of sin: It hurts the Church as a community. In particular the priest's sin.

Passion according to John
The love of God the Father, the grace of the Lord Jesus Christ, *comunione dello Spirito Santo* [the fellowship of the Holy Spirit]
Reflection; Terce

---

1 The apostolic constitution *Regimini Ecclesiae universae* (Government of the Universal Church) was issued by Pope Paul VI on 15 August 1967.
2 See Exodus 20:2.

Talk 15: The testimony of the confessional.

Pater [Father]

(Let all the confessionals speak, especially those that have been deserted by confessors and penitents.)

don Orione

- God–Father is waiting. Confession: mortal sins, venial sins (Pius XII's words). The apostles of all times have drawn their strength to evangelise from frequent confession. Maybe this is why today there is a shortage of great apostles. *Dire tutto al confessore* [To tell the confessor everything].
- Confession is the source of happiness and joy.

Card. Tisserant's Testament

Filius [Son]

Camus

Augustine: *vulnera Xristi merita mea!* [the wounds of Christ are my wages!] Tisserant: Christ has suffered so much for us. The confessional is a witness to the mercy of our Lord Jesus Christ. We need to seek this mercy and holiness! 'God who did not spare His own Son but gave Him up for me . . . will He not also give us all things with Him?' (St Paul).[1]

Comunione dello Spirito [Communion in the Holy Spirit]

- The special work that the Holy Spirit does in the sacrament of penance.

The retreat is a time to seek the 'idol' that prevents us from entering communion with God.

Servant of God Jan Balicki

- Particular gratitude for every confession, especially retreat confessions!

Concluding meditation; The Way of the Cross; Sext; None; *Angelus*; Adoration of the Blessed Sacrament; Rosary (II), (III)
[Reading:] *Marialis cultus*[2]
Vespers

'Life without the key'

Talk 16: *Testimonianza delle chiavi* [The testimony of the keys].

- Revelation: 'I have the keys . . .' '*Non temere, Io tengo le chiavi*' ['Fear not, I hold the keys'].[3]
- Christ shares these 'keys' of the kingdom of heaven, the power to bind and loose with Peter; He shares it with the Church.[4]

Card. Ottaviani

- The keys of knowledge: from the preaching of the Gospel,

1 See Romans 8:32.
2 See n. 3, p. 177 [11 March 1981].
3 See Revelation 1:17–18.
4 See Matthew 16:19.

as long as it is preached fully, without omissions and distortions. People have the right to such preaching. The responsibility of theologians. Bishops, in communion with Peter's successor, are responsible for such preaching of the Gospel (*carisma della verità* [the charisma of truth]). This is a kind of '*ananke*', *determinatio* ['necessity', destiny]; 'woe to me if I do not preach the gospel'.[1]

- The keys of power. The power in the Church comes entirely from Christ: *potestas ordinis* [the power conferred by holy orders] – *potestas iurisdictionis* [the power of jurisdiction]. This is a paternal power, its nature is that of service, but it nevertheless still remains a power. The contemporary Church has a special need for this power.

Bismarck
German bishops
Pius IX

- The power of bishops comes from Petrine primacy: Christ gives the keys to Peter, some mosaics portray Peter offering the keys to Christ (*testimonianza delle chiavi!* [the testimony of the keys!]).
  St Boniface: *Ecclesia non est derelinquenda sed regenda* [the Church is not to be abandoned but to be controlled].[2]
  Veritas fatigari potest, sed vinci et falli non potest [The truth can be impeded, but it cannot be conquered nor deceived].
- The keys of power entail a burden! (*iugum* [yoke])

Anticipated Matins; *Veni Sancte Spiritus* [Come, Holy Spirit]

Talk 17: *Maria – Testimone della famiglia* [Mary – Witness of the family]

- *Familia*/Family. The mystery of God: *creda alla famiglia!* [believe in the family!]

  The charter of God's rights in the family. Sacrament. The lack of faith is the primary cause of the crisis of the family.

  Maria – testim. della f. Nazaret [Mary – the witness of the family from Nazareth] – Mary builds her family seeking Christ. In this way She enters more deeply into the mystery of His Father.

Faber
Card. Ottaviani

  Family: the mystery of God in Christ and in the Church.

1 See 1 Corinthians 9:16.
2 See n. 4, p. 92.

- *Maria – testimone della famiglia umana* [Mary – the witness of the human family]. Cana of Galilee: the sixth word of Mary in the Gospel ('they have no wine').[1] 'O woman', my hour has not yet come.[2] Likewise on the cross: 'Woman, behold, your son'.[3]

  Mater hospitalitatis [Mother of hospitality] [illegible]: She says to everyone: 'do whatever my Son tells you'.[4] Let our workplace be also our family.

Card. Bacci Ratzinger

- The image of the Mother belongs to the common treasury of European culture.

The Mother of the Church: *testimone dell'intera famiglia umana* [the witness of the entire human family].
We glorify God when we are witnesses to the family following Mary's example.

Rosary (I); Eucharistic Adoration and Benediction; Holy Hour; Compline
[Reading:] Kasper, *Jésus le Christ*; *Communio*;[5] and others

13 March

Intentions
Morning meditation: '*Erit vobis sanguis in signum . . . iustificavit Ipse iustus . . .*' ['The blood shall be a sign for you . . . the righteous one shall make many to be accounted righteous . . .'][6]
[Reading:] (*Regimini* and others)
Holy Mass; Prayers; Lauds

Talk 18: Bearing witness with prayer.

J. Bielatowicz

- One cannot be a witness to Christ without prayer. Christ brought the hymn of glory sung by heaven to earth – Christ prayed all the time.
- *Christus oratur a nobis ut Deus noster, orat pro nobis ut . . . orat in nobis ut caput nostrum* [We pray to Christ as our God, Christ prays for us (as our Priest) and He prays in us as our head] (Augustine).[7]

1 See John 2:3.
2 See John 2:4.
3 See John 19:26.
4 See John 2:5.
5 *Communio* is an international journal of theology. It was founded in 1972 by Hans Urs von Balthasar, Henri de Lubac and Joseph Ratzinger.
6 See Exodus 12:13 and Isaiah 53:11.
7 See Saint Augustine, 'Exposition of Psalm 85', in *Expositions of the Psalms*, vol. 4, trans. Maria Boulding, ed. John E. Rotelle (New York, 2002), pp. 220–45.

- This refers in particular to the breviary: *anamnesi di Gesù tramite le ore! Celebrazione dell'opera salvifica di Cristo* [remembering Jesus through the liturgy of hours! The celebration of Christ's work of salvation]. (The breviary) should be prayed *come testimonianza (a) del largo cuore* [as a testimony (a) of a great heart]. It is a prayer that is important for the whole Church.
  (b) The breviary should be *testimonianza della preghiera comunitaria* [a testimony of the communal prayer]. Christ and the entire Church pray with us. The theology of prayer groups – their meaning in the Church. The breviary is the source of our sanctification and apostolate (*'sub gravi!'* ['under the pain of mortal sin!']). The future of the Church depends on it.
  (c) The breviary should be *testimonianza della preghiera incessante* [a testimony of unceasing prayer]. [How to pray 'always'?] . . . *continua* [continuous].
- If we pray like this (the breviary) – at some point our prayer will become the eternal heavenly liturgy.

Good Friday; Reflection; Rosary (II) – part

Talk 19: The testimony of conscience (*sacrarium della coscienza* [the sanctuary of conscience]).

- *G[audium et] S[pes]* on conscience. It was possible to break the tables of the law. It is not possible to 'break' conscience. It resounds with God's voice. *Pedagogia divina* [Divine teaching]: conscience is in communion with the law, with grace, with glory.

Förster

- Man discovers the law in his conscience. *Non autonoma sed theonoma* [Not autonomic but theonomic]. Conscience should be raised by the Church. The Holy See. Not only is conscience the voice of God in man, it is also a dialogue with God.
- The greatest tragedy of man is not to acknowledge sin (*agnoscamus peccata* . . . [let us acknowledge our sins . . .]). Hence the examination of conscience. Through such an examination, our conscience becomes the sanctuary of our returns (like the prodigal son).

St Jerome

6, Konf. XIX Świadectwo sumienia = (sacrario della coscienza)

– GS – o sumieniu). Tablice dekalogu można było rozbić. Sumienia „rozbić" nie można. Rozbrzmiewa w nim głos Boży. Pedagogia divina: Sumienie jest zjednoczone z Prawem, z Łaską, z Chrystusem –

Förster

– wszystko to sumienie odbiera w prawo (non autonoma sed theonoma) sumienie ma być wychowywane przez Kościół. Stolica Apost. Sumienie nie jest tylko głosem Boga w człowieku – jest także dialogiem z Bogiem

– największa tragedia człowieka jest nie uznawać grzechu (agnoscimus peccata ...) Stąd rachunek sumienia. Poprzez taki rachunek sumienia staje się sanktuarium naszych powrotów (jak syn marnotr.)

św. Hier.

– Znakiem postępu jest wrażliwość na (zaniedbane) opuszczenia (zaniedbania, p. omissiones)

– w sumieniu człowiek spotyka Boga mówiąc o swych przewinieniach (dostrzec): co innego występuje „contra tales et talia" pora świadectwem dobrego sumienia

– sumienie kapłańskie jest szczeg. sanktuarium, w którym Bóg mówi takie rzeczy, których nie mówi gdzie indziej – ale to też pociąga szczególną odpowiedzialność.

6a Meditatio synthetica

7. [Via Crucis] → L. 18[15]

8. ~~Tertia~~ Sexta, Nona, Ang.

9. Ador. Euch. (z Ojcem)

10. Cor. Ros (I, III) – II)

11. Vesp.

12. Konf. XX Świadectwo Kościoła

Vis corpus Christi aedificare? ama — Paulus VI

– Trzeba budować Kościół jeden: jedność Kościoła buduje się przede wszystkim na kolanach! Służba Kościołowi jedynym jest źródłem szczęścia!

– Trzeba budować Kościół święty (sancta): świętość Kościoła buduje się przez [illegible] na ziemi. Sancta et semper purificanda. Sposa amata di Cristo e madre dei peccatori. Kościół jest święty, choć jest [illegible] naszych słabości.

– Trzeba budować Kościół powszechny (universalis): jest powszechny, gdyż [illegible] Chrystus swoją moc [illegible], zbawczą – jest nie powszechny, chociaż się rozrósł bardzo i z trudem. „Reszta" eschatologiczna. „Reszta" wybrana przez Łaskę. Jest powszechny Kościół ponieważ pracuje dla wiecznego zbawienia wszystkich.

APPUNTAMENTI

Powszechność Kościoła ma swój wymiar eschatologiczny i kosmiczny

pytanie: czy budujesz Kościół katolicko??

– Trzeba budować Kościół apostolski: dzięki apostołom zaczął się w dniu Zielonych Świąt i trwa z pokolenia do końca świata. Służbę Kościołowi traktować jako wszystko ofiarowany przez Chrystusa Apostołom.

- Sensitivity to (culpable) omission (failure) (*p. omissionis* [the sin of omission]) is a sign of progress.

St Pius X
chi lo sa?
[who knows this?]

- In his conscience man, under God's eyes, decides on his destiny (*destini*): What else will there be left '*contra tales et talia*' ['in the face of this and suchlike'] apart from the witness of good conscience?
- Priestly conscience is a special sanctuary in which God speaks words that He does not speak elsewhere – but this also entails a special responsibility.

Concluding meditation
(The Way of the Cross) → 6.15 p.m.
Sext; None; Angelus; Eucharistic Adoration (seven words); Rosary (I), (III), (II); Vespers

Marialis cultus
[Devotion to Mary]

Talk 20: The testimony of the Church.
vis Corpus Christi aedificare? [Do you want to build the Body of Christ?] Paul VI.

- We have to build one (*una*) Church: The unity of the Church is built, above all, on one's knees! Service to the one Church is a source of happiness!

Card. Tisserant's Testament

- We have to build a holy (*sancta*) Church: The holiness of the Church is already being built here on earth. *Sancta et semper purificanda* [Holy and always in need of being purified].[1] *Sposa santa di Cristo Madre dei peccatori* [Holy Bride of Christ, Mother of sinners]. The Church is holy despite all our weaknesses.
- We have to build a catholic (*universalis*) Church: It is catholic because Christ acts in it with His messianic power of salvation; it is catholic even though it grows slowly and with difficulties. The eschatological 'remnant'. The 'remnant' chosen by grace.[2] The Church is catholic because it works for the eternal salvation of all.

  The catholicity of the Church has its eschatological and cosmic dimension.

  Question: Am I building the Church in a 'catholic' way?

Fr Misiałowicz
parish priest from
Brzozów (17th c.)

Augustine
Card. Newman

- We have to build an apostolic Church: The Acts of the

1 See *Lumen gentium*, chapter I.
2 See Isaiah 10:22–23.

Apostles began on the day of Pentecost and, in a sense, will last until the end of the world.

To perceive the service to the Church as a holy gift given by Christ to the apostles.

Pius IX: the fifth attribute – the Church is 'persecuted'!

The testimony of the Church is always the sun to humankind because the Church shines with the light of Christ Himself.

Reflection; Anticipated Matins

The Way of the Cross (*oratio ad S. Spiritum* [prayer to the Holy Spirit]) (21)

I – Is the work of redemption more delightful to me than any other earthly work? Let it absorb me ever more!

II – Do bishops' and priests' sins not make Christ's cross heavier than others' sins? Let every Mass bring a conversion.

III – *Copiosa apud Eum redemptio* [With Him is plenteous redemption]![1] Is our love for Christ '*copiosa*' ['plenteous']? Especially when *peccata omissionis* [sins of omission] are considered! Let me never commit them again!

Reflections on the Eucharistic liturgy

IV – Who can explain the degree of Mary's Eucharistic contemplation? And my Eucharistic contemplation during the Holy Mass – Mother, help me!

V – Who should be the Simon of Cyrene more than the priest? Hence: every Holy Mass should be a fervent Eucharistic prayer. Lord, make it happen!

VI – The Veil of Veronica: a sign of dialogue between Christ and a soul redeemed by Him. The priest ought to show the spirit of compensation, atonement: especially during the Holy Mass.

VII – '*ex Tua largitate*' ['from Your bounty'] – here in this bread: body; in wine: blood. Am I '*hilaris dator*' ['a cheerful giver']? In the service of the Lord and my brothers? Jesus, let me be one!

VIII – *Parola del Signore* [The word of the Lord]. Do I love the word of God? Do I live it out? Do I share it willingly? – Lord, help me live by Your word!

IX – Jesus falls for the third time for the priests who celebrate

1 See Psalm 129 (130):7.

the Eucharist and receive the body and blood of the Lord in the state of mortal sin. Let me always be in communion with You.

X – *Victima pura – sancta – immaculata* [Pure – holy – immaculate victim]. Therefore He requires His priests to have *indivisum cor* [an undivided heart] (celibacy) – and He demands priestly chastity. Jesus, help me!

XI – When He was being nailed to the cross, Christ was obedient to the Holy Spirit: on the cross and in the Eucharist. Am I obedient to the Holy Spirit living in the Church? Let me be ready to make any sacrifice!

XII – Man: the priest of the universe. To convert the world to God, not to be converted to the world. Let me celebrate the sacrifice on the altar of the world, while mortifying the world within myself.

XIII – Mary takes Christ in Her arms for the sake of people, for the sake of the Church. Do I celebrate the Eucharist in this spirit? Mother, I ask you to help me with this!

XIV – *Pascha nostrum* [Our Passover]. If we die with Christ, together with Christ we will be glorified in resurrection.[1] Lord, let me find paschal joy in the Holy Mass among the problems of everyday life.

Final prayer to the Holy Spirit; Eucharistic Adoration and Benediction; Concluding meditation; Compline

14 March

Intentions; Morning meditation: '*Vivo Ego – nolo mortem peccatoris*' ['As I live – I do not want the death of the wicked'][2]
Holy Mass; Prayers; Lauds

Final talk: *Testimone fedele* – (Faithful witness).

- For I have come into the world to bear witness to the truth. Everyone who is of the truth hears my voice.[3] Every man, in particular the priest, comes into the world for this reason.
- Christ: Amen = yes (not 'yes' and 'no', but 'yes').

  Contemporary man has a special need for this 'amen'

1 See Romans 6:5.
2 See Ezekiel 33:11.
3 See John 18:37.

– 'yes'. No one can offer certainty that they do not have. Christ is the 'rock' (God is the 'rock'). The 'schizophrenic' of the twentieth century (Miłosz[1]) needs the 'amen', the 'rock'.

Miłosz

- Christ, the faithful witness, began His way with faithful witnesses who were ready to die. (St Thomas More.)
- What can be greater than to hear the words 'my faithful witness' from Christ! (Revelation). For the price of 'white' or 'red' martyrdom.
- We are to follow Christ, the faithful witness – and, as faithful witnesses, lead others in His steps.

John XXIII
[illegible]

Thankgiving; Blessing; Magnificat
AMDG /UIOGD[2]

1 Czesław Miłosz (1911–2004) was a Polish poet, prose writer and translator. In 1980 he was awarded the Nobel Prize in Literature. In the poem *Treatise on Morals* (1947), he referred to 'contemporary schizophrenia' as a 'feeling that my deeds / are not done by me, but somebody else'.

2 See p. xxi.

28 February – 6 March 1982
Retreat in St Matilda's Chapel
Led by Prof. S[tanislas] Lyonnet SJ[1]

28 February Vespers; *Veni Creator* [Come, Creator (Spirit)]

Talk 1 (Introduction):

(a) St Paul.

(b) John XXIII's 100th birthday[2] – '*exercitia spir.*' ['Spiritual Exercises'] of St Ignatius.
Journal of a Soul:[3] it is possible to see how John XXIII prepared – or rather was being prepared by the Holy Spirit – through the school of St Ignatius, for great tasks: above all the Council – the greatest event of our century. The sense of one's littleness – an instrument in God's hands – open to the inspirations of the Holy Spirit.

(c) The spirit of this retreat should be in accordance with this, and we need to ask for this grace.

Adoration of the Blessed Sacrament; Anticipated Matins; Meditation; Adoration; Rosary (III); Compline

1 March Intentions
Morning meditation: '*assumam vos mihi in populum, et ero vester Deus: aliquando non populus, nunc autem populus Dei*' ['I will take you for my people, and I will be your God: once you were no people but now you are God's people'][4]
Holy Mass; Prayers; Lauds

Meditation 2 (Talk): The presence of God is constitutive of the retreat.

This is the same God in whom Paul believed

The presence of God in prayer and through prayer.
God: God of revelation: God of existence.

---

1 Stanislas Lyonnet SJ (1902–86) was a theologian, Bible scholar and linguist. He lectured at the Jesuit Institute of Lyon-Fourvière and in 1942 was appointed professor at the Pontifical Biblical Institute in Rome.
2 Pope John XXIII was born on 25 November 1881.
3 Giovanni XXIII, *Il giornale dell'anima* (Rome, 1964); English edition: Pope John XXIII, *Journal of a Soul*, trans. Dorothy White (Westminster, MD, 1965).
4 See Exodus 6:7 and 1 Peter 2:10.

In the Old Testament: the revelation to Moses 'in the burning bush' – 'I Am'!!![1] Yahweh – He does not give His Name(!) – He is revealed in being and action as mercy (*Rahamim*) = 'motherly' goodness – Father the Shepherd (Ezekiel 34) – Bridegroom –

God, who is near, enters into friendship (Vatican II, *D[ei] V[erbum]*),[2] enters into communion (Ignatius): adoration, thanksgiving, worship.

Complementary meditation:

(a) God reveals His closeness. He comes to meet us. He wishes to enter into communion . . .

At the same time: communion through the 'night' (St John of the Cross). In this 'darkness' there is closeness, the growing closeness of Him who Is.

(b) God: Abraham = He who Is, and the God of our fathers, the God of our faith (how all these spheres are related: Israel – Christianity – Islam, and all these to the 'religions' of the Far East, and to 'atheism').

Terce

Meditation 3 (Talk): *Benedictus Pater Domini nostri Jesu Xristi* [Blessed be the Father of our Lord Jesus Christ].[3]

'*Paternità*' [Fatherhood] – the New Testament – completely new concepts and dimensions (obviously this is different from 'Jupiter': '*paternità*' in the naturalistic sense of pagan religion) – precisely for this reason the Old Testament avoided calling God the Father directly; at most: 'like father, like mother', Father, Lord of heaven and earth . . .[4] Jesus spoke to God in this way, in accordance with the Old Testament tradition, and straight afterwards: **Yes. Father!**

For the first time! Everything comes from You; and no one knows the Father except the Son, and no one knows the Son

1 See Exodus 3:14.

2 *Dei verbum* (The Word of God), the Second Vatican Council's Dogmatic Constitution on Divine Revelation, was promulgated by Pope Paul VI on 18 November 1965.

3 See 2 Corinthians 1:3.

4 See Matthew 11:25 and Luke 10:21.

4a [Medit. compl.]

a) Bóg objawia swoją bliskość. Wychodzi na spotkanie. Pragnie obcować...
Równocześnie: obcowanie przez owe „Jan od †" = w tej „ciemności" jest właśnie bliskość, następująca bliskość Tego, który Jest.

b) Bóg: Abrahama = Ten, który jest i Bóg ojców, Bóg naszych czasów
jak nawiązuje się do wiary Abrahama: Izrael – chrześcijaństwo – islam // a to wszystko razem do „religie" Bł. Człowieka // oraz do „ateizmu"

5. Tertia

6. III Medit. (konf): Benedictus Pater Domini nostri Jesu Christi

„Ojcostwo" – N. Test. – zupełnie nowy przełom i wymiar [oczywiście jest to całkiem coś innego niż „Jupiter": „pater noster" w znaczeniu naturalistycznym w religii pogańskiej] – właśnie etap powstaje St. Testament nie tak nazywanie Boga swoim Ojcem // wyjątki: „jak ojciec, jak matka" / „Ojcze, Panie nieba i ziemi"... tak Jezus zwraca się z tradycji St. Test, a zaraz potem: [Tak, Ojcze!] bo tak podobało się! ... wszystko jest od Ciebie; i nikt nie zna Ojca jeno Syn, ani Syna nikt nie zna tylko Ojciec [to tekst synopt. – a równocześnie: Jan niczego nie dodał do tego: jest cały Jan]

i ten, komu Syn zechce objawić

I odtąd stale w ustach Jezusa aż do Ogrójca, Golgoty...

Stąd: filii per Filium → per naturam
→ per gratiam

filii (filiatio adoptiva) – bo Chrystus daje nam udział w swoim życiu Syna: tchnienie b. wiele! ojcowskość między nami a Chrystusem więź, która może być tylko porównana do więzi Trynitarnej

APPUNTAMENTI

[Dobry Pasterz, / winorośl „eucharystii" / krzew winny – latorośle i inne]

6a {Via Crucis
medit. compl. ad 6.

7. [Sexta, Nona]

[Praca apost.: przygot.]

except the Father.[1] (This is a synoptic text – and at the same time: John did not add anything: so typical of John.)

And since then the word is constantly on Jesus' lips until Gethsemane, until Golgotha . . .

and anyone to whom the Son chooses to reveal

Hence: *filii per Filium* [sons through the Son].

↓ ↓

per naturam [through nature]

per gratiam [through grace]

filii – (*filiatio adoptiva*) [sons – (adopted sonship)] because Christ grants us participation in the Son's life: there are many texts!

↘

(The Good Shepherd, the 'Eucharistic' speech,
the true vine – the branches, and others.)

There is a bond between Christ and us that can be compared only to the Trinitarian bond.

The Way of the Cross; Complementary meditation on Talk 3; Sext; None; (Apostolic work: preparation); Rosary (II), (III); Litany of the Holy Name of Jesus; Litany of the Polish Nation; Eucharistic Adoration (Meditation 3 continued); Vespers

Meditation 4 (Talk):

St Ignatius (John XXIII): *sacra indifferentia* [holy indifference] – this is an attachment to the holy will of God – the spirit of the Beatitudes – the joy of the Holy Spirit.

Bergson
[illegible]
Chesterton

On the other hand: care to prepare for spiritual struggle, etc. – the principle of using goods, making use of them in freedom.

Solution: not in possession – but in donation (cf. *G[audium et] S[pes]* 25).[2]

Garaudy
de Foucault

[The solution does not lie in the transfer of 'possession' to eternal life: not here – but 'there' – even though there is a basis for this in the biblical and liturgical language.]

Sacra indifferenza [Holy indifference] – the basic condition of our spiritual and apostolic life.

1 See Matthew 11:27, Luke 10:22, and John 10:15.

2 *Gaudium et spes* (Joy and Hope), the Second Vatican Council's Pastoral Constitution on the Church in the Modern World, was promulgated by Pope Paul VI on 7 December 1965.

Anticipated Matins

Meditation 5 (Talk): Genesis 1–11: prehistory.

History: begins with Abraham!

It begins in this spirit: (*sacra indiff.* [holy indifference]): call – promise, God's initiative – Abraham's faith: the words '*credere* – to believe' and '*iustitia* – justice' appear for the first time in the Bible.[1] Isaac – the son of the promise; the trial of Abraham's faith: so that he trusts God Himself.

(*adorare* [to adore] = to let God give man whatever He wants)

(*credere* [to believe] = *pisteuein* = to make certain, constant)

↓ ↘ Through the act of faith man opens up to God's action.

Man '*si abbandona*' ['surrenders himself'] = surrenders himself to God.

Rosary (I); Eucharistic devotion

Concluding meditation (revision and expansion of the afternoon topics, which can be brought together with the topic of '*fides*' ['faith']. In the morning: '*Deus*' ['God'] – in the afternoon: '*fides*' ['faith'])

Compline; Thanksgiving

2 March

Morning prayer intention

Meditation: I return to yesterday's reflections again: God, faith

Holy Mass; Prayers; Lauds

Meditation 6 (Talk):

According to St Ignatius: 'man' – 'sinner'. God – when He wants to allow man to come particularly close to Him – lets him recognise his own degradation.

Analysis of sin in Genesis 3: Above all, sin consists in an inner attitude, 'like gods'.[2] The Tempter wants to make us doubt God's 'honesty' and love. God is 'jealous' of man. In this way sin 'removes' man from God: God does not push man away; man moves away. As a consequence, man → against man: man – woman, brother – brother; egoism (hatred).

St Paul. Romans: 'I see in my members another law . . .'[3]

Sin: offence to God (*disprezzo di Dio, in quanto ci dona lo Spirito Santo* [contempt of God, as [He] gives us the Holy

1 See Genesis 15:6.

2 See Genesis 3:5.

3 See Romans 7:23.

Spirit]) – *universalità del peccato* [the universality of sin] – hence: everyone may sin: commit the sin that others have committed.

St Ignatius: shows the Crucified One: let us give thanks!

Meditation (complementary): *peccatum* [sin] – *peccatum originale* [original sin] – *peccata mundi* [the sins of the world]
Litany of the Sacred Heart of Jesus, Blessed Virgin Mary, St Joseph

Meditation 7 (Talk):

Sin: how could God allow this? Pauline subject – in particular: the sin of the chosen people: Israel (Romans!): analysis!

Romans, exegesis!

Three chapters:[1] The Gentiles received mercy 'thanks to' the disobedience of Israel, their unfaithfulness.

Thus: unfaithfulness may be used by God! The essence of Israel's unfaithfulness consisted in their feeling of 'self-sufficiency', in the feeling of 'justice' (– here a digression: Job!) . . . Jonah . . .

This is Paul's theology of history.

God enclosed everything in disobedience in order to show mercy to all!

Divine goodness: in delivering us from sin, in forgiving us our sins (Augustine, Thérèse of the Child Jesus[2]).

Abisso della misericordia [The abyss of mercy].

The Way of the Cross; Complementary meditation on Talks 6 and 7; Sext; None; *Angelus*; Passion according to Mark; Apostolic work: preparation; Rosary (III), (I); Litany of the Polish Nation; Adoration of the Blessed Sacrament; Vespers

Meditation 8 (Talk):

Following St Ignatius: '*Regnum Christi*' ['Kingdom of Christ'].

According to the Gospel ↘	According to St Paul
Servant of God John XXIII	→ great harvest ↙
	until He has put all His enemies under His feet – that God may be everything to everyone[3]

1 See Romans 9–11.
2 St Thérèse of the Child Jesus (1873–97) was a French Discalced Carmelite nun. Also known as Thérèse of Lisieux and the Little Flower, she was canonised by Pope Pius XI in 1925.
3 See 1 Corinthians 15:25–28.

This kingdom is the work of Christ, His '*impresa*' ['undertaking'] – it is a task, an undertaking to which Christ calls us. He calls for our collaboration, calls us to put it into practice – He calls, always respecting human freedom: 'follow Me'[1] – this was (and is) a call to a difficult life too, to an often ungrateful mission, to suffering – and all this is motivated by love (!)

John XXIII's prayer, which he repeated after St Ignatius every day (analysis!).

A letter of the missionary I.J.[2] – a martyr among the Iroquois, as the fruit of the meditation '*de Regno*' ['on the Kingdom'].

Anticipated Matins

Meditation 9 (Talk):

Love that descends: this is the Bible: the Old and the New Testament – complete novelty in relation to Greek thought (the love described there only 'ascends'). This is '*Incarnatio*' – incarnation as the subject of St Ignatius's *exer. spir.* [Spiritual Exercises]. Secondly: the Most Holy Trinity's work for the salvation of man. Although man, humankind, does not think of this salvation.

God becomes man so that man – humankind – in Him could return to God. The masterpiece of love: He became one of us and assumed human nature after the fall!

He becomes man by our human consent (Mary! *fiat!* [let it be!]) – a new 'gentle' trait of this love.

St Bernard's words: *Totus mundus exspectat!* [The whole world is waiting!]

Gratitude to the Most Holy Trinity; gratitude to Mary, the Mother of Christ and our Mother.

Rosary (II); Litany of the Blessed Virgin Mary; Celebration – Eucharistic Adoration; Concluding meditation (synthesis of Meditations 8 and 9); Compline (thanksgiving)

3 March

Daily intention; (Morning prayers)
Meditation

1 See Mark 2:14.

2 This is probably a reference to St Isaac Jogues SJ (1607–46), a Jesuit priest, missionary and martyr who worked among the Iroquois and other Native populations in North America. For a comprehensive bibliography of his letters and writings, see Francis Talbot, *Saint Among Savages: The Life of Saint Isaac Jogues* (San Francisco, 2002), pp. 453–4.

[*'Dabo legem meam . . . in tabulis cordis carnalibus . . . superscribam eas non atramento, sed Spiritu Dei vivi'* ['I will write my law . . . on tablets of human hearts . . . not with ink but with the Spirit of the living God'].[1] In relation to yesterday's afternoon reflection.]

Holy Mass; Thanksgiving; Prayers; Lauds

Claudel, *L'Otage* [The Hostage]

Meditation 10 (Talk): *O admirabile commercium* [O wonderful exchange!] – the way in which God's gift is given. (*Modus*): *modus sponsalitius* [(Mode): nuptial mode] – matrimony – mutual gift! This is precisely what happens in the incarnation – and in the entire salvific economy: this is what is '*novum*' ['new'] about the New Testament – what is fundamentally *novum*.

Significant words on Christ–Judas

Christ becomes the Bridegroom and spouse of the Church – and of man, in order to save him with the gift of His divinity, His redemption.

Passion of Our Lord Jesus Christ according to Matthew

Christ loved with the truest love, accepting that which is human (*divinum–humanum*) [divine–human]!

– '*Verbum caro factum est*' ['The Word became flesh'].[2]

– the secret: love.

Complementary meditation: 'redemptive' love, 'redeem' (buy back) – and at the same time, it is a 'gift' and it is mutual
Litany of the Holy Name of Jesus

Meditation 11 (Talk):

- *BV Maria: fide credidit, fide concepit – fide!* [Blessed Virgin Mary: through Her faith She believed, through Her faith She conceived – through Her faith!]

  The circumstances of the Nativity – utter poverty, there was no place for them in the inn:[3] God seemed not to have cared about the way in which His Son was born on earth – the manger: how are we to reconcile this with the messianic expectation of the 'King'?
- Further 'paradoxes': Simeon's prophecy: 'for the falling and

1 See Jeremiah 31:33 and 2 Corinthians 3:3.
2 See John 1:14.
3 See Luke 2:7.

the rising of many'. . . a sword will pierce through your own soul.[1]

- Faith: a re-evaluation of all human values: at the end God's power is revealed (Nietzsche).
- Continuation: the escape to Egypt.

  For Mary all this was the first sign that this Child did not belong to Her(!) – He belongs to all(!)
- Cont. 'the finding of the twelve-year-old Jesus' ('*sposalizio di Dio e la mediocrità*' ['God's marriage with ordinariness']).

  Mary 'pondered all these things in her heart'[2] – let us ask Her to help us penetrate into the heart of this mystery. Mary experiences 'the night of faith'! (St Thérèse of the Child Jesus: not a curtain, but a wall) and in all this She 'surrendered Herself' (*abandono*) to God – like Abraham; She did so, above all, under the cross.

The Way of the Cross; Complementary meditation on Talks 11 and 10; Sext; None; *Angelus*; (Apostolic work: preparation); Rosary (I) (II); Litany of the Polish Nation; Adoration of the Blessed Sacrament

Meditation 12 (Talk): (*admirabile commercium* [wonderful exchange]).

St Ignatius: *meditatio: duo vexilla* [meditation: the two standards].[3] *Xristum Deum pro nobis tentatum . . . : nos tentati in Xristo – in Xristo viatores* [Christ God, who was tempted for our sake . . . : we, who are tempted in Christ – pilgrims in Christ]. The specific temptations that Christ had to face were messianic in nature. If Christ had met the conditions set by the tempter, He would have been considered the Messiah by His contemporaries; likewise in other situations (cf. Porphyry's and others' writings). Yet Jesus rejected this 'spectacular' mode of action in this situation (and in others).

- He rejects the means of external authority, omnipotence, importance, etc.

1 See Luke 2:34–35.

2 See Luke 2:19.

3 The meditation on the two standards is part of St Ignatius of Loyola's Spiritual Exercises. Its focus is a battle of two armies, one under Christ's standard and the other under Satan's.

- Why does He act like this? To show that He finds His source of power only in God Himself. (*abandono heroico* [heroic surrender]).

Anticipated Matins; Litany of the Saints

Meditation 13 (Talk):

Human means are acceptable, but we must not put all our trust and hope in them. We have to put them in the Holy Spirit: (*visum est Spiritui Sancto et nobis* [it has seemed to the Holy Spirit and to us]).[1] It was the same during Paul's travels – the initiative came always from the Holy Spirit – and it is so in the entire Acts of the Apostles: a series of initiatives of the Holy Spirit – '*avvinto dallo Spirito Santo*' ['bound in the Holy Spirit'][2] – with these words St Paul summarises his apostolic work, and any true apostolic work, very well.

According to St Ignatius, in order to find God's will:

- The first condition is '*indifferenza totale*' ['total indifference'].
- The second condition: prayer (Holy Mass) – to sacrifice our will to God so that He accepts and confirms it.

Seeking God's will (not only human solutions) in everything – this is the model of apostolic work.

This is very important for those who are to lead the Church.

Rosary (III); Celebration – Eucharistic Adoration; Concluding meditation: (in particular: synthesis of Talks 12 and 13); Litany of the Blessed Virgin Mary; Litany of St Joseph; Compline

4 March

Daily intention; Prayers
Meditation: *Ego transibo . . . est Transitus Domini (Pascha)* [I will pass . . . it is the Lord's Passover].[3] Exodus – retreat – situations;
Holy Mass; Prayers; Lauds

Meditation 14 (Talk):

St Paul: In order for God to act through His instrument, this instrument ought to have a sense of its weakness! (*ad Cor.* [Letter to the Corinthians]): First, he speaks about the weak-

1 See Acts 15:28.
2 See Acts 20:22.
3 See Exodus 12:11–12.

nesses he has experienced, about '*stimulus carnis . . . qui me colaphizet*' ['a thorn in the flesh . . . to harass me']:[1] Paul felt weak, lonely . . . And then the Lord told him (in relation to the great apostolic task in Corinth): My grace is sufficient for you(!)[2] Hence the famous words in the letter to the Corinthians: 'for I decided to know nothing among you except Jesus Christ'[3] – (different obstacles, in particular 'false brothers'[4]); 'The Lord gave me strength' . . . [5] the Gospel has been received . . . the Lord will liberate me, help me: Hope and trust in grace itself!

Complementary meditation:
'*Sufficit tibi gratia mea*' ['My grace is sufficient for you'][6] – this brings a lot of reflections and conclusions!! One could say that this is what the fundamental approach is, though (occasionally) there are splinters of other thoughts. Apart from this, there is the central problem of trust/resignation.

(Passion of Our Lord Jesus Christ according to Luke); Terce

Meditation 15 (Talk):
(Relating to different passages in St Ignatius: three degrees of humility and others.)

Desire to imitate Christ: reading different excerpts from the biography of St Ignatius – imitation in suffering and humiliation: the resistance of 'nature' – the supernatural 'motive' (imitation of Christ) – aim: the glory of God and salvation of souls.

Let us ask for the grace of loving our suffering, humiliations and crosses for the sake of Christ.

(Also on previous days: act of 'slavery');[7] Prayer for the gifts of the Holy Spirit; The Way of the Cross; Complementary meditation; Sext; None; *Angelus*; (Apostolic work: preparation); Rosary (III); Litany of the Blessed Virgin Mary; Litany of St Joseph; Litany of the Polish Nation; Adoration of the Blessed Sacrament (my grace is sufficient for you); Vespers

1 See 2 Corinthians 12:7.
2 See 2 Corinthians 12:9.
3 See 1 Corinthians 2:2.
4 See 2 Corinthians 11:26.
5 See 2 Timothy 4:17.
6 See 2 Corinthians 12:9.
7 See n. 4, p. 43 [21 December 1966].

Meditation 16 (Talk):

The Eucharist: It is an act of covenant in accordance with the tradition of the old covenant; therefore it also includes people's '*impegno*' (involvement): an active response! – the renewal of the covenant in Joshua's times (a great text when it comes to the conscious and free response of Israel)[1] – the whole liturgy should be understood against this background; in particular, the Holy Mass should be understood as 'participation' of the people of God(!)

We have a synthesis of the whole Bible, from the first words of the Book of Genesis to the last words of Revelation, in the Eucharist.

Complementary meditation: On the great significance of the covenant for the entire concept of religion – especially for Christianity: for Christian life, for Christian existence.

Meditation 17 (Talk):

The Eucharist – the covenant: 'new and everlasting covenant' – here a connection with Jeremiah: on the 'New' covenant, which is the law set out by God, yet not given 'externally', but as an inner gift of the Eucharist: in the place of the 'law' (Jeremiah) speaks of the 'Spirit'[2] –

In its essence the covenant is a 'gift of the law'.

- here: a commentary by St Thomas:
  Law – Spirit – Love
- here: a quotation from St Thérèse of the Child Jesus:
  The Eucharist – food: my love will be a source of strength for you, and without it you will not be able to love.

Rosary (I); Adoration and Eucharistic celebration; Penitential psalms; Holy Hour; (Rosary (II)); Compline; (Thanksgiving)

5 March

Daily intentions; Prayers
Meditation: ('*Judica causam meam; defende, quia potens es, Domine*' ['Plead my cause and redeem me; O Lord, for You are powerful'])[3]
Holy Mass, Prayers; (Thanksgiving); Lauds

1 See Joshua 24:1–28.
2 See Jeremiah 31:31–33.
3 See Psalm 118 (119):154.

Meditation 18 (Talk):

The agony of Jesus: the things that precede the agony – and the agony itself.

First Friday.

(John): before: In the 'speech' at the Last Supper Christ speaks about His unity with the Father, about the glory that He has been given by the Father at the beginning. He says: 'I desire' that they may be with me where I am.[1] This happens before the agony – and then, during the agony: 'My soul is very sorrowful, even to death'; 'remain here, and watch with me'; 'He fell on His face';[2] 'His sweat became like great drops of blood'.[3] Christ wants to share our human weakness until the very end. He speaks in a human way and shows His humanity, human weakness!! ('what I will' – not βούλομαι [to want to], but [θέλω (to be ready to, to wish)]).[4] (Pascal: Christ will be in agony even until the end of the world, we must not sleep during that time.)[5] The suffering of Jesus, the agony, *fiat* [let it be], is the strength of so many martyrs.

St Thérèse of the Child Jesus: To suffer with Jesus, to 'comfort' Jesus in His agony is to work towards salvation, towards the sanctification of souls: '*mihi fecistis*' ['you did it to me'].[6]

Service to the Sacred Heart of Jesus.

Passion of Our Lord Jesus Christ according to John

Complementary meditation: (one has to maintain and deepen the practice of being with Jesus in His agony: service to the Sacred Heart of Jesus – offered in reparation)
Terce

Meditation 19 (Talk):

Death – the highest revelation of love: Jesus' love for the Father, and the Father's love for the Son, and the Father and Son's love for man.

'To die' (to suffer death) and 'to give life' are two different things. Not only does Jesus suffer death from His enemies, but He gives life! Jesus' death was not only suffered, but also willed with a 'redemptive', 'atoning' intention.

1 See John 17:24.
2 See Matthew 26:38–39 and Mark 14:34–35.
3 See Luke 22:44.
4 See Mark 14:36.
5 Blaise Pascal, *Pensées*, Introduction by T. S. Eliot (New York, 1958), p. 148.
6 See Matthew 25:40.

There are many details showing that Jesus willingly chooses death (before He is arrested, He shows His power in front of Pilate).

The motivation for this choice is not '*in recto*' ['directly'] the sin itself – but His love for the Father, for humankind: '*pro nobis*', *pro me* ['for us', for me] (He gave Himself for us, for me).[1]

Jesus' death is an expression of the Father's love for humankind, an expression of His mercy: 'He who did not spare His own Son . . .'[2] '*tradidit*' ['gave over'] – at the same time: the Father's love for Christ (the Son): '*communicavit*' ['communicated'] His love to the Son – and 'entered into communion' with the Son in love.

Hence: to give life: '*comunicare con il Padre nell' Amore*' ['to commune with the Father in Love'].

Act of 'slavery';[3] Prayer for the gifts of the Holy Spirit; The Way of the Cross; (Continuation of Meditations 18 and 19); Sext; None; Angelus; (Apostolic work – preparation); Adoration of the Blessed Sacrament: seven words!; Rosary (III), (I); Litany of the Polish Nation; Vespers

Meditation 20 (Talk):

- Christ finds glory in the greatest destruction of the cross, the greatest display of (human) weakness. Hence constant references in the liturgy: *crux gloriosa!* [glorious cross!] etc. Many references.
- This tone of the Bible and liturgy can be explained by the fact that it is not about 'death', but about 'giving life out of love': *comunione con il Padre nell'amore* [communion with the Father in love].

Anticipated Matins; (Litany of the Sacred Heart of Jesus)

Meditation 21 (Talk):

- In the passion and death on the cross – the glorification of Christ (His glory).
- Yet everyone 'accepted' death as death and destruction.

  The only person who believes '*fide nuda*' ['with naked faith'] in the resurrection: the Mother of God. The whole

1 See Titus 2:14.

2 See Romans 8:32.

3 See n. 4, p. 43 [21 December 1966].

Church is in Her alone at that time(!) Mary's consolation is the knowledge that Jesus is happy in God. The state of the other people's souls: the apostles, enemies, Mary Magdalene – the disciples in Emmaus – all in the same state.

Women: Jesus makes them apostles to the apostles . . .

- And then: the Fact: all authority in heaven and on earth has been given to me . . . go, therefore, and make disciples of all nations.[1]
- *Christus est resuscitatus tamquam primitiae!* [Christ has been raised from the dead as the firstfruits!][2] We are all going to be raised from the dead in Him. The Mother of God has already seen it.
- One must never separate death from resurrection: It is one single mystery, one single key to the renewal of the world: *(novus) homo!* [(new) man!].

Rosary (II); (Prayers for Good Friday); Eucharistic celebration – adoration
Concluding meditation: synthesis of the day
Litany of the Blessed Virgin Mary; Litany of St Joseph; Compline; (Thanksgiving)

6 March[3]

Daily intentions; Prayers
Morning meditation: *Bonus est Dominus sperantibus in Eum, animae quaerenti Illum! Gloria Tibi Verbum Dei* [The Lord is good to those who wait for Him, to the soul that seeks Him! Glory to You, Word of God][4]
Holy Mass; Thanksgiving; Prayers; Lauds

Meditation 22 (Talk):

Solemnitas solemnitatum: [The solemnity of solemnities] [is] *Pentecoste* [Pentecost], which constitutes one single mystery with the Passover (Easter – Ascension). The 'law' written upon our hearts – with the Spirit of the Living God '*Digitus Paternae Dexterae*' ['Finger of the Divine Hand'].[5]

St Thomas: *Lex Nova = Spiritus S. (vel Ipse vel sua activitas in cordibus nostris, qua istam legem facit)* [the new law = the Holy Spirit (either He or His actions in our hearts, through

1 See Matthew 28:18–19.
2 See 1 Corinthians 15:23.
3 The final talk of the retreat was delivered by John Paul II. The full text (in Italian) is available at: https://w2.vatican.va/
4 See Lamentations 3:25.
5 See the hymn *Veni Creator Spiritus* (Come, Creator Spirit).

which He sets out the very law)]. Hence: *principaliter ipsa gratia* – (*in quantum gratia* – *iustificat*) – *secundarie: 'Littera'* – *Lex uti Littera.* ('*Littera*' *sola* '*occidit*', even if it were '*Littera*' (!) *N. Legis* itself) [most importantly, it is grace itself – (in so far as it is grace – which justifies) – secondly: the 'letter' – the law as the letter. (The 'letter' on its own 'kills', even if it were the 'letter' (!) of the new law itself)].[1]

Vatican II: '*maturitas christiana*': (*ubi Spiritus ibi libertas*) ['Christian maturity': (where the Spirit is, there is freedom)];[2] our task is to bring people up to this '*maturitas*' ['maturity'] – our contemporaries expect this. But: this is above all about God's actions! Not man's.

Final words; Blessing; Thanksgiving; *Salve Regina*
UIOGD[3]

1 See 2 Corinthians 3:6.
2 See 2 Corinthians 3:17.
3 See p. xxi.

20–26 February 1983
Retreat in St Matilda's Chapel
Led by Cardinal J[oseph] Ratzinger

20 February 6.00 p.m.; Vespers; *Veni Creator* [Come, Creator (Spirit)]

Introduction. Talk (1):

1. The baptism of Christ – 'led up into the wilderness'.[1] Wilderness – the place of the Absolute, the place of grace – the retreat ought to be a 'wilderness'.
2. The wilderness is the place of death – this is where temptations are born.
3. Going into the wilderness, Jesus enters the history of His people: their journey and temptations in the wilderness. Jesus – Moses. To convert is to enter into the history of the chosen people. The priests of today should make a pathway through the wilderness of contemporary times.

Eucharistic Adoration; Anticipated Matins

Meditation: 'Christ's Hour'[2] began with His baptism in the Jordan. His 'wilderness' lasted until the words 'my Father, why hast Thou forsaken Me?' spoken on the cross.[3]

Compline; Preparation; Reading: 'Pascha nostrum' [Our Passover]

21 February Daily morning prayer

Meditation: '*ut, per annua quadragesimalis exercitia sacramenti, et ad intelligendum Christi proficiamus arcanum, et effectus eius digna conversatione sectemur*' ['that through the yearly observances of holy Lent we may grow in understanding of the riches hidden in Christ and by worthy conduct pursue their effects'].[4]
Lauds

---

1 See Matthew 4:1.

2 See John 2:4.

3 See Mark 15:34.

4 See the Collect for the First Sunday of Lent.

Liturgical meditation (2): *Converte nos, Deus, salutaris noster* [Convert us, O God, our saviour].[1]

(a) *Converte! – convertimini!* – [Convert! – let all of you be converted!]

optio fundam. [fundamental option] → Rejection of self-fulfilment – in the sense of autonomy – '*avere*' ['to have']: acceptance of love – '*essere*' ['to be'] to allow God to form us.

(b) '*ut nobis opus quadragesimale proficiat*' ['that we may benefit from the works of Lent'].[2] Discipline is a condition of true progress.
– On the meaning of the 'Stations' of Lent.
Today: *S. Petri in vinculis!* [Feast of St Peter in chains!]:[3] prayer for all those who are persecuted for their faith.

(c) The reading explains more fully the continuation of the prayer '*mentes nostras coelestibus instrue disciplinis*' ['instruct our minds by the heavenly teaching'].[4]

Reflection: There is an evangelical sense in finding self-fulfilment in love and through love, 'whoever loses his life for my sake and the gospel's will save it'.[5]

(Matthew); Terce

Christological meditation (3):
'*descendit*' ['descended'] – unpopular word: (due to the idea of God, and also the idea of the 'cosmos' – but what is unpopular above all is 'in-equality').

– irreplaceable word: if God 'descends', what is 'low' becomes 'high' – but first there has to be 'highness': God's Majesty and His Reign over the entire creation.

'*descendit*': the descent of the Divine into the human
the descent of the reign onto the cross

1 See the Collect for Monday in the First Week of Lent.
2 See the Collect for Monday in the First Week of Lent.
3 See Acts 12:1–7.
4 See the Collect for Monday in the First Week of Lent.
5 See Mark 8:35.

'but a body hast Thou prepared for Me' (Hebr.):[1] 'obedience becomes incarnated'. Incarnation responds to the essence of the Son–Word in a special way.

The response to the Father is in this Word.

In this response we are to become the body of Christ. All this is contained in '*descendit de coelis*' ['descended from heaven'].

The Way of the Cross (on what has been said above); Sext; None; Preparation (suffering); Holy Mass; Thanksgiving; Adoration of the Blessed Sacrament; Rosary (II), (III); Vespers

Christological meditation (4):

Incarnatus est de Spiritu Sancto [(He) was incarnate by the Holy Spirit].

What does it mean that Jesus lived a human life as a child, as an adolescent, as an adult?

Child: He was incarnate of the Virgin and, at the same time, the human inheritance of Abraham and Adam. 'Childhood' has a special meaning in Christ's teaching: To be a child means to be able to say 'Father': the way to enter into divinity.

'The poor' – 'children' (a poor one – a child).

The Greeks: eternal children (Plato); admiration for reality – not technocracy.

To be a child means to be able to say 'Mother'. He learnt to say 'yes' to God from His Mother.

Nazareth. Family; home as the Church; hidden life. Work, poor and humble Church; the new covenant does not begin in the Temple, but in the manger and the house in Nazareth.

Vita publica [Public life] entails loneliness. Disappointment with one's friends. Loneliness with God.

(Anticipated) Matins; Litany of the Polish Nation

Christological meditation (5):

We return to *I Dom. Quadrag.* [First Sunday of Lent]: Temptation.

Christ and the Tempter use words from the Old Testament.

1 See Hebrews 10:5.

(The issue of the relationship of the two Testaments: Marcion, Harnack, E. Bloch,[1] *theologia liberationis* [liberation theology], where Moses is a model of Christ.)

The temptation of bread: The Messiah is he who always gives bread to all (i.e. material goods). Christ gives 'bread' in the Eucharistic sense. Response: 'man shall not live by bread alone, but by every word . . .'[2] The bread is not enough, one needs truth! The temptation contains a lie: it makes a partial aspect absolute.

Questions of conscience: Does God (the word of God) have priority?

On the importance of fasting (!) the patriarch's answer.

Two further temptations: the elimination of the need for redemption.

Reference to the Ignatian meditation on the two standards.[3]

Rosary (I); Eucharistic Adoration; Litany of the Blessed Virgin Mary, St Joseph, the Holy Name of Jesus; Concluding meditation; Compline [illegible]

22 February: Feast of the Chair of St Peter

Daily morning prayers; Meditation, prayer: 'but I have prayed for you that your faith may not fail';[4] Lauds

Liturgical meditation (6):

Lect. Is [Reading from Isaiah] *feria III* [Thursday]. (Matins.)

Isaiah: My word that goes forth from my mouth; it shall not return to me empty.[5] The mystery of Christ is deeply connected to the mystery of Mary: In Her the Word of God does not remain empty. It is received in the world: the soil of the Church: 'She kept the Word in Her heart'.[6] In Her heart the soil

---

1 Marcion of Sinope (*c.*85–160) was an early Christian leader and theologian. He rejected the Hebrew Bible and argued that the wrathful God of the Old Testament was a separate entity from the all-forgiving God of the New Testament.

Adolf von Harnack (1851–1930) was a German Lutheran theologian and historian. He challenged the authenticity of doctrines that arose in the early Christian Church, and rejected the Gospel according to John, questioning its historical value.

Ernst Bloch (1885–1977) was a German Marxist philosopher. His book *The Principle of Hope* influenced theologians such as Jürgen Moltmann.

2 See Matthew 4:4.

3 See n. 3, p. 197 [3 March 1982].

4 See Luke 22:32.

5 See Isaiah 55:11.

6 See Luke 2:19.

of humanity became fertile. Mary 'found self-fulfilment' in Her complete availability! This is the answer to contemporary atheisms. *Feminismo* [feminism]: (?) the result of the rejection of Mariology in Protestantism (?) The consequences in ecclesiology: The Church is not a product of human structures and plans. The Marian mystery is inscribed deep into it: the ripening in the spirit of 'availability': the opening up to God's action!

Reflection: Let the Church – through the Marian mystery inscribed into its nature – become a fertile soil for the Word. Let me – through the consecration to the Immaculate One, through the 'holy slavery' – become a fertile soil for the Word in the Church every single day!

Terce; (Mark); Litany of the Polish Nation

Christological meditation (7):
Cathedra S. Petri [The Chair of St Peter]. Peter's answer to Christ's question 'Who do men say that the Son of Man is?'[1] constitutes the very core of Christology. Mark: you are the Christ,[2] Matthew, Luke. From among many names, what remained in the end is *Christos*, Lord (*Kyrios*), Son of God. This is what we find in Matthew: 'You are the Christ, the Son of the living God'.[3] This answer explains all of the other names and concepts. The dogma of the Church is expressed in it. In the light of the Gospel, the centre of Jesus' life was His relation with the Father. Hence: Son.

The calling of the twelve apostles, that is, the birth of the Church, originated in Jesus' prayer to the Father. Peter's declaration of faith constitutes, as it were, the second stage in the birth of the Church. Peter shared in the inner (*intimità* [intimacy]) communion of Christ with the Father – through his faith born out of this he could become the 'rock'.

(Transfiguration)

(Gethsemane): *Abba*. Prayer.

My Father – Our Father; the participation of the Church community 'we' in relation to Christ's Father 'I'.

1 See Matthew 16:13.
2 See Mark 8:29.
3 See Matthew 16:16.

The Way of the Cross (in the context of Meditations 6 and 7); Sext; None
Reading and preparatory meditation (on suffering)
Holy Mass; Thanksgiving; Rosary (III), (I); Eucharistic Adoration; Vespers

Christological meditation (8):

'*Consubstantialis*' (*homo-ousios*) ['Consubstantial'] – the central term of the Christological dogma. It fully corresponds to the tradition of the Bible and the apostolic faith (see Meditation 7) from the perspective of Christology and soteriology. There is no contradiction between the 'biblical' and the 'Greek'.

The question of freedom lies in the centre of soteriology – freedom is the divine dimension of man. Freedom in truth. The liberation of man without his divinisation is an illusion.

The Council of Nicaea used the philosophical term '*consubstantialis*' to explain the biblical words 'Son of God': 'I glorify You, Father . . .'

The Council of Chalcedon: the unity of divine and human nature in Person.

The Third Council of Constantinople: The duality of natures does not destroy human freedom, but forms (gives birth to) it: 'I have come down from heaven not to do my own will, but the will of Him who sent Me, the Father'[1] – this unity of human will and divine will through love lays the ground for the unity of Christ's self.

The transformation of human freedom in every person also takes place in a similar way: the laboratory of human freedom (soteriological aspect).

Reflection; Anticipated Matins; Litany of the Sacred Heart of Jesus; Litany of the Blessed Virgin Mary

Christological meditation (9):

Passover. In Israel it was celebrated in the family, at home (not in the Temple!). Passover was an annual return to the divine foundation, the leaving of chaos.

In this way Passover became a Christian feast, celebrated in the family of the Church – opposing the forces of chaos and destruction. This has its contemporary meaning.

1 See John 6:38.

Israel inherited Passover from the nomads for whom it was the festival of spring. Hence the conclusion: we are on the way. You were a wanderer.

Christian Passover – passing over. We are on the way to a different life, to a different homeland. The Church is not a fortress, but an open city. To believe means to 'leave' the night, chaos 'behind' – just as Jesus 'left' it 'behind': Maundy Thursday. We are to leave it behind with Him – towards *mysterium paschale* [the paschal mystery].

Rosary (II); Eucharistic Adoration; Concluding meditation; Compline [illegible]; Litany of St Joseph; Penitential psalms

23 February Daily prayers
Meditation: '*in corde susperscribam . . . non atramento, sed Spiritu Dei vivi*' ['I will write on hearts . . . not with ink but with the Spirit of the living God'].[1]
Holy Mass; Thanksgiving; Act of Consecration to the Blessed Virgin Mary; Prayers to the Holy Spirit; Lauds

Liturgical meditation (10):

Prophet Jonah. The Jews demand signs – so does our generation. Marxism: Christianity has had enough time to change the world . . . signs: in the domain of earthly life. Many accept these views at least partially. '*Haec generatio signa quaerit*' ['This generation seeks signs'][2] – the sign that will be given . . . '*vedere Gesù*' ['to see Jesus']. The Rosary, the Way of the Cross, and other prayers allow us to see Jesus.

The credibility of Jonah: Nineveh really lived in sin. The prophet was unbiased. The great cities of our times need apostles of penance, of repentance.

Jonah is a paschal figure: he gives himself up to death out of love for Israel, 'throw me into the sea'.[3]

The sign of Jonah: love that conquers death.

Reflection; Terce; (Luke); Litany of the Polish Nation

Christological meditation (11):

Christ died praying: *Eli, Eli . . . In manus Tuas* [My God, my God . . . Into Thy hands].[4] Psalm 21: messianic: the subject

1 See Jeremiah 31:33 and 2 Corinthians 3:3.
2 See Luke 11:29.
3 See Jonah 1:12.
4 See Matthew 27:46 and Luke 23:46.

proper of this psalm is Jesus . . . The last words of Jesus express complete obedience to the Father.

The words uttered at His death are closely connected to the words spoken at the Last Supper. The Eucharist emerges from this unity. Hence the Eucharist is not only a supper, but an anticipated sacrifice. All the sacrifices of the old covenant are fulfilled in this sacrifice.

The figure of Yahweh's Servant (Isaiah) – higher than all other prophets, '*sacramentum futuri*' ['sacrament for the future'] (Isaiah).

The tradition of Jeremiah: the new covenant.

Cena – Croce – Risurrezione: fanno uno indiviso misterio pasquale [the Supper – the Cross – the Resurrection: they form one single undivided paschal mystery]. The supper (the Eucharist) also anticipates the resurrection: '*transsubstantiatio mortis*' ['transubstantiation of death'].

The Way of the Cross; Sext; None
Reading and preparatory meditation (suffering: [illegible])
Adoration of the Blessed Sacrament; (Litany of the Saints); Rosary (I), (II); Vespers

Christological meditation (12):
Mysterium Paschale di Gesù. s. Giov. [The paschal mystery of Jesus according to St John] two parts 1–13, 13–21.

The washing of the feet. To be a Christian means allowing one's feet to be washed (reactions of Judas and Peter). The washing of the feet is an act of love that can be accepted only through love. Accepting it is also love.

The washing of the feet – the sacramental, ecclesial meaning ('to wash one another's feet':[1] community), the ethical meaning.

St Augustine's interpretation: in between the ideal of contemplative purity and apostolic, pastoral worries one ought to 'get one's feet dirty', on one's way to meet Christ for the sake of one's neighbours and the world.

Christ washes 'our feet' every day when we pray 'forgive us our trespasses'.

1 See John 13:14.

Reflection: how to apply it to my own life
Anticipated Matins; Litany of the Holy Name of Jesus; Litany of the Blessed Virgin Mary; Litany of St Joseph; *Veni Sancte Spiritus* [Come, Holy Spirit]

Christological meditation (13):

Homo factus est [(He) became man][1] = He faced death, He met death. The entire biological setup is destined to die. The spiritual essence defies death because it lives to love.

The dispute about the resurrection originated in the translation of biblical concepts. Two biblical traditions: the tradition of the 'confession' – (*confessionale*) – the tradition of the 'narrative' (*narrativo*). The oldest text (the core) is possibly the words: 'The Lord rose from the dead and appeared to Peter'. The '*narrativa*' ['narrative'] tradition tries to explain how the events unfolded.

Paul (1 Cor.) begins with death: Christ died in accordance with the Scriptures (i.e. in accordance with the Old Testament) for our sins (hence death was not a punishment for sin, but liberation from death). He was buried; He descended to the dead; then He was seen (*ὤφθη*). 'He rose again on the third day in accordance with the Scriptures, He appeared to Peter'.

The tomb. The resurrection took place before the decomposition of the body could begin (Ps. 15!).

Death is part of the world that exists. Real resurrection (not only a conceptual one) does not cease to be man's desire. The resurrection is the revelation of God's power! The same power that was revealed in the creation.

Rosary (III); Eucharistic Adoration; Concluding meditation; Compline; Preparation

24 February

Intentions; Daily prayers
Meditation: '*Ipse liberabit te de laqueo venantium et a verbo maligno*' ['For he will deliver you from the snare of the fowler and from the malicious word'][2]
Holy Mass; Thanksgiving; Lauds

Liturgical meditation (14):

Liturgical catechesis on prayer. Against the views that question the necessity of petitionary prayer (and which are based

1 See John 1:14.
2 See Psalm 90 (91):3.

on the illusion of human self-sufficiency) – It is Jesus who teaches us petitionary prayer.

God is the final power, which at the same time is goodness, pure goodness and the source of all good.

God is power and love. The ethical order comes together with the ontic order.

Gnosis: religion separated from faith. Prayer is substituted with the development of the inner self ('emptiness').

What can we ask for? For everything that is good. To present the entire reality to the omnipotent Father.

Prayer separates light from darkness in us – moral good and evil – and directs the process of conversion (Luke: 'give the Holy Spirit . . .').[1]

Prayer in the name of Christ is the path to become an adopted son of God.

Seek God – you will find joy in the Holy Spirit (cf. *collecta de die!* [the collect for the day!]).

Reflection on my own prayer and its history
Terce; (John); Litany of the Polish Nation

Christo-Ecclesiological meditation (15):

Contemporary view: Jesus – yes: Church – no. We get to know Jesus through everything: through learning.

Yet we can get to know Jesus authentically only through prayer, because Jesus has revealed Himself in prayer. A certain '*con-naturalitas*' ['connaturality'] or '*sym-pathia*' ['compassion'] is necessary. Christ: 'No one can come to me except through the Father'.[2]

The need for theology – but above all for the theology of saints, which is rooted in love.

The Church – the body of Christ is the real condition of knowing Jesus: we get to know Christ in this 'we', which is permeated with God's love.

Man cannot 'force' God to let him know Him – this knowledge can only be the fruit of God's initiative.

1 See Luke 11:13.
2 See John 6:44.

Jesus entered Israel's tradition of the old covenant and drew His existential relation to God from it: 'Our Father'.

The mystery of Christ and the mystery of the Church are inseparable from each other until the end of the world.

The Way of the Cross: Glory be to the Father + and to the Son + and to the Holy Spirit: the passing through the reality of sin and beyond this reality – to the glory in which God exists and gives beginning to everything.

Preparatory reflection: suffering
Reading: *Collegialité du Synode* [Collegiality of the Synod]
Sext; None; Adoration of the Blessed Sacrament; Rosary (II), (III); Vespers

Ecclesiological meditation (16):

Ecclesiology has its origin in Luke's description of Pentecost. The apostolic Church: '*perseverantes in doctrina Apostolorum*' ['they devoted themselves to the Apostles' teaching'],[1] the holy Church: '*assidui in oratione et in fractione panis*' ['. . . devoted themselves to the prayers and the breaking of bread'], the one Church: '*unum solum cor et anima una*' ['of one heart and soul'][2] – catholic: the gift of tongues, since the first day the Church has spoken in all languages: the catholic Church does not 'entail' the multiplicity of particular Churches, but it 'gives birth' to this 'multiplicity': '*dilatamini*' ['widen your hearts'].[3]

The day of Pentecost already contains the entire history of the Church. The apostolic missions end in Rome. Rome becomes the heir and centre of catholicity.

Luke's ecclesiology is pneumatological and at the same time Christological; spiritual and at the same time specific . . .

Reflection; Anticipated Matins; Litany of the Blessed Virgin Mary, St Joseph

Ecclesiological meditation (17):

Communio (*koinonia* [community]) Hebr. *chaburah* (*cooperativa* [cooperating]).

The Church is Jesus' '*koinonia*', the *koinonia* of His Passover – *Communio* [Community] – only between people

1 See Acts 2:42.
2 See Acts 4:32.
3 See 2 Corinthians 6:13.

(*chaburah*) according to the Old Testament. According to the Old Testament, there is no *communio* between God and man, there is only the covenant. According to the New Testament, there is *communio* between God and man. The Old Testament opposed pagan beliefs because of God's transcendence. The Greeks accepted communion between people and gods.

The teaching of the New Testament, however, is not a result of hellenisation, but an entirely new reality, which is essential for the New Testament: the radical novelty of Christianity. Incarnation is a new synthesis created by God Himself. St Paul: *koinonia nel Sangue di Cristo . . . nel Corpo di Cristo . . .* [communion in the blood of Christ . . . in the body of Christ . . .][1] The Eucharist opens the human self to the transcendent God in His deity: 'deifies' man.

This 'communion' has its foundation in the hypostatic union: *communio* of the divine (nature, will) and the human (nature, will).

The communion with God in Christ as the foundation of the Church is the source of communion between people ('we' of the Church).

Pastoral reflection: for a deeper consideration or even resignation from Holy Communion for the sake of a better Communion, which also involves an act of solidarity with those who wish to, but cannot receive Holy Communion.

Koinonia means the 'Eucharist' and 'community'.

Rosary (I); Litany of Our Lord Jesus Christ, Priest and Victim; Eucharistic Adoration; Holy Hour; Compline

25 February

Intentions; Daily prayer
Meditation: '*Ipse peccata multorum tulit et pro transgressoribus rogavit*' ['He bore the sin of many, and made intercession for the transgressors'][2]
Holy Mass; Thanksgiving; Consecration to the Blessed Virgin Mary; Prayers to the Holy Spirit (daily); Lauds

Liturgical meditation (18)

De iustitia christ. [On Christian justice]. We find two soteriological concepts: '*compassio Dei*' ['God's compassion']; St Bernard: '*Deus non patitur, sed compatitur*' ['God does not

1 See 1 Corinthians 10:16.
2 See Isaiah 53:12.

suffer, but He co-suffers']. This sheds light on the question of '*compatheia Dei*' ['God's compassion']. '*Cor meum*' ['my Heart'] about God.

(The Eucharist: *personalismo profetico* [prophetic personalism]). Lenten Friday liturgy focuses our attention on Calvary:[1] He who suffered death without sin, He suffered death – for us – even though the prophet maintains that every person is responsible for their own sins only.

The Gospel: 'unless your righteousness exceeds . . .'[2] 'excessive' (excess). God is an 'excess, abundance'. Christians ought to be capable of giving, of 'exceeding'; this gives birth to spiritual joy.

This leads us to the antitheses in the Sermon on the Mount, 'it was said to the men of old'[3] (God spoke through Moses); but I say to you[4] (God speaks through Me.)

Cf. *postcommunio* [prayer after Communion].

Reflection: about this 'excess' – in the Church teaching (*H[umanae] V[itae]*, *F[amiliaris] C[onsortio]*)[5] and in personal life. The methodology of homily(!)
Terce; Litany of the Polish Nation

Meditation on priesthood (19):

The calling of Peter. Luke: the miraculous catch of fish. Before that, Peter called Jesus 'Master'; afterwards: 'Lord'.[6]

The description of the first calling: Andrew and his brother Simon:[7] Come! Look! Without seeing there is no 'experience' (*gustare* [to taste, to grasp]).

Before that they called Jesus 'Rabbi', after meeting Him: 'We saw Christ = Messiah'.[8] There are elements of calling contained in this: *ubi habitas*? [where are you staying?] – come and see.[9]

---

1 The readings for the First Friday of Lent are Ezekiel 18:21–28 and Matthew 5:20–26.

2 See Matthew 5:20.

3 See Matthew 5:21.

4 See Matthew 5:21–44.

5 The encyclical *Humanae vitae* (Of Human Life) was issued by Pope Paul VI on 25 July 1968. The apostolic exhortation *Familiaris consortio* (Of Family Partnership) was promulgated by Pope John Paul II on 22 November 1981.

6 See Luke 5:5–11.

7 See Matthew 4:18–22.

8 See John 1:41.

9 See John 1:38–39.

To throw nets when He says so – these elements have to be repeated in every vocation.

Both disciples have the awareness of the 'Lamb of God',[1] so they also have the awareness of their own guilt: 'depart from me, O Lord, for I am a sinful man'.[2] *Initium sapientiae timor Domini* [The fear of the Lord is the beginning of wisdom].[3] Only he who has the awareness of his sinfulness can preach repentance in an authentic way.

Videte Eum et illuminamini! [Look to Him and be radiant!][4]

'They beckoned to their partners in the other boat':[5] being called with others, and through others. Together they form '*koinonia Petri*' ['Petrine community'] (+ James, John), and at the same time the seeds of the future Church.

'To be a disciple' is to let Jesus 'catch' you. The calling is not only a personal thing; it finds fulfilment in the community of the Church; through the Barque of Peter.

The Way of the Cross (Passion [?])
(Preparatory consideration: suffering); (*Collegialità a Sinodo dei Vescovi* [Collegiality at the Synod of Bishops])
Rosary (III), (I); Adoration of the Blessed Sacrament (seven words); Chaplet of the Five Wounds of Christ; Vespers

Meditation on *spiritualità sacerdotale* [priestly spirituality] (20):
Dominus pars haereditatis meae et calicis mei [The Lord is the portion of my inheritance and my cup].[6]

The tribe of Levy did not receive any portion at the division of the Promised Land.[7] God Himself was their inheritance, the secure foundation of their life, even in the material sense. The psalm which contains these words is a priestly psalm. At the same time, this psalm goes beyond the old covenant and gestures towards Christ.

This belonging to God, a special dependence on Him, a permanent readiness to receive His commands, is a source of special joy.

---

1 See John 1:36.
2 See Luke 5:8.
3 See Proverbs 9:10.
4 See Psalm 33:6 (34:5).
5 See Luke 5:7.
6 See Psalm 15 (16):5.
7 See Joshua 13:14.

There is no true priesthood without the readiness to leave one's goods. Celibacy belongs to this context: one should seek an existential justification for it in this context.

The life of the priest is wholly focused on the Eucharist. It is our entire inheritance.

'We have left everything . . .' '. . . will receive a hundredfold . . .'[1]

Reflection; Litany of the Sacred Heart of Jesus; Litany of the Blessed Virgin Mary, Litany of St Joseph; Anticipated Matins

(Liturgical) meditation *de sabato* [on Saturday] (21):

Collect: '*Ad Te corda nostra, Pater aeterne, converte, ut nos, unum necessarium semper quaerentes et opera caritatis exercentes, Tuo cultui praestes esse dicatos*' ['Turn our hearts to You, eternal Father, and grant that, seeking always the one thing necessary and carrying out works of charity, we may be dedicated to Your worship'].[2]

Repentance: from a distant country (i.e. from the land of sin), like the prodigal son.[3] Two brothers: the elder and the younger. The older (the symbol of Israel) is faithful, but jealous (because he would also like to have the goods of the 'distant country'), even though his Father tells him: 'all that is mine is yours'.[4]

Primary conversion: *ad Te* [to You!] to God Himself.

The primacy of God: '*unum necessarium*' [the one thing that is necessary],[5] and then '*opera caritatis*' ['the works of mercy'].

A recollection of the ember days (*quattuor tempora* [four seasons]) (Lenten; week 1): an ancient tradition – for some time connected to the priestly vocation: Wednesday – Friday – Saturday.[6]

Cf. *postcommunio de sabato* [prayer after Communion on Saturday].

1 See Matthew 19:27–29.

2 See the Collect for Saturday in the First Week of Lent.

3 See Luke 15:13.

4 See Luke 15:31.

5 See Luke 10:42.

6 The ember days, four separate sets of three days within the same week (Wednesday, Friday and Saturday) traditionally set aside for fasting and prayer, used to be considered especially suitable for the ordination of clergy.

Rosary (II); Eucharistic Adoration; Concluding meditation; Compline; Preparation

26 February[1] Intentions; Daily prayer

Meditation: '*omnibus mutationibus multa subesse quae . . . fundamentum habent in Christo, qui est heri et hodie, Ipse et in saecula*' ['beneath all changes there are many realities which . . . have their ultimate foundation in Christ, who is the same yesterday and today, and forever'].[2] Through Him united with Mary.

(Consecration to the Blessed Virgin Mary; Prayer to the Holy Spirit); Holy Mass; Thanksgiving; Lauds

Liturgical meditation *de Dominica* [on Sunday] (22)

The covenant with Abraham (Genesis). Faith is worth life and death. It is worth binding one's fate to it.

God also gives Himself in the covenant: He binds His 'Fate' with the covenant. He confirms it with the death of His Son. He becomes fully involved with man.

Final words; Thanksgiving; Blessing; *Salve Regina*
UIOGD[3]

1 The final talk of the retreat was delivered by John Paul II. The full text (in Italian) is available at: https://w2.vatican.va/

2 *Gaudium et spes* 10.

3 See p. xxi.

11–17 March 1984
Vatican Retreat
Led by Cardinal A[lexandre] do Nascimento[1]

~

11 March Vespers; *Veni Creator Spiritus* [Come, Creator Spirit]

Introductory talk 1:

St Mark: '*venite in disparte*' ['come away all by yourselves'].[2]

Come! (in relation to freedom) come with your personal story, with your cross.

Come = '*essere in tensione*'... '*essere in lotta*' ['to be in tension'... 'to be in struggle']. In response the Church offers us retreats: (*vacare Deo*): *solus cum Solo* [(to be free for God): alone with the Only One].

'*Deja las otras cosas*' ['Leave other things'] (St Charles Borromeo) – *purificazione* – *intercessione* – *contemplazione* [purification – intercession – contemplation].

(The canonisation of St Paula Frassinetti[3] – people, the holy Church and the mother of saints): to live a saintly life is to somehow make God present in the history of humankind.

Venite – *accipite iugum* [Come – take the yoke][4]

Venite – *benedicti Patris mei* [Come – O blessed of my Father][5]

Adoration of the Blessed Sacrament; Lenten Lamentations I;[6] Anticipated Matins; Concluding meditation; Compline
Reading: Card. Ratzinger: *Behold the Pierced One*.[7]

---

1 Alexandre do Nascimento (b. 1925) is an Angolan Cardinal of the Catholic Church. He was elevated to the cardinalate by Pope John Paul II in 1983, and served as Archbishop of Luanda from 1986 to 2001.

2 See Mark 6:31.

3 St Paula Frassinetti (1809–82) founded the Congregation St Dorothea. She was canonised on 11 March 1984 by Pope John Paul II.

4 See Matthew 11:29.

5 See Matthew 25:34.

6 Lenten (or Bitter) Lamentations (Polish: *Gorzkie żale*) is a religious devotion that developed in Poland in the eighteenth century. It is primarily a sung reflection on the Passion of Christ.

7 Joseph Ratzinger (Pope Benedict XVI), *Schauen auf den Durchbohrten: Versuche zu einer spirituellen Christologie* (Einsiedeln, 1984). English edition: *Behold the Pierced One: An Approach to a Spiritual Christology*, trans. Graham Harrison (San Francisco, 1986).

12 March

Intentions; Prayers
Meditation: (*vacare Deo* [to be free for God])
Holy Mass; Thanksgiving (intercession), as usual; Lauds

Meditation 2: **Dio/God**

The end point of the human mind's pursuit. At the same time, He completely surpasses human reason (Pascal).

Ricerca [search]/pursuit, that permeates the whole of the Old Testament.

Psalms: **The Face of God!**

– in medieval theology/philosophy: Person.

Vultum Tuum, Domine, requiram [Thy face, Lord, do I seek][1] – this also contains a simultaneous desire to be seen by God.

Cercare Dio = cercare il bene, evitare il male [To seek God = to seek good, to avoid evil].

Bergson

On mystics and mysticism: They bear witness to what is the ultimate future of man: man – '*essere in lenta maturazione*' ['to be in a slow process of growth'] / 'to lift up our eyes to heaven': *levare oculos.*[2]

Passion according to Mark; Prayer for the gifts of the Holy Spirit; Terce

Newman

Descartes

Meditation 3: **Man: 'I'**

Quis est Deus? [Who is God?] – St Thomas.

– Newman: I and my Creator.

– Descartes: *Cogito – ergo sum* [I think – therefore I am].

'I' versus 'God'.

Io davanti a Dio [I before God]: What am 'I'? The body and the spirit, spatio-temporal being: historical.

Lucretius

Who am 'I'? A person open to the other (others), open to God.

Creator – Pater Sanctus – Erus totius bonitatis [Creator – Holy Father – Lord of all goodness] (Thomas). He who gives without expecting anything in return – all good that exists in creatures is found in God, its Source (Fount).

Sext; Rosary (II); Meditative reflection; The Way of the Cross [illegible]; None; Adoration of the Blessed Sacrament; Rosary (III); Penitential psalms; Vespers

1 See Psalm 26 (27):8.

2 See John 17:1.

Meditation 4: (Ps. 104) **Divine providence:**

Dostoyevsky
St Thomas
Merton

Creatures sing the glory of the Creator.

The life of all accidental beings comes from God.

Dogma consolatore della Div. Providenza [The consoling dogma of Divine Providence]: God supports the existence of everything (Matthew's words about the lilies of the field).[1]

The call to love every creature (animals, plants) cf. *Prex Euch IV* [Eucharistic Prayer IV]: the praise of God's wisdom. The Book of Wisdom: 'For Thou lovest all things that exist'.[2] The special place of man (*nobilitas*: dignity).

Baudelaire

Man–woman: a Trinitarian reflection.

Card. Newman: text on providence.

Reflection; Anticipated Matins; Litany of the Blessed Virgin Mary, St Joseph

Meditation 5: ***Mysterium iniquitatis*** **[The mystery of evil]**[3] **sin:** '*salvare gli uomini dai loro peccati*' (*ad Tessal.*) ['save the people from their sins' (Letter to the Thessalonians)].[4]

The light of faith is necessary to understand the mystery of sin: when faith fades away, the awareness of sin fades away too.

Cicero
Thomas

Christ: '*si*' ['yes']; *peccatum* – '*non*' [sin – 'no'].

Peccatum = *non oboedire* [Sin = not to obey]; *iniquitas* [injustice]; *ingratitudo* [ingratitude]; *impietas* [impiety]; breaking up the friendship with God; a rejection of a free person given to the Absolute: Father.

What does sin mean in my personal life?

Death – the effects of sin.

Bernanos

Hell – Bernanos = not to be able to love any more.

Lord, I entrust my freedom into Your hands.

Have mercy, Lord, have mercy!

Rosary (I); Litany of Loreto; Eucharistic Benediction; Concluding meditation; Compline
Reading: J. Ratzinger, others

13 March

Intentions; Prayers
Meditation: *amor – providentia – peccatum* [love – providence – sin]
Holy Mass; Thanksgiving; Daily intercessions; Lauds

1 See Matthew 6:28.
2 See Wisdom 11:24.
3 See 2 Thessalonians 2:7.
4 The quoted passage comes from Matthew 1:21.

Meditation 6: ***Redemptio* [Redemption]**

St Paul: *quis me liberabit?* [who will deliver me?][1]

Greek philosophers [illegible] Asia Africa

Deus tantum dilexit mundum, ut Filium Suum Unigenitum mandavit . . . [God so loved the world that He gave His Only Son . . .][2] (*dedit* = *donum* [gave = gift]). The gift expresses the Giver; the present = represents the giver.

Christ – the gift from the Father.

St Paul: on all the gifts that preceded this highest gift: gifts of nature, gifts of culture, also Asian, African: great figures.

Jesus Christ – the Second Adam.

St Paul

The Father who did not spare His own Son but gave Him up for us all, will He not also give us all things with Him?[3]

Verbum caro factum est [The Word became flesh].[4]

Prayer for the gifts of the Holy Spirit; Passion of Our Lord Jesus Christ according to St Mark; Terce

Meditation 7: **Incarnation – gospel: *Magister* [Teacher]**

Christ – the Gift from the Father – the Son who is consubstantial with the Father: everything was made in Him and everything remains in Him.

This Gift came to us as a defenceless child.

The Teacher (Master): His teaching is directed at the innermost part of man ('*cuore*' ['heart']) – and awakens the depth of humanity in every man.

New criteria related to exercising power.

Demanding teaching – at the same time: the boundary of forgiveness is extended.

Rivelatore [Revelatory] (student–Master) – '*io e mio Redentore*' ['I and my Redeemer'].

He revealed the mystery of the Father and His own mystery (cf. *Dei verbum*):[5] He preached the words of God: the same word is given to us, to keep it and to pass it on.

Sext; Rosary (III); Meditation continued; The Way of the Cross (of Pope Paul VI); None; Adoration of the Blessed Sacrament; Rosary (I); Litany of the Saints; Vespers

---

1 See Romans 7:24.
2 See John 3:16.
3 See Romans 8:32.
4 See John 1:14.
5 See n. 2, p. 190 [1 March 1982].

Meditation 8: **Prayer**

Cyprian, Thomas Aquinas and many others. S. Weil

Lord, teach us how to pray! – Our Father:[1] Prayer for all and everyone.

Our Father, who art in heaven: trust (*fiducia* [trust]): we are His sons.

Hallowed be Thy name – Name – Being – concept of God.

Thy kingdom come – announced and launched by Christ.

Thy will be done – holiness: to fulfil God's will.

Give us this day our daily bread – natural and supernatural.

And forgive us our trespasses as we forgive those who trespass against us –reconciliation with God and with people.

Mauriac

Lead us not into temptation – we acknowledge our weakness.

But deliver us from evil: from the Prince of this world!

The temptation of the non-existence of satan is to be fought with the sacraments and devotion to the Blessed Virgin Mary.

Anticipated Matins; Litany of the Sacred Heart of Jesus; Litany of the Blessed Virgin Mary; Litany of St Joseph

Meditation 9: ***'Go-el'***

– *Redentore – Riscattatore* [Redeemer – Saviour] – (*Go-el*).[2]

L[umen] G[entium]: The Son of God has united Himself in some fashion with every man.[3] (In relation to African culture: *bantu* [human beings]). Man in personal union with God – God is the head of all humankind.

Rosary (II); Litany of Loreto; Eucharistic Benediction
Concluding meditation: ('*Go-el*' ['Redeemer'] – Act of Consecration to the Immaculate Heart of Our Lady)
Compline
Reading: Ratzinger, others

14 March

Intentions; Prayers
Meditation: forgive us our trespasses in Christ '*go-el*' ['redeemer']
The Way of the Cross; Holy Mass; Thanksgiving; Daily intercessions; Rosary (I); Lauds

1 See Matthew 6:9–13.

2 *Go-el* is a Hebrew term meaning 'redeemer'. In the Bible and the rabbinical tradition, it refers to a person who, as the nearest relative of another, is charged with the duty of restoring the rights of another.

3 Cf. *Gaudium et spes* 22.

Newman

Meditation 10: **The passion of the Redeemer**

Calvary – the Lamb of God[1] – through the eyes of St John the Evangelist, who heard these words by the Jordan from John the Baptist together with the song of Yahweh's Servant (from Isaiah)[2] – with all the messianic content and the content speaking of the passion.

Ps. 21: 'they have pierced my hands and feet . . .' to the words 'My God, my God, why hast Thou forsaken me?'[3] At Calvary, John, son of Zebedee, finds the confirmation of these Old Testament words on the passion – at the same time, there are the words of Christ Himself: 'The good shepherd lays down his life for the sheep'[4] . . . to 'This is my Body which is given for you.'[5] 'This is my Blood . . .'[6]

Adoration of the Blessed Sacrament; Prayer for the gifts of the Holy Spirit; Terce

Meditation 11: **Mother**

Newman

'*Iuxta Crucem Tecum stare*' ['By the cross with Thee to stand'][7] – '*Fiat*' ['Let it be'] by the Annunciation.[8]

Newman: 'in the light of the Blood of Christ' . . .

St Gregory
Augustine
Card. Wyszyński

Where are we, regarding the departure from sin?

The sensitivity of conscience that we find in saints is indispensable in the life of priests.

St Gregory, St Augustine, Sixtus.

The great humility of saints.

The Prison Notes.[9]

Ps. 50: '*cor contritum et humiliatum* . . .' ['a broken and contrite heart . . .'][10]

Sext; Jubilee celebrations at a general audience; None; Rosary (II); Vespers

---

1 See John 1:29.
2 See Isaiah 52:12–53:13.
3 See Psalm 21 (22):16 and 1.
4 See John 10:11.
5 See Luke 22:19.
6 See Mark 14:24 and Matthew 26:28.
7 See the hymn *Stabat Mater Dolorosa* (The Sorrowful Mother Stood).
8 See Luke 1:38.
9 Stefan Wyszyński, *A Freedom Within: The Prison Notes of Stefan Cardinal Wyszyński*, trans. Barbara Krzywicki-Herburt and Walter J. Ziemba (San Diego, 1984). Originally published as Stefan Wyszyński, *Zapiski więzienne* (Warszawa, 1983).
10 See Psalm 50 (51):17.

Card. Wyszyński

Meditation 12:

'*Cor contritum et humiliatum*' ['a broken and contrite heart'][1] – a condition for becoming a new man: God creates a new man. Justification is the work of God: the analogy with the act of creation: the day of resurrection: Receive the Holy Spirit![2]

CIC [Code of Canon Law]
R. Aron
Pius XII

The salvation of many depends on others.

The virtue of repentance – and the sacrament of penance! St John of the Cross.

Anticipated Matins; Litany of the Holy Name of Jesus; Litany of the Blessed Virgin Mary, Litany of St Joseph

Meditation 13: ***De Spiritu Sancto* [On the Holy Spirit]**

'*Vultum Tuum Domine requiram – a Dio Creatore*' ['Thy face, Lord, do I seek – to God the Creator'].[3]

Idem – a Dio Redentore [The same – to God the Redeemer].

Nunc: idem – a Dio Spirito Sancto [Now: the same – to God the Holy Spirit].

The Holy Spirit is given to us – Gift – the Spirit of the Father, the Spirit of Christ (the Holy Spirit – the symbol of water (!)).

The Holy Spirit who spoke through the prophets: the relationship with the Word.

St Paul: The Holy Spirit dwells in us as in a temple.[4]

Christ's promise is fulfilled in churches that are persecuted: the Holy Spirit will teach you what you ought to say![5]

'Another Counsellor'![6]

(R. Brown)

'*Sanctificator*' = Sanctifier.

Isaiah: the vision of six Seraphim – Holy, Holy, Holy[7] – and he touched the mouth of the man, the prophet, with a coal, purifying it.[8]

Holiness: the essential attribute of God, the attribute of the Absolute.

---

1 See Psalm 50 (51):17.
2 See John 20:22.
3 See Psalm 26 (27):8.
4 See 1 Corinthians 3:16.
5 See Luke 12:12.
6 See John 14:16.
7 See Isaiah 6:3.
8 See Isaiah 6:6–7.

(a) holiness: transcendence – *relationes inter-trinitariae* [inter-Trinitarian relations]
supernaturale est 'suum naturale' [supernatural is 'natural to itself']

(b) holiness in a moral sense – in relation to creatures, 'to make people become partakers of the divine nature'.[1]

Rosary (III); Litany of Loreto; Eucharistic Benediction
Concluding meditation: on the holiness of God: God is love
Reading: Ratzinger and others
Compline

15 March

Intention; Prayers
Meditation: Isaiah: Holy, Holy, Holy . . . a burning coal[2]
Holy Mass; (Thanksgiving; Daily intercessions); Lauds

Meditation 14: **Holiness**

Exiit Seminator seminare . . . Semen [The Sower went out to sow . . . Seed]:[3] The word of God sown in a well-disposed soul bears fruit: *meta-noia* [a change of mind]: a new scale of values that is put in practice with effort and struggle: this is the path to our sanctification and holiness: *imitare Christum* [to imitate Christ] – human will united with the will of God.

s. Joan della † [St John of the Cross]
Aristotle

Christian holiness is for every day.

Deus mirabilis in sanctis suis [God is wonderful in his saints].[4]

Saints: their likeness to Christ: 'he will also do the works that I do'.[5]

To bear witness before all, including nonbelievers – and to leave the rest to God, who '*scrutatur corda*' ['searches hearts'].[6]

Prayer for the gifts of the Holy Spirit; Passion of Our Lord Jesus Christ according to Luke; Terce

Meditation 15: **Friendship with God – prayer**

Amor naturalis: *auto-conservazione della natura* [Natural love: self-conservation of nature].

1 See 2 Peter 1:4.
2 See Isaiah 6:3–7.
3 See Luke 8:5.
4 See *Lumen gentium* 50.
5 See John 14:12.
6 See Romans 8:27.

Amicitia – solummodo inter personas [Friendship – only between persons].

Confidenza fra i cuori – communio personarum [Trust between hearts – community of persons].

Vatican II: *sancti sunt amici Dei: amicitia inter Deum et hominem: 'vocavi vos amicos . . .'* [saints are God's friends: the friendship between God and people: 'I have called you friends . . .'].[1]

Spiritus S. habitat in nobis = amicitia [The Holy Spirit lives in us = friendship]: hence, to open one's heart to God, to speak to Him, to talk to Him: **prayer, contemplation.**

Maritain

The witness of St Thomas Aquinas (more came about from the power of his prayer than the effort of his spirit).

St John Vianney's testimony about one of his parishioners.

Dio stima l'amicizia dei suoi fedeli [God values the friendship of his faithful].

The fruitfulness of the intercession of saints can be explained in this way.

Sext; Rosary (II); Reflective meditation; The Way of the Cross; None; Adoration of the Blessed Sacrament; Rosary (III); Vespers

Meditation 16: ***Communio Sanctorum* [The communion of saints]**

Humankind threatened by 'deindividuation'! Contemporary man.

Christianity counters this with the reality of '*communio*' (κοινωνία [community]): the communion with God through Jesus Christ, through the mystery of incarnation; the communion of saints.

'The Spirit of the Lord God is upon me' (Isaiah)[2] – it refers *in prima persona* [personally] to Christ Himself. In turn – in Him and through Him – to the entire people of God: '*baptizati sumus in eodem Spiritu*' ['we were baptised in one Spirit'].[3]

St Thomas

The mark of holiness is above all: love, and all the theological and moral virtues.

'*Motiones Spiritus S.*' ['Movements of the Holy Spirit'].

1 See John 15:15.
2 See Isaiah 61:1.
3 See 1 Corinthians 12:13.

L[umen] G[entium]: Our weakness is supported by the intercession of saints in heaven.

Anticipated Matins; Litany of the Blessed Virgin Mary; Litany of St Joseph

Meditation 17: **The holiness of the Church**

L[umen] G[entium]. Ecclesia – instrumentum unionis cum Deo = instrumentum sanctitatis! [The Church – an instrument of union with God = an instrument of holiness!] All those who have been sanctified and are constantly being sanctified in the Church bear witness to this. The Church has the means to sanctification.

At the same time, sinners also belong to the Church. Tertullian's opposing point of view has long been rejected. For the Church is a merciful Mother.

Everyone in the Church has been called to holiness.

Rosary (I); Eucharistic Benediction; Penitential psalms; Holy Hour; Litany of our Lord Jesus Christ, Priest and Victim
Reading: Ratzinger and others
Compline

16 March

Daily intentions
Meditation: (*Vultum Tuum, Domine, requiram* [Thy face, Lord, do I seek])[1]
Holy Mass; (Thanksgiving; Daily intercessions); (Litany of the Polish Nation); Lauds

Shakespeare

Meditation 18: **Priests**

Holiness in priests: a special calling to holiness related to the vocation and priestly life. Above all: the Eucharist (*gratias agentes quia nos dignos habuisti astare coram Te et Tibi ministrare* [giving thanks that You have held us worthy to be in Your presence and minister to You]).[2]

St John the Evangelist – he alone took part in the bloody sacrifice at Calvary. It was also him who presented the 'heavenly liturgy' to us in the Book of Revelation.

Priest: he is either a man of living faith, or 'nothing' (a burden to himself).

All the good in the world has its beginning in Christ's sacrifice. The priest is an instrument.

1 See Psalm 26 (27):8.
2 See Eucharistic Prayer II.

Dante Woe to the world in which there would be no priests!

Constant gratitude for the priesthood in the Eucharistic Heart of Our Lord Jesus.

Prayer for the gifts of the Holy Spirit; Passion of Our Lord Jesus Christ according to John; (Litany of our Lord Jesus Christ, Priest and Victim); Terce

Meditation 19: ***Maria Virgo et Mater*** **[Mary: Virgin and Mother]**
So many moments, so many years with Jesus the Redeemer. She was redeemed in a special way. The highest moment – the
Newman moment that was also 'His hour'.[1]

Mary – the Mother of Her Creator (Newman). Mary's
(R. Brown) divine motherhood remains in a special relationship with the mystery of redemption (*Go-el* [Redeemer]).

The Bethlehem night – Cana of Galilee – this has to be read in the full messianic context, in the context of Calvary. The Immaculate Conception – the Assumption: the special fruit
[illegible] of redemption: She was redeemed in an '*eminenter*' ['exalted']
Saladin way.

The wonderful relationship between Mary's motherhood and the ministry of the priests of the Church.

Sext; Rosary (III); Reflective meditation (the Mother of Christ – priesthood); The Way of the Cross (Friday); None; Eucharistic Adoration (seven words of Our Lord on the Cross); Rosary (I); Vespers

Bernanos Meditation 20: **BMV –** ***et sacerdos*** **[Blessed Virgin Mary – and the priest]**
Motherly love in human experience. The personal experience of the retreat leader – and of every human being.

1 Cor. 13: the hymn to love: motherly love comes closest to this ideal.

Mary – in relation to Christ, in relation to everyone who belongs to Her mystical body, *L[umen] G[entium]* VIII (*Salvifici doloris*).[2]

Card. Wyszyński Act of Consecration to the Blessed Virgin Mary: consecration through 'slavery';[3] *Soli Deo per Mariam* [To God alone

1 See John 17:1.
2 The apostolic letter *Salvifici doloris* (Of Salvific Suffering) was delivered by Pope John Paul II at St Peter's Basilica in Rome on 11 February 1984, the liturgical Memorial of Our Lady of Lourdes.
3 See n. 4, p. 43 [21 December 1966].

through Mary][1]– the Act of Consecration of 25 March.[2]

Litany of the Sacred Heart of Jesus; Litany of the Blessed Virgin Mary; Litany of St Joseph; Prayers for Good Friday; Anticipated Matins

Mauriac
Le Goff
Balzac

Meditation 21: **Purgatory**

(a) At the end of your life, you will be judged by your love (St John of the Cross).

(b) Purgatory: the priest – neither hot not cold.[3]

'*zelus domus Tuae comedit me*' ['zeal for Thy house has consumed me'].[4]

St Catherine of Genoa
St Theresa of Avila

John XXIII's *Journal of a Soul.*[5]

We will be judged by love – *imparare Cristo* [to learn Christ][6] – gentleness of conscience – love for people, especially children.

The meaning of purgatory: standing still in love.

It is important that we make our Lord our centre of gravity.

Rosary (II); Eucharistic Benediction; Concluding meditation and the Chaplet of the Five Wounds of the Lord Jesus; Compline

17 March[7]

Intentions; Prayers; Morning meditation; Renewal of the act of holy slavery to the Blessed Virgin Mary; Holy Mass; (Thanksgiving; Daily intercessions; Litany of the Polish Nation); Lauds

St Augustine

Meditation [22]: **Eternal life**

Man – *essere in progetto – in tensione* [to be in formation – in tension]. The end: '*La fine di quella tensione* [The end of that tension]: death shall be no more, neither shall there be mourning nor crying . . .'[8]

'*Non sunt condignae passiones huius temporis in comparatione ad futuram gloriam*' ['The sufferings of this present time are not worth comparing with the glory to come'].[9]

---

1 *Soli Deo per Mariam* was Cardinal Wyszyński's episcopal motto.

2 On 25 March 1984, in the Jubilee Year of the Redemption, Pope John Paul II consecrated the world and 'all individuals and peoples' to the Immaculate Heart of Mary in St Peter's Square in Rome.

3 See Revelation 3:16.

4 See Psalm 68:10 (69:9) and John 2:17.

5 See n. 3, p. 189 [28 February 1982].

6 See Ephesians 4:20.

7 The final talk of the retreat was delivered by John Paul II. The full text (in Italian) is available at: https://w2.vatican.va/

8 See Revelation 21:4.

9 See Romans 8:18.

'*Tra noi e voi è stabilito un grande abisso*' ['Between us and you a great chasm has been established'].[1]

Great, perfect friendship, *intimità con la Persona della SS-ma Trinità* [intimacy with the Person of the Most Holy Trinity].

'What no eye has seen, nor ear heard, nor the heart of man conceived . . .'[2]

'Come, O blessed . . .'[3]

The 'personalist' nature of eternal bliss.

St Augustine

The mystery is concealed for us to find in earthly life.

Vultum Tuum desidero: in Lumine videbimus Lumen! [Thy Face I desire: in Light we see Light!][4]

Final words; Thanksgiving; Blessing

1 See Luke 16:26.
2 See 1 Corinthians 2:9.
3 See Matthew 25:34.
4 See Psalms 26 (27):8 and 35:10 (36:9).

sabato **5** gennaio

s. Amelia

Saturday Samstag Samedi
СЪБОТА Sábado السبت

January Januar Janvier
ЯНВАРЬ Enero يناير

Ex. Spir. 1985. 24.II – 2.III.
/abp Glorieux/

(24.II) 9.18

1. Vesp.
2. Veni Creator
3. Konf. Medyt. (I)

Tworzymy wspólnotę rekol. W centrum: Chrystus. Duch Św.!, który mówi „wszystko"
Znajdujemy się w pośrodku Kościoła: w Rzymie – i w świecie. Kościół przygotowujący się do Paschy.
W Post – przez nawrócenie.
Temat: Symbol wiary.
Wspomnienie z Matką Kościoła, z Lourdes: słowa do ś. Bernadetty: [illegible] Matka Boża, [illegible] za [illegible] –

4. Ador. Euch.
5. Cor. Ros. (III) Lit. SS. Cordis / BMV / 2 ja.
6. Compl.

/ Lektury /

(25.II)

1. Int.
2. Medyt. („Ja jestem pośrodku nich")
3. Sacramentum {Grat. act. / [illegible] / Ant. Mar. / SS. Spir. / Cot. [illegible]

M	G	V	S	D	L	M	M	G	V	S	D	L	M	M	G
16	17	18	19	20	21	22	23	24	25	26	27	28	29	30	31

24 February – 2 March 1985
Exercitia Spiritualia [Spiritual Exercises]
Led by Archbishop [Achille] Glorieux[1]

~

24 February 6.00 p.m.: Vespers; *Veni Creator* [Come, Creator (Spirit)]

Talk. Meditation (1):

We form a retreat community. In the centre: Christ. The Holy Spirit, who speaks 'inside us'.

We are at the core of the Church: in Rome – and in the world. The Church prepares for Passover.

Lent – is a calling!

Topic: The symbol of faith.

In unity with the Mother of the Church from Lourdes: St Bernadette's words: Holy Mary, Mother of God, pray for me, a poor sinner.

Eucharistic Adoration; Rosary (III); Litany of the Sacred Heart of Jesus, Blessed Virgin Mary, St Joseph; Compline; Reading

25 February Intentions

Meditation: 'I am in the midst of them'.[2]

Holy Mass; Thanksgiving; Daily prayers; Act of Consecration to Virgin Mary; Prayer to the Holy Spirit; Litany of the Polish Nation; Lauds

Talk. Meditation (2):

(*Credo* [Creed]) Only God can properly speak of God: many times and in various ways . . . God spoke . . . , in the last days He has spoken by a Son.[3]

Symbolus Apostolorum [The Apostles' Creed]: the Trinitarian structure – *symbolus baptismalis* [the baptismal creed].

(The ecumenical meeting near Trent:)

---

1 Achille Marie Joseph Glorieux (1910–99) served as Secretary of the Pontifical Council for the Laity (1966–69), Titular Archbishop of Beverley (1969–99), Apostolic Pro-Nuncio to Syria (1969–73) and Apostolic Pro-Nuncio to Egypt (1973–84).

2 See Matthew 18:20.

3 See Hebrews 1:1–2.

Baptism gives us divine life: Bl. Elizabeth of the Trinity: the life of the Trinity in us!

The crisis of faith in our age (*malecredenti* [people of little faith]).

It was different: in the first centuries of Christianity, when catechumens prepared to receive baptism: the enthusiasm of faith.

Monotheism: Islam (prayer – creed).

The remembrance of Damascus! Contrast: Western secularism. Cardinal Journet: *segreto di Dio* [the secret of God].

One God – Creator!

Reflection; Credo of the People of God;[1] Passion according to Matthew; Terce

Talk. Meditation (3):

solidarity with the persecuted

An analysis of secularism, indifference, in the Christian world (West). The signs of renewal: conversions from Islam! To what extent are believers responsible for the current situation? (*G[audium et] S[pes]*)[2] – Marxism – Soviet: USSR: the situation of religion, an uncompromising war against religion.

Concluding meditation: 'Only God can properly speak of God . . .'
Sext; None; The Way of the Cross (Trinitarian); (On the Holy Spirit – reading and meditation); Adoration of the Blessed Sacrament; Rosary (II), (III); (Reading texts); Vespers

Talk. Meditation (4):

The history of religion – before 4000 BC we know practically nothing.

Genesis: Babel – Abraham '*pater credentium*' ['the father of all believers'].[3]

Moses: God's name is 'He who IS'.[4]

The revelation of divine Fatherhood – first, in the collective sense: the liberation of Israel from Egypt; then: the prophets.

God is omnipotent (as opposed to pagan gods).

God is holy (the Ten Commandments). Omnipotence permeated with love.

1 The Credo of the People of God is a profession of faith written by Pope Paul VI and published in the motu proprio *Solemni hac liturgia* (This Solemn Liturgy) on 30 June 1968.

2 See n. 2, p. 192 [1 March 1982].

3 See Romans 4:11.

4 See Exodus 3:14.

Liturgy – full of worship and adoration of the divine majesty (so that we do not fall into habit!) The ideal of the 'Church in prayer'. The example of African parishes!

'*Te Deum laudamus . . . Te per orbem terrarum sancta confitetur Ecclesia*' ['We praise you, O God . . . To the ends of the earth your holy Church proclaims her faith in you'].

Reflection; Credo of the People of God; Anticipated Matins

Talk. Meditation (5):
(*Credo . . . in Creatorem coeli et terrae* [I believe . . . in the Creator of heaven and earth]).

Man – as the custodian of creation. The aim: the glory of God. *Canticum 3 Puerorum ab fornace* [The Canticle of the Three Youths in the furnace].[1] Human being: man and woman – in the image and likeness of God. This is connected with 'be holy' (St Elizabeth of the Trinity).[2]

The history of salvation is tightly linked to human history. The history of salvation moves from the 'missionary mandate' of Christ to the history of evangelisation: Europe, Africa, (Asia) – America. 500 years.

Since the eighteenth and nineteenth centuries – the industrial age (*L[aborem] E[xercens]*).[3] Among the effort of 'ruling over the earth' – there is an expectation of 'new heavens and a new earth' (2 P.).[4] Man has a personal vocation (*G[audium et] S[pes]*).

Rosary (I); Litany of the Blessed Virgin Mary, Holy Name of Jesus, St Joseph; Eucharistic Adoration
Concluding meditation: (on the love of God)
Compline

26 February Daily intentions; Prayers
Meditation: only God can speak about Himself
Holy Mass; Thanksgiving; Prayers [illegible]; Litany for the Homeland; Lauds

Talk. Meditation (6): Creation (cont.)
More on creation: Great progress in how the world is ruled.

1 See Daniel 3:23–91.
2 See n. 2, p. 151 [25 February 1980].
3 The encyclical *Laborem exercens* (Through Work) was issued by Pope John Paul II on 14 September 1981.
4 See 2 Peter 3:13.

Words of appreciation for human achievements *iuxta* [in accordance with] Genesis! Numerous statements: Paul VI, JP II – initiatives: because these new developments simultaneously give rise to new threats – and moral deviations (sex, life, genetics, 'space'). At the same time: famine and backwardness. The future of humankind – in danger.

All this is connected with the topic of creation; the place of the human being in the cosmos! American cosmonauts read Genesis 1 during a space flight. As if a continuation of the psalm: '*Coeli enarrant gloriam Dei*' ['The heavens are telling the glory of God'].[1]

Reflection; Prayer to the Holy Spirit; Passion of Our Lord Jesus Christ according to Mark; Credo of the People of God; Terce

Talk. Meditation (7): The Covenant.
After the original sin – the flood and Noah (the covenant with Noah) – Babel. The covenant with Abraham – the offspring of Jacob: Israel – the slavery in Egypt: Moses – liberation – Mount Sinai – the covenant.

The 'gratuitousness' of being chosen by God: a formal commitment on Israel's part. The rite of the covenant: blood.

The Ark of the Covenant, the Tablets of Stone – then the period of the Temple.

Israel broke the covenant more than once, but they always returned to it, remembering the testimony of God's love: God-Beloved. The old covenant – preparation for the new covenant.

Reflective meditation: (on the love of God)
The Way of the Cross; Sext; None; (Reading, reflection – on the Holy Spirit); Adoration of the Blessed Sacrament; Litany of the Saints; Litany of the Sacred Heart of Jesus; Litany of the Blessed Virgin Mary; Litany of St Joseph; Litany of our Lord Jesus Christ, Priest and Victim; Rosary (III), (I); Vespers

Talk. Meditation (8): (Christology).
The most developed part of the Creed speaks about Jesus Christ. (Two names: Mary . . . Pilate . . .)

Jesus of Nazareth: Parables – simple language – actions full of humanity. Jesus loves. Many, many details from the Gospels. When He is alone, He prays, talks to the Father . . .

1 See Psalm 18:2 (19:1).

However, this human image of the life of Jesus of Nazareth cannot reveal His divine mystery yet!

(Reflection); Anticipated Matins

Talk. Meditation (9):

Jesus provoked reaction among His contemporaries: His miracles, His actions, His teaching. Hence the question: Who do men say I am?[1] Peter's response. 'No one knows the Son except the Father, and no one knows the Father except the Son . . .'[2] and 'He who has seen me has seen the Father';[3] 'I and the Father are one':[4] the violent reaction of the Jews.[5]

'Father, glorify Thy Son with the glory which I had with Thee before the world was made.'[6] Hence the Prologue to the Gospel of John. 'I believe in Jesus Christ . . . our **Lord'**.[7] Cf. Peter's speech on the day of Pentecost.[8] Paul to the Philippians: '. . . God has highly exalted Him . . .'[9] The very core of Christian faith: 'Christ is Lord.'[10] Martyrs died for this truth.

Apocalypse. 'I am the Beginning . . . and the End.[11] Come, Lord Jesus'. Liturgy: a re-evaluation of words!

Rosary (II); Eucharistic Adoration
Concluding meditation: (on the love of God)
Compline

27 February Intentions; (Prayers)
Meditation: (You are the Christ, the Son of the living God)[12]
Holy Mass; Thanksgiving; Prayers; Act of Consecration to Virgin Mary; Prayers to the Holy Spirit; Litany for the Homeland; Lauds

Talk. Meditation (10):

Angelus: who was conceived by the Holy Spirit, born of the Virgin Mary – Immaculate Conception – Divine Motherhood

1 See Matthew 16:13.
2 See Matthew 11:27.
3 See John 14:9.
4 See John 10:30.
5 See John 10:31–39.
6 See John 17:4.
7 See the Apostles' Creed.
8 See Acts 2:14–36.
9 See Philippians 2:9.
10 See Philippians 2:11, Romans 10:9 and 1 Corinthians 8:6.
11 See Revelation 22:13, 20.
12 See Matthew 16:16.

– Visitation of St Elizabeth. *Mater Praecursoris* [Mother of the Precursor]. Magnificat – in line with the spirituality of Israel. Bethlehem: The Word became flesh and dwelt among us:[1] 'a body hast Thou prepared for me – I have come to do Thy will'.[2] Presentation: Temple: '*Lumen*' ['Light'].[3] Cross: a sign that will be spoken against[4] – 'a sword that will pierce through'.[5]

Terce
(Audience with Minister Gromyko)[6]

Talk. Meditation (11):

Audio-recorded: Encounters with Jesus of Nazareth, beginning with the calling of the disciples, others . . . e.g. in Lazarus' house, Zacchaeus . . . finally, the Good Thief on Calvary.

Jesus' perspective.

Reflective meditation: seeking the retreat's perspective through the audience mentioned above: *Christus Princeps Pacis* [Christ, Prince of Peace].[7]
The Way of the Cross; Adoration of the Blessed Sacrament; Sext; None; Penitential psalms; Litany of the Holy Name of Jesus, Blessed Virgin Mary, St Joseph; Rosary (I), (II); Vespers

Talk. Meditation (12):

The institution of the Eucharist in the context of the commandment of love: 'having loved His own who were in the world, He loved them to the end'[8] – the new commandment in unity with the sacrament of love; with the gift of the Holy Spirit: Person – Love.

John 15: 'As the Father has loved me, so have I loved you';[9] '– love one another, as I have loved you'[10] – in this spirit, communion with Jesus: the Eucharistic Communion.

Reflection; Anticipated Matins

1 See John 1:14.
2 See Hebrews 20:5–7.
3 See Luke 2:32.
4 See Luke 2:34.
5 See Luke 2:35.
6 Andrei Gromyko (1909–89) served as Minister of Foreign Affairs of the USSR (1957–85). Pope John Paul II met Gromyko on 24 January 1979 and 27 February 1985.
7 See Isaiah 9:6.
8 See John 13:1.
9 See John 15:9.
10 See John 13:34.

Talk. Meditation (13): Gethsemane.

The final days before the passion as related by the Synoptics: the disagreement over primacy, anticipation of the passion, Peter's reassurances. Christ enters into His passion out of sovereign freedom. And then Gethsemane: prayer and suffering, in which Isaiah's prophecy about the Servant of Yahweh is fulfilled: He carried the full weight of the disobedience of the first Adam and his offspring: the entire inheritance of sin. 'If it be possible, let this cup pass from me' . . . 'not as I will, but as Thou wilt'.[1] Parallels between the temptation in the wilderness and the prayer in Gethsemane.

The apostles: 'Watch with Me' . . . and pray that you may not enter into temptation . . .[2] Let us be going, the hour has come . . .[3]

(Talking to Muslims about Gethsemane.)

Rosary (III); Eucharistic Adoration
Concluding meditation: (Eucharist – Gethsemane)
Compline; Reading

28 February Intentions; prayers
Morning meditation: (Love – Eucharist)
Holy Mass; Thanksgiving; Prayers; Act of Consecration to Virgin Mary; Prayers to the Holy Spirit; Litany for the Homeland; Lauds

Talk. Meditation (14): Passover.

'I have power to lay down my life . . . and I have power to take it again . . .'[4] With the awareness of this, and after the prayer in Gethsemane, Jesus goes to meet those who came to arrest Him. Before *Synedrium* [the Sanhedrin]: sentenced to death. Before Pilate: death sentence – crucifixion – death on the cross. Defeated – He triumphs!: 'I have power to take it again'.

Peter on the day of Pentecost: '*Deus Eum resuscitavit a mortuis*' ['God raised Him from the dead'].[5] Since the resurrection, Jesus is seated at the right hand of the Father.

Passover: catechumens received baptism.

1 See Matthew 26:39.
2 See Mark 14:38.
3 See Mark 14:41–42.
4 See John 10:18.
5 See Acts 3:15.

Reflection; Passion of Our Lord Jesus Christ according to Luke; Terce

Talk. Meditation (15): *Spiritus S.* [The Holy Spirit].
'He will take what is mine and declare it to you.'[1] The revelation of the Holy Spirit is gradual: In the work of creation, especially in the human being . . . The Holy Spirit as a person is not distinct in the Old Testament. This is something that the New Testament brings.

Pentecost: the apostles receive the light of understanding Scripture and the courage to bear witness (before the *Synedrium* [Sanhedrin]). The Holy Spirit in the Acts of the Apostles, in Paul's apostolate, in his mission – the Council of Jerusalem. 'It has seemed good to the Holy Spirit . . . and to us . . .'[2] The Holy Spirit acts in the sacraments: the forgiveness of sins; charismata (cf. Vatican II).

The Council especially emphasises the work of the Holy Spirit in holiness (*vocatio ad sanctitatem* [call to holiness]).[3]

He is in us and works in us.

Reflective meditation: (the rhythm of 'departure' and 'arrival'); (Texts: Testament); The Way of the Cross
(Reading: reflection on *Reconciliatio et paenitentia*)[4]
Sext; None; Adoration of the Blessed Sacrament; Litany of the Saints; Litany of Our Lord Jesus Christ, Priest and Victim; Litany of the Blessed Virgin Mary; Litany of St Joseph; Rosary (II), (III); Vespers; Reading

Talk. Meditation (16): *Ecclesia*: The Church.
Rome – the Church – seen from the nunciatures in Muslim countries (*kafir* [infidel]). The Church in the countries of persecutions: the witness borne by priests(!) Bukowiński?[5] How does one see the Church from this perspective in the light of the Council documents?: *L[umen] G[entium]. G[audium et] S[pes]*: laity(!): Cardijn.[6] The pioneers of evangelisation

1 See John 16:14.
2 See Acts 15:28.
3 See *Lumen gentium*, chapter V.
4 The post-synodal apostolic exhortation *Reconciliatio et paenitentia* (Reconciliation and Penance) was issued by Pope John Paul II on 2 December 1984.
5 Bl. Władysław Bukowiński (1904–74) was a Polish Roman Catholic priest who served in the diocese of Karaganda in Kazakhstan. When he visited Poland between 1963 and 1973, he met the future Pope John Paul II, who was then serving as Archbishop of Kraków. Pope Francis proclaimed Bukowiński Venerable in 2015. He was beatified on 11 September 2016.
6 Joseph Leo Cardijn (1882–1967) was a Belgian cardinal of the Roman Catholic Church. He founded the Young Christian Workers movement.

in Korea – Victoire . . . on Madagascar[1] – some Council texts.

All these facts are a testimony to the Holy Spirit's work in the Church.

Anticipated Matins

Talk 17: A continuation of personal testimony from the nunciature (Damascus, Cairo).[2]

Eastern Churches: great attachment to the Church Fathers. Very good turnout, very good priests, (female) vocations, small but lively communities. *Copti* [Copts]: orthodox and catholic: devotion to Our Lady (Holy Family), also Muslims. Does providence not have special plans for these people? Churches? The Copts and Patriarch Shenouda (!) – dynamism: common declaration with Paul VI.[3] Richness of their liturgy.

Good relations of Christians with the authorities, yet at the same time, their underprivileged social position.

The meaning of the Council. The dialogue with Islam is difficult. Muslims' religious zeal. We will need centuries to bring Christians and Muslims together through their faith in one God: but we trust in the work of the Holy Spirit.

Christian–Muslim religious groups: common prayer.

Rosary (I); Eucharistic Adoration; Holy Hour; Compline; Reading

[1 March] Intentions; Prayers
Morning meditation: (You are the Christ, the Son of the living God)[4]
Holy Mass; Thanksgiving; Act of Consecration to Virgin Mary; Prayers to the Holy Spirit; Prayers; Litany for the Homeland; Lauds

Talk. Meditation 18: *Communio Sanctorum* [The communion of saints].

The article that was later introduced into the Apostles' Creed (fourth century) is missing in other creeds.

Communio Sanctorum [The communion of saints] –

---

1 Bl. Victoire Rasoamanarivo (1848–94) was a Catholic activist from Madagascar who devoted her life to the poor and the sick. She was beatified by Pope John Paul II on 9 May 1985.

2 See n. 1, p. 235 [24 February 1985].

3 The Coptic Patriarch Shenouda III of Alexandria visited the Vatican and met Pope Paul VI in May 1973. A common declaration issued at the conclusion of the visit demonstrated that there were no more theological discrepancies between the Coptic and Roman Catholic churches.

4 See Matthew 16:16.

according to the apostolic and biblical tradition: common participation in spiritual goods, in goods coming from 'holiness' (e.g. in St Paul).

This is most visible in the Eucharist. Other sacraments also belong to all Christians, likewise the word of God, tradition, the Magisterium, etc.

The communion between the dead and the living, 'until we all attain to the fullness of Christ'.[1]

Reflection; Passion of Our Lord Jesus Christ according to John; Terce

Talk. Meditation 19: *Remissionem peccatorum* [The forgiveness of sins].

This article refers not only to '*Penitentia secunda*' ['second penance'] but first of all to '*Penitentia prima*' ['first penance']: to baptism. The Niceno-Constantinopolitan Creed: '*Confesso unum baptisma in remissionem peccatorum*' ['I confess one baptism for the forgiveness of sins']. The Synod of 1983, Exhortation *Reconciliatio et paenitentia* [Reconciliation and Penance]:[2] Lent, the spirit of penance, acts of penance.

Concluding meditation: examination of conscience; The Way of the Cross; Sext; None (Reading: *Dives in misericordia*, reflection)[3]
Eucharistic Adoration; Penitential psalms; Litany of the Sacred Heart of Jesus, Blessed Virgin Mary, St Joseph; Rosary (III), (I); Lenten prayers; Reading; Vespers

Talk. Meditation (20): '*Carnis resurrectionem*' ['The resurrection of the body'].

Eschatology. Divine life in us – oriented towards eternal life, eternity. In the Old Testament – few testimonies: Job, Wisdom ('their hope is full of immortality')[4] – soul/body; person; risen Christ – the model for the resurrection of the body: (the Councils). How will bodies be resurrected? (1 Cor. 15): certainty and mystery!

The meaning of Easter.

Reflection; Anticipated Matins

1 See Ephesians 4:13.
2 See n. 4, p. 242 [28 February 1985].
3 The encyclical *Dives in misericordia* (Rich in Mercy) was promulgated by Pope John Paul II on 30 November 1980.
4 See Wisdom 3:4.

Talk. Meditation (21): '*Vitam aeternam*' ['Life everlasting'].

Christ's words: 'that they know Thee, Father, Him whom Thou hast sent, the Son': and this is eternal life.[1] 'He who eats my flesh . . . has eternal life.'[2]

We cannot understand eternal life using our concepts.

Paul: struck blind by a great light! Mary – assumed into heaven. '*Satiabor cum apparuerit gloria Tua*' ['I shall be satisfied with beholding Thy glory'].[3]

Particular judgement/Last Judgement (Mt. 25).

'At the evening of life, we shall be judged on our love.'[4]

'You did it to Me'[5] – this is important to everyone, including those who do not know God.

'The righteous will go into eternal life.'[6]

Seeing God 'face to face'[7] (John, Paul).

'*Cenabo cum illo*' ['I will eat with him'][8] . . . (Apocalypse).

'Into Thy hands I commit my spirit.'[9]

Through Mary.

Rosary (II); Eucharistic Adoration; Concluding meditation; Reading; Compline

2 March[10]

Intentions; Prayers
Meditation: (*Totus Tuus . . . et omnia mea . . .* [Entirely Yours . . . and all that is mine . . .])
Holy Mass; Thanksgiving and prayers; Act of Consecration to Virgin Mary; Prayers to the Holy Spirit; Lauds

Concluding talk (22):

Gratiarum actiones: mutuae [Acts of thanksgiving: mutual].

For the Lord Jesus, who was present among us. For the Mother of Christ.

'*Pater noster*' ['Our Father']: We pray for the glory of God, for the radiation of the kingdom, for the will of God to be

1 See John 17:3.
2 See John 6:54.
3 See Psalm 16 (17):15.
4 See the *Catechism of the Catholic Church*, 1022.
5 See Matthew 25:40.
6 See Matthew 25:46.
7 See 1 Corinthians 13:12 and 1 John 3:2.
8 See Revelation 3:20.
9 See Luke 23:46.
10 The final talk of the retreat was delivered by John Paul II. The full text (in Italian) is available at: https://w2.vatican.va/

fulfilled. How far does contemporary reality seem to be from what the Gospel says about the will of God. We pray for bread (famine in the world). The final supplications are about the moral order, in relation to the difficult situation of the contemporary world.

Final words; Magnificat; Blessing
AMDG UIOGD[1]

1 See p. xxi.

16–22 February 1986
Exercitia Spiritualia [Spiritual Exercises] Led by Father [Egidio] Viganò[1] (*Rettore Magnifico* SDB [Rector Major of the Salesians of Don Bosco])

~

16 February 6.00 p.m.: Vespers; *Veni Creator* [Come, Creator (Spirit)]

Introductory talk 1:

Lenten period (*Kairos* [the right moment]): catechumenate; *pedagogia ecclesiale* [Church teaching].

Exercitia spiritualia [Spiritual Exercises].

First Sunday of Lent: reading: profession of faith among temptations.

Wilderness – the Holy Spirit – fasting. *Kenosis/ascesis* [Self-emptying/ascesis].

Topic: Vatican II – as a source of inspiration and, above all, new conversion (Paul VI).

Programme – pastoral aim: to return from the wilderness with Jesus in order to save people.

Eucharistic Adoration; Anticipated Matins; Concluding reflection; Compline; Reading

17 February Intentions; Morning prayers; (Meditation on Holy Mass); Holy Mass; Thanksgiving; Prayers; Litany for the Homeland; (Prayers to the Holy Spirit); Lauds

Talk 2: **Church – mystery, *Mysterium***

(a) *Mysterium* [mystery] and history. St Paul, *L[umen] G[entium]*.

– Blindness to the mystery that does not lead to liberation,

---

1 Egido Viganò SDB (1920–95) was a prominent theologian who served as the seventh Rector Major of the Salesians of Don Bosco (1977–95), and confessor of Pope John Paul II. John Paul II dedicated to him the apostolic letter *Iuvenum Patris* (Father of the Youth) issued on 31 January 1988, the first centenary of St John Bosco's death.

lunedì **21** gennaio

s. Agnese

Monday Montag Lundi
ПОНЕДЕЛЬНИК Lunes الاثنين

January Januar Janvier
ЯНВАРЬ Enero يناير

Ex. Spir. 1986. 16.II – 22.II

P. Viganò (Rett. Magg. SDB)

(16.II.) g. 18.

1. Vesp.

2. Veni Creator

3. I Conf. introduction
Cras. civil – pasty kairos; katechumenat / pedagogia ecclesiale
exercitia spir.
I, więź. G. Patre: czytanie: uznanie ciąży porod. pokus.
Postquia – Duch Święty – post / kairos / ascesis /
Tematyka: Vaticanum II – jako źródło inspiracji a przede wszystkim źródło nowego nauczania (Tavi?)
Program – cel pastor.: wrócić z Jezusem z pustyni, aby zbawić człowieka

4. Ado. Euch.

5. Matut. antycip.

6. Refl. stat.

7. Compl.

Lecturae

M	G	V	S	D	L	M	M	G	V	S	D	L	M	M	G
16	17	18	19	20	21	22	23	24	25	26	27	28	29	30	31

but to new enslavement (ideological oppression, new idolatry).

- A new opening to the mystery: a new inspiration of the Holy Spirit (*E[vangelii] N[untiandi]*).
  : This is the mystery of the Father: love – creation.
- The reality of the 'world' (Paul VI).
  : This is the mystery of the Son – *contra* [against] 'political explanations', one has constantly to seek to reveal the identity and absolute originality of the mystery of the Son.
  : This is the mystery of the Spirit – against all contemporary rationalism, history confirms the presence of the Spirit. Hence: call to holiness (*vita consecr.* [consecrated life]).

God is love = creation, redemption, sanctification. *Transform.* [transformation]; (*Mysterium Dei* [The mystery of God] is fulfilled in history).

(Reflection); Terce

Talk 3: **Church – *Mysterium***

(b) *Vita nello Spirito* [Life in the Spirit] = holiness.

Participation in the divine life through the mediation of the Trinitarian 'movement'. From the Father through the Son in the Holy Spirit – towards the Father through the Son in the Holy Spirit.

Contra [against]: contemporary anthropocentrism – *Protagonista ultimo* [the ultimate protagonist] – the Holy Spirit! The whole topic is connected with Him: holiness.

St Paul: 'in Christ' – 'in the Holy Spirit'.

The Spirit transcends our 'I' and 'we' (psycho-sociology).

Three divine 'dynamisms' of holiness in man – faith, hope, love – three modes of being – the greatest: love. The world needs this new life in the Spirit urgently.

Paul – the Spirit working in man; Luke – the Spirit working in the community, in the Church. These interventions of the Holy Spirit recur in history: Vatican II – the new Pentecost.

[Life in the Spirit – it gives direction to a person's behaviour and provides orientation for apostolic and pastoral work.]

Sext; None; (Concluding meditation); The Way of the Cross; (*Angelus*); Adoration of the Blessed Sacrament; Rosary (II), (III); Reading; Litany of the Holy Name of Jesus, Blessed Virgin Mary, St Joseph; Vespers

Talk 4: **Church – Mysterium**

(c) The grace of unity.

Holiness – life in the Spirit – life of faith, hope, love, ultimately focused on love: the love of God and man – indivisible. Pastoral love.

The path of love is man. To reveal His love, God became a poor man. Christ is the source of this love.

In between the two poles of love – God; man – the unity of heart: the grace of unity between '*interiorità*' ['internal life'] and '*operosità*' ['actions'].

(Quotations from the documents of Vatican II.)

St Francis de Sales; St Camillus de Lellis; St John Bosco; the Council's recommendation is *promuovere una nova spiritualità (apostolorum) dell'apostolato* [to promote new apostolic spirituality]. Contemplation and action: two complementary dimensions.

Christ laid down His life for us – we – ours – for our brothers (John).[1]

(Anticipated Matins)

Talk 5: **Church – Mysterium**

(d) Beatitudes (Eight Beatitudes).

The spirit of the Beatitudes is indispensable for all Christians: the world cannot be transformed and offered to God without this (Vatican II).

Beatitudes (Mt., Lk.) – in a way, this is Christ's autobiographical synthesis.

Particular attributes of love; 'above' the commandments – expressions of evangelical witness.

The fullest commentary on the Eight Beatitudes – the life of Jesus, as well as Mary and saints – structural analysis of the Beatitudes: (four elements) . . . . ??

These are true evangelical energies that can transform the world.

1 See 1 John 3:16.

Conclusion: To love like God loves means to implement the spirit of the Eight Beatitudes in our lives.

Rosary (I); Eucharistic Adoration; (Prayers); (Concluding meditation); Compline; Reading

18 February Intentions; Morning prayers; (Meditation on Holy Mass); (Prayers to the Holy Spirit); Holy Mass; Thanksgiving; Prayers; Litany for the Homeland; Lauds

Talk 6: **Church – *Sacramentum* [Sacrament]**

(a) '*Essere Chiesa*' ['To be the Church'].

We are not a religious association etc. We are the body of Christ. The Church is *mysterium et sacramentum* [mystery and sacrament].

One could say: In the Church *Mysterium* [mystery] becomes a sacrament. The sacrament existing in history. Church – sacrament and the seven sacraments = 'we' as the body of Christ ('*biologia mystica*' ['mystical biology']).

'*Essere Chiesa*' = *sentirsi membra vive e corresponsabili* = *vivere in comunione* ['To be the Church' = to be living and responsible members = to live in communion].

God – *Communio!* [community!] (Trinity) – *Mysterium* [mystery] – Church.

If the Church is '*sacramentum*', that is a 'sign', then Christians (the Church as a whole) are to bear witness (cf. *L[umen] G[entium]; G[audium et] S[pes]*) = *martyrium* [witness].

The more secularism and atheism spread in the world, the more urgent this witness is.

The sacraments (especially the Eucharist) and the sacrament: '*ecclesiogenesi*' ['ecclesiogenesis'].

[All this as 'material' for the examination of conscience: '*essere Chiesa*' ['to be the Church'] = to fight against sin, to work with redemption.]

Terce; (Passion according to Matthew)

Talk 7: **Church – Sacrament**

(b) *Essere pastori nella Chiesa San.* [To be shepherds in the Holy Church].

- Vatican II as a Copernican revolution – *sacerdotium commune fidelium* [common priesthood of the faithful]

- risen Christ – the Only Highest Priest
- the fullness of *ministeriale* [ministerial] priesthood – in episcopacy.

Christ: Prophet, Priest, Shepherd – He does not have a successor, He only has '*ministri*' ['ministers'] (*vicarii, delegati* [vicars, delegates]).

Hence: '*essere pastori*' = *essere strumenti che fanno visibile Cristo* ['to be shepherds' = to be instruments that make Christ visible].

Pastori [Shepherds] (bishops):

(1) *successio apost.* [apostolic succession]
(2) *collegialità episcop./corpus episc.* [episcopal collegiality/ the episcopal body]

[In what does '*communio*' ['communion'] of priests with Peter consist? *communio et participatio* [communion and participation].]

(3) *sollicitudo universalis* [universal care] (missionary tasks).

(1), (2), (3) – the novelty of Vatican II *quoad consecr. episc.* [regarding episcopal ordination]).

- '*essere presbyteri*' ['to be priests']! (*L[umen] G[entium], P[resbyterorum] O[rdinis]*)
- *Pastori* [shepherds] called to celebrate the sacrament of the Church! *Populus acquisitionis, gens sancta!* [A people of His possession, a holy nation][1]

[*originalità del minister.* [the originality of the ministry]. The new covenant.]

Sext; None; (Concluding meditation); The Way of the Cross; Adoration of the Blessed Sacrament; Rosary (III), (I); Penitential psalms; Reading; Litany of the Sacred Heart of Jesus, Blessed Virgin Mary, St Joseph; Vespers

Talk 8: **Church – Sacrament**

(c) *Essere Curia del Papa nella Chiesa* [To be the Papal Curia in the Church].

1 See 1 Peter 2:9.

'Presidenza dinamica nella carità' ['Dynamic leadership in love'] *e 'complesso anti-romano'* [and the 'anti-Roman complex'].

Due atteggiamenti spirituali: (apertura – resp. min.?) [Two spiritual attitudes: (opening – ministerial responsibility?)].

Knowledge and implementation of Vatican II.

Nuova evangelizzazione [The new evangelisation].

Ministero della santificazione [Ministry of sanctification].

Si governa animando – si anima governando [It governs by enlivening – it enlivens by governing].

Ministero di Pietro nella collegialità – è personale se si esercita non sostituendo da istituzione – [Peter's service in collegiality – it is personal if one undertakes it and it cannot be replaced by institutions].

(*Principio della sussidiarietà* [The principle of subsidiarity]).

Alcune priorità [Several priorities]:

(1) *applicazione del Vat. II* [implementation of Vatican II]
(2) *apertura alla comunion(e), all'ecumenismo, altre religioni etc.* [openness to the communion, to ecumenism, to other religions, etc.]
(3) relation to the particular Churches
(4) *apertura al laicato* [openness to the laity]
(5) *spirito di servizio, bontà* [spirit of service, goodness].

Paul VI's words.
Prayer to St Peter.

Anticipated Matins

Talk 9: **Church – Sacrament**
(d) *Essere religiosi o laici nella Chiesa* [To be the clergy or the laity in the Church].

No 'state' in the Church is self-sufficient, but there is a mutual openness and interdependence.[1]

***Vita consacrata* [Consecrated life]:** *radicalità delle esigenze del Vangelo* [the radicality of the Gospel's demands]
– *Pastori – forma gregis* [Shepherds – the role model for the flock]

1 See the *Catechism of the Catholic Church*, 837.

Laici [**laity**] (the Church), *Popolo di Dio, servitori del mondo* [people of God, servants of the world] – to permeate the entire earthly reality with the spirit of the gospel ('secularisation – secularism')
– *spiritualità apostolica!* [apostolic spirituality!]

Conclusion of the day's topic.

Rosary (II); Eucharistic Adoration; (Prayers); (Concluding meditation); Compline; (Reading)

19 February Intentions; Morning prayers; (Meditation on Holy Mass); Holy Mass; Thanksgiving; Prayers; Litany for the Homeland; (Prayers to the Holy Spirit); Lauds

Talk 10: **Church: the source of life**

(a) The Word of God/*Parola di Dio.*

Shepherd – the herald of the Word of God. Christ – the fullness of the Word. *Verbum incarnatum* [the incarnated Word], and full of grace and truth.[1]

Bread of the Word: One cannot be a shepherd if one does not draw sustenance from this Word. *D[ei] V[erbum]*: two tables!

The Word of God: divine teaching: One has to be convinced that the Word comes from God who loves us: '*ascolto dell'amore*' ['listening to the love'] as the canvas for prayer (St John Bosco) and *ascolto orante* [prayerful listening].

Following from that: ministry of the word (as the fruit of prayer) – against superficiality. Christ is present in His word, in the word of the Church.

St John: we proclaim to you the eternal life![2]

Terce; (Passion of Our Lord Jesus Christ according to Mark)

Talk 11: **Church: the source of life**

(b) The Eucharist.

Quotations from Vatican II.

What is illuminated the most in the Eucharist is the definiteness of the *Mysterium* [Mystery]: sacramental realism.

1 See John 1:14.
2 See 1 John 1:2.

'*Tutto il bene specifico della Chiesa*' ['All the specific good of the Church'].

Qui si concentra la N. et eterna Alleanza [Here is the centre of the New and eternal Covenant].

Christ is present in the Eucharist – He is present in the priest who makes an offering – He is present in the offering under the forms of bread and wine.

Constantly to renew the Eucharistic meditation: *mystagogia eucharistica (ad Hbr!!!)* [Eucharistic mystagogy (Letter to the Hebrews!!!)].

The optics of the new and definitive covenant.

(Absolute novelty / the originality of the Eucharist.)

The Eucharist – gratitude – completely focused on the Father, from the Son and sons in the Son.

The Eucharist – *ecclesio-genesis* [the genesis of the Church]. The Eucharist gives birth to the Church as the body of Christ in the history of humankind and humanity – the meaning of the Eucharistic communion.

Being included in Christ gives birth to brotherly love between people. The most complete fulfilment of the *Mysterium* [Mystery] and the sacrament.

Sext; None; (Concluding meditation); The Way of the Cross
(Audience of President Gemayel)[1]
Eucharistic Adoration; (Litany of the Saints); Prayers; Rosary (I), (II); Reading; Vespers

Talk 12: **Church – the source of life**

(c) *Riconciliazione* [Reconciliation]: reconciliation, penance.

The Synod of 1983: a dangerous picture of tensions, conflicts. Is reconciliation still possible?

Reconciliation as a 'dimension' of the mystery: 'horizontal' reconciliation entails 'vertical' reconciliation (interhuman reconciliation + reconciliation with God). This reconciliation is the fruit of redemption, whose source is the infinite mercy of the Father. The Father achieves reconciliation through the Son (in the Holy Spirit).

1 Amine Gemayel (b. 22 January 1942) was president of Lebanon from 1982 to 1988. Pope John Paul II received him in the Vatican on 19 February 1986.

The dignity of the penitent (the one who undertakes penance): penitential acts + sacramental grace are expressed in conversion. This, in turn, constitutes the 'experience' of Christ's Passover. This is the fulfilment of the Church.

Everyone in the pilgrim Church should live out such conversion – reconciliation.

Reconciliation – as a historic power that the Church puts forward against historical materialism, where everything is reduced to struggle as the only means to bring justice into the world.

The power of reconciliation is always the 'great novelty' of the Gospel.

Litany of the Holy Name of Jesus, Blessed Virgin Mary, St Joseph; Anticipated Matins

Talk 13: **Church – the source of life**

(d) *Sequela radicale* [Radical imitation].

Sequela – propria ai Pastori [Imitation – typical of Shepherds]. Like: in the calling of the apostles: to work with Christ for the kingdom, to leave all behind.

Total *'disponibilità' alla volontà del Padre* ['availability' to the will of the Father]. Cf. *P[resbyterorum] O[rdinis]* – in all that comprises pastoral service. (*P[resbyterorum] O[rdinis].*)[1]

This is connected to the following characteristics: humility – chastity in celibacy – voluntary poverty – difficult studies, necessary to face the challenge of evangelisation in the contemporary world – the ability to be with others.

Kenosis [self-emptying] – vigilance! (necessary in every age).

(Conclusion of the whole day.)

Rosary (III); Eucharistic Adoration; Prayers; (Concluding meditation); Reading; Compline

20 February Intentions; Morning prayers; (Meditation on Holy Mass = on the Eucharist); Holy Mass; Thanksgiving; Prayers for the Homeland; Prayers to the Holy Spirit; Lauds

Talk 14: **Church '*in missione*' ['on its mission']**

(a) *Originalità della pastorale* [The originality of pastoral work].

1 See n. 1, p. 160 [28 February 1980].

Mutua interazione e complementarietà [Mutual interaction and complementarity] *doctrina* ⟷ *pastorale* [doctrine ⟷ pastoral work]. Doctrine in its nature is 'pastoral', because it is oriented towards man. This doctrine, in its essence, is also 'religious' (it is 'religion'), but this essence has various and diverse consequences for human life too. The social teaching of the Church responds to a particular need of our times.

Christ came to teach new 'religion', which is grounded not in myths, but in persons, facts: the religion of 'the Father who loves the world'. From this follows '*la pastorale*' (pastoral work) that is sensitive to all dimensions of human life.

Terce; (Passion of Our Lord Jesus Christ according to Luke)
!! '*Ut qui sine Te esse non possumus, secundum Te vivere valeamus*' ['Since without You we cannot exist, may we be enabled to live according to Your will'][1]

Talk 15: **Church '*in missione*' ['on its mission']**
(b) Evangelisation.

The Synods of 1974, 1977. Quotations from Vatican II!! (*G[audium et] S[pes]*); (*altre* [others]).

Eternal and contemporary questions (*G[audium et] S[pes]*) – man seeks convincing answers. This is the rationale for evangelisation, which has to move with the times (the new evangelisation) which takes into account the principle of religious freedom.

Evangelisation has to take place in a dialogue with cultures (with culture).

Evangelisation in the fullness of truth (not 'partial'): *mysterium* [mystery] – the world: *verità salvifica in nuova metodologia* [salvific truth in new methodology].

Veritas liberabit vos – non: novitas liberabit vos [The truth will make you free – not: novelty will make you free].[2] This is connected with (and supported by) the charism of infallibility, also: '*religiosum obsequium*' ['religious obedience'].

The significant point of the extraordinary Synod: catechism, textbooks.

Academic '*interscambio*' ['exchange'] between faith and human sciences.

1 See the Collect for Thursday in the First Week of Lent.
2 See John 8:32.

Evangelical mission has to be grounded in proper apostolic 'teaching'.

Quotations from Vatican II.

Let us thank the Lord for having called us to preach the Gospel in these critical times!

Sext; None; Litany of the Blessed Virgin Mary, St Joseph; (Concluding meditation); The Way of the Cross (Eucharistic); Eucharistic Adoration; Rosary (II), (III); Litany of Our Lord Jesus Christ, Priest and Victim; Prayers; Vespers

Talk 16: **Church '*in missione*' ['on its mission']**
The poor/peace.
(c) *Opzione per i poveri e per la pace* [option for the poor and for peace].

Christ – the poor: One of them.

The Gospel of the poor (Mary, *Fiat* [Let it be]).[1] Poor all the way to the crucifixion.

L[umen] G[entium] – poverty serves the freedom of spirit.

Evangelical poverty – not only does it correspond to the lack of material goods, but also to the right attitude to them.

Evangelical poverty – it is a challenge both in relation to the West and the East. It brings a clear perspective for the whole apostolic and pastoral work in the Church.

Peace. Sin gave birth to hatred in human history; its consequences. *Christus est Pax nostra* [Christ is our Peace].[2]

At the same time, peace is the criterion for various human actions. Also for the pastoral work of the Church. The tasks of the laity – broad and diverse.

Anticipated Matins

Talk 17: **Church '*in missione*' ['on its mission']**
(d) *Martyrio e la Croce* [Martyrdom and the Cross], the Synod of 1985 (*non pessimismo, ma la speranza* [not pessimism, but hope]).

In Christ: *desiderio della sofferenza redentiva* [desire for redemptive suffering].

In the Church – this redemptive suffering is continued. It is testified to by various texts of Vatican II; 1 Cor.!

1 See Luke 1:38.
2 See Ephesians 2:14.

The gift of martyrdom: characteristic traits of a martyr(!). Witness borne to Christ: *mihi vivere est Christus* [for me to live is Christ].[1]

'Bloodless' martyrdom – among persecutions.

Missione apostolica può essere vissuta nell'azione o meglio nella passione [Apostolic mission can be lived out in action, or better, in suffering].

La presenza della passione e della Croce – parte constitutiva della missione della Chiesa [The presence of suffering and the Cross – a constitutive part of the mission of the Church].

Reasumptio [Conclusion].

The protagonist of the (apostolic) mission: '*la grazia di Dio*' ['the grace of God']. St Paul's words: by the grace of God I am what I am . . . etc.[2]

Rosary (I); Eucharistic Adoration; Prayers; Holy Hour; Reading; Compline

21 February Intentions; Morning prayers; (Meditation on the Most Holy Eucharist); Holy Mass; Thanksgiving; Litany for the Homeland; Prayers to the Holy Spirit; Lauds

Talk 18: **Church and eschatology**

(a) *Dono di giovinezza* [The gift of youth].

Caducità [Transience]: Transience, perishability of all that is created. Also of the 'sacrament', as far as it partakes in this transitoriness.

'Only love never ends.'[3]

L[umen] G[entium] VII: (*indoles eschatol. Ecclesiae* [the eschatological nature of the Church]).

Eschatology brings in the perspective of everlasting novelty. It began with Passover and the reception of the Holy Spirit. This perspective permeates the whole life of the Church. The sacraments, holiness, consecration, the apostolate of the laity.

This '*tensio eschatologica*' ['eschatological tension'] imprints a mark of youthfulness on every period of Church history.

For this reason, the Church views anything that brings true progress in the history of humankind amicably. Eschatological orientation (the kingdom of God) stimulates this progress.

1 See Philippians 1:21.
2 See 1 Corinthians 15:10.
3 See 1 Corinthians 13:8.

Giovinezza – e Risurrezione [Youthfulness – and Resurrection].

'*Opzione per i giovanni*' ['option for the youth']. Youth always signifies a new beginning(!) – (provided that it does not fall into degradation – deviation), so we should pass on the entire Vatican II to the young; during the Council the Church worked to 'rejuvenate' its face.

The Church – the youthfulness of the world.

Terce; Passion of Our Lord Jesus Christ according to John

Talk 19: **Church and eschatology**

(b) *Forza della Speranza* [The power of Hope].

Speranza è forza più di costruire che di aspettare [Hope is a power that creates rather than waits].

Denouncers of Christianity and creators of contemporary ideology suggest – against hope – that man ought to take his future into his own hands (creator of history).

Vatican II (*G[audium et] S[pes]*): the dynamism of the pilgrim Church, originating in Passover and Pentecost, is also expressed in the structures of earthly life.

In between 'already' and 'not yet'!

The risen Christ and Mary (assumed into heaven) intercede, intervene in history ('already').

'Not yet' – hence the entire effort of the struggle with the evil present in the world (dynamism).

Hope is connected with courage (bravery), St Pius X said: the greatest obstacle in apostolic work is fearfulness and cowardice of the 'good'.

The opposite is '*parrhesia*' ['sincerity'], courage and freedom of spirit, whose ultimate perfection is Christ.

In turn: patience and resilience (rooted in paschal powers). In this way: *pregustare e vivere i beni del 'già' e 'non ancora'* [to foretaste and live the benefits of 'already' and 'not yet'].

Healthy optimism; faith in the victory of good over evil. *Formare* [To form] Christian communities permeated with the spirit of such hope. An appeal to priests and their hope.

Sext; None; (Concluding meditation); Litany of the Blessed Virgin Mary, St Joseph; The Way of the Cross; Litany of the Sacred Heart of Jesus; Eucharistic Adoration; Rosary (III), (I); Vespers

Talk 20: **Church and eschatology**

(c) *Comunione con la Città futura* [Communion with the future City].

Heavenly Jerusalem: Saints and the blessed are united with the pilgrim Church in Christ. This mutual union is expressed through cult, through supplications for the intercession of saints.

L[umen] G[entium] VII: *communio Sanctorum* [the communion of Saints] – oriented towards the good of salvation.

Parousia: the coming of the Lord: 'the day of the Lord.'[1]

The second Adam: Mt. 25!: 'those who are His.'[2] He will reveal Himself in His full beauty. The body of Christ; creatures will partake in the glory of the sons of God (Romans 8).

Christ returns the kingdom to the Father.

The resurrection of the body.

Paradiso [Paradise]: the fullness of love and happiness.

The fullness of communion. Seeing 'face to face.'[3]

This eschatological dimension ought to be integrated into the whole pastoral 'strategy' of the Church.

'*attrattiva del Paradiso*' ['attraction of Paradise'] (St John Bosco).

(Unfortunately, these days we speak too little '*de Novissimis*' ['of the Last Things'].)

Quotation from the Apocalypse: 'the dwelling of God is with men' . . . 'I make all things new.'[4]

(Anticipated Matins for the Feast of the Chair of St Peter)

Talk 21: **Church and eschatology**

(d) Christ: The Alpha and the Omega.[5]

This truth seems to find a particular expression in the Constitution *G[audium et] S[pes]*. Risen Christ.

Christ: The Alpha and the Omega is also the true centre of all the reflections at this retreat.

1 See 1 Thessalonians 5:2, Acts 2:20 and 2 Peter 3:10.
2 See Matthew 25:31–46.
3 See 1 Corinthians 13:12.
4 See Revelation 21:3–5.
5 See Revelation 1:8.

The Synod of 1985: The orientation of the Church is Christocentric; it is not oriented towards itself.

Christ: the firstborn of all creation.

Christ: the consubstantial image of the Father.

Christ: *Homo Novus* [New Man] – He restores the original solidarity to humankind: *figli nel Figlio* [sons in the Son]. New creation begins in Him. He 'brings everything together' in Himself.

All shepherds find the centre and common rhythm to their life and work in Him. 'He must increase, but I must decrease.'[1] To lead everyone and everything to Christ.

Rosary (II); Eucharistic Adoration; Prayers; (Concluding meditation); Reading; Compline

22 February: Feast of the Chair of St Peter[2]

Intentions; Daily prayers; (Meditation: on the Eucharist); Holy Mass; Thanksgiving; Prayers for the Homeland; (Prayers to the Holy Spirit); Lauds

Talk 22: **Mother of the Church**

(Council discussions – *L[umen] g[entium]* VIII.)

The analysis of *L[umen] g[entium]* VIII.

(a) Mary in the life and work of Christ.
(b) Mary in the life and work of the Church.
Paul VI: the Mother of the Church!
(At the conclusion of the third session of Vatican II):
Auxilium Episcoporum [Help of Bishops][3] – and all the people of God.
? (1888) St John Bosco: *Auxilium Christianorum* [Help of Christians].
Madonna: The Mother of all good that is being done in the Church and through the Church. The Mother of difficult moments!

---

1 See John 3:30.

2 The final talk of the retreat was delivered by John Paul II. The full text (in Italian) is available at: https://w2.vatican.va/

3 The closing speech of the third session of the Second Vatican Council was given by Pope Paul VI on 21 November 1964. At the end of the speech he addressed the Blessed Virgin Mary with the following words: 'O, Virgin Mary, Mother of the Church, to you we recommend the entire Church and our ecumenical council! You, *Auxilium Episcoporum*, Help of Bishops, protect and assist the bishops in their apostolic mission, and all those priests, religious and laymen, who help them in their arduous work'.

In particular: *Auxilium Petri (in successoribus) et Curiae Rom.* [Aid of Peter (and his successors) and of the Roman Curia].
(von Balthasar: *Maria – et Petrus* [Mary – and Peter] in the process of the 'constitution' of the Church).

(c) *L'icona escatologica della Chiesa* [The eschatological image of the Church].
Mary and the Church together are the 'new Eve'.
The glorified Mary is the beginning of the eschatological fulfilment of the Church.

Let the Mother of the Church plead for us so that what has been achieved through these Spiritual Exercises may bear fruit.

Final words; Magnificat; Blessing
UIOGD[1]

1 See p. xxi.

lunedì **11** febbraio

N. S. di Lourdes

Monday Montag Lundi
ПОНЕДЕЛЬНИК Lunes

February Februar Fevrier
ФЕВРАЛЬ Febrero

Exercitia spir. 1987.

P. Kolvenbach

8.III – 14.III.

8.III. 19.18

1° Vesp. Dom. I Quadragesimae

2 Compl.

I conf/Medit 1: De conversione

teraz nas prowadzi liturgia tych dni W. Postu.

40 dni: konwersja 40 lat — 40 dni: obraz historii

Paschalnej ludzkości zbawionej w Chrystusie

W pierwszej paschy (egipskiej) poprzez wyzwolenie na-
stępuje Bóg wiąże z sobą lud wybrany — aby
w dziejach tego ludu być poświęcanym; i
przez to wszelkie ostateczne zwycięstwo

50 dni: obraz tej Radości, której uczestnicy
w nas już obecne

Ta pamięć i historia ... spełnienie

Pustynia — droga do Ziemi Obiecanej. Pustynia
— wiadomo, że wśród doświadczeń tego życia trzeba stale i ciągle wszystko zaufać Bogu.

Pokusa w ... 40 dni Chrystusa na pustyni: (o ca-
łość) obraz nawrócenia paschalnego / ...
Maryi)

3. Benedictio SS-mi

Compl.

Lectura
Corona Ro...
Lectio ...
Lit. SS Cordis
BMV
S. Jos.

V	S	D	L	M	M	G	V	S	D	L	M	M	G	V
1	2	3	4	5	6	7	8	9	10	11	12	13	14	15

7/S.W. 42/323

8–14 March 1987
Exercitia Spiritualia [Spiritual Exercises] Led by Father [Peter-Hans] Kolvenbach [SJ][1]

8 March (6.00 p.m.): Vespers for the First Sunday of Lent; Introduction

Talk 1 (Meditation): *De conversione* [On conversion].

Let us follow the liturgy of these Lenten days.

Forty days: commentaries of the Church Fathers – forty days: image of human history.

Passover: humankind redeemed in Christ once and for all.

[From the first (Egyptian) Passover, through all the ones that follow, God fights for His chosen people – so as to be defeated in the history of this people and, thus, achieve final victory.]

Fifty days: image of the joy which nobody can take away from us.

The Church [illegible] – history and eschatology of fulfilment.

Wilderness – the path to the Promised Land. Wilderness – a sign that, first and foremost, one has constantly to trust God among various experiences of this life.

Temptation at the end of Christ's forty days in the wilderness: (complete).

The image of paschal conversion (Mary's [illegible]).

Benediction with the Blessed Sacrament; Lenten Lamentations;[2] Rosary; Anticipated Matins; Litany of the Sacred Heart of Jesus, Blessed Virgin Mary, St Joseph; Compline

9 March Morning prayer intentions

Meditation: 'God fights for His people . . .'[3] (from yesterday: meditation)

Holy Mass; Thanksgiving; Litany for the Homeland; Lauds

---

1 Peter Hans Kolvenbach SJ (b. 1928) was the 29th Superior General of the Society of Jesus (1983–2008).

2 See n. 6, p. 221 [11 March 1984].

3 See Exodus 14:14.

Talk 2 / Meditation:

The Book of Leviticus – the institution of the old covenant priesthood in contrast to the new covenant priesthood (Hebrews). Not a break, but fulfilment. Nevertheless: everything is 'different' through the novelty of Christ's Passover. No man can take the place of the only Mediator of the new and eternal covenant.

At the same time, however, the only Mediator 'needs' priests – humans.

Just like the priests mentioned in Leviticus, they have the *ministerium* (*mediationem*) [service (mediation)] of the Word of God. This is '*verum sacrificium intellectus*' (*Padri Capadoc.*) ['a true sacrifice of the intellect' (the Cappadocian Fathers)].

Likewise, the ministers of the new covenant remain bound to the Temple, which is Christ – the Eucharist and our Passover. This bond extends as far as spiritual 'identification': it is no longer I who live, but Christ who lives in me (Paul).[1]

Likewise – just like the Levites – the ministers of the new covenant undertake the task of blessing in the name of God: by the power of Christ. In Him, the priest is a 'mediator' between God, who gives Himself (offers Himself) to humankind, and man, who in him and with him stands before the infinitely Holy God.

Reflection after the talk; Terce; Passion of Our Lord Jesus Christ according to Matthew; Rosary (II)

Talk 3 / Meditation:

'You shall be holy; for I the Lord your God am holy'.[2]

While other divine perfections leave reflections (*vestigia* [vestiges]) in creatures – holiness is entirely within God. Holiness – it is the very being of God, deity in itself.

For man, this holiness is a complete 'surprise' (*sorpresa*): cf. Paul, Peter, the rich young man in the Gospel, Isaiah(!). All our attempts at comprehending holiness – to understand God – fail to reach this reality – the mystery of God – holiness that 'exceeds' everything.

1 See Galatians 2:20.

2 See Leviticus 19:2.

'Saints' – each and every one of them – 'reflect' some 'trait' of this absolute, transcendent holiness of God on the level of (sinful) creation.

In the economy of the old and new covenant (that is, in history that God writes 'together' with man), God 'separates' His people from everything that is 'un-clean', 'un-holy': *sacrum – profanum* [the sacred – the profane]. Nevertheless, this 'sacred separation' does not close the abyss between the holiness of God and the imperfection/sinfulness of creation.

This 'abyss' cannot be 'filled' with sacrifices of creatures. It can be 'closed' only with the sacrifice of the gift (*dono e perdono* [gift and forgiveness]), which we find in the event of Abraham–Isaac. And the fulfilment: in the sacrifice of Christ (the Eucharist).

This is the only source (*medium*) *sacramentum* [(medium) sacrament] of our sanctification in the Holy Spirit: be holy.

(Blessed Virgin Mary.)

Sext; None
Meditation continued: Holiness of God – *Trinitas* [Trinity] – Love
Learning; Reading
The Way of the Cross; Adoration of the Blessed Sacrament; Penitential psalms; Rosary (III); Litany of the Holy Name of Jesus, Blessed Virgin Mary, St Joseph; Reading; Vespers

Talk (4) Meditation:

'When the Son of Man comes . . .' (Mt. 25).[1]

The Gospel today. The Son of Man is poor. The Risen One is poor too. And the Church is poor when it comes to 'means' – it has to 'beg', asking those who do not know faith yet to believe, and yet from the perspective of the salvation of the world, this is a matter of life and death.

You are 'poor' – and yet He is 'rich': rich, because He is always ready to give, to offer gifts. St Josaphat:[2] poverty – paschal abundance = '*di passaggio*' ['temporary'].

'The poor save the world' – the poor transform the world.

Christ chooses the poor: *optio pro pauperibus* [option for

1 See Matthew 25:31.

2 St Josaphat Kuntsevych OSBM (*c.*1580–1623) was a monk and archbishop of the Ukrainian Greek Catholic Church, who was killed at Vitebsk in the Polish–Lithuanian Commonwealth (now in Belarus) as a victim of sectarian violence.

the poor]; not in the political sense, but in the evangelical sense, with ethical implications.

Poverty – not: resignation, but: choice out of love (*dives . . . factus est pauper . . . ut nos divites faceret*) [(rich . . . He became poor . . . so that He might make us rich)].[1]

This paradox is embodied in the Eucharist. The Church has to live with this paradox, being patient against the forces that seem to 'overtake' it in justice and in support of the underprivileged classes.

Anticipated Matins

Talk (5) Meditation:

'When did we see Thee a stranger . . . ?' (Mt. 25).[2]

The Son of Man – poor, but free in His poverty. This is not contempt for earthly goods. This is the 'poverty in spirit', which corresponds to the very '*esse*' ['being'] of Christ: the Son of God who always fulfils the will of the Father. The Son of God who 'deprived' Himself of everything – who, 'though He was rich, yet for our sake He became poor, so that by His poverty we might become rich'.[3]

Hence the 'rich' can also be poor in spirit – and vice versa: the poor who is not poor in spirit.

Such 'poverty' lies at the foundation of the Eight Beatitudes.

Christ's 'poverty' remains in fundamental agreement with the liberation of man from various forms of social disadvantage: from evil that hurts people in different ways. Christ did not preach and did not implement social reforms. The core of transformation is indeed the evangelical truth of poverty.

Rosary (I); Benediction and adoration of the Blessed Sacrament; Concluding meditation; Reading; Compline

10 March

Morning meditation: (You shall be holy for I the Lord your God am holy . . .)[4]
Holy Mass; Thanksgiving; Prayers; Litany for the Homeland; Prayers to the Holy Spirit; Lauds

1 See 2 Corinthians 8:9.
2 See Matthew 25:38.
3 See 2 Corinthians 8:9.
4 See Leviticus 19:2.

Talk (6) Meditation:

'When you pray, say: Our Father . . .'[1]

Lord, teach us to pray . . .[2] In response, Christ reveals his own life in these supplications, which are His petitions, requests: this is the Spirit of the Son: the life of the Son. Whenever we say this prayer, we have to enter into the life of the Son, in the Spirit, who cries in our hearts: *Abba!* Father![3] 'Our Father' is the synthesis, the reconciliation of the disciples' prayers, and before that, of all the prayers of the psalms and the whole Old Testament. This prayer (Our Father) integrates us into the paschal act of Christ: deliverance from evil (*libera nos a malo* [deliver us from evil]).

The entire 'Our Father' is permeated with the realism of the reconciliation with the Father achieved by Christ in the Holy Spirit: Thy will be done on earth as it is in heaven. From the reconciliation with the Father to the reconciliation with people (forgive us . . . as we forgive those who trespass against us) . . . do not lead us into temptation . . .

If Christ had not spoken the words of the Lord's Prayer, no human being would have been able to 'invent' this prayer.

(Blessed Virgin Mary – final prayer); (Reflection after the talk); Terce; Passion of Our Lord Jesus Christ according to Mark; Rosary (III)

Talk (7) Meditation:

'And in praying do not heap up empty phrases . . .'[4] What is important is not the number of words, but the openness of the heart to the Father in the Holy Spirit. St Paul speaks in the same spirit, calling us to give thanks to the Father always and for everything.[5] Prayer is not measured by the number of words that could 'ensure' that the petitions are heard – but by this continual thanksgiving for everything. Paul's prayer is, above all, the contemplation of God's actions in us and in everything. At the same time, it is a 'realistic' prayer, without any 'euphoric' optimism.

1 See Luke 11:2.
2 See Luke 11:1.
3 See Galatians 4:6.
4 See Matthew 6:7.
5 See Ephesians 5:20 and 1 Thessalonians 5:17–18.

Paul's thanksgiving refers not to the past, but to the present: it is a thanksgiving for what the Father does all the time by the power of Christ's redemption. The prayer of our life – and the life of our prayer. For we are 'God's fellow workers'.[1]

Paul's prayer comes close to the prayer of Christ Himself. It is an unending thanksgiving coming from the human heart. The petitions included in Christ's prayer also take the form of thanksgiving.

The Eucharist.

Didache:[2] We give thanks to you, our Father . . .

(The Church prays with the Mother of God, giving thanks.)

Sext; None; Meditation (continued); The Way of the Cross; Adoration of the Blessed Sacrament; Litany of the Saints; Rosary (I); Vespers
Learning; Reading; Litany of the Sacred Heart of Jesus, Blessed Virgin Mary, St Joseph

Talk (8) Meditation:

The prayer of the Mother of God. She does not say anything about Her prayer Herself. Her prayer is Her constant openness to God. It is the prayer of silence, especially under the cross.

Magnificat – a prayer that is completely Hers – and at the same time fully belongs to the tradition of Israel (especially the Canticle of Anna,[3] the Psalms), hence it is not-Hers.

Magnificat does not break Mary's silence – it is a part of it. This silence consists in a careful listening to the 'words of the Holy Spirit'. This was Mary's prayer.

Mary's Son learnt the prayer of His people from His Mother. In this way, He got to know the word of God, which was the expression of God's will regarding Himself, the Messiah, and the salvation of humankind. 'Everything written about Me in the law of Moses and the Prophets and the Psalms must be fulfilled'.[4] This 'must' is not an expression of fatalism, but of love. 'Did you not know that I must be in my Father's house?'[5]

To pray the Psalms with Mary.

1 See 1 Corinthians 3:9.

2 *Didache* (or *The Teaching of the Twelve Apostles*) is an early Christian treatise (dated *c.* first–second century) and one of the oldest extant catechisms.

3 See 1 Samuel 2:1–10.

4 See Luke 24:44.

5 See Luke 2:49.

St Robert B. [Bellarmine]:[1] '*electa elegi*' ['I chose the chosen'].

Eastern liturgy: Mary is all 'listening': She intently listens to the word of God. Her freedom finds expression in Her maidenly and motherly 'yes': *Electa elegi* [I chose the chosen].

Anticipated Matins

Talk (9)/Meditation:

'*Panem nostrum cotidianum*' ['Our daily bread'].[2] Christ, the Son of a poor family from Nazareth, knew the worth of daily bread. 'Bread' is the symbol of 'the work of God', but also the fruit of human work. Human work – and all human activity – is permeated with God's act of creation.

This is also evoked by the bread and wine on the Eucharistic altar. The Lord has chosen the fruits of human work which are the cheapest and most basic.

St Paul's words point to the necessity of sharing things with others (with the hungry): The Eucharistic bread delivers a particularly harsh judgement here: in this way the Eucharist becomes a sign of 'exit' (*exodus*) for all forms of human egoism. Christ radically 'gives' Himself to all in the form of bread (and wine).

Here is the source of all prayer in the Church and the entire apostolate.

(Prayer – through Mary.)

Rosary (II); Eucharistic Benediction and Adoration; (Reading); (Concluding) meditation; (Daily prayers); Compline

11 March

Intentions; Morning prayers

Private meditation: (Christ has given Himself in prayer: 'Our Father' – and in the sacrament: Eucharist)

Holy Mass; Thanksgiving; Litany for the Homeland; Lauds; Rosary (I)

Talk (10) Meditation:

'*Signum Jonae profetae . . .*' ['The sign of the prophet Jonah . . .']:[3]

---

1 St Robert Bellarmine SJ (1542–1621) was an Italian cardinal and Archbishop of Capua. He played an important role in the Counter-Reformation. He was canonised in 1930 by Pope Pius XI and named a Doctor of the Church.

2 See Luke 11:3 and Matthew 6:11.

3 See Matthew 12:39.

Jonah as the sign of Christ. It is a 'strange' sign – it may even cause scandal; it seems to stand in contrast to what Christ is . . .

But: 'something greater than Jonah is here'.[4]

Christ is a sign in which we find the identity of truth: God who is truth itself acts in Him and through Him. 'I am the truth . . .':[5] Truth – Person.

This 'sign' also contains a signpost for all those who preach this truth – they are only messengers (*ambasciatori* [ambassadors]): they are to be faithful to the truth (*fedeltà creatrice* [creative fidelity]), but in this truth they are also to be 'creative': in the power of His Spirit: the Spirit of truth.

theology

The Lord gave the 'sign of Jonah' in Christ to all humankind, to people of all times, experiencing evil and death. And Christians are to carry this sign to the Nineveh of the contemporary world.

(Reflection after the talk); Terce; Passion of Our Lord Jesus Christ according to Luke

Talk 11/Meditation:

'*Quanta generatio signum quaerit*' ['How much this generation seeks a sign'] . . .[6] These words are still topical. You are better and better at statistics and projects, but you are less and less able to interpret 'the signs of the times':[7] that which is the most significant at the turn of the millennium. (*G[audium et] S[pes].*) That which God says through facts and events.

For God wanted, as Emmanuel [illegible] 'God with us',[8] 'to write' with us, with humankind, our history.

One must not understand God's 'signs' in an automatic way – in the way in which Job's friends interpreted his experiences. That which is the experience of people, humanity, nations, has to be interpreted 'in the sign of Jonah'!

Spirit – the God of truth leads to the fullness of truth.

Reading (interpreting) the signs of the times must not be

4 See Matthew 12:41.
5 See John 14:6.
6 See Mark 8:12.
7 See Matthew 16:3.
8 See Matthew 1:23.

done according to an ideological key, even if it appears to be well-grounded – but according to the sign of Jonah: something greater than Jonah is here, something greater than Solomon . . .[1]

One must not forget that the interpretation of the signs of the times is always liable to fall into the traps of 'the father of lies';[2] and he also finds many points of leverage in us.

Vatican II (*G[audium et] S[pes]*) firmly reminds us of the only key with which the Church and humankind should open 'the signs of the times': the crucified and risen Christ: the foolishness of God – wiser than human wisdom, the weakness of God – stronger than human strength.[3]

(Prayer to the Blessed Virgin Mary); Sext; None; Meditation (continued); The Way of the Cross; Adoration of the Blessed Sacrament; Litany of the Saints; Rosary (II); Vespers

(Learning; Reading); Litany of the Holy Name of Jesus, Blessed Virgin Mary, St Joseph

Talk (12) Meditation:

!'Arise, go to Nineveh . . .'[4] Missionary call. In the Old Testament, Israel lived with the vision of nations coming to Israel (to Jerusalem). The risen Christ commanded the apostles: 'go to' all the nations of the world.[5] The missionary mandate.

This missionary 'tension' corresponds to the mystery of the Good Shepherd who 'seeks' each lost sheep to lead it back to the flock. Hence the moral 'necessity' of evangelisation in the contemporary world.[6] The Christian cannot get absorbed by the transitory 'world', but by the power of his faith, he should reveal and embody the 'eternal world'.

The 'world' – especially the contemporary world – intimidates. Christ gives courage: 'I am with you . . .';[7] 'All authority in heaven and on earth has been given to me';[8] 'I have overcome the world'.[9] Thus, the mission of the Church is not fulfilled in

1 See Matthew 12:41–42.
2 See John 8:44.
3 See 1 Corinthians 1:25.
4 See Jonah 1:2.
5 See Matthew 28:19.
6 See 1 Corinthians 9:16.
7 See Matthew 28:20.
8 See Matthew 28:18.
9 See John 16:33.

a vacuum: this is the world in which God is present and He acts by the power of the paschal mystery of Christ. Nevertheless, God often is unknown. Christ has left the epiphany of this unknown God in the hands of His disciples, in the hands of the Church.

Jonah is afraid of his mission, he disbelieves . . . God converts him . . . and Jonah converts Nineveh. He becomes an instrument of the salvific will of the merciful God. Therefore one should start with the conversion of one's own heart . . .

(Prayer to the Blessed Virgin Mary); Anticipated Matins

Talk (13) Meditation:

Jonah urged people to convert – and Nineveh listened to him. He who is 'more than Jonah' – found resistance: Christ was therefore 'less than Jonah'.

And then Christ 'does penance': He gives Himself away to be humiliated and crucified: 'emptied Himself, taking the form of a servant',[1] just like it was prophesied in the canticles about the Servant of Yahweh(!): 'He emptied Himself, being equal with God': He gave up everything that He 'had', to remain who He 'was': Love.

The cross – a complete 'revolution' in the world of concepts and values.

This 'revolution' found an echo in Saul–Paul: 'I counted all things as refuse . . . in order that I may gain Christ'.[2]

One is often tempted radically to separate God and the Servant: the cross and glory. The fourth Gospel most fully binds the former to the latter: God 'gives up' all forms of glory except for one: to be love!

To be the gift that gives life.

In this way Christ is 'more than Jonah'.

We ought to seek this very likeness to Him!

(Prayer to the Blessed Virgin Mary); Rosary (III); Eucharistic Benediction and Adoration; Concluding meditation; Reading; Compline; (Prayers)

---

1 See Philippians 2:7.
2 See Philippians 3:8.

12 March

Intentions; Morning prayers
Private meditation: ('A sign . . . something greater than Jonah is here')[1]
Holy Mass; Thanksgiving; Lauds; (Rosary (II)); Litany for the Homeland

Talk (14) Meditation:

'Queen Esther prayed for her people.'[2]

Today the Church prays with Esther, who, risking her own life, saved her people (the Old Testament and the festival of Purim): between the throne – the place of exaltation, and the cross – the place of death. (The figure and prophecy of Christ, who died, so that we can live . . . : '*rovesciamento*' ['reversal'] – and transubstantiation (*transsubstan.*).)

(St Basil) God laid on Him (Christ) the sins of us all: this is, so to say, 'the second descent into hell' in order to uproot creatures 'against God', bringing into the world 'God with us' (Emmanuel): 'for us and for our salvation' (the same formula of faith in Rome, Antioch, Alexandria) – in this way Christ establishes a new relationship between 'us', the people of *communio Redemptionis* [communion of Redemption]. This is an essential foundation of the 'together' (unity) of all people, above all, all Christians (ecumenical): 'because all men sinned';[3] 'One has died for all.'[4]

(Prayer to the Blessed Virgin Mary); Terce; Passion of Our Lord Jesus Christ according to John

Talk (15) Meditation from the Gospel:

'Who of you, if your son asks you for bread, will give him a stone?' How much more your Father who is in heaven![5]

A child . . . is a symbol of the gratuitousness of the kingdom of God, the gratuitousness of grace. A child is trustful, believes its parents . . . Father cannot disappoint his child . . . ; in this sense – if we want to 'enter the kingdom' – we have to become 'like children.'[6]

A child as a 'model-example': not its 'immaturity', but its

1 See Matthew 12:41.
2 See Esther 4:17–19.
3 See Romans 5:12.
4 See 2 Corinthians 5:14.
5 See Matthew 7:9–11.
6 See Matthew 18:3.

simplicity and the trust in truth – the truth that comes from the Father.

Christ is the first who remains faithful to this 'model': complete confidence in what comes from the Father (through Gethsemane right to the cross).

> It is here that a whole spiritual tradition originates – up to St Thérèse of the Child Jesus.

So the certainty of faith as personal trust: confidence put in the Father. 'Whoever receives Me, receives Him who sent Me.'[1] In this way the 'child of the kingdom' partakes in paschal joy: 'that your joy may be full'.[2]

(Prayer to the Blessed Virgin Mary); Sext; None; Meditation (continued); The Way of the Cross; Adoration of the Blessed Sacrament; Rosary (III); Vespers
(Learning; Reading); Litany of Our Lord Jesus Christ, Highest Priest; Litany of the Blessed Virgin Mary, St Joseph

Talk (16) Gospel Meditation:

(1) 'Ask, and it will be given you . . .'[3]
To ask – to give. To knock – and it will be 'opened'. Asking comes from faith. Our love is always preceded by God's love: 'He first loved us'.[4] Faith on the part of the one who asks is always already the fruit of that love. 'Thou wouldst not seek Me, if thou hadst not found Me.'[5]

(2) At the same time, God does not separate His gifts, and, what is more, the coming of His kingdom, from our prayer.

---

1 See Mark 9:37.
2 See John 16:24.
3 See Matthew 7:7.
4 See 1 John 4:19.
5 Blaise Pascal, *Pensées*, Introduction by T. S. Eliot (New York, 1958), p. 149. Pope John Paul II offered a reflection on this quotation in his general audience of 27 December 1978: 'A good many men have described their search for God along the ways of their own lives. Even more numerous are those who are silent, considering everything they have lived along these ways as their own deepest and most intimate mystery: what they experienced, how they searched, how they lost their sense of direction and how they found it again. Man is the being who seeks God. And even after having found him, he continues to seek him. And if he seeks him sincerely, he has already found him; as, in a famous fragment of Pascal, Jesus says to man: "Take comfort, you would not be looking for me if you had not already found me." This is the truth about man. It cannot be falsified. Nor can it be destroyed.'

(3) The prayer in the garden of Gethsemane: Alone with the Father. He encounters the Father's silence. 'If it be possible . . .'[1] 'All things are possible to Thee . . .'[2] The response is His renewed readiness to fulfil the redemptive mission: 'Thy will'.[3]

(4) Hence this prayer in the garden of Gethsemane is the model of all prayer: and its fruit is, above all, the transformation of our will. What is revealed is, so to speak, the very heart of petitionary prayer (Cf. also the prayer at the resurrection of Lazarus: supplication and thanksgiving[4]).

(Prayer to the Blessed Virgin Mary); Anticipated Matins

Talk (17) Meditation:

'Father will give good things to those who ask Him'[5] . . . According to Luke: He will give the Holy Spirit . . .[6] That good gift is the Holy Spirit.

Through St John's eyes: Christ's pierced side on the cross is the very 'moment' of this gift: the Holy Spirit. The beginning of Pentecost – the birth of the Church. Blood and water are the signs of death.[7] It is simultaneously death that gives life. For St John this dead body on the cross is already the body of resurrection, of glory.

The mystery of the pierced side: the mystery of the blood spilt in sacrifice, the mystery of the water that Jesus spoke about at the Feast of Tabernacles: the rivers of living water shall flow.[8] In this way Christ invited everyone to quench the thirst of the soul in Him.

What is more: he who seeks to quench the thirst of his soul in Him will become the spring of living water for others.

Hence: the coming of the enlivening Spirit is strongly connected with the salvific death of the Redeemer.

1 See Matthew 26:39.
2 See Mark 14:36.
3 See Luke 22:42.
4 See John 11:41–42.
5 See Matthew 7:11.
6 See Luke 11:13.
7 See John 19:34.
8 See John 7:38.

The pierced side: *Cor ad cor loquitur* [Heart speaks to heart]. Augustine: *redeamus ad cor . . .* [let us return to the heart]. The Heart of the Saviour: the source of life in the Spirit: the mystery of wounded love.

(Prayer to the Blessed Virgin Mary); Rosary (I); Eucharistic Benediction and Adoration; (Reading); Holy Hour; Compline; (Prayers)

13 March

Intentions; Morning prayers
Private meditation: (the mystery of the Pierced Side: *Cor Jesu* [the Heart of Jesus])
Holy Mass; Thanksgiving; Prayers; Litany for the Homeland; Prayers to the Holy Spirit; Rosary (I); Lauds

Talk (18) Meditation:

'When you are offering your gift at the altar . . .'[1] The Sermon on the Mount . . . We are going to the Upper Room . . . Christ, before He institutes the altar of the new and eternal covenant, shows the apostles that it is necessary to be cleansed – and to accept Himself as the Servant!

'Go, be reconciled . . .'[2] The Lord knows that human life is always full of tensions and conflicts. He wants this life always to be permeated with the spirit of His service and reconciliation.

Unity in Christ does not erase differences and varieties, it does not erase diversity – it entails them and supports them. Using these varieties and differences to direct them towards oppositions and hatred: this is how the Prince of this world works. The Spirit of Christ, the service of the gospel, direct this diversity into unity through reconciliation.

Christ is new peace: He reconciled two into one . . . He has broken down the dividing wall of hatred . . .[3] by forgiving His own enemies (*dona et pardona* [give and forgive]) on the cross.

(Prayer to the Blessed Virgin Mary); Prayers and hymns for Good Friday

1 See Matthew 5:23.
2 See Matthew 5:24.
3 See Ephesians 2:14. This refers to the wall that divided the court of the Jews from the court of the Gentiles in the Jerusalem temple. Christ metaphorically broke it down and reconciled the two groups into one.

Talk (19) Meditation:

'Unless your righteousness abounds more . . .'[1] The Sermon on the Mount.

This is not about a new moral system, but the existing system that becomes more deeply permeated with the mystery of the love and mercy of God Himself: the righteousness of the kingdom! 'Be perfect, as your heavenly Father is perfect'.[2] New justice = the response of love, which comes from God: not '*eros*', but love that 'descends' from the Father – *Agape*!

The Sermon on the Mount 'translates' the experience of the Son into the language of commandments or counsels. In this sense, John will say that 'love is keeping God's commandments'.[3] These commandments protect all that is truly and deeply human. In this spirit, the Sermon on the Mount explains e.g. the fifth or sixth commandment of the Decalogue . . .

Evangelical behaviour is to be a reflection of the love of the Father, who comes forward, who extends His hand first . . . From this perspective, the final word is 'love for enemies'. This love implies perceiving, in him who is your 'enemy', a child of God.

Man cannot love like this – cannot love with the love that is God's, unless he recognises that he is loved by God – and hence he is in the order of grace. This is the 'righteousness that abounds more . . .'[4]

(Prayers to the Blessed Virgin Mary); Sext; None; Meditation continued; Rosary (II) – during the Way of the Cross; (Learning; Reading)
Eucharistic Adoration; seven penitential psalms (seven words of Christ on the cross); [Prayer] to the Five Wounds of the Redeemer; Rosary (III); Litany of the Sacred Heart of Jesus, Blessed Virgin Mary, St Joseph; Vespers

Talk (20) Meditation:

'But I say to you . . .':[5] the essence of morality and its source in the law of God are confirmed in the Sermon on the Mount:

---

1 See Matthew 5:20.
2 See Matthew 5:48.
3 See 1 John 5:3.
4 See Matthew 5:20.
5 See Matthew 5:22–44.

'I have come not to abolish the law and the prophets, but to fulfil them'.[1]

Christ states: 'But I say to you' from this very position. This is, so to speak, the absolute appeal, confirmed with the cross and resurrection.

Christ – the new Moses. 'I am the Lord your God, who brought you out of . . . the house of bondage'.[2]

This liberating love of God lies at the foundation of the law (Decalogue). Love – law: Love gives power to the law; the law serves to fulfil love.

The Beatitudes in the Sermon on the Mount are not as much moral norms as they are an expression of unity with Christ as the fullest embodiment of the Beatitudes. At the same time, they emphasise the joyful aspect of this unity with Christ in everything, through which He Himself 'has fulfilled the law'[3] – joyful in the eschatological dimension.

We are called to the freedom to which Christ liberated us: 'But I say to you . . .' St Paul: 'not having a righteousness of my own, based on law . . .':[4] Christ – the source of justification.

(Prayer to the Blessed Virgin Mary); Anticipated Matins

Talk (21) Meditation: 'and then come and offer your gift . . .'[5] (from the Sermon on the Mount). What is the relationship between 'reconciliation with man' and a 'sacrifice' offered to God? In other words, between the dimension of spirituality 'for people' (in a way, horizontal) and the dimension 'for God' (vertical). Christ says: 'and then come and offer your gift' – this means: the entire dimension 'for people' has to be rooted in the dimension 'for God'. At the same time, the dimension 'for God' has to translate into the dimension 'for brothers'. This is the eternal centre of evangelical spirituality.

'Secularisation' = 'not coming back to the altar' . . . The system of human values: justice, brotherhood, solidarity, originate in Christianity, which contemporary civilisation

1 See Matthew 5:17.
2 See Exodus 20:2.
3 See Romans 13:8.
4 See Philippians 3:9.
5 See Matthew 5:24.

acknowledges, but from which it also distances itself. Christ is [illegible], but only 'man for others', without any connection with the paschal reality: the cross – the resurrection.

The Church is engaged in the human dimension of the civilisation of love as a consequence of the paschal mystery, which constantly purifies and deepens everything that the human dimension forms in a human way.

Hence we have always to 'come back' and offer our gifts with Christ. The kingdom of God is already present in the world. All that is human finds its fulfilment only in the risen Lord, in the transcendental kingdom, which is the gift of God. Without this – the spiritual hunger will always remain . . .

(Prayer to the Blessed Virgin Mary); The Way of the Cross [illegible]; Concluding meditation; (Reading); Compline

14 March

Intentions; Morning prayers
Private meditation: (The Sermon on the Mount: liberating love as the foundation of the law)
Holy Mass; Thanksgiving; Litany for the Homeland; Prayer to the Holy Spirit [illegible]; Lauds

Talk (22) Meditation: *Transfiguratio* – Transfiguration of the Lord – as if a lamp that shines in the darkness.

'Father, glorify Thy name':[1] The Father shall be glorified when the human body is 'transfigured'.

'We await a Saviour, who will change our lowly body to be like His glorious body . . .'[2]

Those present: Moses and Elijah. When Moses came down from Mount Sinai, the skin of his face shone.[3] Christ speaks with Moses about His own 'Exodus', *grande Pascha* [great Passover]. In this way Christ 'takes over' the leadership of the people of God at a definitive stage: Paul: 'And the rock was Christ'.[4]

In the glory of transfiguration Christ, confirmed by the voice of the Father, is Him who shall be 'sacrificed'.

1 See John 12:28.
2 See Philippians 3:20–21.
3 See Exodus 34:29.
4 See 1 Corinthians 10:4.

God wished to 'transfigure' His people already in the first exodus. It is here that the new exodus begins: This is my beloved Son, with whom I am well pleased.[1] For this reason the Father loves Me, because I lay down My life . . .[2]

The apostles: 'when they lifted up their eyes, they saw no one but Jesus only'[3] – and our 'exodus' to the Easter Night of the Lord shall end in a participation in His resurrection and glory.

(Concluding prayer with the Blessed Virgin Mary); Conclusion; Final words; Magnificat; Blessing
UIOGD[4]

1 See Matthew 3:17.
2 See John 10:17.
3 See Matthew 17:8.
4 See p. xxi.

21–27 February 1988
Exercitia Spiritualia [Spiritual Exercises] Led by Archbishop [James Aloysius] Hickey, USA Wash[ington][1]

~

21 February (6.00 p.m.): Exposition of the Blessed Sacrament; Sunday Vespers

Talk 1/Meditation:

'*O Jesu vivens in Maria . . .*' ['O Jesus living in Mary'] (The Marian Year).

Redemptoris Mater [Mother of the Redeemer][2] – Pius IX's words. Mary under the cross and together with the Church: this is the starting point of all our reflections.

Marian cult in America since the times of Columbus – Mississippi: the river of Immaculate Conception; the Mother of Immaculate Conception – the patron saint of the United States; Washington: the national shrine, like so many others around the world and in different countries.

[illegible] – everyone – sons of Mary through grace, like Christ '*per naturam*' ['through nature']. Mary has a lot to say to us – a lot to say to the contemporary world.

Eucharistic Adoration; Lenten Lamentations;[3] Anticipated Matins (for the Feast of the Chair of St Peter); (Reading); Compline

---

1 James Aloysius Hickey (1920–2004) was an American cardinal and Archbishop of Washington, DC (1980–2000).

2 Pope John Paul II proclaimed a Marian Year from Pentecost 1987 to Assumption 1988. In his encyclical *Redemptoris Mater* (Mother of the Redeemer), issued on 25 March 1987, John Paul II wrote: 'the Marian Year is meant to promote a new and more careful reading of what the Council said about the Blessed Virgin Mary, Mother of God, in the mystery of Christ and of the Church, the topic to which the contents of this Encyclical are devoted. Here we speak not only of the doctrine of faith but also of the life of faith, and thus of authentic "Marian spirituality," seen in the light of Tradition, and especially the spirituality to which the Council exhorts us. Furthermore, Marian spirituality, like its corresponding devotion, finds a very rich source in the historical experience of individuals and of the various Christian communities present among the different peoples and nations of the world. In this regard, I would like to recall, among the many witnesses and teachers of this spirituality, the figure of Saint Louis Marie Grignion de Montfort, who proposes consecration to Christ through the hands of Mary, as an effective means for Christians to live faithfully their baptismal commitments.'

3 See n. 6, p. 221 [11 March 1984].

Exercit. Spir. – 1988

21. – 27. II [abp Hickey] USA Wash.

21. II. g. 18

1. Expositio. SS-mi
2. Vesp. dom.
3. I Conf. / Medit.

„Jesu vivens in Maria ..." / Rola Maryi „Redemptoris Mater". – Sługa Pius IX: Maria pod krzyżem wraz z Kościołem: I punkt wyjścia wszystkich rozważań

Kult Maryjny w Ameryce od czasu Kolumba – Missisipi: rzeka Niep. Pocz. / Matka Niep. Pocz. – Patronka Stanów Zjedn. (Washington: sanktuarium narodowe, jak tyle innych na rzecz Maryi i nagrody)

Marianum – pragnę – cywilizacji Maryi, przez której, jak Chrystus „per universum" // Maryja ma nasze oczy do przyjaźni – oczy do poznania współczesnego świata //

4. Adorat. Euch.
5. Godzina święta
6. Matut. laud.: Coll. S. Rosarii
7. Compl. | Lectiones

22 February Intentions; Prayer for the gifts of the Holy Spirit
Morning meditation: Our life is hidden with Christ in God[1]
Holy Mass; Thanksgiving; Petitionary prayers; Rosary (II); Lauds

Meditation (2): *Stabat Mater Dolorosa* . . . [The Sorrowful Mother stood . . .][2] (*La fede di Maria* [Mary's faith]).

(a) Did not Mary under the cross experience the 'night' that St John of the Cross writes about – 'the dark night of faith' [illegible] – versus 'the darkness of unbelief'.
'The foolishness of God – is wiser than men; the weakness of God – is stronger than men.'[3]
(b) What is the 'darkness' of contemporary humanity?
Cognitive scepticism in relation to truth – and, simultaneously, the exaltation of 'technological success' without any regard for human dignity and true values.
(c) The Church appreciates the value of real technological progress – but it is guided, first and foremost, by the affirmation of the value and dignity of the human being. The Church tries to be close to everyone, especially young people.
'*Crux fidelis* . . .' ['Faithful cross . . .']

Reflection; Passion of Our Lord Jesus Christ according to Matthew; Terce; Litany of the Holy Name of Jesus

Meditation (3): (*La dimensione della fede di Maria* [The dimension of Mary's faith]).
'*Beata, quae credidisti*' ['Blessed are you who believed'].[4]

(a) Mary's faith: the inheritance of Israel's faith, which was 'exalted' in Mary. Listening to the Word of God Himself, She conceived the Word–Son in Her soul before She conceived Him in Her body. Speak, Lord, for Thy handmaid is listening.[5]
(b) The readiness to receive and fulfil the Word of God (*disponibilità* [readiness]). This readiness is related to the

1 See Colossians 3:3.
2 See n. 1, p. 29.
3 See 1 Corinthians 1:25.
4 See Luke 1:45.
5 See 1 Samuel 3:9–10 and Luke 1:38.

'poverty in spirit'. It is related to Her virginity. Unyielding faith (*perseverante* [persevering]) – She never hesitated, a true '*Virgo fortis*' (*mulier fortis*) ['strong Maiden' (strong woman)].

(c) Model of faith for the shepherds of the Church: Faith should be the dominant element of our life, no matter how full of human problems and earthly tasks it is. Faith as a readiness to receive the Magisterium of the Church (example: Monsignor Fitzgerald: infallibility).

Sext
Meditation continued: Annunciation – the first self-revelation of God–Trinity
The Way of the Cross; None; Adoration of the Blessed Sacrament; Litany of the Saints; Rosary (III); Litany of the Blessed Virgin Mary, St Joseph; Reading; Vespers

Meditation (4): (*Maria Madre della nostra fede* [Mary – Mother of our faith]).

Mater Salvatoris – ora pro nobis [Mother of the Saviour – pray for us].

(a) To stand under Christ's cross like Mary and John – to bear witness to the person and love. This witness cannot be substituted by any 'ideology' – any abstract thought system (cf. Rahner). There can be no 'gospel' without Christ: crucified and resurrected. To avoid this, we have to stand by Mary. Then Christ will be a living person for each of us (Paul VI – quotation).

(b) Bearing witness to Christ, we can never cease to remind people what standards He has set for us. If we stand under the cross with Mary, we shall not lack courage to do this. For these are standards that come from the very essence of Christian faith. This is sometimes connected to the true '*martyrium*' ['testimony, martyrdom']: a sign of contradiction to fashionable trends. (Cf. Paul VI – *H[umanae] V[itae].*)

Anticipated Matins; (Tuesday, St Polycarp)

Meditation (5): (*La Regina dei martiri* [The Queen of martyrs]).

Regina martyrum – ora pro nobis [Queen of martyrs – pray for us].

(a) Although contemporary culture objects both to '*Regina*'

nie uchylali się do tej odwagi. Ta to
bowiem wymaganie, które wypływa z samego wnętrza wiary chrześcij. – Czasem łączy się
to z prawdziwym „martyrium". Często
spotyka wobec urodzonych pogłos. (Cf.
Vatic. II – 110.)

14. Matut. anticip. (Feria VI, s. Polyc.)

15 Medit. (V) [La Regina dei martiri]

Regina martyrum – ora pro nobis

a) Chociaż kultura współczesna wymaga za-
chwiania i wobec „Regina" i wobec „marty-
rów" – to jednak „Regina martyrum"
ma w odniesieniu do Maryi pełne uza-
sadnienie. Trzeba jeszcze bardziej pogłębić
treść tego wezwania, nawiązując do boga-
tej tradycji.

b) Maryja, która uczestniczyła we wszystkich
Tajemnicach życia Chrystusa, pod krzyżem
„uczestniczy w Jego Golgocie" – oto
„martyrium cordis". To martyrium
jest źródłem nowej płodności w Duchu Ś.:
uczestniczy w rodzeniu się i wychowaniu
wszystkich przez wieki.

c) Czy nie potrzebny dziś być prawdziwym
świadkiem Chrystusa, jeśli zabraknie
pomocy nas Maryi.

16. Ror. Ros. (I) — Godzina czytań.

17. adorac. Euch. — Lecture: Espérer pour tous (v. Balthasar)

18 (Medit. s...)

19 Compl.

['Queen'] and to '*martyres*' ['martyrs'], it is fully justified to call Mary '*Regina martyrum*' ['the Queen of martyrs']. The content of this name should be further developed in relation to a rich tradition.

(b) Mary participated in all mysteries of Christ's life; She participates in 'His Hour' under the cross – this is '*martyrium cordis*' ['martyrdom of the heart']. This martyrdom is a source of special fertility in the Holy Spirit: it partakes in the giving of birth to and raising of the sons of God through grace.

(c) We cannot be true witnesses to Christ if Mary is not near us.

Rosary (I); Eucharistic Adoration; Intercessory prayers
Reading: *Dare We Hope* (v. Balthasar),[1] others
(Concluding meditation); Compline

23 February Intentions; Prayer for the gifts of the Holy Spirit
Morning meditation: (our life is hidden with Christ in God)[2]
Holy Mass; Thanksgiving; Prayers [illegible]; Rosary (III); Lauds

Meditation (6): (*Umiltà* [Humility]).

Mater humilitatis ora pro nobis [Mother of humility, pray for us].

(a) At the foot of the cross Mary participates in this: 'He humbled Himself (*humiliavit Semetipsum*) . . . *propterea Deus exaltavit Eum* [therefore God has highly exalted Him]'.[3] Through Her humility Mary takes part in the 'humiliation' of God–Man. Humility opens a special space in Mary's heart, which is filled with the glory of God.

(b) The 'humiliations' of the Church, the suffering of the Church, the humility of the Church: not only persecutions by the enemies of the Church, but also indifference of so many contemporaries.

The Church stands with Mary at the foot of the cross.

1 Hans Urs von Balthasar, *Dare We Hope*, trans. David Kipp and Lothar Krauth (San Francisco, 1988). John Paul II read this book in the French translation: *Espérer pour tous*, trans. Henri Rochais and Jean-Louis Schlegel (Paris, 1987).

2 See Colossians 3:3.

3 See Philippians 2:8–9.

The 'humility' of the Church – following the example of the Mother of the Church.

(c) Reflection *post medit.* [after the meditation].

Terce; Passion of Our Lord Jesus Christ according to Mark

Meditation (7): (*Mater misericordiae – ora pro nobis* [Mother of mercy – pray for us]).

Autorità della Chiesa [Authority of the Church]. (*Autorità* [Authority].)

(a) The authority of Christ was based on the mission that He received from the Father. His authority was revealed in His actions, in the 'signs' He gave, and in the words of truth that He preached. Ultimately: in His death and resurrection.

(b) Mary was fully aware of this 'authority' of Christ, Her Son: redeeming authority that has brought salvation to humankind: 'I did not come to judge but to save'.[1] Salvation – it is a work of merciful love: Mary participates in this work as the Mother of mercy.

(c) The 'authority' of the Church and in the Church should always stem from and correspond to what constituted the redeeming authority of Christ. The Mother of mercy wishes to help us with this.

Sext; (Meditation continued); The Way of the Cross; None; Adoration of the Blessed Sacrament; Penitential psalms; Litany of the Sacred Heart of Jesus; Rosary (I); Litany of the Blessed Virgin Mary; Litany of St Joseph
Reading: von Balthasar
Vespers

Meditation (8): (*Obbedienza* [Obedience]).

(a) '*Fiat voluntas Tua*' ['Thy will be done'][2] – reference to priestly ordination.

Mary's whole life – as a response to the will of God through intent listening to the Word of God: as at the Annunciation. In this way, She participated in the obedience of the Son and in the work of salvation.

(b) The Church – obedient to Christ; following from this

1 See John 12:47.
2 See Matthew 6:10.

'*sentire cum Ecclesia*' ['to think with the Church'] as an expression of obedience within the Church. Not 'formal' obedience, but obedience based on truth and spiritual freedom.

Let us imitate the Immaculate One with obedience and love.

Matins (anticipated)

Meditation (9): (*Libertà* [Freedom]).

Mary's freedom – Christian freedom.

(a) To be obedient to God who is the Creator of our freedom – this cannot be in conflict with freedom (Guardini?).[1] Mary's obedience – is an obedience of love, hence an obedience of freedom.

(b) Mary teaches all Christians that in order to find true freedom, one needs to be able to 'lose' it. This is the condition of the 'freedom for which Christ has set us free':[2] He set us free, liberating us from the bondage of sin to its very roots.

'*Volo quidquid vis* [I want whatever you want]
volo quia vis [I want it because you want it]
volo quomodo vis [I want it in the way you want it]'.[3]

Rosary (II); Intercessory prayers; Eucharistic Adoration
Reading: v. Balthasar, others
(Meditation: *de oboedientia* [on obedience]); Compline

24 February Intentions
Morning meditation: (Our life is hidden with Christ in God)[4]
Prayer for the gifts of the Holy Spirit; Holy Mass; (Thanksgiving; Petitionary prayers); Rosary (I); Lauds

Meditation (10): (*La Chiesa in servizio* [The Church in service]).

'At the evening of life, we shall be judged on our love' (St John of the Cross).[5]

1 Romano Guardini (1885–1968) was an Italian-German Catholic priest, theologian and academic. He lectured at the Universities of Berlin, Tübingen and Munich.
2 See Galatians 5:1.
3 A prayer attributed to Pope Clement XI (1700–21). See *Handbook of Prayers* (Princeton, NJ: Scepter Publishers, 1995), p. 288.
4 See Colossians 3:3.
5 See also the *Catechism of the Catholic Church*, 1022.

(a) Christ and the Gospel are an inexhaustible source of inspiration to an active love of our neighbours, especially those who are the most in need (the sisters of Mother Teresa). And this – despite the most radical of criticisms (Marx).
(b) Seeking that which is eternal (the kingdom of God) does not divert our attention from earthly things. On the contrary: it is an inexhaustible inspiration to acts of love to our neighbours, to serving those who are in need.
(c) *Suscipe, Domine, universam meam libertatem . . . Amorem Tuum et gratiam Tuam mihi dones . . . nec aliud quidquam ultra posco* [Take all my freedom, Lord . . . Give me Your love and Your grace . . . I ask for nothing more].

Terce; (Passion of Our Lord Jesus Christ according to Luke)

Meditation (11): (*La tenerezza della Chiesa-Madre* [The tenderness of the Church–Mother]).

(a) (the American writer O'Connor . . .)[1] A lack of empathy to other people – on the surface substituted with the notion of 'the quality of life' – is the symptom of our age. This is related to the separation from God, from the crucified Christ and from Mary under the cross.
(b) The service of the Church to those who suffer should be of Marian nature; without this we shall never fully understand the depth of man and his suffering; our 'empathy' will remain superficial or it will vanish completely.

To stand under Christ's cross – means to 'touch' His suffering in all the people who suffer.

Mary – the Mother of the Church.

Sext; Meditation continued; The Way of the Cross; None; Adoration of the Blessed Sacrament; Litany of the Saints; Litany of the Sacred Heart of Jesus; Litany of the Blessed Virgin Mary; Litany of St Joseph; Rosary (II); Reading; Vespers

1 Mary Flannery O'Connor (1925–64) was an American writer and essayist who in her writing frequently examined questions related to her Roman Catholic faith, morality and ethics. Her major works include the novels *Wise Blood* and *The Violent Bear It Away*, and the collection of short stories *A Good Man Is Hard to Find.*

Meditation (12): (*Servire i poveri di spirito* [To serve the poor in spirit]).

Servire pauperibus . . . in spiritu [To serve the poor . . . in spirit] (reference to Washington). The cross of Christ, at the foot of which stands Mary, is the power of this service. This service is often undertaken in the 'loneliness of faith' (Cardinal Lustiger).[1] To fulfil it, we can never separate ourselves from the cross, from the Gospel, from the teaching of the Church. The cross is the 'fullness' of Christ's message.

Mother Teresa: people are hungry for God. This is the deepest poverty. Preach the word of God to us!

Matins (anticipated)

Meditation (13): (*Dire 'Chiesa' è dire 'Missione'* [To say 'Church' is to say 'mission']).

(a) Mary visits Elizabeth to tell her the 'good news': this is a pre-model of evangelisation, which is the mission of the Church.

(b) Mary shows that the 'mission' is a necessity for the Church: a commandment to love people and peoples (*urget nos* [it urges us]), cf. St Francis Xavier.

Mary says 'Do whatever my Son tells you',[2] and the Son says 'make disciples of all nations':[3] love is universal.

(c) Missionary work involves the whole Church – all the bishops in unity with the Successor of St Peter. Like Mary, we should take Christ to all the dimensions of human reality.

Rosary (III); (Intercessory prayers)
Reading: v. Balthasar, others
Eucharistic Adoration; Meditation continued; Compline

25 February Intentions; Prayer for the gifts of the Holy Spirit
Meditation: Our life is hidden with Christ in God[4]
Holy Mass; Thanksgiving; Prayers; Rosary (II); Lauds

1 Aaron Jean-Marie Lustiger (1926–2007) was a French cardinal, Bishop of Orléans (1979–81) and Archbishop of Paris (1981–2005).
2 See John 2:5.
3 See Matthew 28:19.
4 See Colossians 3:3.

Meditation (14): (*Sacerdoti – uomini trasformati in Xristo* [Priests – people transformed in Christ]).

(a) If Cana of Galilee was a kind of anticipation of the Upper Room and the institution of priesthood (the transformation of water into wine) – then the Last Supper was an actual transformation of people–apostles into the priests of Christ.
(b) Christ wants one thing only: to fulfil the will of the Father. Priest: it is no longer I who live, but Christ who lives in me.[1] Hence the priest is a man whom Christ 'possesses', whom He can 'use'. A man who acts '*in persona Christi*' (*alter Christus*) ['in the person of Christ' (another Christ)].
   Do our hearts 'burn' within us?[2]
   Let us pray to the Mother of priests.

Reflection; Terce; (Passion of Our Lord Jesus Christ according to John)

Meditation (15) (*Sacerdoti – chiamati alla preghiera* [Priests – called to prayer]).

(a) On the cross Christ entrusts Mary to John, and John to Mary. This refers to all people as the disciples of Christ, and in particular to priests (as '*alter Christus*' ['another Christ']) – due to their ordination.
(b) It is for this reason (among others) that we are called to prayer in a special way, to maintain in our hearts the presence of Her who 'kept all these things in Her heart'.[3]
(c) This is also linked to the need to receive the sacrament of penance: to confess also '*ex venialibus*' ['venial sins'] (K. Rahner).
(d) The source of trust and apostolic courage is in prayer: 'Take heart, it is I'.[4] St Paul: 'I know whom I have believed . . .'[5]

1 See Galatians 2:20.
2 See Luke 24:32.
3 See Luke 2:19.
4 See Mark 6:50.
5 See 2 Timothy 1:12.

(e) The perfection and centre of priestly prayer – is in the Eucharist (celebration – and adoration).
Mother of the Eucharist – pray for us.

Sext; Meditation continued; The Way of the Cross; None; *Angelus*; Adoration of the Blessed Sacrament; Litany of the Saints; Litany of the Blessed Virgin Mary; Litany of St Joseph; Rosary (III); Vespers

Meditation (16) (*Sacerdoti – uomini di castità consacrata* [Priests – people of consecrated chastity]).

(a) Celibacy – chastity (unmarried state) consecrated to God – (in the past it was linked with the ordination to the diaconate) relates us to the Mother of God – Virgin – in a special way.
The 'fertile' virginity of Mary shaped the 'style' of chastity for the kingdom of God in the Church. It was a reflection of the virginity of Christ Himself. Virginity – a sign of undivided love, open to everyone, not limited to one's own family.
(b) Jesus – Mary – John, united in the cross. Celibacy is an expression of sacrificial love (*amore sacrificale*). Therefore, we have to make sure that our celibacy does not degrade into any form of egoism, narrowness or spiritual 'meanness'.
(c) It is difficult to maintain celibacy without prayer, without spiritual sacrifice, without inner discipline.
Queen of priests – pray for us.

Reflection; Matins (anticipated)

Meditation (17): (*La gioia del sacerdote* [The joy of the priest]).

(a) We call Mary the Mother of priests because She helps us find joy in the priesthood of service. Even among persecutions and suffering (St Maksymilian Kolbe).[1]
(b) As priests we can enter human matters not as 'observers', but '*in persona Xti*' ['in the person of Christ']. The main source of priestly joy is the Eucharist, the celebration of the Eucharist. Then: the sacrament of penance – the joy of serving human souls and consciences.

1 See n. 3, p. 68 [2 September 1971].

(The retreat leader makes numerous references to his experiences as well as the words of popes, bishops, especially the US Conference, theologians, spiritual leaders, etc.)

(c) The joy coming from priestly service in relation to the sick and suffering. Separately: on the joy of elderly priests who have completed their work.

Causa nostrae laetitiae – ora pro nobis [Cause of our joy – pray for us].

Rosary (I); Eucharistic Adoration; Petitionary prayers
Reading: v. Balthasar, others
Holy Hour; Compline

26 February Intentions; Prayer for the gifts of the Holy Spirit
Meditation: ('Our life . . .' cont.)
Holy Mass; Thanksgiving; Prayers; (Rosary (III)); Lauds

Meditation (18): (*In communione mysteriorum* [In communion with the mysteries]).

(a) '*O Jesu, vivens in Maria, veni et vive in me . . . in communione mysteriorum Tuorum*' ['O Jesus, living in Mary, come and live in me . . . in communion with Thy mysteries'] (Fr Olier).[1] The seventeenth-century French school of Sulpicians (Bérulle, Olier . . . but also St Louis-Marie Grignion).[2]

A Christian is a person who has the Spirit of Christ (Fr Olier). In this context Olier asks Jesus, who lives in Mary, to come and live in everyone (who has seen Mary has seen Christ, and who has seen Christ has seen Mary).

(b) Thus, through Mary, Christians have access to the mysteries of Christ, to all His mysteries – from the incarnation to *mysterium paschale* [the paschal mystery].

(c) The Church, following Mary – tries to introduce us into the mysteries of Christ with its own example.

---

1 Jean-Jacques Olier ss (1608–57) was a French Catholic priest and the founder of the Society of Saint-Sulpice (the Sulpician Order).

2 Pierre de Bérulle, Cong. Orat. (1575–1629) was a French Catholic priest, cardinal and statesman. He established the Congregation of the French Oratory and is considered the founder of the French school of spirituality (his disciples included St Vincent de Paul and St Francis de Sales).

(d) Reflection: How much do I owe to Mary (in learning, experiencing, preaching the mysteries of Christ! In loving them!)?

Terce; Liturgy for Good Friday: prayers, hymns

Meditation (19): (*Corpus mysticum* [Mystical body]).

(a) According to the tradition of the Fathers, just like Eve was made from Adam's rib when he was asleep – the Church was made from the body of Christ during His passion and agony on the cross.
(b) The Church is the body of Christ in the sense of the multitude of cells (organs) that participate in its life, at the same time everyone works for the good of the whole organism according to the measure of the 'gift' they have received.[1]
(c) The multitude that enables the 'communion' and mutual givenness 'is built into' the unity of the body. The collegial unity of bishops united with Peter in his successors contributes to this in a special way.

    Mary helps us live out this *mysterium* [mystery] (Mother of the Church).

Sext; Meditation continued; The Way of the Cross; None; (*Angelus*); Adoration of the Blessed Sacrament; Litany of the Most Precious Blood of Jesus; Chaplet of the Five Wounds of Christ; Litany of the Sacred Heart of Jesus; Litany of the Blessed Virgin Mary; Litany of St Joseph; (Reading); Vespers

Meditation (20): (*Exspectantes Beatam Spem* [Awaiting Our Blessed Hope]).[2]

(a) The retreat leader, beginning with his personal memories and experiences, emphasises the significance of living faith in the last things (death, judgement), *beata spes aeternitatis in Deo* [blessed hope of eternity in God]. And the significance of living them out in the spirit of faith, as it was done in the authentic Christian tradition.
(b) Mary, who is a witness to Her Son's death on the cross,

1 See Ephesians 4:7.
2 See Titus 2:13.

shows us *beatam spem vitae aeternae* [the blessed hope of eternal life] in the best way.

(c) Death is a painful 'passage'; in the light of the paschal mystery of Christ this 'passage' is translated as a definitive 'transformation' (*transformatio*) of that which is bodily, mortal and sinful – into that which is spiritual, supernatural and holy. This perspective also explains the mystery of purgatory (*Purgatorium*): extra-terrestrial 'purification' in the fire of God's love in order to become deserving of God's holiness.

'*In paradisum deducant te Angeli* . . .' ['May the Angels lead you into paradise . . .'][1]

Matins (anticipated)

Meditation (21): (*Nostra Madre nella fede* [Our Mother in the faith]).

(a) Cana – Golgotha. In the kingdom of Her Son, Mary intercedes for us just like She did in Cana. At the foot of the cross She 'drank from the cup' from which Her Son drank.[2]

In heaven the Church lives the fullness of life, in which the Blessed Virgin also partakes.

(b) Heaven: A space that Christ made for man in God (Ratzinger).

(c) Mary intercedes for us – and Her prayer is always contained 'within' the will of God.

Mary teaches us how to desire fervently the heavenly Jerusalem, which is so 'far away' from the mindset of the contemporary world. As if the final reality was an 'obstacle' to being responsive to people's earthly needs.

Ave Regina coelorum [Hail, Queen of heaven].

Rosary (II); Eucharistic Adoration
Concluding meditation: (let Our Lady help me deepen *communio mysteriorum Xti, quae ad spem vitae aeternae referunt* [the communion with the mysteries of Christ that relate to the hope of eternal life])
Compline

1 See the antiphon *In paradisum* (Into paradise).

2 See Mark 14:38; Matthew 26:39; Luke 22:42; and John 18:11.

27 February

Intentions; Prayer for the gifts of the Holy Spirit
Meditation: (*gratitudinis erga BMV pro communione mysteriorum Christi* [gratitude to the Blessed Virgin Mary for the communion with the mysteries of Christ])
Holy Mass; Thanksgiving; Prayers; Rosary (II) – parts; Lauds

Concluding meditation 22:

(*Quodcumque dicetur vobis, facite* [Do whatever He tells you]).[1]

Mary with John under the cross.

From this place She repeats again, in a poignant way, 'Do whatever He tells you' – the words from Cana. These are the last words of Mary recorded in the Gospel.

Conclusion; Final words; Blessing; Magnificat
UIOGD[2]

1 See John 2:5.
2 See p. xxi.

12–18 February 1989
Exercitia Spiritualia [Spiritual Exercises] Led by Cardinal G[iacomo] Biffi[1]

12 February ('Lenten Lamentations');[2] Exposition of the Blessed Sacrament; Vespers for the First Sunday of Lent

Opening meditation (1):

Contemplation – silence (listening to the word of God). '*Ascolta, Israele*' ['Hear, O Israel'][3] – *solitudine* [solitude] (to stand alone before the majesty of infinite God).

Communio cum Deo – cum tota Ecclesia [Communion with God – with the whole Church].

(In these couple of days.)

Eucharistic Adoration; Eucharistic Benediction; Litany of the Sacred Heart of Jesus; Litany of the Blessed Virgin Mary, St Joseph; Meditation continued; Compline; Reading

13 [February] Intentions; Prayers; Private meditation: contemplation; Holy Mass; Prayers; Thanksgiving; (Rosary (II)); Lauds

Meditation (2): ***ad Ephesios 1*** [Letter to the Ephesians 1]

God's eternal plan.

'He chose us before the foundation of the world . . .'[4]

- we have eternal life in God
- our pre-existence
- *praedestinati ad gloriam* [predestined for glory][5]
- That which exists has always existed in some form.

In human experience, this is in conflict with the knowledge of our transience, destructibility.

Dilemma – either an eternal plan or a coincidence (*casus*

1 Giacomo Biffi (1928–2015) was an Italian cardinal and Archbishop of Bologna (1984–2003).
2 See n. 6, p. 221 [11 March 1984].
3 See Deuteronomy 6:4.
4 See Ephesians 1:4.
5 See Ephesians 1:12.

and this plan has been communicated to us!!

[accident]). Man often gives in to the temptation of 'coincidence'.

The knowledge of the plan – victory over that temptation.

Conclusion: we need a response to the plan.

I choose Him who has chosen me!

The plan is fulfilled through God's givenness: *Pneuma* [Breath, Spirit].

Hence: we dwell in a world permeated with deity (*invasi* [permeated]): in a supernatural world.

Enlightened secularism, laicism etc. reject this. God is Emmanuel.

Lord, make my heart bigger (St Catherine of Siena).

Reflection; Terce

Meditation 3: (*ad Eph.* [Letter to the Ephesians]).

God is the Father of our Lord Jesus Christ.[1]

God's plan is Christocentric.

(*ad Col* [Letter to the Colossians]): all things were created in Him – and for Him.[2] The firstborn of all creation:[3]

In Him man can recognise himself in his theological nature. (Christianity = Christ).

The world tries to categorise Christ: 'one of . . .'

Yet: Christ is the Only One.

The Only One – because He is alive (not through our faith, but by Himself).

People can be divided into those who recognise Christ as living (believers) or dead (nonbelievers); 'I AM'.[4]

He alone is the Lord of the universe (because He is living) – apart from Him death is the master of everything.

He is the Lord, because everything exists in Him – He is our Lord, my Lord.

This is a source of great joy: that we belong to Him (the source of salvation). St Ambrose.

Conclusion: inviolable fidelity to the Lord.

There is no knowledge of Christ without love of Christ.

1 See Ephesians 1:3.
2 See Colossians 1:16.
3 See Colossians 1:15.
4 See Exodus 3:14.

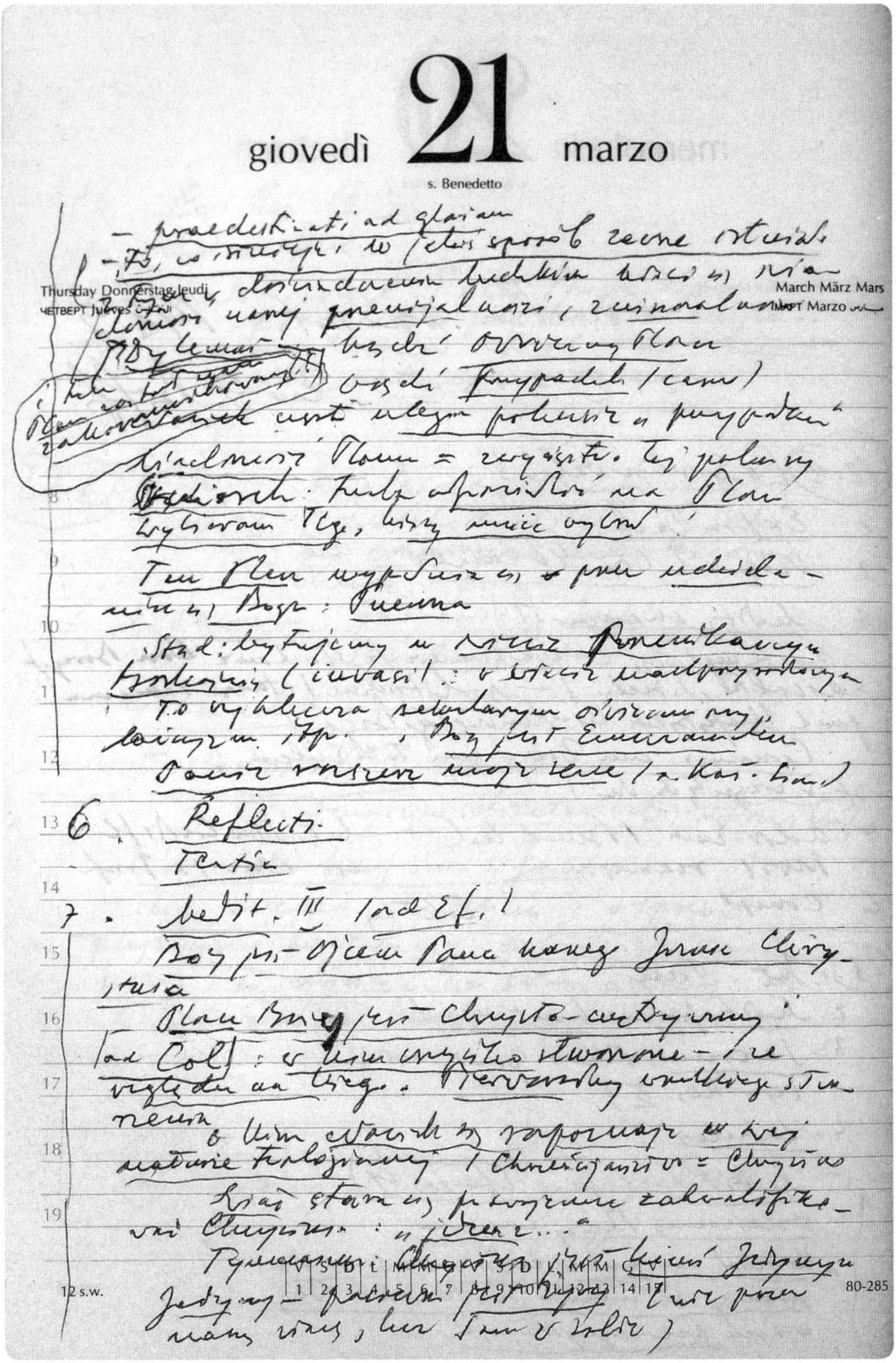

giovedì **21** marzo

s. Benedetto

Thursday Donnerstag Jeudi — March März Mars

ЧЕТВЕРТ Jueves — МАРТ Marzo

– praedestinati ad gloriam
– To, co mówiąc w jakiś sposób zewnętrznie ostateczne
[illegible] doświadczeniem ludzkim wszystkim na
[illegible] naszej przewidywalności, zwyczajności
Dylemat: — będzie obiektywny Plan
— będzie Przypadek (chaos)
[illegible] ulegam pokusie przypadku
Świadomość Planu = zwycięstwo tej pokusy
Wyjaśnić: trudno oprzeć się na Planie
wybierając Tego, który mnie wybrał
Ten Plan wyraża się w przeznaczeniu [illegible] w Bogu: Pneuma
Stąd: być tajemnicą w świetle Przenikania Bóstwa, [illegible] w świetle wszechobecności
To wyjaśnia sekularyzm obecnego [illegible] Bóg jest Emmanuelem
Ponieważ wszystkie moje serce (św. Kat. [illegible])

6. Reflecti.
Tertia

7. Medit. III (ad Ef.)
Bóg jest Ojcem Pana naszego Jezusa Chrystusa
Plan Boży jest Chrystocentryczny (ad Col): w Nim wszystko stworzone – ze względu na Niego. Pierworodny wszelkiego stworzenia
o Nim człowiek się zapoznaje w swej naturze teologicznej (Chrześcijanin = Chrystus)
Lecz stara się przyjmować zakotwiczenie w Chrystusie: w Jezusie...
Przyjmowanie Chrystusa jest [illegible] Jedynym
Jedynym – pozostanie jest [illegible] (nie poznamy więcej, lecz Tam w Niebie)

12 s.w. — 80-285

(Passion of Our Lord Jesus Christ according to Matthew); Reflection continued; The Way of the Cross; Adoration of the Blessed Sacrament; Sext; None; Reading; Litany of the Saints; Daily prayers; Rosary (III); Vespers

Meditation 4:

Our bond with Christ – first of all: faith, hope, love.

Memoria [Remembrance]: do this in memory of me[1] (*memoria*).

The Church is a constant *memoria* [remembrance] of Christ.

The Eucharist – *memoria 'obiettiva'* ['objective' remembrance].

The remembrance of who Christ was allows us to understand who we are: He is the Saviour – we – the saved etc.

Our '*memoria*' ['remembrance'] – the remembrance of Christ – makes our lives a response given to God.

In this way we achieve gratitude: *memoria della memoria di Dio* [remembrance of God's remembrance].

Memoria Xristi [Remembrance of Christ] = at the same time our own history.

Man (especially contemporary man) is a pilgrim suffering from amnesia (*smemorato* [forgetful]).

A Christian community that lives with memory protects man and society against the malaise of 'contemporaneity'. The bond with the tradition and history is broken.

Anticipated Matins (Ss Cyril and Methodius)

Meditation 5:

Obbedienza (obedience): There is one Lord – Christ, and we are all His servants (*ministri* [ministers]). The Church is a servant of Christ, who Himself became a servant. The Church is not, however, a servant of the world, even though together with Christ it serves the world.

The starting point is the Eucharist. The Eucharist is, above all, obedience, which is also expressed in the celebration.

Obedience to the truth – (*a quocumque dicatur* [no matter who it is spoken by]) [illegible].

Obedience to the faith – that is obedience to God's plan, which sometimes 'surprises' us (*sorpresa* [surprise]).

1 See Luke 22:19.

Finally: we are to be obedient to Christ, who Himself became obedient unto death:[1] 'Thy will be done'[2] (*preghiera tremenda* [awe-inspiring prayer]).

The will of God is a mystery. We know signs: *voluntas signi/ metaforice dicta* [the will of the sign/in a metaphorical sense]. We have to read them in the right way.

Rosary (I); Eucharistic Adoration and Benediction; Litany of the Holy Name of Jesus; Litany of the Blessed Virgin Mary, St Joseph; Concluding reflection; Reading; Compline

14 February: Feast of Ss Cyril and Methodius

Intentions; Morning prayers
Meditation: *Cristo è vivo* [Christ is alive]
Holy Mass; Thanksgiving; Prayers; Rosary (III); Prayer to the Holy Spirit; Lauds

Meditation 6: *(Il regno scuro): mundus* [(The kingdom of darkness): the world] [illegible].

Redemption 'presupposes' evil – the evil of sin, which exists: it 'awaits' redemption – *Christus 'Redemptor intrinsecus'* [Christ the 'inner Redeemer'].

Original sin (*pecc. originale*) . . . is of non-human origin ('*origo angelica*' ['angelic origin'] – L. Bloy[3]).

Satan – the father of lies[4] – according to Christ: enemy . . .

Through him 'sin came into the world'.[5]

Man comes into the world with him: the likeness to Christ is 'broken', and it awaits renewal.

The 'world' – the whole 'organisation' of elements that under the influence of the 'father of lies' forms an opposition against Christ and His work: 'the world hates you, because it also hates Me'.[6]

Personal sin.

Retreat: to renew the awareness of my numerous infidelities, e.g. devoting more time to 'godly matters' than to God Himself, and other similar things.

1 See Philippians 2:8.
2 See Matthew 26:42.
3 Léon Bloy (1846–1917) was a French thinker and novelist. His works explored various dimensions of his Catholic faith.
4 See John 8:44.
5 See Romans 5:12.
6 See John 15:18–19.

The 'lost sheep' (St Ambrose's prayer).

Reflection; Terce

Meditation 7: (*Felix ruina* [Happy fall]).

To understand sin, one has to look at the cross. It bears witness to sin (evil) and the greatness (dignity) of man. Christ also cannot be understood without sin nor sin without Christ. *Redemptor*: *Gŏél* [Redeemer (Latin): Redeemer (Hebrew)].

The Church of the apostles knew that the crucifixion conformed to the will of God: Peter – Paul – in this sense one can speak of *'positività' del peccato* ['positivity' of sin] – Ambrose.

The rationale behind such a viewpoint is God's mercy – '*o felix ruina*' ['o happy fall']!

The primacy of mercy.

! Creating the world according to a Christocentric plan, God has chosen a world that would express mercy. The Gospel: 'more joy . . .'[1]

(Purgatory – a kind of retreat (Cardinal Schuster))[2]
Reflection continued; The Way of the Cross; (Passion of our Lord Jesus Christ according to Mark); Adoration of the Blessed Sacrament; Sext; None; Penitential psalms; Daily prayers; Rosary (I); Vespers

Meditation 8: (*L'unico Maestro* [The only Teacher]).

Unus est Magister vester – unus – vester [You have one Master – one – yours][3] – in Him – and through Him – the revelation of God has been completed.

There are two (main) topics in Christ's teaching: (1) The Father – the Parable of the Prodigal Son, others – We can accept the 'world' (with its suffering) only when we receive the Father (Newman – Solovyov).[4] In the nineteenth century a new worldview was formed: to retain the conclusions of Christianity (brotherhood between people), introducing different premises: man without God. (2) The kingdom = the world is in the holy hands of God's power; (although contem-

1 See Luke 15:7.

2 Bl. Alfredo Ildefonso Schuster OSB (1880–1954) was a Benedictine monk and served as a cardinal and Archbishop of Milan (1929–54). He was beatified by Pope John Paul II on 12 May 1996.

3 See Matthew 23:10.

4 Vladimir Sergeyevich Solovyov (1853–1900) was a Russian philosopher, theologian and writer. He played an important role in the spiritual revival of the late nineteenth and early twentieth century.

poraneity does not seem to accept this): to live as if God did not exist. It is true that God chose 'loss' in this world – He has made this 'loss' the foundation of His reign.

Anticipated Matins

Meditation 9: (*La parabola* [The parable]): Lk. (the good Samaritan).

The core of the law: love of God and neighbour. 'Who is my neighbour?'[1] Jesus replies with a parable: the priest–Levite (perhaps afraid of ritual uncleanliness) – the Samaritan.

'Who is my neighbour?' – who proved 'neighbour to the man in need?'[2]

The concept of the 'neighbour' is an *a priori* concept – in the parable: dynamic! What does the term 'neighbour' cover?

Xtus [Christ] does not command us to love 'humanity', 'classes', but our neighbour! – This is the ethical meaning of the parable.

Moreover: the theological meaning – the synthesis of the history of salvation: the man who fell among robbers (the fallen man). The Samaritan – Christ (the first 'neighbour'), who institutes the sacrament to return health to man – the Church to which Christ entrusts the care of the 'beaten' man. Being '*debitores*' ['debtors'], we become '*creditores*' *Christi* ['creditors' of Christ].

Rosary (I); Eucharistic Adoration and Benediction; Litany of the Sacred Heart of Jesus; Litany of the Blessed Virgin Mary; Litany of St Joseph; Concluding reflection; Reading; Compline

15 February

Intentions; Morning prayers
Meditation: (*de Div. Misericordia* [on Divine Mercy])
Holy Mass; Thanksgiving; Prayers; (Litany of Polish Saints); Rosary (I); Prayer to the Holy Spirit; Lauds

Meditation 10:

Christ – the Church: the Bridegroom – the Bride.

Adam – Eve, to the Bride of the Lamb in the Apocalypse.[3]

Il misterio nuziale [The nuptial mystery].

1 See Luke 10:29.
2 See Luke 10:36.
3 See Revelation 19:7.

Bella o brutta? [Beautiful or ugly?] The Church is presently accused of being 'ugly'. And yet – despite everything – she was chosen by the divine Bridegroom, who loved His Bride. And love creates beauty. Hence: admiration for the beauty of the Church–Bride is born out of faith and contemplation. The Church – a multidimensional reality.

Sancta o peccatrice? [Holy or sinful?]/*Simul sancta et peccatrix* [Simultaneously holy and sinful] – Luther.

Ambrose: '*[Ecclesia] ex maculatis immaculata [potest esse]*' ['the immaculate [Church can be composed] of sinners'] – God can make sinners and weaklings into the instruments of His grace.

Journet

Ecclesiology is not Synagogology!

The announcement of the kingdom is not '*profezia*' ['prophecy']. The kingdom is already fulfilled in it. *Sancta et semper purificanda!* [Holy and always in need of being purified!][1]

Ambrose: *Ecclesia sicut luna* [The Church is like the moon]: it does not shine with its own light, but the light coming from Christ.

Reflection; Terce

Meditation 11:

Chiesa frutto dello Spirito S. e Madre [Church, the fruit of the Holy Spirit and Mother].

The Church is rooted in eternity – Christ, seated at the right hand of the Father, sends the Holy Spirit. The Holy Spirit is the source of holiness – in the objective and subjective sense (*il 'santo'* ['holy'] – *e il 'sacro'* [and 'sacred']).

Objective sacredness: the word of God (Sacred Scripture), the sacraments, the apostolic succession (*Sacro* [Sacred]). Christ gives the Church these elements of objective sacredness, which remain there even if the people in the Church are not holy.

They should, nevertheless, live up to this '*sacrum*' ['sacredness'] through personal (subjective) holiness.

The Church – Mother/Fathers: analogy to Eve – united with

1 See *Lumen gentium* 8.

Adam like the Church is united with Christ, and she gives birth to the adoptive children of God.

L[umen] G[entium] VIII on Mary – '*typus*' ['type'] of the Church.

The Church is a mother, not only a servant and guardian of the deposit – but also a mother! This is a fundamental difference.

Christ – the only Redeemer. Simultaneously: every man '*in Xristo et per Xristo*' ['in Christ and through Christ'] partakes in redemption (*cor-redemptio* [co-redemption]). Every man partakes in the motherhood of the Church too. St Paul: In Christ I gave birth to you![1]

The Church – sign = it is a visible prophetic sign: it anticipates the kingdom in its eschatological fulfilment.

Reflection continued; The Way of the Cross; (Passion of Our Lord Jesus Christ according to Luke); Adoration of the Blessed Sacrament; Sext; None; Reading; Litany of the Saints; Rosary (II); Vespers

Meditation 12:

(*Nozze eterne – Maria* [Eternal nuptials – Mary]).

Since God decided to enter the covenant of eternal nuptials with man in an ineffable way, through the incarnation of the Son–Word, hence: the special place of the Mother of the incarnated Word. She becomes '*primizia*' ['the first fruits'], '*prima redempta*' ['the first one redeemed'] – '*alma Mater Redemptoris*' ['the nourishing Mother of the Redeemer'].

The objective holiness of the divine motherhood and the subjective holiness in Her are perfectly consistent. Her '*fiat*' ['let it be'] is a brief synthesis of this.

Hence: Her presence in Cana of Galilee.

The symbol of eternal nuptials: Her concern for the nuptial drink (Eucharist) – Mary Help of Christians.

Woman, behold, Your Son . . .[2]

First: Eve the mother of the living; Mary – the mother of renewed life.

Our attitude to Mary – filial!

1 See 1 Corinthians 4:15.

2 See John 19:26.

Anticipated Matins

Meditation 13:

(*Missione apostolica* [Apostolic mission]).

The divine plan opens this mission.

The calling of the apostles – selection; 'He went up into the hills . . .'[1] – this also has a symbolic meaning.

Jesus calls those whom He desires . . .[2] This is decisive: He desired . . . And it is the same with their successors.

They had different characters, also deficiencies – different social and political orientations. They all, however, have become new men.

They are sent out by the power of 'being with Christ' – just like Christ: He is sent – in the Father.

Sent out to preach the Gospel.

They receive the power to 'cast out demons' (Mk)[3] – this means '*mali del mondo*' ['the evil of the world'], but above all, this means the destruction of the reign of the Evil One.

The calling of the apostles is also a fruit of Christ's prayer. This prayer of Christ – of the Father – gave birth to the apostles and all who belong to this succession (bishops, priests).

Rosary (III); Eucharistic Adoration and Benediction; Litany of the Holy Name of Jesus; Litany of the Blessed Virgin Mary; Litany of St Joseph; Concluding reflection; Reading; Compline

16 February

Intentions; Morning prayers
Meditation: (*De Div. Misericordia* [On Divine Mercy])
Holy Mass; Thanksgiving; Prayers; (Litany of Polish Saints); Rosary (II); Prayer to the Holy Spirit; Lauds

Meditation 14:

The calling of the first disciples (apostles): Andrew, Simon Peter and others.

- John: the seven-day structure, parallel to the seven days of creation (Genesis); then: Cana of Galilee – nuptials – the eschatological feast.
- *Ri-creazione del mondo* [Re-creation of the world]:

1 See Mark 3:13.
2 See Mark 3:13.
3 See Mark 3:15.

'Let there be' – Genesis,[1] and 'Come' – John.[2]

- John's disciples: some of them followed Christ, some stayed with John.

  Fra: relativo e definitivo [Between: relative and definitive].
- 'Where are you staying?':[3] the divine calling is of a definitive and irreversible nature: for your whole life (difficult for the contemporary generation).
- Come, see[4] = experience! You have found yourself in the centre!
- Moreover: Christ knows what is in man.[5] He knows the inner side of man, and man's 'past' – and 'future' (examples: Simon Peter, Nathanael).
- Not only this: He has already found each of us (called us). The encounter is the moment of finding.
- This short passage from John contains an amazing Christology (cf. text).
- Let us ask for the gift: so that we can always remain those who are fathoming Christ. And this means: that which is constantly new (*ricercatori di Cristo* [people searching for Christ]).

Reflection; Meditation; Terce

Meditation 15:

(Mk) Fishermen – by the lake: 'Follow Me'. And they left their nets and followed Him.[6] Almost all of them had previous contact with Jesus (John writes about this).

Getting to know Christ (*vide* [see] Paul: '*scio, cui credidi*' ['I know whom I have believed']).[7]

Pescatori di Cafarnaum sono stati pescati [The fishermen of Capernaum have been caught] and they became '*pescatori di uomini*' ['fishers of men'].[8]

1 See Genesis 1:3.
2 See John 1:39.
3 See John 1:38.
4 See John 1:39.
5 See John 2:25.
6 See Mark 1:17–18.
7 See 2 Timothy 1:12.
8 See Mark 1:17.

- *distacco* [parting] (they left) – *sequela* [imitation] (they followed Him); '*sequela*' entails '*distacco*'; '*sequela*' will be followed by '*missio*' (mission). All this is important for apostolic calling always and everywhere.
- *distacco* (*fuga mundi* [escape from the world]) – with regard to 'riches' (material goods); with regard to people, family (the issue of priestly testament).
- Luke: 'they left everything'[1] – to leave 'everything' in order to find 'Everything' in Christ.

Christ Himself has given up everything – up to the destruction of His naked body on the cross – in order to become the Redeemer – Saviour – of us all.

Reflection; The Way of the Cross; (Passion of Our Lord Jesus Christ according to John); Adoration of the Blessed Sacrament; Sext; None; Reading; Penitential psalms; Rosary (III); Vespers

Meditation 16:

(The unsuccessful and successful catch).

After the resurrection: a miraculous fish catch (John).

The (seven) apostles have already experienced the truth of the resurrection. At the same time they are a bit 'disoriented' with regard to their future tasks: 'I am going fishing . . .'[2] – the others went with him. They did not catch anything. This is what happens when in our actions we lack connection with Christ.

After Jesus spoke to them, they cast the net again. They caught 153 fish. (What does this number signify?) Some see in it a symbol of the universality of salvation and the mission of the Church.

The net was not torn – this also shows the Church as a community of salvation.

'It is the Lord.'[3] During the unsuccessful catch, they are a group of people – it is a human initiative. During the second catch – they are the Church in which Christ works.

Prayer.

Anticipated Matins

1 See Luke 5:11.
2 See John 21:3.
3 See John 21:7.

Meditation 17:

(Eucharist – Peter).

(John cont.) Meal – a symbol of the Eucharist.

The community of the Church – the Eucharist – apostolic mission. 'Have you any food?'[1] Christ first asks, and then He Himself gives that which He receives as a gift. In the Eucharist: our gift of bread and wine is transubstantiated by the power of the Holy Spirit (That which is 'ours' is at the same time God's: '*de Tuis donis ac datis*' ['from the gifts that You have given us']).

Jesus – Peter: a conversation that testifies to the greatness of love: it is greater than any sin.

Just before this: after Peter's denial, Christ looked at Peter

Ambrose

and Peter wept bitterly.[2]

Mistero della pastoralità partecipata [The mystery of pastoral participation]. Christ – the sole Shepherd of the Sheepfold – says to Peter: 'tend my sheep!'[3]

Carità pastorale è per prima la carità per Cristo [Pastoral love is primarily love for Christ]: 'Do you love me?'[4]

Card. Newman

In John's text discussed above: Peter represents every believer [illegible] and shepherd. This is a text that testifies to the 'primacy of Peter' (the pastoral line of Peter and his successors). The Church is permanently young, authentic, *affascinante* [fascinating]. The unconditional mercy of God to man and the world has been revealed in Peter.

Rosary (I); Eucharistic Adoration and Benediction; Litany of Our Lord Jesus Christ, Priest and Victim; Litany of the Blessed Virgin Mary, St Joseph; 'Holy Hour'; Compline; Reading

17 February

Intentions; Morning prayers
Meditation: (*Vocatio: Misericordia Div.* [Calling: Divine Mercy])
Holy Mass; Thanksgiving; Prayers; (Litany of Polish Saints); Rosary (III); Prayer to the Holy Spirit; Lauds

Meditation (18): (*celibato – proposta evangelica* [celibacy – evangelical proposal]).

---

1 See John 21:5.
2 See Luke 22:61–62.
3 See John 21:16.
4 See John 21:15–17.

martedì **2** aprile

s. Francesco di P.

Tuesday Dienstag Mardi · ВТОРНИК Martes · April Avril · АПРЕЛЬ Abril

pojmowania działalności tworzenia z Chry-stusem. –

– Na wschód Jeziora zarzucenie sieci [illegible] 153 ryby. (Comunione [illegible]) [illegible] symbol powszechności zbawienia w mocy Krzyża.

– Sieć się nie rozerwała – to tylko oznacza [illegible] na koniec jako wypełnienie zbawienia

8 – „Pan jest"

9 Przy śniadaniu [illegible] grupę ludzi [illegible] z Kościołem, w którym działa Chrystus.

10 – Modlitwa

11 17 Matut. anticip.

18 (Medit. XVII) (Eucharistia – Piotr)

(cd. [illegible]) Posiłek – symbol Eucharystii.

– Wspólnota osób. – Eucharystia – miejsce apost. „Uczniowie [illegible]" – Chrystus napełnił [illegible] – a z kolei oddaje sam siebie, [illegible] w darze. W Eucharystii: nasz dar chleba i wina zostają przemienione mocą Ducha Świętego (To, co „nasze" jest zarazem Boże: „de tuis donis ac datis")

16 – Sieć – Piotr: rozmowa, [illegible] o Tym, jak wielka jest miłość i [illegible] jako [illegible] grzech.

Już przedtem: po zaparciu się Chrystus spoj-rzał na Piotra – i Piotr gorzko zapłakał

[illegible] – Ministero della paternità partecipa-ta, Chrystus – [illegible] Pasterz [illegible] miłości do Piotra [illegible] miłujesz?

Carità pastorale è [illegible] carità per Cristo: „miłujesz Mnie?"

'Extraordinary' charisma: 1 Cor. 7; Mt. 19, celibacy for the kingdom of God . . . Let him who is able to understand it, understand it! For the heavenly kingdom: eschatological meaning – prophetic meaning. Ecclesiological meaning: the kingdom is already present in the mystery.

We need to remember the unpredictable forces that have been invested in the history of the people of God.

Contemporary situation: the absolutisation of sex (Freud), which is absurd and brings about a destruction of essential human values. This is a particular challenge for Christians: celibacy, virginity 'restores value', restores dignity to masculinity and femininity.

(Contemporary pastoral work): There is no point in seeking to 'reconcile' the gospel and the sins (deviations) of contemporary times. To reconcile is to reduce(?). The only way: to preach, to bear witness!

St Ambrose: *Il segno della presenza del Re* [The sign of the King's presence].

Verso celibato sacerd. [towards priestly celibacy].

Reflection; Terce

Meditation 19: (*Impegno ecclesiale* [Ecclesial commitment]).

The fact that Christ remained celibate (against the Old Testament Jewish tradition) is of deep significance. It means: Christ is the Bridegroom (*lo Sposo*) – scriptural testimony. Christ being the Bridegroom points to a higher 'nuptial' reality; Ephesians, the Bridegroom of the Church–Bride. In Christ one can find an exemplary dimension of any nuptial relationship.

What does it mean that Christ is the Bridegroom of the Church? The answer is in Ephesians 5: He nourishes her, cleanses her and leads her to holiness.[1]

We find all these tasks in the ministerial priesthood. *Sacerdotium – est sacramentum Christi-Sponsi* [Priesthood – is the sacrament of Christ–Bridegroom].

Hence the practice of celibacy of priests in the (Western and

1 See Ephesians 5:25–30.

Eastern) Church. (Differences between the Eastern Church and the Western Church.)

The conditions of celibate life:

(1) love for Christ, which has to be constantly renewed
(2) love for the Church as the Bride of the priest
(3) to love people with the love of Christ–Saviour (pastoral love)
(4) *BMV – archetipo dell'amore sponsale di Dio* [Blessed Virgin Mary – the archetype of God's spousal love].

Reflection; The Way of the Cross; Adoration of the Blessed Sacrament; Reading; Sext; None; Friday, 3.00 p.m.; Rosary (I); Vespers

Meditation 20: (*L'orazione dell'essere* [The prayer of being]).

Christ: the prayer of eternity, '*preghiera eternizzata*'. Augustine on priests: '*Homo Dei*' ['Man of God']. Prayer has to be an expression of the priest's whole '*esse*' ['being']. His entire 'being' should emanate prayer. Prayer is born from what one loves. Sin (as a state of the soul) extinguishes prayer in us. If prayer returns, sin has to subside.

The priest's prayer is usually 'crowded' with people, their problems, their intentions. Personal prayer. Communal prayer. They are connected in a particular way in the priest's life. To pray for everything, i.e. for each of one's own and others' needs. In spontaneous words too.

[Reading:] Ephesians; Anticipated Matins

Meditation 21: (*I sentimenti fondamentali dell'orante* [Fundamental feelings of the supplicant]).

Il sentimento della vuotezza . . . (vanità della vanità) [The feeling of emptiness . . . (vanity of vanities)].[1] Man and all the creatures come from nothingness . . . the need to contact 'Him who IS'.[2]

Sentimento della presenza [The feeling of presence]: the entrance into 'everything' that has been united with the divine thought: the divine plan.

Sentimento del Cristo vivo [The feeling of the living Christ]:

1 See Ecclesiastes 1:2.
2 See Exodus 3:14.

Christ who is alive – crucified and risen from the dead: He is alive.

Sentimento della volontà del Padre [The feeling of the Father's will]: through Christ, especially in His sacrifice.

Per lo Spirito Santo [Through the Holy Spirit]: the source of all life in the body of Christ, the Church. To be the Church means to be in the Holy Spirit.

With the awareness of evil which is present in the world. This also means: with the awareness of the cross, that is, the redemption, which is working in the world, overcoming evil.

And, simultaneously, with the feeling of beauty that comes from God. (This is a kind of destination point in this process, which started with *sentimento della vuotezza* [the feeling of emptiness].) This feeling of beauty is a type of fulfilment of Christian prayer, through which the world becomes an epiphany of God.

Rosary (II); Eucharistic Adoration and Benediction; Litany of the Sacred Heart of Jesus; Litany of the Blessed Virgin Mary; Litany of St Joseph; Concluding reflection; Reading; Compline

18 February[1]

Intentions; Morning prayers
Meditation: (*de Sacerdotis alloquendo* [on the priest's address])
Holy Mass; Thanksgiving; Prayers; (Litany of Polish Saints); Rosary (I); Prayer for the gifts of the Holy Spirit; Lauds

Meditation 22:

'*Consegna, Signore, la tua grazia*' ['Grant us, Lord, your grace']. Ambrose. We are not innocent – but redeemed. We may fall – but can always rise again. Ambrose.

Conclusion; Final words; Blessing; Magnificat
UIOGD[2]

1 The final talk of the retreat was delivered by John Paul II. The full text (in Italian) is available at: https://w2.vatican.va/

2 See p. xxi.

4–10 March 1990
Exercitia Spiritualia [Spiritual Exercises]
Topic: *Consacrati nella Verità* [Consecrated in the Truth]
Led by Father [Georges Marie Martin] Cottier OP[1]

~

4 March

6.00 p.m.: ('Lenten Lamentations');[2] Exposition of the Blessed Sacrament; Vespers for the First Sunday of Lent

Introductory meditation (1): (John 20:31).

Ecclesia ex natura sua – missionaria [The Church is missionary in its nature] (*L[umen] G[entium]*).

The main topic based on the Gospel of St John: the gospel of the Son's and the Holy Spirit's mission.

Mission through witness: witness borne by people from Abraham through Moses to John the Baptist – and from the apostles through the Church until our times.

Above this human witness – there is the witness of Jesus Christ.

'If you knew the gift of God':[3] We are all in a situation (danger) of superficiality in relation to the divine reality: in relation to the gift.

Eucharistic Adoration; Eucharistic Benediction; Meditation continued; Reading; Compline

5 March

Intentions; Prayers
Morning meditation: ('if you knew the gift of God')
(Prayer to the Holy Spirit); Holy Mass; Prayers; Thanksgiving; (Rosary (II)); Lauds

---

1 Georges Marie Martin Cottier OP (1922–2016) was a Swiss cardinal and Titular Archbishop of Tullia (2003–16). He was a professor of theology at the Universities of Geneva and Fribourg, and served as secretary of the International Theological Commission and Pro-Theologian of the Pontifical Household.
2 See n. 6, p. 221 [11 March 1984].
3 See John 4:10.

Meditation 2: (John 1:7).

St John the Baptist: he came to bear witness to the light.[1]

He was not the light, but came to bear witness to the light: He Who comes after me – is the light; He was before me.[2]

Faced with this light everyone has to make a fundamental choice: for or against the light. The drama of life and death – truth and 'lie'.

Witness – he who bears witness to the light (this is much more than a simple report of facts). John the Baptist – I am the voice: I am the voice of one crying in the wilderness . . .[3] (Origen's commentary).

The Lord's messenger leads to the meeting with Christ.

Reflection; Prayer to the Holy Spirit; Terce; Passion of Our Lord Jesus Christ according to Matthew

Meditation 3: (John 1:34).

Why are you doing this? (baptising?) . . .[4] I baptise with water; but among you stands He who baptises with the Holy Spirit and power.[5]

Witnesses – Scripture: *memoria* [memory]. Recorded testimonies and witnesses.

John the Baptist is a teacher (*maestro*) of the history of salvation – the history of people (Israel, the Church) and also every person.

The history of salvation helps us understand Christ (yet at the same time Christ is the final key to the understanding of this history).

Among you stands one whom you do not know.[6] This is permanently true in the history of the Church, the history of the mission. All this constantly reveals the paradigm of the Baptist: service and transparency.

Sext; None
Reflection continued: (Paul VI: our times need witnesses)
The Way of the Cross; Adoration of the Blessed Sacrament; Reading, etc.; Litany of the Saints; Prayers; Rosary (III); Vespers

1 See John 1:7.
2 See John 1:8, 15.
3 See John 1:23.
4 See John 1:25.
5 See John 1:26, 33.
6 See John 1:26.

Meditation 4: (*amicus Sponsi* [the friend of the Bridegroom]) John 3:29.

John the Baptist: 'Behold, the Lamb of God, who takes away the sins of the world':[1] the Old Testament figures. In the New Testament (beginning with John the Baptist's words) the 'Lamb of God' is an expression of redemption: Christ – Redeemer – 'who takes away the sins of the world'.

'He on whom you see the Spirit descend'[2] (the fulfilment of Isaiah). John the Baptist saw and bore witness: This is the Son of God.[3] John's witness originates in the witness of the Holy Spirit.

Next day two of John's disciples, hearing again 'Behold, the Lamb of God!', follow Jesus. John the Baptist is a perfect example: to lead to Christ. This is the synthesis of the old covenant, and at the same time an anticipation of the Church's mission.

Anticipated Matins

Meditation 5:

'What do you seek?' Jesus asks the two disciples of John.[4]

'Rabbi, where are you staying?' If Andrew tells his brother Simon 'we have found the Messiah' after this meeting (likewise Philip to Nathanael), it means that (says Thomas Aquinas):[5] he recognised the Messiah because he desired it very much.

Jesus says to Simon: 'You shall be called Petrus'.[6]

Nathanael: 'Can anything good come out of Nazareth?' Philip: 'Come and see'. Jesus: 'Before Philip called you, I knew you'. Nathanael: 'You are the King of Israel' (a messianic title).[7]

Christ – the Gate to heaven; He who descends from the Father (Jacob the patriarch in Bethel).

Rosary (I); Eucharistic Benediction; Litany of the Holy Name of Jesus; Litany of the Blessed Virgin Mary, St Joseph; Concluding reflection; Compline

1 See John 1:29.
2 See John 1:33.
3 See John 1:34.
4 See John 1:38.
5 See John 1:41.
6 See John 1:42.
7 See John 1:46–49.

6 March

Intentions; Morning prayers
Meditation: (He whom you do not know stands among you)[1]
Holy Mass; Thanksgiving; Prayers; Rosary (III); Prayer to the Holy Spirit; Lauds

Meditation 6: (*amico dello Sposo* [the friend of the Bridegroom]).[2]

(*Jo baptizat* [John baptises] – the disciples – *Christus – discipuli Eius* [Christ – His disciples].)

No one has any power unless it has been given from above[3] – these words refer to John the Baptist and his spiritual power, but they also refer to earthly power (cf. the conversation with Pilate).

On the friends of the Bridegroom: there is a reference to Yahweh's covenant with Israel here – revealed by the prophets (Hosea, others) in relation to spousal love, that is, to the very beginning, to the primal sacrament.

The friend of the Bridegroom rejoices . . .[4] He must increase, but I must decrease[5] (John the Baptist).

(St Paul continues this thought, speaking of Christ as the only Bridegroom of the community.) Furthermore: Book of Revelation.

Witness as the Bridegroom. Bridegroom–Witness. Joy is part of bearing witness – even in adverse conditions, secularism, persecutions.

Reflection; Terce; Passion of Our Lord Jesus Christ according to Mark

Meditation 7:

Witness/*Testimonio superiore* [Higher witness] – the witness of Christ Himself, the witness of the Word that came into the world but His own people received Him not:[6] the great drama of human history. To receive – and not to reject the witness of the Word. What is at stake is the truth that God is true, that God is truth.

The mission of the Church faces an adverse climate at this central point: scepticism – nihilism – they undertake a search

1 See John 1:26.
2 See John 3:29.
3 See John 19:11.
4 See John 3:29.
5 See John 3:30.
6 See John 1:9–11.

for the truth in such a way that they make sure they will never find it. Secularisation brings about various forms of relativism. The fact of religion is accepted, but nothing is said about the truth of religion – the entire climate shaped by 'mass media'. The result: there is no certainty; there are opinions.

What is the task of those who bear witness? He who believes in the Son has life![1]

Sext; None; Reflection continued; The Way of the Cross; (Reading and others); Adoration of the Blessed Sacrament; Penitential psalms; Rosary (I); Vespers

Meditation 8:

Testimonianza superiore di Giovanni [The higher witness of John] in the context of John 5 . . . where Jesus says, 'the Father has Himself borne witness to Me', which arouses fierce opposition from the Jews. 'I and the Father are one'.[2]

Jesus calls John '*Lampas ardens*' ['Burning lamp'] (commentary by St Thomas). He was to lead to Christ. Christ Himself is the light, truth and life.

Jesus refers to the Scriptures: 'they that bear witness to Me'.[3] He refers to Moses, who bears witness to Him (law).

Scrutare la Scrittura [To examine the Scriptures] *in fede* [in faith]. Knowledge (biblical–exegetical) enlivened by faith!

Anticipated Matins

Meditation 9:

'If you do not believe the scriptures, how will you believe my words?' (John).[4] 'You refuse to come to Me that you may have life . . .' (John) . . . [5]

> The mission of the Church in the contemporary world, where man lives outside that which is essential, removed from his own self and from God, inner emptiness – 'neither cold nor hot – lukewarm' (to the church in Laodicea). [6]

1 See John 3:36.
2 See John 5:37 and 10:30.
3 See John 5:39.
4 See John 5:47.
5 See John 5:40.
6 See Revelation 3:16.

[*G[audium et] S[pes]* 21. Man '*alienato a se stesso*' ['alienated from himself'] – he has to find the desire for God inscribed in his humanity.]

How can you believe? (since you do not seek the glory that comes from God, but receive glory from one another).[1] '*Gloria*
? *Iehovae*' ['Yahweh's glory'] is He Himself.

The works that I am doing bear witness to Me: that the Father has sent Me: the witness of the Father Himself – the sign that 'the Father is in Me and I am in the Father'.[2]

Signs – miracles. But Christ's signs (*semeion* [sign]) go well beyond miracles. He Himself is the greatest sign. Signs belonged to the economy of the old covenant.

Rosary (II); Eucharistic Adoration and Benediction; Litany of the Sacred Heart of Jesus; Litany of the Blessed Virgin Mary; Litany of St Joseph; Concluding reflection; Reading; Compline

7 March

Intentions; Morning prayers
Meditation: (The Father has borne witness to Me)[3]
Holy Mass; Thanksgiving; Prayers; Rosary (I); Prayer for the gifts of the Holy Spirit; (Litany of Polish Saints); Lauds

Meditation 10:

Signs (*semeia*) – revelation of the redemptive power of God, the coming of the Messiah, finally: eschatological meaning.

At the same time, signs (*semeia*) allow us to learn about the whole drama of human freedom. Signs awaken faith, but they are also met with rejection (disbelief). They require a response of faith. John the Evangelist showed this in his writing, which records only some of the miracles/signs.

(Text by St John of the Cross: God has said everything in Christ, so to seek further signs or revelations is a sort of offence to God.

In our times there is an excessive search for those further 'revelations'.)

The Father has borne witness to the Son.

Reflection; Terce; Passion of Our Lord Jesus Christ according to Luke

1 See John 5:44.
2 See John 10:38.
3 See John 5:37.

Meditation 11:

John 6 [illegible] *de signis* [on signs]: the sign of the multiplication of bread. 'Make the people sit down'.[1] The gathering of people is 'inscribed' in the Eucharist. The apostles are to feed them with one bread because through this they form a unity.

'They were about to take Him by force to make Him king.'[2] They interpreted the sign incorrectly: in the sense of a political messiah. The danger of interpreting the 'signs' according to one's preconceptions. Faith cleanses.

De Lubac/Joachim of Fiore

An eternal problem: earthly messianism: the kingdom of this world. In the old covenant, such a kingdom (the liberation from slavery and the Promised Land) is only a figure. Some liberation theologians did not overcome this temptation.

The Vatican takes a clear stance regarding the evangelical needs of the 'world' – but this is something completely different from political messianism.

Sext; None; Reflection continued; Reading; The Way of the Cross; Adoration of the Blessed Sacrament; Litany of the Saints; Rosary (II); Vespers

Meditation 12:

Jesus walks on the sea. 'Do not be afraid' (John . . .).[3]

The healing of a man blind from his birth: 'who sinned, this man or his parents, that he was born blind? It was not that this man sinned, nor his parents, but that the works of God might be made manifest in him'.[4]

Our contemporaries are very sensitive to human suffering. At the same time, they are very insensitive to sin, hence the question: how to reconcile evil (suffering) with the existence and goodness of God? Insensitivity to sin makes the answer more difficult. Philosophers as well as 'theologians' very often turn into Job's friends who lead the way to blasphemy.

(Digression: Leibniz – an attempt at 'justifying' God (?!))

Only theology, which is born in prayer, can give the answer.

Jesus anointed the eyes of the man born blind with the clay.

1 See John 6:10.
2 See John 6:15.
3 See John 6:20.
4 See John 9:2–3.

„teologowie" często zamieniają się w przyjaciół Hioba, którzy torują drogę do bluźnierstwa.

[Dygresja: Lesbun – próba „usprawiedliwienia" Boga (?!)]

Odpowiedź może dać tylko teologia, musi się wznieść z praktyki.

— Oczy ślepo-urodzonego Jezus pomazał błotem (śliną), kazał mu iść do sadzawki Siloe. Rozmowa z faryzeuszami, którzy go wypytywali... (powrót)

17 Matut. anticipatum

18 Medit. XII.

(cd.) Ale faryzeusze są podzieleni między sobą: „ktoś jest od Boga, skoro ... sabat – jakże mógłby takie znaki uczynić, gdyby Bóg z nim nie był?" – Ty co mówisz o Nim? – jest Prorokiem – Badanie uzupełniające okoliczności tego uzdrowienia.

Podobnie „uzdrowienie" w ich oczach sprawia, że ludzie odchodzą z prawdy.

świadek staje się ostatecznym

Faryzeusze: „Ten człowiek (tj. Jezus) jest grzesznikiem. Urodzony w ślepocie: „czy jest grzesznikiem, nie wiem – wiem, że nie widziałem, a teraz widzę." I dalej: „wiemy, że Bóg grzeszników nie wysłuchuje..." – „Ten człowiek jest posłany od Boga"

Finał. Chrystus się objawia w Synu Człowieczego?? – „Kto nim jest?" – „Ten, który z tobą mówi" – „Wierzę, Panie"

„Przyszedłem na świat, aby ci, którzy nie widzą, widzieli, a ci, którzy widzą, by zaślepli." ... radować się w sobie – sens odpowiedzi danej przez

He told him to go to the pool of Siloam.[1] A conversation with the Pharisees, who are aggressive . . .[2]

(Break)
Anticipated Matins

Meditation 13: (Cont.) But the Pharisees are divided among themselves. 'He is not from God, for he does not keep the Sabbath – how can a man who is not from God do such signs?'[3]

What do you think about Him? He is a prophet.[4] Additional interrogation of his parents. They are intimidated.[5]

Similar 'intimidation' often makes people part ways with the truth.

The witness becomes the defendant

Pharisees: this man (i.e. Jesus) is a sinner. The man who had been blind: 'Whether he is a sinner, I do not know; one thing I know, that though I was blind, now I see'.[6] And then . . . 'We know that God does not listen to sinners . . .'[7] 'This man has been sent from God'.

Conclusion. Christ: 'Do you believe in the Son of Man?' – 'And who is he?' – 'He who speaks to you' – 'Lord, I believe'.[8]

'I came into this world so that those who do not see may see, and that those who see may become blind'[9] (because they are self-righteous, the meaning of Christ's response to the Pharisees).

We constantly have to ask ourselves about the essential motives of our behaviour!

Rosary (III); Eucharistic Adoration and Benediction; Litany of the Holy Name of Jesus; Litany of the Blessed Virgin Mary; Litany of St Joseph; Concluding reflection; Reading; Compline

8 March

Intentions; Morning prayers
Morning meditation: (on the Spirit of truth)
Holy Mass; Thanksgiving; Prayers; (Litany of Polish Saints); Rosary (II); Prayers to the Holy Spirit; Lauds

1 See John 9:6–7.
2 See John 9:13–34.
3 See John 9:16, 33.
4 See John 9:17.
5 See John 9:18–23.
6 See John 9:25.
7 See John 9:31.
8 See John 9:35–38.
9 See John 9:39.

Meditation 14:

The raising of Lazarus – a particularly important *semeion* [sign].

Conversation with Martha: 'Your brother will rise again'.

Martha: '. . . at the last day'.

Jesus: 'I am the resurrection and the life. He who believes in Me, though he die, yet shall he live'.[1] Physical death, the death of sin; both are meant here.

Mary: the anointing of Jesus' feet in Bethany (after Lazarus was raised from the dead). Before the raising of Lazarus, Mary says less than Martha, but more or less the same: if you had been here, Lazarus would not have died.[2]

Jesus wept. Humanity. Faced with his friend's human death. *Ad Rom.* [Letter to the Romans]: death came into the world through sin.[3] The 'wages' of sin.[4]

The death of Christ ⟷ the death of Socrates. An analogy, more differences. Plato: thanks to philosophy we learn how to die.

Presently: a tendency to forget about death. Much attention is paid to earthly suffering.

Banalisation of sin, *aborto* [abortion], euthanasia. Against the gravity of life. This is connected to the gravity of death. The perspective of the Judgement, the resurrection of the body, life everlasting.

Terce

Meditation 15:

The consequences of the sign of the raising of Lazarus. On the one hand: the awakening of faith in Christ, which is expressed in His triumphal entry into Jerusalem. On the other hand: The Sanhedrin is about to decide to kill Jesus. A political argument: 'It is expedient that one man should die . . .':[5] True common good is not directed against a person, but it is for the sake of a person.

---

1 See John 11:23–25.
2 See John 11:21.
3 See Romans 5:12.
4 See Romans 6:23.
5 See John 11:50.

Caiaphas' words: he is unaware of the proper sense of the prophetic words that he utters: Christ was indeed to die for the people, to gather into one the children of God who are scattered abroad . . .[1]

We move on to the witness of the Holy Spirit. Nicodemus (John 3): Christ's works (signs) bear witness to His having come from God. Jesus: you have to be born anew. Nicodemus: How? Jesus: of water and the Holy Spirit . . .[2]

Nicodemus, however, is a man of the letter of the law; Jesus: the wind blows[3] . . . breath – the Spirit.

Sext; None; Passion of Our Lord Jesus Christ according to John; Reflection continued; The Way of the Cross; Adoration of the Blessed Sacrament; Reading; Penitential psalms; Rosary (III); Vespers

Meditation 16:

Jesus to Nicodemus: 'God so loved the world that He gave His only Son, that whoever believes in Him should not perish but have eternal life . . .' '. . . For God sent the Son into the world, not to condemn the world, but that the world might be saved through Him . . .'[4]

Then about the light (*Luce*) and darkness . . . the whole passage surpasses any commentary.

On the Holy Spirit:

'If any one thirst, let him come to Me – and drink.

Out of his heart shall flow rivers of living water'. This He said about the Spirit, which as yet had not been given, because Jesus was not yet 'glorified'.[5]

He is the Paraclete: Counsellor – Advocate, whose coming Christ promised to the apostles before His departure.

'If a man loves Me, he will keep My word, and My Father will love him, and we will come to him and make our home with him . . .' (John).[6]

'When He, the Spirit of truth, comes, He will guide you into

1 See John 11:51–52.
2 See John 3:3–5.
3 See John 3:8.
4 See John 3:16–17.
5 See John 7:37–39.
6 See John 14:23.

all the truth, for He will take what is Mine and declare it to you.'[1] 'He will bear witness to Me, and you will also be witnesses . . .'[2]

'If I do not go away, the Counsellor will not come to you, but if I go, I will send Him to you. And when He comes, He will convince the world of sin and of righteousness and of judgement' (John 16).[3]

Radix peccati [The root of sin] – rejection of faith.

'The victory that overcomes the world – our faith.'[4]

Anticipated Matins

Meditation 17:

We live in the age of a 'rediscovery' of the Holy Spirit in the Church. It is connected with a deepened awareness of the Church: the mystery of the Church.

The Holy Spirit is the source of the New Law (Thomas Aquinas). The primacy of the theological virtues, the gifts of the Holy Spirit, the sacraments. Christian vocation is a divine vocation. Hence we need sensitivity (*docilitas* [docility]) to the work of the Holy Spirit.

'He who has seen Me has seen the Father' . . .[5]

'The Father is in Me and I am in the Father' . . . 'He who loves Me will be loved by My Father, and we will come to him and make our home with him.'[6] In these words – the very core of mystical life.

At present, 'mystical experience' is sought through human practice only. Mysticism is only possible on the basis of the gift of the Holy Spirit: the theological virtues and the gifts of the Holy Spirit.

Today there is a certain confusion in this area.

Rosary (I); Eucharistic Adoration and Benediction; Litany of Our Lord Jesus Christ, Priest and Victim; Litany of the Blessed Virgin Mary; Litany of St Joseph; Holy Hour; Compline; Reading

1 See John 16:13–14.
2 See John 15:26–27.
3 See John 16:7–8.
4 See 1 John 5:4.
5 See John 14:9.
6 See John 14:11, 21, 23.

9 March: Feast of St Frances of Rome

Intentions; Morning prayers
Meditation: If I go, the Counsellor will come[1]
Holy Mass; Thanksgiving; Prayers; Rosary (III); Prayer for the gifts of the Holy Spirit; (Litany of Polish Saints); Lauds

Meditation 18:

I am the light of the world . . . I am the truth[2] (John 7, John 8). Man is made for truth. With due respect for the critical mindset, one cannot but notice that this mindset also contains a strategy not to seek the truth, not to find the truth, not to accept the truth.

Despite the appearance of intellectual coherence (reliability), it is a fundamental evasion. Life that parts ways with what is the deepest and most essential in the human being.

Man is made for truth. Truth versus certainty.

If this inner attitude is missing, one will never meet Christ: Christ is the light, the truth, the image of the Everlasting Father. He is the Word. If man does not receive this Word, he remains lonely and imposes the image that he himself produces on the world, creation and the Creator.

Terce; Reflection

Meditation 19:

A friendly attitude to Jesus among His and our contemporaries that, nevertheless, does not lead to the acceptance of the whole truth about Him: to faith. (Likewise, when it comes to certain 'chapters' of the moral teaching of the Church, in particular on social issues.) These are precious things, but they are incomplete!

When you have lifted up the Son of Man, then you will know that I AM.[3]

If you continue in my word, you will know the truth, and the truth will make you free (liberate you)![4]

There are, however, many who set freedom against the truth. For them, freedom itself is the truth and the source of

1 See John 16:7.
2 See John 8:12 and 14:6.
3 See John 8:28.
4 See John 8:31–32.

truth – it creates truth. What man wants – becomes the truth, versus: man wants (should want) that which is the truth.

The condition is: not to be a slave, but a son (Gal.).[1] This is the condition for accepting the truth, the condition of faith: 'If I tell the truth, why do you not believe Me?'[2] '... You are of your father the devil, he was a liar from the beginning...'[3] This lie gives birth to death. 'The father of lies' is a murderer.

We are faced with a dramatic struggle that takes place in the entire spiritual domain (cf. Eph. 6): It is not enough to reduce evil to human (creation's) mortality only.

'Before Abraham was, I AM.'[4]

European issues[5]

Sext; None; Reflection continued; The Way of the Cross; Adoration of the Blessed Sacrament; Reading; Friday, 3.00 p.m.; Rosary (I); Vespers

Meditation 20:

'Are you the king? . . . I was born, and I have come into the world, to bear witness to the truth . . .' 'My kingship is not of this world.'[6]

The pagan concept of the state: man lives in the dimension of the state – according to the Gospel, the dimension of man is transcendent and thence come all human rights, beginning with the right of religious freedom... The kingship of man...

'Every one who is of the truth hears My voice.'[7]

John's description of the passion of Christ is a testimony to His kingship.

Pilate: 'what is truth?'

Pilate: 'I find no crime in Him.'[8]

1 See Galatians 4:7.
2 See John 8:46
3 See John 8:44.
4 See John 8:58.
5 This probably refers to the political developments in East-Central Europe leading to the dissolution of the Soviet Union. In June 1989 Lech Wałęsa became the first democratically elected non-communist president of Poland after World War II. This was followed by revolutions in other East-Central European countries and the fall of the Berlin Wall in November 1989. John Paul II was a prominent opponent of communism and firmly supported the Solidarity movement. During his first pontifical visit to the Polish People's Republic (as present-day Poland was called in the communist era) in 1979, he offered spiritual support and encouragement to people living under communism. During the Mass he celebrated in Warsaw, he famously prayed: 'Let Thy Spirit descend and renew the face of the earth, the face of this land!'
6 See John 18:33, 37, 36.
7 See John 18:37.
8 See John 18:38.

The 'king of the Jews', wearing the crown of thorns – 'here is the man' – the crowds demand: 'crucify Him'. 'He has made Himself the Son of God'! 'I have power to release you, and power to crucify you . . .'

'You would have no power unless it had been given you from above'.[1]

'If you do not sentence this man, you are not Caesar's friend'; 'we have no king but Caesar'[2] – for a believing Jew this was something horrible. The 'father of lies' triumphs.

The title: 'Jesus of Nazareth, the King of the Jews'.[3]

'When I am lifted up from the earth, I will draw all men to Myself'.[4]

Anticipated Matins

Meditation 21:

We return to John 6: The Eucharist.

'Seek the food which endures to eternal life . . .'[5] His listeners recall God's 'signs' in history: the manna in the wilderness – 'I am the bread of life'[6] – this bread is, above all, the truth that we receive in faith. Faith.

'All that the Father gives me will come to Me . . .' 'I am the bread which came down from heaven' . . . (– murmur –) 'no one can come to Me unless the Father draws him':[7] faith is a gift.

Christ moves from the topic of faith to the Eucharist. 'Unless you eat the flesh of the Son of Man and drink His blood, you have no life in you.'[8]

'As the living Father sent Me (the Father who is life), and I live because of the Father – so he who eats Me will live because of Me'.[9]

---

1 See John 19:5–11.
2 See John 19:12, 15.
3 See John 19:19.
4 See John 12:32.
5 See John 6:27.
6 See John 6:35.
7 See John 6:37, 41, 44.
8 See John 6:53.
9 See John 6:57.

(Many disciples left Him after these words): a hard saying.[1]

Man encloses himself within his boundaries, he does not want to open up to divine life.

'It is the spirit that gives life, the flesh is of no avail'.[2]

To the twelve: will you also go away?

You have the words of eternal life.[3]

The Eucharist – embodies and prepares the dwelling of God in us.

Rosary (II); Eucharistic Adoration and Benediction; Litany of the Sacred Heart of Jesus; Litany of the Blessed Virgin Mary; Litany of St Joseph; Concluding reflection; Compline; Reading

10 March[4]

Intentions; Morning prayers
Meditation: (The Spirit gives life)
Holy Mass; Thanksgiving; Prayers; (Litany of Polish Saints); Rosary (III); Prayer for the gifts of the Holy Spirit; Lauds

Meditation 22:

John's Gospel on Mary.

(1) Cana of Galilee: 'the mother of Jesus', 'woman' . . . 'my hour has not yet come – do whatever He tells you!'[5]
(2) Golgotha: 'Woman, behold, Your son . . .'; 'behold, your Mother'.[6]

('Woman') – a proclamation of Mary's spiritual motherhood. 'The disciple whom He loved': 'As the Father has loved Me, so have I loved you'[7] – Love is the life of the Church.

'Woman' – the Bride (*Sposa*): *Maria – Chiesa* [Mary – the Church]. *L[umen] G[entium]* VIII: 'new Eve': in Mary the Church finds its perfection. John received a special mission: to take Mary for his Mother. The whole Church is with him. We are at the heart of the covenant.

The Mother of the Church – the Mother of the mystical body.

1 See John 6:60.
2 See John 6:63.
3 See John 6:67–68.
4 The final talk of the retreat was delivered by John Paul II. The full text (in Italian) is available at: https://w2.vatican.va/
5 See John 2:3–5.
6 See John 19:26–27.
7 See John 15:9.

Associata non solo all'umanità del Verbo Incarnato, ma anche alla sua missione [Bound not only to the humanity of the Word Incarnate, but also to His mission].

I entrust the fruits of the retreat to Mary.

UIOGD[1]

Conclusion; Final words; Blessing; Magnificat

1 See p. xxi.

17–23 February 1991
Exercitia Spiritualia [Spiritual Exercises] Led by Archbishop [Ersilio] Tonini[1]

17 February 6.00 p.m.: ('Lenten Lamentations');[2] Exposition of the Blessed Sacrament; Vespers for the First Sunday of Lent

Introductory meditation (1):

The time of grace. To stand under the cross with Mary and like Mary. In this dramatic moment: the Middle East.[3]

The topic of '*Chiesa omnia è mia speranza*' ['The whole Church is my hope'].

The Holy Spirit works through human events: Islam.

The West (Europe). A challenge for the Church. The Apostolic See at the centre of the mystery of redemption. Believers, but also nonbelievers, are waiting. What is needed the most: holiness (analogy: the period of the Reformation).

Simone Weil
Pasolini

Eucharistic Adoration; Eucharistic Benediction; Meditation continued; (Reading); Compline

18 February Intentions; Prayers
Morning meditation: (*Paraclitus* [Paraclete])
Holy Mass; Prayers; Thanksgiving; Rosary (II); Lauds

---

1 Ersilio Tonini (1914–2013) was an Italian cardinal and Archbishop of Ravenna-Cervia (1975–1990).

2 See n. 6, p. 221 [11 March 1984].

3 Reference to the Gulf War (2 August 1990 – 28 February 1991) taking place in Iraq and Kuwait. John Paul II repeatedly appealed for peace in the Middle East, and he referred to the Gulf War in his 1991 encyclical *Centesimus annus* (The Centenary): 'I myself, on the occasion of the recent tragic war in the Persian Gulf, repeated the cry: "Never again war!". No, never again war, which destroys the lives of innocent people, teaches how to kill, throws into upheaval even the lives of those who do the killing and leaves behind a trail of resentment and hatred, thus making it all the more difficult to find a just solution of the very problems which provoked the war. Just as the time has finally come when in individual states a system of private vendetta and reprisal has given way to the rule of law, so too a similar step forward is now urgently needed in the international community. Furthermore, it must not be forgotten that at the root of war there are usually real and serious grievances: injustices suffered, legitimate aspirations frustrated, poverty, and the exploitation of multitudes of desperate people who see no real possibility of improving their lot by peaceful means.'

Meditation 2:

Spirito S. inviato nella Chiesa huius temporis [The Holy Spirit sent to the Church of our times]. *Tempo di Chiesa – tempo della persona* [The time of the Church – the time of the person]. The Holy Spirit is always sent to a person (*Prima – Maria* [Firstly – Mary]): He is sent to each and every one in their personal uniqueness, into their inner selves. This is the aim of the retreat. To find one's 'self'. *Devorant tempora et devorantur a tempore* ['Wasting away time, and being wasted away by time'].[1] The retreat – a time for the Holy Spirit.

Tutto preceduto dalla Grazia [Everything is preceded by grace]. The retreat – *tempo primo* [the most important time]. The Bridegroom is close. The joy of being a Christian. Let us not impede the Spirit.

Incarnazione di Cristo nei cristiani [The incarnation of Christ in Christians].

Prayer to the Holy Spirit; Terce; Passion of Our Lord Jesus Christ according to Matthew

Meditation 3:

'For this reason the Father loves Me, because I lay down My life . . .'[2] – the meaning and value of every inner act – 'Simon, do you love Me?':[3] on this path every act acquires meaning. The meanings may change according to what is inside oneself. This is the aim of the retreat too: 'new eyes', to see great things (*magnalia* [great things]) in small things, 'to see Him who sees'.

The Holy Spirit reveals (to everyone) things that have been hidden for ages. The Church is a space of great divine plans. Everyone is willed, well thought-out by God: *speranza cristiana* [Christian hope].

Meditation continued: The Holy Spirit reveals God's eternal plans to people who live in time. The space of this revelation is the 'self', the inner man.

Thanks to this light, the inner man discovers God's

1 See Augustine, *Confessions*, Book IX, Chapter IV.
2 See John 10:17.
3 See John 21:15.

greatness in small, ordinary things (*magnalia* [great things]). The Church: the space of God's plans being revealed in the Holy Spirit.

The Way of the Cross; Sext; None; Reading, etc.; Eucharistic Adoration; Litany of the Saints; Rosary (III); Vespers

Meditation 4:

The Church is a caring Mother – and like a Mother, she deserves gratitude. As well as particular institutions that comprise the Church. For example, the seminary (as well as the Curia). Particular people: priests, tutors, but also other people who are sometimes very modest (e.g. sacristans etc.) . . . parents!

Concern for people, for the youth, so that they are safe from evil and retain the treasure that they have: heart – conscience (Augustine: *cum conscientia turbata universum turbatum* [if the conscience is troubled, everything is troubled]). Moreover (and above all): an amazement at the fact that 'I am' – the gift of being, the miracle of existence – the gift of vocation!

The gift of service to the Church (service in the Curia – service to the universal Church).

Anticipated Matins

Meditation (5):

The divine gift of the human mind: The future depends on how this gift is used – what becomes of man depends on . . . humanity! The Church is a guardian – and it stands on guard. Mind – truth 'made subordinate' to its own freedom, destroyed by freedom.

It 'is' not, but it 'creates itself'. The defence of truth is a con-
! dition for the defence of man, morality, civilisation.

The Church undertakes this defence: it teaches how to use the gift of the human mind (reason).

Rosary (I); Litany of the Holy Name of Jesus, Blessed Virgin Mary, St Joseph; Eucharistic Adoration and Benediction; Meditation continued; Compline

19 February Intentions; Prayers
Morning meditation: (*Paraclytus* [Paraclete])
Holy Mass; Prayers; Thanksgiving; Rosary (III); Lauds

Meditation (6):

The Church in contemporary times – and for these times: and each of us for these 'great and terrible' times (Paul VI). It is not '*tempo neutro*' ['neutral time']. Many issues have become clear (e.g. Marxism). It is rather a time of radical alternatives. What does the Holy Spirit say to the Church in these times? '*Nolite obdurare corda vestra*' ['Do not harden your hearts'][1] – a call to holiness, to selfless love – '*elencho*' ['rejection'] of all that is
Peguy against such love: '*amor carnale*' ['carnal love'] (St Catherine of Siena), being dependent on human favours etc. Eyes fixed on Christ – filial fear.

Terce; Prayer to the Holy Spirit; Passion of Our Lord Jesus Christ according to Mark

Meditation 7:

(Cardinal Bea)[2] Holy fear of God and anxiety for the souls of our close ones. *Ne nos inducas in tentationem* [Lead us not
Manzoni into temptation].[3] Fear of God comes together with trust in God: God wants my good more than I do, and He knows better what that good is. The sin of the first parents was already a
Newman negation of this attitude.

Cognar de Lubac The holy fear of God reduces anxiety (human fear), and it gives courage that comes from God's love instead. This gives courage and fortitude to others (*per amore di Dio* [for the love of God]).

Following in Mary's steps!

(*Placent Deo, quibus Deus placet* [God finds pleasure in those who find pleasure in God].)

Meditation continued:

Original sin – the negation of the fear of God, which is a complete and selfless act of trust (because of God) – Mary: the affirmation of this fear, which is the fullness of trust.

The Way of the Cross; Sext; None; Reading etc.; Adoration of the Blessed Sacrament; Penitential psalms; Rosary (I); Vespers

1 See Hebrews 3:8.

2 Augustin Bea SJ (1881–1968) was a German cardinal and biblical scholar at the Pontifical Gregorian University. He was the first president of the Secretariat for Promoting Christian Unity and served as the personal confessor of Pope Pius XII.

3 See Matthew 6:13.

30 martedì aprile

Pio V papa

Tuesday Dienstag Mardi ВТОРНИК Martes — April April Avril АПРЕЛЬ Abril

Newman
Congar
de Lubac

chcę ~~[illegible]~~ mojej dalszej [illegible] już tyle razy, i lepiej co, co jest celem [illegible] — grzech pierworodny właśnie być przezwyciężeniem tej postawy dziecka Bożego. Boża wyzwala, tzn. to bojaźń [illegible], natomiast daje męstwo i Bożej miłości. [illegible] rodzi to męstwo i odwaga (per amore di Dio)

Po śladach Maryi!

(Placuit Deo, quibus Deus placuit)

8\. Medit. reasumpt.

grzech pierworodny — negacja bojaźni Bożej, która jest zaufaniem całkowitym i bezwarunkowym (Bogu, w Bogu) — Maryja i afirmacja takiej bojaźni, która jest pełnią zaufania.

9\. Via Crucis

10\. Lex. [illegible] — Lectura etc

11 Adhor. [illegible]

12 Psalmi poen.

13 Cor. Ro. (Z)

14\. Vesp.

15\. Medit. (VII)

Znaczenie prowadzenia każdego w ramach Stolicy Apost. Aug. i Ecclesia Mater i Ecclesia in mundo — Ecclesia in Ecclesia (Ecclesia in qua sumus). Stał na pięciu walki [illegible] Cath. di Siena: o walce duchowej między Tym, co pochodzi z Łaski, a Tym, co od grzechu wewn. i zewn. od szatana (Ojciec [illegible])

Wezwanie do walki duch. należy do całej tradycji Kościoła i chrześcijaństwa. Czym jest opuszczenie tej walki — [illegible] [illegible] i [illegible].

Przyjęcie [illegible] [illegible] [illegible]

Meditation (8):

The meaning of individual vocation within the Apostolic See. Augustine: *Ecclesia–Mater* [the Church–Mother] and *Ecclesia in mundo – Ecclesia in Ecclesia (Ecclesia, in qua sumus)* [the Church in the world – the Church in the Church (the Church in which we are)]. Hence the tensions and inner conflicts. Catherine of Siena: on the spiritual conflict between that which comes from grace and that which comes from inner and outer sinfulness. From satan (the father of lies).

A call to a spiritual battle belongs to the whole tradition of the Church and Christianity. The result of a resignation from this battle – is testified by e.g. drug addicts and others.

The primacy of the inner man; the primacy of conscience.

Anticipated Matins

Meditation 9:

St Catherine of Siena (cont.). Encouraging words – this is what the youth are waiting for: to keep yourself for Christ. Innocence entrusted to God. The meaning of the confession of children, young people. The light of Christ is still alive in them (the grace of baptism).

Devotion to the Holy Spirit.

Devotion to the passion of Christ: there is a unique fullness of the Father's revelation in this passion and death.

Celebration of the mysteries and liturgy: '*Divina pati*' ['to accept the divine judgement'] – *maiora te quaeras!* [seek things which are greater than you!] – to be prepared to stand before God, to stand with the 'price of the Redeemer's blood'.[1]

Rosary (II); Eucharistic Adoration and Benediction; Litany of the Sacred Heart of Jesus, Blessed Virgin Mary, St Joseph; Meditation continued; Reading; Compline

20 February

Intentions; Prayers
Morning meditation: (the Father will give the Holy Spirit to those who ask Him . . .)[2]
Holy Mass; Prayers; Thanksgiving; (Rosary (I)); Lauds

1 See 1 Corinthians 6:20.
2 See Luke 11:13.

Meditation (10):

God. It is not easy to speak about Him. The contemporary mindset has reduced Him to a 'religious need' – *reductio ad hominem* [reduction to man]. Various groups that have contributed to this.

Despite this reduction, the Church bears – and has to bear – witness to the living and true God, who has revealed Himself in Jesus Christ.

When speaking about God, it is easier to focus on the authenticity of a subjective feeling than on the authenticity of the truth of God. Sometimes an atheist can have a deeper sense of God as Someone unfathomable than a believer.

Qual è il mio modo di essere credente? [What is my way of being a believer?]

Examples . . .

The Church carries in itself the good of all people: the highest good; *Creatore che si fa Pastore* [the Creator who becomes a Shepherd].

On God – with inner trepidation.

Prayer to the Holy Spirit; Terce; Passion of Our Lord Jesus Christ according to Luke

Meditation (11):

The word of God. Genesis 1–3: the foundation of monotheism: Judaism – Christianity – Islam – the word of God: God undertakes a universal plan of salvation . . . God saves.

Modernità [Modernity]: everything has its beginning in '*cogito*' ['I think']: thought creates reality. God is a limitation (*limite* [limit]).

Human '*cognoscere*' ['to understand'] means to become richer by understanding reality, the divine thought. Hence: from '*cognoscere*' to '*laudare Deum*' ['to glorify God'] for all His gifts (the gift of being, life).

Meditation continued: '*modus essendi christiani*' ['the Christian mode of being'] – with a touch of the reduction to '*humanum*' ['what is human'] and of '*modernità*' ['modernity']. We have to strive to purify the Christian mode of being!

The Way of the Cross; Sext; None; Reading; Adoration of the Blessed Sacrament; Litany of the Saints; Rosary (II); Vespers

Meditation (12):

The theology of creation is a fortress against all forms of immanentism. *Siamo pre-ceduti!* [We are pre-conceived!] Moreover: the first motive for thanksgiving – creation – gift. Ontology – ethics. Civilisation in which human products obscure the work of the Creator.

Creation: the root of the community of the Church – *Chiesa di Dio* [the Church of God].

This is also the root of our priesthood: *Omnibus debitor sum* [I am a debtor to all] – the universal priesthood: (oriented towards everyone and everything). Hence: the will to regain (*recuperare* [recover]) everything for God.

Anticipated Matins

Meditation (13):

Theology of the incarnation: What my Father has given Me no one is able to snatch out of My hand:[1] Creation – incarnation. Augustine: *Quid Tibi sum, Domine? . . . Dic animae meae, 'salus tua Ego sum'* [Lord, what am I to You? . . . Say to my soul, 'I am your salvation'].[2] In the incarnation, God is 'for' man, for me, for everyone: *commorimur, conresuscitabimur, conregnabimus* [we die together, we will be raised together, we will reign together].[3]

Corpus natum de Maria Virgine [The body born of the Virgin Mary]: the first stone on which the Church has been built.

Hence: the Church – mission oriented towards all people.

Recapitulatio omnium in Christo [The union of all things in Christ].[4]

Rosary (III); Eucharistic Adoration and Benediction; Litany of the Holy Name of Jesus, Blessed Virgin Mary, St Joseph; Meditation continued; Reading; Compline

21 February Intentions; Prayers
Morning meditation: ('. . . we will come to him and make our home with him')[5]
Holy Mass; Prayers; Thanksgiving; Rosary (III); Lauds

1 See John 10:29.
2 See Psalm 34 (35):3 and Augustine, *Confessions*, Book I, Chapter V.
3 See 2 Timothy 2:11–12.
4 See Ephesians 1:10.
5 See John 14:23.

Meditation (14):

The Church – *Mysterium* [mystery] – *dono di Dio* [gift from God] – not only a community. The *Principio animatore* [animating Principle] is not an idea (ideology), but a Person – Christ, thanks to whom the living God gives Himself to people in the Holy Spirit. In this givenness, the Holy Spirit brings man 'into the centre' of the love between the Father and the Son, which embraces everyone. Hence, He brings man much closer than to the feet of the God of creation, the threshold of the monotheistic reality – He brings man into the centre of the Trinity: the Trinitarian reality.

'I and the Father are one'.[1]

Terce; Prayer to the Holy Spirit; Passion of Our Lord Jesus Christ according to John

Meditation (15):

Spirito filiale (the spirit of filiation) – comes from the Holy Spirit, who is the Spirit of the Father and the Son – it is expressed in the 'I–You', which is a knowledge that I am His, that I speak to Him as the firstborn Son, 'Father, *Abba*', that I am a son with whom He is pleased (*complacentia* [satisfaction]).[2] This creates a special exchange: I want to reciprocate the gifts that I have received and am receiving. Hence, the missionary impulse is born. (*Exempla* [Examples].) Desire to see God.

Meditation continued: (*argumentum centrale* [central argument])
The Way of the Cross; Sext; None; Adoration of the Blessed Sacrament; Reading; Penitential psalms; Rosary (III); Vespers

Meditation (16):

The Apostolic See (Roman Curia): *diakonia* [service] or *koinonia* [community] in a given period in relation to the people who build it. Culture oriented towards future (future as a category of earthly life). Everything assumes worldly dimensions. '*Cattolica*' ['Catholic']: these dimensions are included in the founding principles of the Church (Catholicism). Hence: the special meaning of the Apostolic See.

Tillich

Great traditions of the past: '*Litterae communionis*' ['Testimony of the community']. Help offered to those who are in

1 See John 10:30.
2 See Mark 1:11.

need, e.g. the Church in Eastern Europe – missionary initiatives, great shortages in the countries of the first evangelisation – different ways of caring for people and communities, maternal care – also a concern about the depopulation of Europe. Are we prepared to meet Islam? (*casus* [case]: Iraq).

The foundations of morality.

Anticipated Matins (Feast of the Chair of St Peter)

Pirandello
Maritain
Tolstoy

Meditation (17):

Augustine: *Amore casto di Dio (cercare Dio perché è Dio)* [Pure love of God (to seek God because He is God)]. Not because He can be of use to the self-fulfilment of human life or social order – but because He is Who He IS. The Holy Spirit leads us in this direction. *Dio che cerca di essere cercato* [God who wants to be sought].

Examples: *Lettere dei condannati a morte della resistenza* [Letters of resistance fighters sentenced to death].[1]

This is the greatest grace we should ask for.

Rosary (I); Eucharistic Adoration and Benediction
(Holy Hour): The Lord has laid on Him the iniquity of us all – receive the Holy Spirit, if you forgive the sins of any, they are forgiven[2]
Compline; Litany of Our Lord Jesus Christ, Priest and Victim, Blessed Virgin Mary, St Joseph; Reading

22 February

Intentions; Morning prayers
Morning meditation: (*Misit Deus Spiritum Filii sui in corda vestra clamantem 'Abba Pater'* [God has sent the Spirit of His Son into our hearts, crying, 'Abba Father'])[3]
Holy Mass; Prayers; Thanksgiving; Rosary (III); Lauds

Meditation (18):

In Cathedra S. Petri: ministerium Petrinum: servus servorum Dei – et omnes qui huic ministerio cooperantur [In the Chair of St Peter: the ministry of Peter: the servant of God's servants – and all who work together with this ministry]. This is the place of *praedestinationis et benedictionis* [predestination and blessing], of every '*Pietro, mi ami tu?*' ['Peter, do you love me?']. With this we will stand before Christ *in die iudicii* [on

1 *Lettere di condannati a morte della Resistenza italiana (8 settembre 1943 – 25 aprile 1945)* [Letters of the Italian Resistance Fighters Sentenced to Death], ed. Piero Malvezzi and Giovanni Pirelli (Turin, 1952).
2 See Isaiah 53:6 and John 20:22–23.
3 See Galatians 4:6.

the Day of Judgement], so that He can introduce us to the Father.

Cathedra Petri [The Chair of Peter]: a special concentration of *Mysterium* [Mystery]. Why is Peter still alive? Due to the apostolic succession. Not only due to the retrospective continuity, but also through Christ making Peter present in every successor (Peter, do you love Me?).

That which is important in Peter – and in every successor – is all contained in faith!

Terce; Prayer to the Holy Spirit; Prayer for Good Friday

Meditation (19):

In fide vivo Filii Dei [I live by faith in the Son of God].[1] 'I have prayed for you, Peter, that your faith may not fail'.[2] This is a reference point for *Chiesa della speranza* [the Church of hope].

Peter, do you love Me?; Lord, You know that I love You; Tend my sheep (my lambs). When you were young, you girded yourself and walked where you would. When you are old, another will carry you where you do not wish to go . . .[3]

Martyrium [Martyrdom] – the highest test (expression) of spousal love: to lay down your soul and your body.

What more could the Father have done than to give us His Son? Than to accept His *Martyrium*?

Augustine. *Gaudet mente, qui se videt in Me* [He who sees himself in Me rejoices in his soul].

Let the Pope see himself in the Lord, in Christ – '*frui Domino*' ['to rejoice in the Lord'] – and let him serve likewise!

Meditation continued; The Way of the Cross; Sext; None; Adoration of the Blessed Sacrament; Reading; Litany of the Saints; Act of reparation; Chaplet of the Five Wounds of Christ; Rosary (I); Vespers

Meditation (20):

The Apostolic See, as a special community within the Church, undertakes the ministry of promotion (animation) in relation to other particular and local communities, in particular

1 See Galatians 2:20.
2 See Luke 22:32.
3 See John 21:15–18.

nations, and in a universal dimension (*Bonus Pastor*[1] and earlier documents) from the perspective of the Third Millennium.

Schönborn
Danielou
Claudel

What does '*Bonus Pastor*' ['Good Shepherd'] mean? An invitation to recognise the primacy of a person in the Church and in the work of the Curia. Person – the Holy Spirit. Person – community – the Curia: we have to create a climate of grace. *Prevalenza dello spirito pastorale* [Predominance of the pastoral spirit].

The Spirit of truth: the primary task of the Church is truth: only in truth can we meet. Furthermore: *stupor veritatis!* [astonishment at the truth!].

Stupor Eucharistiae; stupor absolutionis sacram. [Astonishment at the Eucharist; astonishment at the sacramental absolution].

Anticipated Matins (St Polycarp)

Meditation (21):

(The Curia): 'And they devoted themselves to prayer, and to the breaking of bread, and to the apostles' teaching . . .'[2] Community: a climate of grace. Role model – the Mother of Christ. *Modo eminentiore* [Even more eminently]. Her entire being was prepared (by the Holy Spirit) to accept the Son of God, to the *Admirabile Commercium* [Wonderful Exchange] and, finally, to glory. All this: God's own initiative. Finally: obedience (*secundum verbum Tuum* [according to Your word]).[3] Perfect Bridehood?

'*Si*' ['Yes!'] I am all of God – I devote all of myself to God. *Virgo* [Virgin] – suffering.

Stabilitas mentis in Deo [The equilibrium of mind in God] despite all human '*fragilitas*' ['fragility'].

Rosary (II); Eucharistic Adoration and Benediction; Meditation continued; Litany of the Sacred Heart of Jesus, Blessed Virgin Mary, St Joseph; Compline; Reading

1 The apostolic constitution *Pastor bonus* (The Good Shepherd) was promulgated by Pope John Paul II on 28 June 1988.

2 See Acts 2:42.

3 See Luke 1:38.

23 February

Intentions; Morning prayers
Morning meditation: (‘*Gaudet mente qui se videt in Me*’ [‘He who sees himself in Me rejoices in his soul’]) Augustine
Holy Mass; Prayers; Thanksgiving; Prayer to the Holy Spirit; Lauds

Meditation (22):

Memoria creaturale: che siamo preceduti dall’Essere Assoluto. Prima intenzione: memoria dell’origine e della fine. La memoria creaturale crea profondità, fundamentus dignitatis, profondità – umiltà [Memory of the creation: we are preceded by the Absolute Being. First intention: memory of the beginning and the end. The memory of the creation creates depth, fundament of dignity, depth – humility].

The Parish Priest of Ars:[1] I gave you life, what have you done with it?

Memoria dei Misteri: non celebriamo i riti, celebriamo misteri [Memory of the Mysteries: we do not celebrate rites, we celebrate mysteries].

Memoria del futuro [Memory of the future].

Preghiera Trinitaria (ut supra) [Trinitarian prayer (as above)].

Destinatari di promesse – di compiacenza [Recipients of the promises – of kindness].

Conclusion; Final words; Blessing; Magnificat
UIOGD[2]

1 St Jean-Baptiste-Marie Vianney TOSF (1786–1859), known in English as St John Vianney, was a French priest who is venerated as the patron saint of parish priests. He was known for his priestly and pastoral work in the parish in Ars and is often referred to as the ‘*Curé d’Ars*’ (the Parish Priest of Ars).
2 See p. xxi.

8–14 March 1992
Exercitia Spiritualia [Spiritual Exercises] Led by Cardinal [Ugo] Poletti *Vic. Romae Emerit.* [Vicar Emeritus of Rome][1]

8 March

'Lenten Lamentations';[2] Exposition of the Blessed Sacrament; Vespers for the First Sunday of Lent

Introductory Meditation (1):

'*Animus pastoralis*' ['Pastoral spirit'].

A pilgrimage along the roads of Palestine, where our Good Shepherd walked, our absolute example. His presence remains a special gift of those roads, that land (which in other respects is ordinary, similar to so many other places in the Middle East).

'He dwelt in Capernaum'[3] – by the peoples' road (*via gentium* [the road of nations]).

adorare [to adore]
tacere [to keep silent]
godere [to rejoice]
cum Maria: [with Mary:]
a master of listening to the Word.

Eucharistic Adoration; Eucharistic Benediction; Meditation continued; Reading; Compline

9 March: Feast of St Frances of Rome

Intentions; Prayers
Morning meditation: *Verbum – Filius hominis* [the Word – the Son of Man]
Holy Mass; Prayers; Thanksgiving; (Rosary (II)); Lauds

Meditation (2):

The pilgrimage begins in Nazareth: an encounter with the mystery of the Mother of God.

---

1 Ugo Poletti (1914–97) was an Italian cardinal and Vicar General of Rome (1973–91).
2 See n. 6, p. 221 [11 March 1984].
3 See Matthew 4:13.

God's eternal intention to save man – grace: pure gift . . . '*non* [illegible]': man – the Virgin of Nazareth.

Annunciation: Mary's faith – (analogically, Abraham) *obbedienza nell'oscurità* [obedience in the darkness] (!) – *Intermediaria nell'annuncio del Vangelo* [Mediator in the proclamation of the Gospel].

An encounter with the mystery of the Mother of God in the Curia – in everyone's ministry: *servi inutiles* [unworthy servants].[1]

Prayer to the Holy Spirit; Passion of Our Lord Jesus Christ according to Matthew; Terce

Meditation (3):
Nazareth: the mystery of Christ (incarnation – redemption – impoverishment – glorification).

'Truly this man was the Son of God'.[2]

'My food is to do the will of Him who sent Me'.[3]

'He loved the Church and gave Himself up for her'.[4]

(The Son) 'He returned everything to the Father, so that God may be everything to every one'.[5]

[*Gloria di Dio (Padre) – amore della Chiesa* [Glory of God (Father) – love of the Church];

Servizio ai fratelli [Service to the brothers]: this is the summing-up of the mystery of Christ of Nazareth.]

This is also our vocation (the Apostolic See) – not the position – but the quality of service(!).

reflection

The servant of servants – he has the right to be judged, to be criticised, so that he can serve better, so that he can do the will of Christ better (*discernimento* [discernment]).

Meditation continued: 'The servant does not know what his Master is doing . . .'[6]

1 See Luke 17:10.
2 See Mark 15:39
3 See John 4:34.
4 See Ephesians 5:25.
5 See 1 Corinthians 15:28.
6 See John 15:15.

The Way of the Cross: 'The Son of Man came to serve, and to give his life as a ransom for many'[1]

Eucharistic Adoration; Sext; None; (Reading); Penitential psalms; (Prayers); Rosary (III); Vespers

Meditation (4):

Spirito di Nazaret [The Spirit of Nazareth]: the spirit of the Servant (from Isaiah's prophecy), the fruit of Mary and Joseph's care, the fruit of self-education.

Mandato dal Padre [Sent by the Father]: He has not left Me alone, for I always do what is pleasing to the Father.[2]

The spirit of service in relation to our brothers and sisters: He was 'for them' without any limits (good Teacher). Foot washing – a kind of conclusion and synthesis of this attitude.

This spirit – for everyone who serves the universal Church in the Roman Curia.

Anticipated Matins; Litany of the Holy Name of Jesus, Blessed Virgin Mary, St Joseph

Meditation (5):

La vita soprannaturale: [The supernatural life] *dono del Mistero di Gesù* [gift of the Mystery of Jesus]. *Vita che viene dal Padre – vita eterna* [Life that comes from the Father – eternal life].

'He who has seen me has seen the Father' (J . . .).[3]

'I came that they may have life, and have it abundantly'.[4] Life everlasting, so that they may know the Father.

'As adopted sons in the Holy Spirit, we cry: "Abba Father"'.[5]

The state of sanctifying grace, and (that is) the call to holiness: *stato missionario della vita cristiana* [missionary status of the Christian life]. (*Christifideles laici*)[6] many sons of God, but scattered . . .

Every Christian: *canale della grazia* [channel of grace] (*L[umen] G[entium]* 29). Our role model – Mary!

1 See Mark 10:45.
2 See John 8:29.
3 See John 14:9.
4 See John 10:10.
5 See Romans 8:15.
6 *Christifideles laici* (The Lay Members of Christ's Faithful People) is a post-synodal apostolic exhortation of Pope John Paul II issued on 30 December 1988. It offers a reflection on the vocation and mission of the laity in the Church.

Rosary (I); Eucharistic Benediction; Concluding meditation; Compline

10 March

Intentions; Morning prayers
Morning meditation: . . . being in the form of God, . . . He took the form of a servant[1]
Holy Mass; Thanksgiving; Prayers; Rosary (III); Prayer to the Holy Spirit; Lauds

Meditation (6): *Vivere la grazia santificante* [To live in sanctifying grace].

Christ chose Galilee: humble people, poor in spirit, more open to receive the gift of the grace of God.

It is the grace of adoptive sonship (sons in the Son), the same for everyone (the parable of the labourer in the vineyard: each of them receive . . . a denarius).[2]

The Parable of the Sower: collaboration with grace takes various forms, it is of a personal nature . . . It also depends on various vocations.

Sanctifying grace and our response (in love). In this way we become living cells in the body of Christ: living and enlivening. It is true everywhere, as it is true in the Curia.

St Bernard: prayer for grace, for good collaboration with it. The Mother of divine grace.

Terce; Passion of Our Lord Jesus Christ according to Mark

Meditation (7): (*Gesù davanti al peccato* [Jesus confronted with sin]).

On the roads of Galilee Jesus constantly encountered human sin. An encounter and a 'clash'. Sin opposes (sanctifying) grace. Sin is an illness; it is the death of a soul.

Against sin – Christ: the Good Samaritan. Always aware of the fact that sin (the sins of the world) will afflict Him in the form of the agony of Gethsemane and death: the sacrifice of the cross on Golgotha.

Jesus is full of mercy and understanding in relation to sinners. He never rejects them, He defends the woman caught in adultery, and at the same time He says 'do not sin again'.[3]

In the end: the cross is an act of special 'solidarity' with sinful humankind.

1 See Philippians 2:6–7.
2 See Matthew 20:10.
3 See John 8:11.

Hence: pastoral consequences:

(a) a sense of sinfulness
(b) let us not allow sin to own our 'self'
(c) always to have the infinite divine mercy before our eyes.

Mary: the Mother of Mercy.

Meditation continued: (on God's givenness – the Holy Spirit – on the sin against the Holy Spirit)
The Way of the Cross; Adoration of the Blessed Sacrament; Sext; None; (Reading); Litany of the Saints; Rosary (I); Vespers

Meditation (8): (*La gioia di perdonare e di essere perdonati* [The joy of forgiving and being forgiven]).

David: *Miserere mei, Deus . . . lava me a peccatis meis . . . Tibi soli peccavi . . .* [Have mercy on me, O God . . . cleanse me from my sin . . . Against Thee only, have I sinned . . .].[1]

The Pharisee and the Tax Collector.[2]

Sin entered into our human condition. Therefore, one should never be discouraged: 'I am disappointed with myself' can be the other side of well-disguised pride. St John: 'God is greater than our conscience'.[3]

('*Perdono – ma non posso dimenticare*' ['I forgive – but I cannot forget'].)

'And forgive us our trespasses, as we forgive those who trespass against us'.[4]

In addition to that, sins of omission.

Sins against chastity . . . a very insightful analysis.

In the confessional – to make special effort to follow the example of Jesus: 'up to seventy-seven times'.[5]

Anticipated Matins

Meditation (9): *Beatitudini* [Beatitudes].

In Galilee, Christ 'sketched out' what the future Church would look like; in Jerusalem He instituted (fulfilled) it. This 'outline' consists in the announcement of the Eucharist, the

1 See Psalm 50:3–4 (51:1–4).
2 See Luke 18:9–14.
3 See 1 John 3:20.
4 See Matthew 6:12.
5 See Matthew 18:22.

primacy of Peter and the Sermon on the Mount: the Beatitudes.

'The poor in spirit.'

The Roman Curia and the spirit of the Beatitudes.

Manzoni

'The meek, for they shall inherit the earth'[1] (the ability to influence hearts and consciences, among much opposition and persecutions).

Cont. tomorrow.

Rosary (II); Eucharistic Adoration and Benediction; Litany of the Sacred Heart of Jesus, Blessed Virgin Mary, St Joseph; Meditation continued; Compline; Reading

11 March

Intentions; Prayers; Morning meditation; Holy Mass; Thanksgiving; Rosary (I); Lauds

Meditation (10): *Beatitudini* [Beatitudes] (cont.).

The continuation of the examination of conscience in the light of the Eight Beatitudes:

- Blessed are those who hunger and thirst for righteousness:[2] righteous according to the evangelical standards (like '*Justus Joseph*' ['Just Joseph']).[3]
- Blessed are the merciful . . . :[4] mercy has to complement righteousness (righteousness judges; mercy gives and forgives). The Curia – the question of organised mercy.
- Blessed are the pure in heart, for they shall see God:[5] The purity of heart – in a broader and deeper sense than just the 'virtue of chastity'. If your eye is sound (full of light)[6] – the purity of a child: 'they see God'.
- Blessed are the peacemakers . . . :[7] 'the peace of God, which passes all [understanding]'[8] . . . to educate to peace, to make peace.
- Blessed are those who are persecuted for righteousness'

1 See Matthew 5:5.
2 See Matthew 5:6.
3 See Matthew 1:19.
4 See Matthew 5:7.
5 See Matthew 5:8.
6 See Matthew 6:22.
7 See Matthew 5:9.
8 See Philippians 4:7.

(17) III

venerdì **17** maggio

s. Pasquale Baylon

Friday Freitag Vendredi — May Mai Mai

пятница Viernes — май Mayo

1. [illegible]
2. medit. – mattutina
3. [illegible] con Ros [illegible]
4. Laudes
5. medit. (X) Beatitudini (c.d.)

8 [illegible] błogosławieństw

9 – błogosławieni, którzy łakną i pragną sprawiedliwości; sprawiedliwość wg [illegible] ewangelicznej (jak u Justus, Joseph)

11 – błogosławieni miłosierni, albo [illegible] sprawiedliwości ([illegible])

14 – błogosławieni czystego serca, albowiem oni Boga oglądają. [illegible]

– błogosławieni pokój czyniący ..... pokój Boży [illegible] ... wychowywać do pokoju, czynić pokój

18 – błogosławieni, którzy cierpią prześladowanie dla sprawiedliwości [illegible]

„Kościół [illegible]" [illegible]

20 s.w. — G V S D L M M G V S D L M M G V — 16 17 18 19 20 21 22 23 24 25 26 27 28 29 30 31 — 137-228

8 błogosławieństw

> sake . . . :[1] 'if the world hates you, know that it has hated Me first'.[2]

'The Code of Christian Life': a word to the Curia. The See of Wisdom: Mary: The Woman of the Eight Beatitudes.

Terce; Prayer for the gifts of the Holy Spirit; Passion of Our Lord Jesus Christ according to Luke

Meditation 11: (*La Chiesa di Cristo fondata su Pietro* [The Church of Christ founded on Peter]).

For the first time Jesus says the words 'Church: My Church' near Caesarea Philippi (Matthew 16:18).

Peter's declaration.

The announcement of the primacy (*petra* [rock]).

(Succession – Apostolic See – Curia.)

The dogmatic constitution *L[umen] G[entium]*: the Church – *universale sacramento di salvezza* – *popolo di Dio* [the universal sacrament of salvation – the people of God] – sent to the whole world. *Cattedra di Pietro presiede alla carità* [The Chair of St Peter presides in charity].

After the declaration of Peter's primacy – this very Peter proves that he does not judge by God's standards, but by human standards.

This is a very important indicator for everyone in the Curia: to live by faith in the Son of God, who loved me and gave Himself for me.[3]

'I cast my net to catch Your word'.

'The Lord of the harvest' . . . 'where your treasure is, there will your heart be also'.[4]

Meditation continued: 'To judge by God's standards, not by human standards'.

The Way of the Cross; Adoration of the Blessed Sacrament; Litany of the Holy Name of Jesus, Blessed Virgin Mary, St Joseph; Sext; None; Penitential psalms; (Reading); Rosary (II); Vespers

1 See Matthew 5:10.
2 See John 15:18.
3 See Galatians 2:20.
4 See Matthew 9:38 and 6:21.

Meditation 12:

Camminando con Gesù incontro alla vita [Walking with Jesus towards life].

Jesus meets death on the Galilean (and Judean) roads three times:

- a young man of Nain
- Jairus' daughter
- Lazarus.

(A dialogue with Martha) . . .

Encounters with death in a priest's life. Incidents of sudden death: '. . . watch therefore, for you do not know on what day your Lord is coming.'[1]

The death of each of us is 'for the glory of God' (Lazarus).[2] We ought to prepare for it. To prepare for the judgement of God – Mt.: 'you did it to me'; 'you did it not to me.'

Spiritual works of mercy; corporal works of mercy.

Pastoral ministry in Rome: the laity (volunteers) bear special witness. Priests focus more on spiritual works of mercy.

'God is love . . . he who abides in love abides in God, and God abides in him' (John).[3]

Pray for us sinners now and at the hour of our death.

Anticipated Matins

Meditation 13:

(*Gesù conferma la fede degli Apostoli: il Tabor* [Jesus strengthens the faith of the apostles: Tabor].)

Tabor as the 'holy mount' (Peter): we have witnessed the elevation of Christ.

Amid the noise of contemporary civilisation, we need places of contemplation where one can only hear the Father's voice: 'This is my beloved Son . . .'[4]

Moses and Elijah – the Law and the Prophets: what has been added is the commandment of love – this is the entire Law: the Law and the Prophets.

1 See Matthew 24:42.
2 See John 11:4.
3 See 1 John 4:16.
4 See Mark 9:7.

Tabor opens the way to Jerusalem.

'Prayer and fasting': different forms of penance in the life of a priest.

Auxilium christianorum [Help of Christians].

Rosary (III); Eucharistic Adoration and Benediction; (Reading); Meditation continued; Compline

12 March

Intentions; Prayers

Morning meditation: (No one knows the Son except the Father . . .[1] The mystery of Tabor)

Holy Mass; Thanksgiving; Prayers; Rosary (II); Lauds

Meditation 14: (*Verso Gerusalemme* [To Jerusalem]).

Christ versus Abraham: 'Go to the land that I will show you'[2] (analogy between the Old and New Testaments).

St Joseph Cottolengo

Jesus leaves Galilee, His family land (a 'Galilean'), to which He was attached from childhood . . . He was to return there only after His resurrection.

(Everyone is attached to their place of origin.)

Jesus walks with the apostles along the valley of the Jordan – this road has a special significance. (A comparison with many of our ways). The Mount of Temptation lies on this way too (there are also temptations on our ways): a 'carnal man', according to St Paul.[3]

At this point the retreat leader analyses all the temptations that Christ had to face at the end of the forty-day fast.

The Lord Jesus is our support in all temptations. Mary.

Terce; Prayer for the gifts of the Holy Spirit; Passion of Our Lord Jesus Christ according to John

Meditation 15: (*Dal Monte degli Ulivi* [From the Mount of Olives]).

Jesus approaches Jerusalem from the side of Jericho. The Mount of Olives. Near Bethany, the home of Mary, Martha and Lazarus – Jesus' friends.

'No longer do I call you servants, but I have called you friends . . . greater love has no man than this . . . that a man lay down his life for his friends'.[4]

1 See Matthew 11:27.
2 See Genesis 12:1.
3 See 1 Corinthians 2:14.
4 See John 15:15, 13.

Friendship: Jesus-friend and Jesus' friends.

(On priestly friendship in the light of Roman experiences.)

Bethphage – the starting point for the entry to Jerusalem: 'you will find a colt' . . .[1]

Nearby there is the place of 'Our Father':[2] the programme of '*unum esse, unum sentire, unum operari*' ['to be as one, to think as one, to act as one'] is founded on this prayer.

'*Dominus flevit*' ['The Lord wept'] over Jerusalem.[3]

'Would that even today you knew' . . .[4] and finally: from the Mount of Olives Jesus will ascend to the Father and send out the apostles to the whole world, saying 'I am with you always, to the close of the age'.[5]

Meditation continued; The Way of the Cross; Eucharistic Adoration: ('My Body – My Church'); Sext; None; Litany of Christ the Priest, Blessed Virgin Mary, St Joseph; Litany of the Saints; Reading; Rosary (III); Vespers

Meditation 16: (*Luce di Betlemme* . . . [Light from Bethlehem . . .]).

Bethlehem – what does it say to us? The Word became flesh and dwelt among us.[6]

'. . . He gave power to become children of God' (John 1).[7]

Prima Epiphania [First Epiphany] of the eternal plan of salvation. '*Gloria in excelsis Deo*' ['Glory to God in the highest']: the birth of Christ (incarnation of the Word) restores to God the glory that was taken away by sin in the created world. '*Et in terra pax hominibus bonae voluntatis*' ['And on earth peace to people of good will'].[8] At the same time, this is the first epiphany of the Church: the people who participate in it – gathered around the newly born – are Mary, Joseph, the shepherds and the wise men.

Card. Traglia

The epiphany of poverty.

1 See Luke 19:30.

2 The Church of *Pater Noster* (Our Father) is a partially reconstructed Roman Catholic church located on the Mount of Olives in Jerusalem. It stands on the traditional site of Christ's teaching of the Lord's Prayer.

3 The Church of *Dominus Flevit* (The Lord wept) is a Roman Catholic church on the Mount of Olives, opposite the walls of the Old City of Jerusalem. It was fashioned in the shape of a teardrop to symbolise the tears of Christ.

4 See Luke 19:42.

5 See Matthew 28:20.

6 See John 1:14.

7 See John 1:12.

8 See Luke 2:14.

(The problem of the poverty of clergy.)

Solidarity (*carità* [charity]) with people without borders.

The epiphany of persecution (Rome), (Herod).

Epiphany = that which God has chosen, becoming man in the Son–Word.

Anticipated Matins

Meditation 17:

(*Nel Cenacolo per raccogliere l'eredità di Cristo* [In the Upper Room to receive the inheritance of Christ].)

('*eredità*') = inheritance – it is the Church built on Christ's messianic sacrifice.

Christ passes on this inheritance to the apostles in the Upper Room: the Eucharist and the priesthood.

'Go and prepare the Passover for us . . .'[1]

(John 13–17.)

- the vine and the branches
- the high priestly prayer

  Even as Thou art in me, and I in Thee, Father . . . that they also may be in Us . . .[2]
- the Eucharist – '*memoriale mortis Domini*' ['memorial of the Lord's death']

  one single Sacrifice, which lasts and is sacramentally renewed in the Church
- *Sacerdos – alter Christus – in spiritu et veritate* [Priest – another Christ – in spirit and truth].

(Practical pastoral observations.)

Rosary (I); Eucharistic Adoration and Benediction; (Reading)
(*Hora Sancta* / Holy Hour):

Christ, accepting the 'chalice', compensates the Father for all sin in human history, all that is rooted in the original opposition to love, in a superabundant way (as God from God) . . . He creates a 'balance' of love on the part of the creation, on the part of humankind: this, indeed, is redemption.

1 See Luke 22:8.
2 See John 17:21.

This 'balance' of love is permanent and irreversible. It abides in God and, simultaneously, in human history. Through it, human history becomes the history of salvation.

Compline

13 March Intentions; Prayers; Morning meditation (in relation to the Holy Hour); Holy Mass; Thanksgiving; Prayers; (Rosary (III)); Lauds

Meditation 18:

(*Il Getsemani, il tempo della prova e della tentazione* [Gethsemane, the time of the test and temptation].)

Christ – the Son, who is consubstantial with the Father, as a true Man experiences complete desolation: the Father 'does not accept' His supplication, He only accepts His readiness to drink from the 'Cup'. The disciples: 'could you not watch with Me one hour?'[1]

(Paul VI – in the basilica of Gethsemane.)[2]

Because of our limited human understanding, we do not want to 'leave Christ alone'. In His inner self He is always alone with the Father, and yet He expects us to 'be with Him'. At the same time, we ask Him to be with us in our petitions and experiences.

Gethsemane, Christ's call to watch with Him, refers to everyone in the Holy See.

Prayer for the gifts of the Holy Spirit; Reproaches: My people;[3] Terce

Meditation 19:

Il Calvario: Vertice della vita cristiana (militante) [Calvary: the perfection of (militant) Christian life].

On Calvary Christ bore the highest witness to the Father's love. On Calvary: *Passio Christi – Passio Ecclesiae* [Passion of Christ – Passion of the Church].

Paul's 'I complete . . .':[4] the vocation of the Church and every Christian in the cross of Christ. Sin is the 'protagonist' of the crucifixion: He is crucified for our sins. Human hatred and all

1 See Matthew 25:40.

2 Pope Paul VI visited the Basilica of the Agony in Gethsemane during his 1964 Holy Land pilgrimage.

3 See Micah 6:3.

4 See Colossians 1:24.

venerdì **24** maggio

Maria Ausiliatrice

Friday Freitag Vendredi
пятница Viernes

May Mai Mai
май Mayo

– Eucharystia – [illegible] Donum [illegible] sakramentalne

– Sacerdos – alter Christus – in spiritu et veritate

(konkretne uwagi duszpasterskie)

18. Cor. Ros. (I)

19. Ador. Bened. Euch. (Ubi?)

8 20. (Hora Sancta / Godzina Święta)

9 – Chrystus [illegible]

10 [illegible]

11 [illegible]

12 [illegible]

13 [illegible]

14 – [illegible]

15 [illegible]

21. Compl.

16

(13. III)

17

1. [illegible]

18 2. Meditatio matut. – (rozważania do Godziny Świętej)

19 3. Sacrum. Grat. act. Preces.

(Cor. Ros. III)

M	G	V	S	D	L	M	M	G	V	S	D	L	M	M
1	2	3	4	5	6	7	8	9	10	11	12	13	14	15

21 s.w.

4. Laudes

who were and are driven by it take part in the procession of sin ('The world hates Me and it will hate you').[1]

Nevertheless, Christ – in the loneliness of His agony on Calvary – was not alone. The Church was with Him in the persons of the Mother, John, other women and also, to some extent, the Roman tax collector and other unnamed people.

And this has continued through the ages.

Meditation continued:

If the Church is with Christ already on Golgotha . . . this is due to the grace of redemption in which the Church is constituted – like a child in a mother's womb. The sacrifice of the cross 'constitutes' the Church, which will be revealed to the world on the day of Pentecost: the Church will be born into the world like a newly born child.

The Way of the Cross; Litany of the Sacred Heart of Jesus, Blessed Virgin Mary, St Joseph; Eucharistic Adoration; Sext; None; Reading; 'seven words on the cross'; 'Faithful cross' (*Crux fidelis*); Rosary (I); Vespers

Meditation 20:

Il Sepolcro: luogo di partenza della testimonianza del Vangelo [The Sepulchre: the place where witness to the Gospel began].

First witnesses: Women, Mary of Magdala. Only in the evening of that day: the Upper Room – the apostles – 'Peace be with you'.[2]

He who raised Christ from the dead, will return us to life with Him too (St Paul).[3]

Christ died for our sins, He was raised on the third day,
? and He appeared.[4] The apostle mentions all the post-paschal theophanies:

- If Christ has not been raised, then our preaching is in vain and our faith is in vain.[5]
- He accepted death and was raised from the dead for all without exception(!)

1 See John 15:18.
2 See John 20:19.
3 See Romans 8:11.
4 See 1 Corinthians 15:3–5.
5 See 1 Corinthians 15:14.

'Being raised from the dead, He will never die again.'[1]

Outside Him there is no salvation. 'Receive the Holy Spirit . . .'[2]

Anticipated Matins

Meditation 21:

(*Il Cenacolo: la presenza e l'opera dello Spirito S. nella Chiesa e in noi* [The Upper Room: the presence and work of the Holy Spirit in the Church and in us].)

The election of Matthias.

Pentecoste [Pentecost].

Christ Himself revealed the Holy Spirit (*Il vero Rivelatore dello Spirito S. è Gesù stesso* [The true Revealer of the Holy Spirit is Jesus Himself]): according to John.

The apostle could understand what the mission of the Holy Spirit (Paraclete) in the Church and in each of us is from Christ's words – in particular in His farewell speech in John.

This is testified to by the rich pneumatology of St Paul (numerous quotations).

'Do not quench the Spirit.'[3]

In the Church: 'It has seemed good to the Holy Spirit and to us . . .'[4] (the apostles, the Church).

The fruits of the Holy Spirit/the gifts . . .

'*O Lux beatissima* . . .' ['O Light most blessed . . .'][5]

To live in the Holy Spirit!

Through Mary.

Rosary (II); Eucharistic Adoration and Benediction; Meditation continued; Compline

14 March

Intentions; Prayers
Morning meditation: (*Il vero Rivelatore dello Spirito S. è Gesù stesso* [The true Revealer of the Holy Spirit is Jesus Himself])
Holy Mass; Thanksgiving; Prayers; (Rosary (I)); Lauds

(Concluding) meditation 22:

(*Predica di Ricordi* [Preaching the Testimony].

1 See Romans 6:9.
2 See John 20:22.
3 See 1 Thessalonians 5:19.
4 See Acts 15:28.
5 See the hymn *Veni Sancte Spirit* (Come, Holy Spirit).

Conclusioni e prospettive sacerdotali [Conclusions and pastoral perspectives].)

- *Passa la scena di questo mondo* [The form of this world is passing away].[1]
- *Tutto posso in Quello che mi conforta* [I can do all things in Him who strengthens me].[2]
- '*in Meam commemorationem*' ['in memory of Me'].[3]
- *ministri della Misericordia* [ministers of Mercy].
- *discepoli e testimoni* [disciples and witnesses].

(Liturgy of the Hours, Rosary)

- *ci ha chiamati amici* [He called us friends].
- *Resta con noi!* [Stay with us!].[4]

Affidamento a Maria [Devotion to Mary].

Madre della Perseveranza [Mother of Perseverance].

mente assorbita dallo Spirito Santo di Dio [mind absorbed by the Holy Spirit of God].

Conclusion; Final words; Blessing; Magnificat.
UIOGD[5]

1 See 1 Corinthians 7:31.
2 See Philippians 4:13.
3 See Luke 22:19.
4 See Luke 24:29.
5 See p. xxi.

28 February – 6 March 1993
Exercitia Spiritualia [Spiritual Exercises] *Capella Redemptoris Mater* [Mother of the Redeemer Chapel] Led by [Bishop] Jorge [Arturo Agustín] Medina Estévez (Chile – Rancagua)[1]

28 February ('Lenten Lamentations');[2] Exposition of the Blessed Sacrament; Vespers for the First Sunday of Lent

Introductory meditation (1):

The time of grace. Working together with grace – conversion – the awareness of sin – humility – glorification of God (*ad laudem suae gratiae* [for the glory of one's grace]) – love.

Silence – inner opening to God who speaks (St Joseph – *Grande Silenzioso* [the Great Silent One]) – 'examination' (*esame*) of life – practical resolutions.

In the spirit of Mary – with Her intercession: '*fiat*' ['let it be'] – I am coming to fulfil Your will – Thy will be done.

Eucharistic Adoration; Eucharistic Benediction; Meditation continued; (Reading); Compline

1 March Intentions; Prayers
Morning meditation: (*ad laudem maiestatis gratiae Tuae* [to the praise of Your glorious grace] – Eph. 1)[3]
Holy Mass; Prayers; Thanksgiving; (Rosary (II)); Lauds

Meditation 2:

Fides [Faith]: 'I have prayed for you that your faith may not fail, and when you have turned again, strengthen your brethren.'[4]

---

1 Jorge Arturo Agustín Medina Estévez (b. 1926) is a Chilean cardinal and Prefect Emeritus of the Congregation for Divine Worship and the Discipline of the Sacraments.

2 See n. 6, p. 221 [11 March 1984].

3 See Ephesians 1:6.

4 See Luke 22:32.

giovedì **30** maggio

s. Felice I papa

Thursday Donnerstag Jeudi
четверг Jueves

May Ma
май Mayo

Exercitia Spirit. 1993

capella Redemptoris 28.II – 6.III

Meditat... [illegible] Jorge Medina Estevez (Chile – Rancagua)

28.II – [„Gardino [illegible]"]

1. Expositio SS-mi
2. Vesp. de Dom. Quadr.
3. Meditatio introductiva (I)

Czas łaski: współpraca z łaską – nawrócenie z świadomości grzechu – pokora – uwielbienie Boga / ad laudem gloriae gratiae – miłość

Milczenie – „otwarcie wewnętrzne na Boga, który przemawia / św. Józef – Grande Silenzioso / – „rachunek" (esame) z życia – konkretne postanowienia –

W duchu Maryi – z Jej [illegible]: „fiat" – idź, bym pełnił Twą wolę – „bądź wola Twoja" –

4. Ador. Euch. / Bened. Euch.
5. Meditatio recapitulativa (Lektura)
6. Compl.

M G V S D L M M G V S D L M M
1 2 3 4 5 6 7 8 9 10 11 12 13 14 15

22 s.w.

1.III

1. Int. [illegible]

Faith/priesthood: *ad Hebr.* [Letter to the Hebrews]: *fondamento di ciò che speriamo* [foundation of what we hope for]: the foundation of the whole life of the Church – faith – sacraments – '*Auctor et Perfectionator fidei nostrae*' ['Pioneer and Perfecter of our faith'][1] (Hebrews).

For a man of faith eternal life is above earthly life. (The opposite – not a negation, but life led 'as if' God and eternal life did not exist.) For a man of faith, the invisible is more real than the visible.

s. Paulus: nollite conformari huic saeculo . . . [St Paul: do not be conformed to this world . . .].[2]

Abraham – Moses – St Joseph – Saul (men of faith); am I truly a man of faith?

The peace and joy that faith brings about.

Increase my faith, Lord.[3]

Terce

Meditation (3):

Blessed Laura Vicuña
Toribio de Mogrovejo

Vita aeterna [Eternal life] (1): I believe in life everlasting (the truth that has been forgotten nowadays). Canonisation/beatification are expressions of this faith.

'Christ is our life – life in Christ – life of grace – earthly life with the perspective of death – '*sic transit gloria mundi*' ['thus passes the glory of the world']. We do not know: how much more? Pilgrim – minister – the minister knows that he is not the owner of earthly goods. At the same time, we are the 'heirs' of eternal goods (co-heirs of Christ).

Meditation continued; Sext; None; The Way of the Cross; Litany of the Holy Name of Jesus, Blessed Virgin Mary, St Joseph; Eucharistic Adoration
Reading: Holy Scriptures, others
Litany of the Saints; Rosary (III); Vespers

Meditation (4):

Vita aeterna [Eternal life] (2).

(St Thomas.) *Desidero mori et esse cum Christo* [I want to die and be with Christ].

---

1 See Hebrews 12:2.
2 See Romans 12:2.
3 See Luke 17:5.

(1) meeting after death
(2) Parousia.

An example of a man of living faith: I am dying; I will be in heaven soon.

Colossians: 'your life is hid with Christ in God'.[1]

Gospel: 'where your treasure is, there will your heart be also' – '*invisibilia*' ['invisible things'] – 'what no eye has seen . . . God has prepared . . .' Different images, above all the 'house'/'my Father's house'.[2]

Catechism

'Feast'/the fullness of communion.

Images of the Apocalypse – Come, Lord Jesus[3] – life everlasting – glory – the fullness of '*essere*' ['being'].

Deus meus et omnia [My God and my all].

Contemplation of absolute beauty; *contemplatio beatificans* . . . [delightful contemplation . . .].

Anticipated Matins

Catechism

Meditation (5): (*Il Cammino verso la Patria* [The Way to the Homeland]).

vocatio finalis – vocatio ad vitam aeternam [final vocation – vocation to eternal life]: God gives man His happiness (*beatitudo*).

'*Beatus*' – *qui est beatus?* ['Blessed' – who is blessed?] in the Old Testament? (many quotations).

Qui in N. Test? [Who in the New Testament?].

Beata, quae credidisti [Blessed is she who believed];[4] (*BMV* [Blessed Virgin Mary]).

Beatus es Simon [Blessed are you, Simon][5] (Peter). Many quotations.

In the Old and New Testaments happiness has a dimension of 'wisdom'.

St Paul: *sapientia Crucis* [the wisdom of the Cross] – happiness that we can understand only in the light of faith.

1 See Colossians 3:3.
2 See Matthew 6:21; 1 Corinthians 2:9 and John 14:2.
3 See Revelation 22:20.
4 See Luke 1:45.
5 See Matthew 16:17.

Mali del mondo: abortus – guerre – ateismo [Evil of the world: abortion – wars – atheism] – sin/rejection of God.

Catechism

Christ weeping over Jerusalem.[1]

Rosary (I); Eucharistic Benediction; Concluding meditation; Reading; Compline

2 March

Intentions; Prayers
Morning meditation: 'He who eats my flesh has eternal life[2]
Holy Mass; Prayers; Thanksgiving; Rosary (III); Lauds

Meditation (6):

'*Beati pauperes*' ['Blessed are the poor'] – meaning (Mt. 5) – those who put all their trust in God (*anawim* [the poor]). 'Do not lay up for yourselves treasures on earth . . . but . . . in heaven'[3] (the perishable – the imperishable).[4] 'It will be hard for a rich man to enter the kingdom of heaven'.[5]

(Judas)

The temptation of riches – one of the greatest dangers to the Church (historically).

– Parables – especially the Rich Man and Lazarus[6]

– Ananias and Sapphira[7]

– Christ did not avoid people of good social standing. Nicodemus. Zacchaeus . . .

Catechism

The Letter of James.[8]

Poverty = heart open above all to God – the commandment of love.

Prayer to the Holy Spirit; Passion of Our Lord Jesus Christ according to Matthew; Terce

Meditation (7): '*Beati miti*' ['Blessed are the meek'].[9]

The prayer of St [Francisco] Solano (a missionary in South America).[10]

In the Old Testament – Moses – also David.

1 See Luke 19:41–44.
2 See John 6:54.
3 See Matthew 6:19–20.
4 See 1 Corinthians 15:53–54.
5 See Matthew 19:23.
6 See Luke 16:19–31.
7 See Acts 5:1–11.
8 See James 2:1–13.
9 See Matthew 5:5.
10 St Francisco Solano y Jiménez OFM (1549–1610) was a Spanish friar and missionary in South America.

In the Gospel – '*Sono mite e umile di cuore*' (*mitis et humilis corde*) ['I am gentle and lowly in heart' (meek and humble in heart)].[1]

Sermon on the Mount.

To Judas: 'Friend'[2] – 'you do not know whose spirit dwells in you'[3] – Shepherd – a lost sheep.

Humilitas, mansuetudo [Humility, meekness] come hand in hand with firmness (the expulsion of the money changers from the Temple), words addressed to Peter – words to the tempters (!)[4] – words at the Final Judgement.[5]

'. . . *quia possidebunt terram*:' for they shall inherit the earth.[6]

Meditation continued; Sext; None; The Way of the Cross; Eucharistic Adoration

'The Eight Beatitudes' – there is a deep connection between the revelation of eternal life: happiness that God wants to give to man – and the 'programme' of evangelical Beatitudes. A logical connection – '*Logica Divina – beatitudo – beati*' ['Divine logic – beatitude – blessed']. Not only the commandments (the Decalogue), but 'Beatitudes'.

Penitential psalms; Rosary (I); Vespers

Meditation (8): (*Beati quelli che piangono* [Blessed are those who mourn]).[7] The raising of Lazarus – 'Jesus wept'.[8]

Perfectus Deus (Perfectus homo) [Perfect God (Perfect man)] (deep sensitivity) – Jesus weeps over Jerusalem.

Cf. Hebrews.

Simeon's words: Mary: participation in Her Son's suffering: Her suffering.

Peter's 'bitter' weeping after the denial.

Paul (three times).

1 See Matthew 11:29.
2 See Matthew 26:50.
3 See 1 Corinthians 3:16.
4 See Matthew 18:5–6.
5 See Matthew 25:31–46.
6 See Matthew 5:5.
7 See Matthew 5:4.
8 See John 11:35.

Later: St Monica's tears; the prayer '*Pro petitione lacrimarum*' ['For the gift of tears'].

Anticipated Matins

Meditation (9):

> *Beati quelli che hanno fame e sete di giustizia perché saranno saziati* [Blessed are those who hunger and thirst for righteousness, for they shall be satisfied].[1]

Righteousness is founded on the law/on truth – the guardians of justice – judges.

Justice – justification.

God Himself is the fullness of righteousness – He is just. About Christ: this Man was just[2] – *Gesù Cristo – giusto* [Jesus Christ – just].

Firstly, just – innocent; secondly, just – justifying; thirdly – . . . The absolute dimension of justice.

Abraham – just, because he believed – with absolute faith.

St Joseph – a just man (Mt.).[3]

Zechariah – Anna – Simeon.

To thirst and hunger for justice (*fame e sete* [to hunger and thirst]) – is the opposite of conformism, of opportunism.

Rosary (II); Eucharistic Benediction; Concluding meditation; Compline

3 March

Intentions; Prayers
Morning meditation: 'Just and Justifying'
Holy Mass; Prayers; Thanksgiving; Rosary (II); Lauds

Meditation (10): (*Beati misericordes* [Blessed are the merciful]).[4]

'*Beati pauperes*' ['Blessed are the poor'] . . . the key blessing.

God is mercy. He is merciful: '*progenie in progenies timentibus Eum*' ['those who fear Him from generation to generation'].[5]

Magnificat.

1 See Matthew 5:6.
2 See Luke 23:47.
3 See Matthew 1:19.
4 See Matthew 5:7.
5 See Luke 1:50.

Benedictus [The Canticle of Zechariah].

The Canticle of Simeon.

In Jesus' teaching: the parable of the prodigal son – the woman of Cana – the ten lepers – and others. Mass healings. Material and spiritual poverty. The woman caught in adultery.

Jesus – Good Samaritan: His whole life and mission are mercy.

Cor misericors Jesu – viscera misericordiae [Jesus' merciful Heart – the heart of mercy].

This '*viscera misericordiae*' ['heart of mercy'] should be a trait of each and every disciple of Christ, in particular every priest – faced with the enormous scope of suffering, poverty and hunger of contemporary man.

Prayer to the Holy Spirit; Passion of Our Lord Jesus Christ according to Mark; Terce

Meditation (11): (*Beati i puri di cuore* [Blessed are the pure in heart]).[1]

'*Cor mundum crea in me, Deus*' ['Create in me a clean heart, O God'].[2]

Purity – in the material world; in the spiritual world: purity of heart.

Catechism

Heart – *intimità, dimora* [intimacy, dwelling], a space of encounter, a space of the covenant with God.

'*Deum videbunt*' ['They shall see God'][3] (transparency), (purity of heart; spiritual poverty).

Shepherds – Nathanael.

On the other hand: many 'impurities' also come 'out of the heart of man.'[4]

St Paul: '*opera carnis*' – '*opera Spiritus*' ['the works of the flesh' – 'the works of the Spirit'].[5]

Spiritual struggle (Eph.) – 'the passions of our flesh.'[6]

The truth of original sin and the triple concupiscence should

1 See Matthew 5:8.
2 See Psalm 50:12 (51:10).
3 See Matthew 5:8.
4 See Mark 7:21.
5 See Galatians 5:19.
6 See Ephesians 2:3.

be remembered against contemporary '*neo-pelagianismo*' ['neo-Pelagianism'].[1]

Purezza del corpo, del cuore, della fede [Purity of the body, of the heart, of the faith].

St Paul: 'I see in my members another law at war with the law of God'.[2]

Christ has set me free from the law of sin and death.[3]

John: on the triple concupiscence ([1] John [2:16]).

A long and painful process of purification.

A peccato meo munda me [cleanse me from my sin].[4]

Litany of the Saints; reading; Rosary (II); Vespers

Meditation (12): '*Beati gli operatori di pace;*' ['Blessed are the peacemakers;'] *saranno chiamati figli di Dio* [they shall be called sons of God].[5]

'God of Peace': God is the maker of true peace.

Messianic times: peace as a good.

Psalms — Peace – a gift from God. *Pax – tranquillitas ordinis* [Peace – calmness of order].

The process of peace-making – gradual.

Christ is our peace Peace with God
Peace with people
Peace with the world . . .
through a reconciliation with God.

'My peace I give to you – not as the world gives do I give to you'.[6]

John: 'Peace be with you' on the evening of the resurrection . . .

. . . I send you . . . if you forgive the sins of any . . .[7]

. . . Peace – the mission of reconciliation.

1 Pelagianism is the belief that Adam's original sin did not corrupt human nature and that human beings are capable of earning salvation by their own efforts, choosing between good and evil. This theological theory, rejected by the Roman Catholic Church as a heresy, was named after the British monk Pelagius (354–420/40).

2 See Romans 7:23.

3 See Romans 8:2.

4 See Psalm 50:4 (51:2).

5 See Matthew 5:9.

6 See John 14:27.

7 See John 20:19, 21, 23.

8

sabato giugno

S. Medardo vescovo

Saturday Samstag Samedi — June Juni Juin

СЪБОТА Sábado السبت — ИЮНЬ Junio يونيه

[illegible] neo-pelagianizmu

[illegible]

[illegible]

Pienezza del corpo, del cuore, della fede

[illegible]

[illegible]

8 [illegible]

9 [illegible]

10 [illegible]

9. Lit. H-ma

11 9. Con. Ros. (II)

12 14. Vesp.

13 15. Medit. (XV) „Beati operatori della pace saranno chiamati figli di Dio"

14 „Bóg pokoju" [illegible]

15 Pokój – [illegible] / Pax – tranquillitas ordinis

16 Proces pokoju – stopniowy [illegible]

Chrystus jest naszym pokojem

17 przez pojednanie z Bogiem

18 „Pokój mój daję wam – nie tak jak daje świat, Ja wam daję"

19 „Pokój wam" [illegible]

„Ja was posyłam" [illegible]

D	L	M	M	G	V	S	D	L	M	M	G	V	S	D
16	17	18	19	20	21	22	23	24	25	26	27	28	29	30

23 s.w. — 159-206

Pokój – posłanie pojednania

[illegible]

The proclamation of the good [news] of the kingdom! Peace be with you (joyful).

– *vinci il male con il bene* [overcome evil with good].[1]

Instruments of peace: to speak the truth – to forget hurts – to pray for wrongdoers – to reject vengeance – to seek good mediators – to avoid words that go against peace – forgive us our trespasses as we forgive those who trespass against us.

Anticipated Matins for the Feast of St Casimir[2]

Meditation (13): '*Beati, qui persecutionem patiuntur propter iustitiam, quia eorum est Regnum Coelorum.*' ['Blessed are those who are persecuted for righteousness' sake, for theirs is the kingdom of heaven'].[3]

- persecution for faith (*odium fidei* [hatred of faith]) in the Old Testament:
  The Book of Esther – 2 Maccabees (?)
- St Ignatius of Antioch (*Letter to the Romans*)[4]
- Roman catacombs bear witness to the martyrs
- the martyrs of our times
- '*Sanguis martyrum – semen christianorum*' ['The martyrs' blood – is the seed of Christians'] (St Maria Goretti – St Maksymilian Kolbe)[5]
- different forms of persecution (and martyrdom): bloodless – common in our times.

The first part of the retreat: the foundations of the imitation of Christ (i.e. being a disciple).

Rosary (III); Eucharistic Benediction; Concluding meditation; Compline

1 Romans 12:21.

2 St Casimir Jagiellon (1458–84) was a prince of the Kingdom of Poland and of the Grand Duchy of Lithuania known for his generosity towards the sick and poor.

3 See Matthew 5:10.

4 *The Letter to the Romans* by Ignatius of Antioch (second century) provides an early Christian reflection on martyrdom. It was written when Ignatius was transported from Antioch to Rome, where he was executed in the Colosseum.

5 St Maria Goretti (1890–1902) was an Italian virgin-martyr and one of the youngest Catholic saints. She was canonised by Pope Pius XII on 24 June 1950. For St Maksymilian Kolbe, see n. 3, p. 68 [2 September 1971].

4 March

Intentions; Prayers
Morning meditation: (Who will deliver me from this body of death?[1] – Divine glory through Jesus Christ)
Holy Mass; Prayers; Thanksgiving; Rosary (II); Lauds

Meditation (14): *S. Giovanni Battista* [St John the Baptist] – *profeta e più che profeta* [a prophet and more than a prophet] – 'He must increase, but I must decrease'[2] – He who comes after me[3] – the 'Bridegroom'.[4]

John's disciples – Andrew – Simon, son of Jonah (Peter).

'Behold, the Lamb of God'– 'they followed Christ'.[5]

John's preaching focused on penance as a condition for salvation. Clear, unambiguous preaching – Herod – John's death.

John – the embodiment of the Eight Beatitudes (in particular: he hungered and thirsted for righteousness).

Prayer to the Holy Spirit; Passion of Our Lord Jesus Christ according to Luke; Terce

Meditation (15): (*La salvezza* [Salvation]).

'*Ad dandam scientiam salutis plebi Eius*' ['You will give knowledge of salvation to His people'].[6]

'*Salvezza*' ['Salvation'] – we all 'need' salvation and a Saviour, who is Jesus Christ: 'apart from Me you can do nothing';[7] the cornerstone – there is salvation in no one else.[8]

The final goal of man: union with God (*visio Dei* [vision of God]). The obstacle: sin. The union with God: holiness. The union with God is the only fulfilment of man.

Salvation – love.

Salvation – gift from God Himself.

Christians cannot be just observers of the drama of salvation. Apostolic challenge.

Sext; None; Meditation continued; The Way of the Cross; Eucharistic Adoration; Reading; Penitential psalms; Rosary (III); Vespers

Meditation [16]: (*Servitori della salvezza* [Servants of salvation]).

1 See Romans 7:24.
2 See John 3:30.
3 See John 1:27.
4 See John 3:29.
5 See John 1:36–37.
6 See Luke 1:77.
7 See John 15:5.
8 See Acts 4:12.

Primo Servo della nostra salvezza – Cristo [The First Servant of our salvation – Christ].

Servo di Jahve [Servant of Yahweh] – 'He took the form of a Servant, and became obedient unto death' . . .[1] I am coming to do Your will . . .

- . . . we are servants (*servi* [servants]).
  All that we are and that we do is to serve.
- *servi inutiles* [unworthy servants].[2]
- *servo – pastore* [servant – shepherd] (*Cristo – Buon Pastore* [Christ – Good Shepherd]).
  I Petri [1 Peter].

Always to have an awareness of our limitations.

Anticipated Matins

Meditation [17]: (*ancora sul Servizio* [still on Service])

'And whoever would be first among you must be servant of all'.[3] Vatican II: *diaconia – ministerium* [diaconate – ministry].

Catechism

('*Prêtre – un homme mangé*' ['Priest – an eaten man'], Chevrier) – *servizio non toglie autorità* [service does not take away authority] – *vicario* [vicar].

A difficult balance between kindness and firmness.

Responsibility and a certain fear.

Catechism

Always available: I belong to others.

Collegialità [Collegiality].

Acting collegially, bishops always act personally.

Demanding *ministerium* [ministry], but it has to be carried out with joy (*hilarem datorem diligit Deus* [God loves a cheerful giver]).[4]

(!)St Toribio de Mogrovejo(!)[5]

Rosary (I); Eucharistic Benediction; Concluding meditation; Compline
Holy Hour: *Primo Servo della nostra salvezza . . . Ancilla Domini . . .* [The First Servant of our salvation . . . The handmaid of the Lord . . .]

---

1 See Philippians 2:7–8.
2 See Luke 17:10.
3 See Mark 10:44.
4 See 2 Corinthians 9:7.
5 St Toribio de Mogrovejo (or Turibius of Mogrovejo) (1538–1606) was a Spanish missionary and Archbishop of Lima.

5 March

Intentions; Prayers
Morning meditation: ('He took the form of a servant'[1] – Servant – Son – Servant – Shepherd)
Holy Mass; Prayers; Thanksgiving; Rosary (III); Lauds

Catechism

Meditation [18]: (*La preghiera* [Prayer]).

'Pray constantly . . .'[2] The awareness of creation and 'createdness' (creation out of nothing) is the basis for prayer. Abraham. The Old Testament.

A book in which the word of God becomes human prayer.

Jesus – prays with the words of the Old Testament, which He learnt from His Mother. Jesus prays in the key moments of His mission.

- the raising of Lazarus
- the high priestly prayer
- the prayer in Gethsemane and on the cross.

Jesus teaches us how to pray (on numerous occasions).

Prayer to the Holy Spirit; Passion of Our Lord Jesus Christ according to John

Meditation [19]: (*La preghiera della Madonna* [The prayer of the Madonna]).

Annunciation – Finding:

- 'She kept all these things, pondering them in Her heart.'[3]
- Cana – Golgotha.
- Pentecost.
- Magnificat (the Song of Mary, the song of the Church).
- *in Dio mio Salvatore* [in God my Saviour].
- *quia fecit mihi magna: opere della Salvezza* [He who is mighty has done great things for me: the work of Salvation].
- *mi chiameranno beata* [they will call me blessed].
- *esalta gli umili* [He has exalted those of low degree].[4]

↓

(the Pharisee and the tax collector).[5]

1 See Philippians 2:7.
2 See 1 Thessalonians 5:17.
3 See Luke 2:19.
4 See Luke 1:47, 49, 48, 52.
5 See Luke 18:9–14.

Jesus Christ, Son of God, have mercy on me – the 'Jesus prayer' of the Eastern Church.

Sext; None; Meditation continued; The Way of the Cross; Eucharistic Adoration; '*Crux fidelis*' ['Faithful cross']; Rosary (I); Vespers

Meditation [20]: (*La fedeltà alla preghiera* [Faithfulness in prayer]).

The difficulties that we encounter in relation to prayer: time (lack of time) – temptation to think that prayer is useless – a view that life itself is a prayer. Life should become a prayer, but it is necessary to meet God in prayer first.

Preghiera – tempo di purificazione [Prayer – time of purification].

Liturgical hours.

Fedeltà [Faithfulness] also in private prayer (and regularity).

Anticipated Matins

Meditation [21]: (*Sul quotidiano*): '*oggi*' [(On the everyday): 'today'].

'Today' (*oggi*) is a gift from God.

'Today' is always connected to 'always'.

(L. Blois: *oggi – adorabile* [today – adorable]).

Daily Mass: The divine 'today' descends onto the human 'today' (Meyendorff).[1]

The greatest event in the history of the world is inscribed into our human 'today'.

Mysterium paschale – Mysterium eucharisticum [The paschal mystery – the Eucharistic mystery].

The 'key' to our 'today' and always.

Rosary (II); Eucharistic Benediction; Concluding meditation; Compline

6 March[2]

Intentions; Prayers

Morning meditation / Holy Mass: The eternal, divine and Trinitarian 'Today' is in the transient human 'today'. For the grace of

---

1 John Meyendorff (1926–92) was a leading theologian of the Orthodox Church of America, a writer and teacher. He served as Dean of St Vladimir's Orthodox Theological Seminary from 1984 to 1992.

2 The final talk of the retreat was delivered by John Paul II. The full text (in Italian) is available at: https://w2.vatican.va/

reconciliation: There can be no Christian unification without (ecumenical) repentance. The ecumenical theme of the retreat.

Holy Mass; Prayers; Thanksgiving; Rosary (I); Lauds

Meditation 22: '*Nelle mani del Padre e sotto lo sguardo di Maria*' ['In the hands of the Father and under Mary's watch']:

'*mondo contemporaneo*' ['the contemporary world']: *olocausto* [Holocaust] – an unprecedented number of the unborn killed before birth.

Rachel plorans filios [Rachel is weeping for her children][1] *et sunt multi* [and there are many of them].

The scope of poverty and the unjust distribution of goods – signs of the weakening of faith.

Doctrino-ethical relativism.

'*La secolarizzazione*' ['Secularisation'] – this is the context into which the Church is called: super-human challenges. They can be undertaken by the power of the Holy Spirit. Christ says: '*nolite timere*' ['do not be afraid']. 'I am with you'; 'I have overcome the world'.[2]

'*In manus Tuas . . .*' ['Into Thy hands . . .'];[3] *sotto lo sguardo di Maria* [under Mary's watch].

Causa nostrae laetitiae [The cause of our joy] *ora pro nobis* [pray for us].[4]

Conclusion; Final words; Blessing; Magnificat
UIOGD[5]

1 See Jeremiah 31:15 and Matthew 2:18.
2 See Matthew 28:10, 20 and John 16:33.
3 See Luke 23:46.
4 See the Litany of Loreto.
5 See p. xxi.

20–[26] February 1994
Exercitia Spiritualia [Spiritual Exercises] *Capella Redemptoris Mater* [Mother of the Redeemer Chapel] Led by Cardinal [Giovanni] Saldarini, Turin[1]

~

20 February (Lenten Lamentations);[2] Exposition of the Blessed Sacrament; Vespers

Introductory talk (1):

Exercitia [Exercises]: '*qualcosa può capitare*' ['something may happen']!

Spirito S. – Parola di Dio ⟷ civiltà anti-tetica che ci abbraccia [The Holy Spirit – the Word of God ⟷ antithetic to the civilisation that surrounds us].

VS – *Veritatis Splendor*

2 Cor.: '*amore immenso che lavora in voi*' ['immense love that works in you'] – the testimony of conscience(!) Paul.

Etica – confronto con l'Altro [Ethics – engagement with the Other].

Gratia Eius in me vacua non fuit [His grace towards me was not in vain].[3]

Abbandonarsi – collaboratori di Cristo [Devoted – collaborators of Christ].

Momento favorevole – lasciamo allo Spirito S. di formarci [The favourable time – let us allow the Holy Spirit to shape us].[4]

Adoration of the Blessed Sacrament; Meditation continued; Compline
Reading: (1) Brandstaetter, *Jezus z Nazaretu* [Jesus of Nazareth];[5] (2) The Martyrs of Podlasie;[6] others

---

1 Giovanni Saldarini (1924–2011) was an Italian cardinal and Archbishop of Turin (1989–99).

2 See n. 6, p. 221 [11 March 1984].

3 See 1 Corinthians 15:10.

4 See 2 Corinthians 6:2.

5 Roman Brandstaetter (1906–87) was an award-winning Polish-Jewish writer, poet and playwright. His acclaimed four-volume novel *Jezus z Nazarethu* (*Jesus of Nazareth*) was published in 1967–73.

6 The Podlasie Martyrs were a group of Greek Catholics from the village of Pratulin who protested against

21 February: Feast of St Peter Damian

Intentions; Prayers
Morning meditation: (*lasciamo allo Spirito S. di formarci* [let us allow the Holy Spirit to shape us])
Holy Mass; Prayers; Thanksgiving; (Rosary (II)); [Litany] 'for the Homeland'; Lauds

Meditation 2: *L'interiorità* [Inner life] (2 Cor. 12:1–6).

'*Conosco un uomo in Cristo che . . . fu rapito al terzo cielo . . . e udì parole indicibili . . .*' ['I know a man in Christ who . . . was caught up to the third heaven . . . and he heard things that cannot be told . . .'][1]

Paul 'boasts' (*si gloria*) in Christ:

- *gratitudine glorificante* [glorifying gratitude]; he 'boasts' of his weaknesses[2]
- *Personalità cristiana – una vera 'novità'* [Christian personality – a true 'novelty'].

ontologica [ontological]: Christ's subjectivity in our 'auto-biography' in Christ (*praese. historicum* [historical presence]).

'Sapere' per 'Sapere' ['To know' through 'knowing'].

'*Abitiamo nella risurrezione*' ['We live in the resurrection'] = (eschatology).

'Christ' – always '*pros ton Theon*' (towards God).[3]

↓ ↘ *uomo del Padre* [man of the Father].

God–Man working in us.

Continuation

Confrontation of the Christian personality in the following dimensions: ontological – historical – eschatological – since it is Christological.

Terce; Passion of Our Lord Jesus Christ according to Matthew

Meditation (3): 2 Cor. 3:15–18.

'*Veniamo trasformati in quella medesima immagine, di gloria, secondo l'azione dello Spirito del Signore*' ['We are

---

the violent process of state secularisation implemented by the Russian Empire. On 24 January 1874, they gathered in front of the local church to demonstrate their opposition. The Russian Army fired at the protesters, killing thirteen of them. They were beatified by Pope John Paul II on 6 October 1996.

1 See 2 Corinthians 12:2–4.

2 See 2 Corinthians 12:5.

3 See John 1:1.

mercoledì **19** giugno

ss. Gervasio e Protasio

Wednesday Mittwoch Mercredi · June Juni Juin
СРЕДА Miércoles · ИЮНЬ Junio

5. Medit. (IIC) 2 Cor. 3, 15–18

„Veniamo trasformati in quella medesima immagine, di gloria, secondo l'azione dello Spirito del Signore"

– experiencia di comunione: widzi siebie w drugim, przede wszystkim w tym „Drugim", który jest przez Chrystusa – refleks Trynitarny: Ojciec w Synu – percorso trinitario.

– transformati wraz w Duchu Świętym – vivificati et conformati ad Christum

– to wszystko – na tle różnych humanizmów laickich, sekularystycznych

D. et V.

– Paulus: Duch Święty pozwalający tylko przez Jezusa Chrystusa, przez Niego też ~~...~~ autentycznie nasze człowieczeństwo. To źródło „nowego humanizmu": humanizm z Ducha Świętego (Dominum et Vivificantem). Ten proces „uczłowieczania", który ma źródło w Duchu Św., się nie ma końca

– Wszędzie wolny: gdzie Duch, tam wolność (humanizm trynitarny: z Ducha przez Syna ku Ojcu) na co dzień, w pracy itd.

– „homo spiritualis"

6. Medit. concl. „debitores Dei et hominum"
transcript

7. Festa, ...

8. Via Crucis / „debitores"

25 s.w.

S	D	L	M	M	G	V	S	D	L	M	M	G	V	S
1	2	3	4	5	6	7	8	9	10	11	12	13	14	15

170-195

transformed through the work of the Holy Spirit, into the same glorious image'].

Esperienza di comunione [Experience of communion]: to see yourself in the other, above all in the 'Other', that is, Christ. Trinitarian reflection: the Father in the Son. *Perichoresis trinitaria* [Trinitarian perichoresis].[1]

Trasformati [transformed] in the Holy Spirit – *vivificati et conformati ad Christum* [called to life and made in the image of Christ].

D[ominum] et Viv[ificantem]!

All this – against various 'lay and secular humanisms'.

Paul: The Holy Spirit can be known only through Jesus Christ; it is also through Jesus that the Holy Spirit shapes our humanity. This is the source of 'new humanism': the humanism of the Holy Spirit (*Dominum et vivificantem*).[2] The process of 'humanisation', which has begun in the Holy Spirit, has no end.

A free man: 'where the Spirit is, there is freedom'.[3] (Trinitarian humanism: from the Spirit through the Son to the Father) for every day, at work, etc. – '*uomo spirituale*' ['spiritual man'].

Concluding meditation resumed: '*debitores Dei et hominum*' ['debtors of God and people']
Terce; Sext; None; The Way of the Cross ('*debitores*' ['debtors']); Eucharistic Adoration (*debitores*)
Reading: Holy Scripture; others; Paul VI's Testament
Litany of the Saints; Litany of the Holy Name of Jesus, Blessed Virgin Mary, St Joseph; Rosary (III)
Reading: 'Letter to Families';[4] the encyclical *Dominum et vivificantem*
Vespers

1 The term *perichoresis* (Greek: περιχώρησις – 'rotation') was used by the Church Fathers to describe the relationship between each Person of the Trinity (Father, Son and Holy Spirit).

2 The encyclical *Dominum et vivificantem* (The Lord and Giver of Life) was promulgated by Pope John Paul II on 18 May 1986.

3 See 2 Corinthians 3:17.

4 In the 'Letter to Families', issued on 2 February 1994, Pope John Paul II welcomed the United Nations' initiative to declare 1994 the International Year of the Family: 'This initiative makes it clear how fundamental the question of the family is for the member States of the United Nations. If the Church wishes to take part in this initiative, it is because she herself has been sent by Christ to "all nations" (Mt. 28:19) . . . Throughout this Year it is important to discover anew the many signs of the Church's love and concern for the family, a love and concern expressed from the very beginning of Christianity, when the meaningful term "domestic church" was applied to the family. In our own times we have often returned to the phrase "domestic church", which the Council adopted and the sense of which we hope will always remain alive in people's minds.'

Meditation 4: *La preghiera della novità* [The prayer of novelty] 2 Cor. 5:6–17.

'*Ormai non conosciamo più nessuno secondo la carne . . . Quindi se uno è in Cristo, è una creatura nuova*' ['From now on, therefore, we regard no one from a human point of view . . . Therefore, if any one is in Christ, he is a new creature'].

Christ known through faith – (Eucharist) – this is not 'possession', this is a communion in faith – this is how the Church–Beloved gets to know Christ.

This is how the Church learns: in prayer, in vigil.

Christ – the perfect shape (fullness) of all prayer in the world: 'Amen' to the Father.

- The fullness of prayer: contemplation.
- This is what the 'novelty' of prayer consists in.
- *Orationi nihil praeponatur* [Nothing should be placed above prayer].
- Such prayer is 'pleasing' to the Father.
- God listens to such prayer.
- Persistent prayer – profession of faith.
- We cannot pray like this 'by ourselves'.
- 'The Spirit Himself intercedes for us'.[1]
- The masters of prayer.

Anticipated Matins

Meditation 5: *La consolazione* [Consolation] 2 Cor. 1:3–5.

'*Sia benedetto Dio . . . Dio di ogni consolazione, il quale ci consola in ogni nostra tribolazione*' ['Blessed be God . . . God of all comfort, who comforts us in all our afflictions'].

The source of comfort: God. Against the fragility of man: fears, humiliations, etc. God forgives all that in order to make us ready for prayer, and He strengthens us in Christ (God's 'strategy' of salvation). '*Consolatio*' ['Consolation'] does not erase experience, but first and foremost explains it.

In relation to this source – there are other '*consolationes*' ['consolations']. But the '*Consolatio prima*' ['highest Consolation'] always remains the *mysterium paschale* [paschal

1 See Romans 8:26.

mystery], the economy of salvation. This is always a consolation in suffering. The 'maternal' consolation (*Consolatio*) of the Holy Spirit.

Rosary (I); Reading; Eucharistic Adoration; Concluding meditation; Compline

22 February: Feast of the Chair of St Peter

Intentions; Prayers
Morning meditation: (the Church crucified)
Holy Mass; Thanksgiving; Prayers; Rosary (III); [Litany] 'for the Homeland'; Lauds

Meditation 6: *Comunione nella purificazione di Gesù Cristo* [Communion in purification through Jesus Christ].

La purificazione [Purification] (2 Cor. 5:1–3).

'. . . *Sospiriamo in questo nostro stato, desiderosi di rivestirci del nostro corpo celeste. È Dio che ci ha fatti per questo e ci ha dato la caparra del suo Spirito*' ['. . . Here indeed we groan, and long to put on our heavenly dwelling. And God, who has prepared us for this very thing, has given us the Spirit as a guarantee'].[1]

Waiting for Christ in faith in order to participate in His resurrection: *rivestirci del nostro corpo celeste: sopravestiti* [to put on our heavenly dwelling: clothed].

This is an original feature of Christianity: *redemptio corporis* [redemption of the body]. Beginning: Christ's resurrection. *Sacramentalità del corpo* [Sacramentality of the body].

Comunione nella purificazione di Gesù Cristo [Communion in purification through Jesus Christ]

Purificazione dell'essere umano nella sua integrità [Purification of the human being in their integrity]. The full meaning of purity: 'to have part in Christ' (Peter).[2]

Terce; Passion of Our Lord Jesus Christ according to Mark

Meditation 7: *La penitenza* [Penitence] (2 Cor. 5:6–10).

'*Perciò ci sforziamo . . . di essere a Lui gradito. Tutti dobbiamo infatti comparire davanti al tribunale di Cristo*' ['We make it our aim . . . to please Him. For we must all appear before the judgement seat of Christ'].[3]

The culture of 'superficiality' (appearances) ⟷ *nolite*

1 See 2 Corinthians 5:2, 5.
2 See John 13:8.
3 See 2 Corinthians 5:9–10.

conformari huic saeculo [do not be conformed to this world].[1] Ascesis. Christian morality is an ascesis. Inappropriate 'division'. ('*Ci sforziamo*' ['We make it our aim'].)

Responsibility: complementing freedom.

Speranza cristiana [Christian hope], different from the various programmes of secularist hope: progress – paradise on earth. Progress in holiness.

Harm done by the division introduced between a 'Christian' and a 'saint' (*L[umen] G[entium]* V).

Penitenza crist. [Christian penance] 'to destroy the old man' – 'to put on the new nature'[2] by the power of the paschal mystery of Christ.

Spiritus poenitentiae [the spirit of penance] (attitude) as a condition for the sacrament of penance.

Sext; None
Reading: Holy Scripture; Paul VI's Testament; *Dominum et vivificantem*; 'Letter to Families'[3]
Meditation continued; The Way of the Cross; Adoration of the Blessed Sacrament; Penitential psalms; Litany of the Sacred Heart of Jesus; Litany of the Blessed Virgin Mary; Litany of St Joseph; Rosary (I)
Reading: 'Letter to Families'; the encyclical *Dominum et vivificantem*
Vespers

Meditation 8: *La riconciliazione* [Reconciliation] 2 Cor. 5:18–21.

'*Tutto questo viene da Dio . . . , che ci ha riconciliati con Sé mediante Cristo . . . Colui che non ha conosciuto peccato, Dio lo trattò da peccato . . . perché noi potessimo diventare per mezzo di lui giustizia di Dio*' ['All this is from God . . . , who through Christ reconciled us to Himself . . . For our sake He made Him to be sin who knew no sin . . . so that in Him we might become the righteousness of God'].

Cristo – Riconciliatore. Apostolo annunzia la riconciliazione – e questo è il suo grande dovere come anche quello della Chiesa [Christ – Reconciler. The apostle announces the reconciliation – and this is his, as well as the Church's, great task] – especially in our times.

Uomo – collaboratore; lasciandosi riconciliare, confessando

1 See Romans 12:2.
2 See Romans 6:6 and Ephesians 4:24.
3 See n. 4, p. 382 [21 February 1994].

i peccati: diaconia, varietà dei carismi [Man – collaborator; to be reconciled, to confess sins: diaconate, various charismata].

Riconciliazione negli ambienti diversi: fra le persone, fra le comunità, fra i popoli. Forza riconciliativa dell'Eucaristia [Reconciliation in different environments: between persons, between communities, between peoples. The reconciliatory power of the Eucharist].

Il Paraclito convincerà il mondo di peccato [The Paraclete will convince the world of sin].[1]

Anticipated Matins

Meditation 9: *L'umiltà* [Humility] 2 Cor. 12:7–13.

'*Perché non montassi in superbia per la grandezza delle rivelazioni, mi è stata messa una spina nella carne, un inviato di satana incaricato di schiaffeggiarmi, perché io non vada in superbia*' ['And to keep me from being too elated by the abundance of revelations, a thorn was given me in the flesh, a messenger of satan, to harass me, to keep me from being too elated'].

A description of Paul (his character). Here, his humility is really moving. He takes pride in his weakness (Jesus in Gethsemane). God's response: my grace is sufficient for you.[2]

Umiltà – verità è nostra forza; quando sono debole, allora sono forte [Humility – truth is our strength; when I am weak, then I am strong].[3] *Kenosis* [Self-emptying].

Rosary (II); Eucharistic Adoration; Concluding meditation; Compline

23 February: Feast of St Polycarp

Intentions; Prayers
Morning meditation: 'purity which amazes'; *beati puri di cuore, perché vedranno Dio* [blessed are the pure in heart, for they shall see God][4]
Holy Mass; Thanksgiving; Prayers; Rosary (I); Litany for the Homeland; Lauds

Meditation 10: *Il coinvolgimento* [Involvement] [2] Cor. 5:14–15.

'. . . *Egli è morto per tutti, perché quelli che vivono, non vivono più per se stessi, ma per Colui che è morto e risuscitato*

1 See John 16:8.
2 See 2 Corinthians 12:9.
3 See 2 Corinthians 12:10.
4 See Matthew 5:8.

per loro' ['. . . And he died for all, that those who live might live no longer for themselves but for Him who for their sake died and was raised'].

The death of Christ is at the same time the death of man as a sinner. This is our great 'fate': Christocentrism: Christ is our new 'centre' in a dynamic sense. Christological concentration.

Impegnarsi del tutto per Gesù Cristo [To commit entirely to Jesus Christ]

St Paul speaks from experience. Simultaneously, this is a new discovery of the mystery of man (cf. *G[audium et] S[pes]*) – hence: *coinvolgimento fino alla fine* [involvement until the end] (*Sancti Polycarpi* [Saint Polycarp]).

coinvolgimento = involvement, preoccupation.

Terce; Passion of Our Lord Jesus Christ according to Luke
Mihi vivere Christus est [For me to live is Christ][1]

Meditation 11: *Il ministerio* [The ministry] (2 Cor. 3:1–3).

'*La nostra lettera siete voi . . . È noto infatti che voi siete una lettera di Cristo composta da noi, scritta non con inchiostro, ma con lo Spirito del Dio vivente . . .*' ['You yourselves are our letter of recommendation . . . And you show that you are a letter from Christ delivered by us, written not with ink but with the Spirit of the living God . . .']

We are not the 'owners' of the Church, we are its servants. The Trinity is at the beginning of any communion in the Church: the Son sent by the Father, sending the Holy Spirit: *lettera di Cristo* [letter from Christ]. Only He is the Author and the Lord. All are 'servants to each other'.

The only right attitude: great love for all. And this is immediately recognised by everyone.

This love is expressed through intercessory prayer, so that 'when the Son of Man comes, He will find faith on earth'.[2] Prayer is the greatest 'engagement'. Especially the prayer of those who do the work of ministry in the Church. Prayer – especially supported by sacrifice.

Is my involvement like this too? *Impegno* [Commitment]?

Sext; None
Reading: Holy Scripture, *Dominum et vivificantem*; 'Letter to Families'; Paul VI's Testament

1 See Philippians 1:21.
2 See Luke 18:8.

Meditation continued; The Way of the Cross; Eucharistic Adoration; Litany of the Saints; Litany of the Holy Name of Jesus, Blessed Virgin Mary, St Joseph; Rosary (II); Vespers

Meditation 12: *Il travaglio* [Suffering] (2 Cor. 6:2–10).

'*. . . in ogni cosa ci presentiamo come ministri di Dio, con molta fermezza nelle tribolazioni, nelle necessità, nelle angosce . . . con parole di verità, con la potenza di Dio.*' ['. . . but as servants of God we commend ourselves in every way, through great endurance, in afflictions, hardships, calamities . . . by truthful speech, and the power of God.']

Salvifici doloris.[1]

Ministri di Dio non devono aspirare a essere trattati meglio del Figlio di Dio [The ministers of God should not aspire to be treated better than the Son of God] – not to lose the readiness to love and forgive even at that time.

Faithfulness faces opposition. The Church does not cease to live in hope.

Anticipated Matins

Meditation 13: *La verità* [The truth] 2 Cor. 11:7–15.

'*In ogni circostanza ho fatto il possibile per non esservi di aggravio . . . Com'è vero che c'è la verità di Cristo in me, nessuno mi toglierà questo vanto in terra d'Acaia*' ['In all circumstances I have done everything possible not to be a burden to you . . . As the truth of Christ is in me, this boast of mine shall not be silenced in the regions of Achaia'].

'*Erit enim tempus, cum sanam doctrinam non tenebunt, sed secundum suam voluntatem*' ['For the time is coming when people will not endure sound teaching, but teaching according to their own likings'] (Tim.).[2]

What I want defines the truth – not: the truth defines what I want.

Annunzio gratuito [Free message]. The truth cannot be purchased. When money speaks, the Gospel keeps silent. Only saints can keep the Gospel 'pure'. '*Martire della verità*' ['Martyr for truth']. Although the truth does not arouse interest.

---

1 The apostolic letter *Salvifici doloris* ('Redemptive Suffering') was issued by Pope John Paul II on 11 February 1984.

2 See 2 Timothy 4:3.

Veritatis splendor.[1]

Acedia = tristezza di doversi impegnare [Acedia = sadness of having to commit].

Comunicare la verità è il primo aspetto della carità [To communicate the truth is the foremost expression of charity].

Il coraggio della verità proviene dalla forza dello spirito [The courage of the truth comes from the fortitude of the spirit].

Rosary (III); Eucharistic Adoration; Concluding meditation; Compline

24 February

Intentions; Prayers
Morning meditation: *Christus nostro 'centro'* [Christ is our 'centre'] = *mihi vivere sit Christus* [for me to live should be Christ][2]
Holy Mass; Thanksgiving; Prayers; Rosary (III); [Litany] 'for the Homeland'; Lauds

Meditation 14: *La iconicità* [Iconicity] (2 Cor. 8:1–9).

'*. . . come vi segnalate in ogni cosa . . . così distinguetevi anche in quest'opera generosa . . . Conoscete infatti la grazia del Signore nostro Gesù Cristo: da ricco che era, si è fatto povero per voi, perché diventaste ricchi per mezzo della sua povertà*' ['. . . as you excel in everything . . . see that you excel in this gracious work also . . . For you know the grace of our Lord Jesus Christ: that though He was rich, yet for your sake He became poor, so that by His poverty you might become rich'].

Rendere evidente Gesù Cristo [To make Jesus Christ visible]

'*Koinonia' delle Chiese – scambio dei doni – economia della condivisione – civiltà dell'amore – 'hilarem datorem diligit Deus'* ['Koinonia' (community, communion) of the Churches – exchange of gifts – the economy of sharing – the civilisation of love – 'God loves a cheerful giver'].[3]

Comunità – un Sacramento permanentemente celebrato – 'Tibi ex Tuis' – ringraziamento [Community – a permanently celebrated sacrament – 'to You from Yours' – thanksgiving]. This is a response to the culture dominated by the spirit of vindication, by a lack of gratitude.

Colletta – 'icona' della Chiesa cattolica [Collect – the 'icon' of the Catholic Church].

1 The encyclical *Veritatis splendor* (The Splendour of the Truth) was promulgated by Pope John Paul II on 6 August 1993.

2 See Philippians 1:21.

3 See 2 Corinthians 2:7.

Cristo – 'icona' di Dio invisibile [Christ – the 'icon' of the invisible God].

Terce; Passion of Our Lord Jesus Christ according to John

Meditation 15: *L'oblatività* [The oblation] (2 Cor. 9:1–9).

'*Conosco bene la vostra buona volontà . . . Già molti sono stati stimolati dal vostro zelo . . . Tenete a mente che chi semina scarsamente, scarsamente raccoglierà*' ['I know your readiness . . . And your zeal has stirred up many . . . The point is this: he who sows sparingly will also reap sparingly'].

The spirit of sacrifice.

St Bernard

'You received without payment, give without payment.'[1]

The key to the social teaching of the Church – not only righteousness, but also love.

Sext; None; Meditation continued; Reading (as above); The Way of the Cross; Eucharistic Adoration; Litanies (as above); Penitential psalms; Rosary (II); Vespers

Meditation 16: *Il perdono* [Forgiveness] (2 Cor. 2:4–11).

'*Se qualcuno mi ha rattristato, non ha rattristato me soltanto, ma in parte almeno, Tutti voi . . . A chi perdonate, perdono anch'io . . . l'ho fatto davanti a voi, davanti a Cristo*' ['If anyone has caused pain, he has caused it not to me, but in some measure, to you all . . . Anyone whom you forgive, I also forgive . . . for your sake in the presence of Christ'].

Dio che perdona [God who forgives].

dove ha abbondato il peccato [but where sin increased] *sovrabbonda la grazia* [grace abounded all the more].[2]

Dives in misericordia.[3]

Vittoria della Chiesa rispetto al mondo [The Church's victory over the world].

Perdoni loro, Padre, perché non sanno che facciano [Father, forgive them, for they know not what they do].[4]

Rimetti a noi come noi li rimettiamo [And forgive us, as we also have forgiven].[5]

1 See Matthew 10:8.

2 See Romans 5:20.

3 The encyclical *Dives in Misericordia* (Rich in Mercy) was promulgated by Pope John Paul II on 30 November 1980.

4 See Luke 23:34.

5 See Matthew 6:12.

Homo misericors salva [illegible] [Merciful man, save . . .].

Non 'uomo misura di tutto' – ma Cristo [Not 'man is the measure of all things' – but Christ].

Dio non si stanca di perdonarci [God never gets tired of forgiving] (Fr Kolbe).

Concentrare la nuova evangelizzazione sul perdono [To make forgiveness the centre of the new evangelisation].

(*Per-dono più che dono* [For-giving more than giving]) *sempre da ricominciare* [always to start anew].

Anticipated Matins

Meditation 17: *La consolazione* [Consolation] (2) (2 Cor. 1:6–11).

'*Quando siamo tribolati, è per la vostra consolazione e salvezza; quando siamo confortati, è per la vostra consolazione . . .*' ['If we are afflicted, it is for your consolation and salvation, and if we are comforted, it is for your consolation . . .'].

Caratteristica di una comunità, che funziona bene. Esistenza delle persone consolanti è propria alla vita cristiana. Il diavolo è scoraggiante et in quel senso influisce sulla civiltà odierna. Il popolo deve essere consolato e consolante [A characteristic of a well-functioning community. The existence of people who offer comfort is appropriate for Christian life. The devil brings discouragement and in this way influences today's civilisation. People have to be able to find comfort and to give comfort].

Consolazione sussiste anche nella ingiustizia sulità [*sic*] [There is consolation even in growing injustice]. *Deus semper maior. Sempre consolante* [God is always greater. He always offers comfort].

Rosary (I); Eucharistic Adoration; Holy Hour; Compline

25 February

Intentions; Prayers
Morning meditation: 'Forgive them, for they know not what they do'[1]
Holy Mass; Thanksgiving; Prayers; Rosary (III); [Litany] 'for the Homeland'

Meditation 18: *L'eterno* [The eternal] (2 Cor. 3:4–11).

'*La lettera uccide, lo Spirito dà vita . . . quanto più sarà glorioso il ministero dello Spirito . . . Se dunque ciò che era effimero*

1 See Luke 23:34.

fu glorioso, molto più lo sarà ciò che è duraturo . . .' ['For the letter kills, but the Spirit gives life . . . will not the dispensation of the Spirit be attended with greater splendour . . . For if what faded away came with splendour, what is permanent must have much more splendour . . .']

Santo Traboccare di speranza in Gesù Cristo [Holy outpouring of hope in Jesus Christ]

L'eterno preme sul presente [The eternal presses on the present]. God's entering into time through Christ. Changing optics. Not '*dopo*' ['later'], but 'now'. The Holy Spirit, the presence of that which is final and definite. This is what the greatness of Christianity and the Church consists in.

Hence: hope = life in the Holy Spirit.

Hope sanctifies the 'world' (the Church present in the world).

Prayers for Good Friday; Terce

Meditation 19: *La morte* [Death] (2 Cor. 4:7–11).

'*Però noi abbiamo questo tesoro in vasi di creta . . . sempre e dovunque portando nel nostro corpo la morte di Gesù, perché anche la vita di Gesù si manifesti nel nostro corpo*' ['But we have this treasure in earthen vessels . . . always carrying in the body the death of Jesus, so that the life of Jesus may also be manifested in our bodies'].

È la Pasqua di Cristo che illumina i contrasti e poi li toglie. In Cristo Dio-Verbo ha vissuto la morte per renderla sorgente di Vita [It is the Passover of Christ that illuminates obstacles and then removes them. In Christ the God–Word experienced death in order to make it the source of Life].[1]

Cardinal Colombo

Life passes. But this is not a one-way process, from life to death. The 'external' man grows old and passes away, but at the same time the inner man grows mature, matures towards eternal life in God.

Paul: *soffrire temporaneo genera gloria e la morte genera la vita* [slight momentary affliction prepares us for an eternal weight of glory and death gives birth to life].[2]

The culture of immanentism has in a way contributed to the domination of death over life. Christ and the Gospel – is

1 Giovanni Colombo (1902–92) was an Italian cardinal and Archbishop of Milan (1963–79).

2 See 2 Corinthians 4:17.

the domination of life over death. The primacy of hope. *Paolo è così* [Paul is like that].

Sext; None; Meditation continued; The Way of the Cross
[Reading:] Brandstaetter: 'The Purest Divine Sacrificial Lamb' from the novel *Jezus z Nazaretu* [Jesus of Nazareth]
Adoration of the Blessed Sacrament; 1st and 2nd Letter of St Peter; Reading (as above); Rosary (I); Vespers

Meditation 20: *La santificazione* [Sanctification] (2 Cor. 6:14–18; 7:1).

'*Quale accordo tra il tempio di Dio e gli idoli? Noi siamo infatti il tempio del Dio vivente . . . portando a compimento la nostra santificazione, nel timore di Dio*' ['What agreement has the temple of God with idols? For we are the temple of the living God . . . making our holiness perfect in the fear of God'].

Timore di Dio [Fear of God] – the primary condition of sanctification, *initium sapientiae* [the beginning of wisdom]. This respect for God has disappeared from contemporary 'lay' culture. Sanctity is the response. We need a new primacy of spirituality. Sanctity within the world. The humanism of sanctity as an antidote for 'corporeal humanism' (Paul's 'life according to the flesh').[1]

The meaning of canonisation and beatification.

Encyclical on sanctity! St Bernard: the saints are waiting.

Anticipated Matins

Meditation 21: *La trinitarietà* [Triunity] (2 Cor. 13:11–13).

'*La grazia del Signore nostro Gesù Cristo, l'amore di Dio e la comunione dello Spirito Santo siano con tutti voi*' ['The grace of the Lord Jesus Christ and the love of God and the fellowship of the Holy Spirit be with you all'].

Decline of Trinitarian awareness: God – the Father, the Son and the Holy Spirit. Not – a general 'Godhead', but Three in One: *Mysterium Communionis* [the Mystery of Communion]. The Living God is *Communio* [Communion], love, not a lonely Absolute. To some extent, '*familia*' ['family'].

The Marian paradigm: a person who stands before the Holy Trinity (the moment of incarnation, annunciation).

1 See Romans 8:12–13.

Rosary (II); Adoration of the Blessed Sacrament; Concluding meditation; Compline

26 February

Intentions; Prayers
Morning meditation: '*mihi vivere Christus est*' ['for me to live is Christ'][1]
Holy Mass; Thanksgiving; Rosary (I); Prayer to the Holy Spirit; [Litany] 'for the Homeland'; Lauds

Meditation (22): *Il profumo di Cristo e il 'sì' di Cristo* [The aroma of Christ and the 'yes' of Christ] (2 Cor. 2:14–17; 1:18–24).

'*Noi siamo dinanzi a Dio il profumo di Cristo fra quelli che si salvano e fra quelli che si perdono*' ['For we are the aroma of Christ to God among those who are being saved and among those who are perishing'].

'*Il Figlio di Dio, Gesù Cristo non fu "sì" e "no", ma in lui c'è stato il "sì"* . . .' ['For the Son of God, Jesus Christ, was not "yes" and "no", but in him it is always "yes" . . .'][2]

'*L'amore di Cristo ci spinge*' ['For the love of Christ controls us'].[3]

Vero apostolo – sposo della Chiesa come Cristo [A true apostle – a bridegroom of the Church like Christ] – *zelus animarum* [zeal of souls] – '*collaboratori della vostra gioia*' ['we work with you for your joy'].[4]

Conclusion; Final words; Blessing; Magnificat
UIOGD[5]

1 See Philippians 1:21.
2 See 2 Corinthians 1:19.
3 See 2 Corinthians 5:14.
4 See 2 Corinthians 1:24.
5 See p. xxi.

5–11 March 1995
Exercitia Spiritualia [Spiritual Exercises] *Capella Redemptoris Mater* [Mother of the Redeemer Chapel] Led by Father [Tomáš] Špidlík SJ[1]

~

5 March

(Lenten Lamentations);[2] Exposition of the Blessed Sacrament; Vespers

Introductory talk (1):

The meaning of the retreat – its sense

Handout

Adoration of the Blessed Sacrament; Meditation continued; Rosary; (Reading); Compline

6 March

Adoration of the Blessed Sacrament; Meditation

The meaning of the retreat: to become open to the work of the Holy Spirit, so that He forms Christ in us

Holy Mass; Thanksgiving; ([Litany] for the Homeland); Lauds

Meditation (2):

Il mistero dell'uomo si comprende solamente in Cristo e attraverso Cristo [The mystery of man can be understood only in Christ and through Christ] (cf. *G[audium et] S[pes]* 22)

Handout

Passion of Our Lord Jesus Christ according to Matthew; Terce

Meditation (3):

Dialogo con Dio [Dialogue with God]

Handout

Concluding meditation; The Way of the Cross; Sext; None; Reading; Litany of the Saints; Vespers

Meditation (4):

Dialogo con il mondo [Dialogue with the world]

---

1 Tomáš Josef Špidlík (1919–2010) was a Czech Jesuit and theologian who specialised in East Christian spirituality. He was a prolific author and the spiritual director of the Czech College in Rome (*Pontificio Collegio Nepomuceno*). He was made a cardinal by Pope John Paul II in 2003.

2 See n. 6, p. 221 [11 March 1984].

venerdì **5** luglio

s. Antonio M. Zaccaria

Exerc. Spirit. 1995

Capella Redempt. Mater 5–11.VII.

Friday Freitag Vendredi
пятница Viernes الجمعة

p. Špidlík SJ

July Juli Juillet
Июль Julio يوليو

5.VII. [Gorzkie Żale]

1. Expositio SS-mi
2. Vesp.

8 3. [Conf. introductoria] (1)

9 Zaproszenie ... zar

teologia

10 do serca

11

4. adorat. SS-mi

12 5. Modlit. różańcowa. Roz. Cap. [Teleview]

13 6. Compl.

14

6.VII.

15

1. Medit. Adorat. SS mi

16

2. Sens rekol.: otwórzmy się na działanie

17 Ducha Ś.: aby On ...

18 3. Laurum ... [illegible]

19 4. Laudes

5 Medit. (1/2)

Handout
Anticipated Matins

Meditation 5:

Dio nel cuore [God in one's heart]

Handout
Rosary (I); Eucharistic Adoration; Concluding meditation; Compline

7 March

Adoration of the Blessed Sacrament

Morning meditation:

(1) 'God spoke': (Christianity versus Buddhism)
(2) Prayer, in a way, creates the world

Holy Mass; Thanksgiving; [Litany] 'for the Homeland'; Lauds

Meditation 6:

Origine del male [Origin of evil]

Handout
Passion of Our Lord Jesus Christ according to Mark; Terce

Meditation 7:

La durezza del cuore [The hardness of heart]

Handout
Concluding meditation: ('*daemonium meridianum*' ['the demon of noonday'])[1]
The Way of the Cross; Rosary; Sext; None; Reading; Penitential psalms; Rosary; Vespers

Meditation 8:

La morte e il giudizio [Death and the judgement]

Handout
Anticipated Matins

Meditation 9:

La penitenza [Penance]

Handout
Rosary (II); Adoration of the Blessed Sacrament; Concluding meditation; Compline

8 March

Adoration of the Blessed Sacrament
Morning meditation: *transitus* [Passover]
Holy Mass; Thanksgiving; [Litany] 'for the Homeland'; Lauds

Meditation 10:

Cristo nei pensatori russi [Christ in Russian thinkers]

Passion of Our Lord Jesus Christ according to Luke

1 See Psalm 90 (91):6.

Meditation 11:

Cristo – anti-Cristo [Christ – anti-Christ]

Terce

Concluding meditation:

(*Christus – Corpus Christi* [Christ – the body of Christ])

Rosary; The Way of the Cross; Sext; None; Reading; Litany of the Saints; Vespers; Rosary

Meditation 12:

Imitazione di Cristo [Imitation of Christ]

Handout
Anticipated Matins

Meditation 13:

Cristo nella Scrittura [Christ in Scripture]

Handout
Rosary (III); Adoration of the Blessed Sacrament

Concluding meditation:

(*Mihi vivere est Christus* [For me to live is Christ])[1]

Compline

9 March: Feast of St Frances of Rome

Adoration of the Blessed Sacrament

Morning meditation: (*Christus – Bonus Pastor* [Christ – the Good Shepherd])
Holy Mass; Thanksgiving; [Litany] 'for the Homeland'; Lauds

Meditation 14:

Cristo meditato [Christ meditated]

Handout
Passion of Our Lord Jesus Christ according to John; Terce

Meditation 15:

La verginità (Virginity – celibacy)

Handout
Concluding meditation; The Way of the Cross (shorter); Sext; None; Reading; Penitential psalms; Vespers

Meditation 16:

L'obbedienza [Obedience]

Handout
Anticipated Matins

Meditation 17:

Passione di Cristo [Passion of Christ]

1 See Philippians 1:21.

Handout
Rosary (I); Adoration of the Blessed Sacrament; Holy Hour; Compline

10 March

Adoration of the Blessed Sacrament
Morning meditation:

'. . . because by Your holy cross, You have redeemed the world . . .'

'God has laid on Him the iniquity of us all . . .'[1] (redemption)

Holy Mass; Thanksgiving; [Litany] 'for the Homeland'; Lauds

Meditation 18:

La risurrezione (Resurrection)

Handout
Prayers for Good Friday; Terce

Meditation 19:

La Chiesa [The Church]

Concluding meditation; The Way of the Cross; Reading; Sext; None; Rosary; Litany of the Saints; Vespers; Rosary

Meditation 20:

Eucharistia [The Eucharist]

Handout
Anticipated Matins

Meditation 21:

Maria (BMV) [Mary (Blessed Virgin Mary)]

Handout
Rosary (II); Adoration of the Blessed Sacrament
Concluding meditation: (Do whatever he tells you)[2]
Compline

11 March

Adoration of the Blessed Sacrament
Morning meditation: *reassumptiva totius exercitii* [concluding the whole retreat]
Holy Mass; Thanksgiving; [Litany] 'for the Homeland'; Lauds

Meditation [22]
Conclusion; Final words; Magnificat
UIOGD[3]

1 See Isaiah 53:6.
2 See John 2:5.
3 See p. xxi.

25 February – [2] March 1996
Exercitia Spiritualia [Spiritual Exercises] *Capella Redemptoris Mater* [Mother of the Redeemer Chapel] Led by Monsignor [Christoph] Schönborn, Archbishop of Vienna[1]

~

25 February 6.00 p.m.: Lenten Lamentations;[2] Exposition of the Blessed Sacrament; Vespers

Introductory meditation (1):

O Lux beata, Trinitas [O blessed Light, Trinity].

Catechism of the Catholic Church

God, infinitely perfect in Himself (*Catechism of the Catholic Church*).

'Rabbi, where are you staying?'[3] It is with these words that the *communio vitae* [communion of life] begins – the Church. *Prima ora* [The first hour]. The beginning.

Adam, where are you?[4]

Previously and since time immemorial: the hour of encounter, *communio* [communion] is in God. In God's heart.

At the beginning of the retreat everyone should remember the hour of their first encounter with God: the beginning to which we can return: where are you staying?

We have found the Messiah:

personal vocation . . . me –
– in the Church the Church

L[umen] G[entium]: the people gathered in the unity of the Father, the Son and the Holy Spirit: *seminarium Verbi* [seminary of the Word].

(*Catechism of the Catholic Church*)

---

1 Christoph Maria Schönborn OP (b. 1945) is the Archbishop of Vienna and President of the Austrian Bishops' Conference. Pope John Paul II made him a cardinal in 1998.

2 See n. 6, p. 221 [11 March 1984].

3 See John 1:38.

4 See Genesis 3:9.

God infinitely perfect – infinitely *adorandus* [to be adored], *amandus* [to be loved].

Fr Garrigou-Lagrange

Called to participate in His life and happiness.

Adoration of the Blessed Sacrament; Meditation continued; Compline

26 February

Intentions; Adoration; Prayers

Morning meditation:

God – infinitely perfect in Himself.

God – who gives Himself.

Seeking man: where are you?

God of the encounter with man – as a person – in the community (the Church).

Deus adorandus, amandus [God to be adored, to be loved].

Holy Mass; Thanksgiving; Intentions; Litany of the Polish Nation; Prayer for the gifts of the Holy Spirit; Act of Consecration to Our Lady; Lauds

Meditation 2: ***Ecclesia – iam ab origine mundi praefigurata*** **[The Church – anticipated from the beginning of the world]**

(*Finis omnium Ecclesia* [The Church is the final goal of everything].)

Lumen gentium – Christus [The Light of nations – Christ] (the goal).

Ecclesia – medium et quasi Sacramentum [The Church – a medium and quasi-sacrament].

Ecclesia [The Church] – in a way, the goal of all creation.

Creatio – fundamentum – Creator [Creation – foundation – the Creator].

God–Creator is the foundation of the entire structure of faith, at the top of which lies the truth of the Church.

Conversio – Conversion to God–Creator, the recognition of one's createdness. In the context of the contemporary mindset, this is the primary conversion.

Ecclesia praefigurata nella creazione [The Church prefigured in the creation].

Simultaneously: *Ecclesia* [The Church] is what the whole creation longs for (Rom. 8).

Augustine: *Ecclesia – mundus reconciliatus* [The Church – the world reconciled].

Terce; Passion of Our Lord Jesus Christ according to Matthew

Meditation 3: ***Coelum et Terra* [Heaven and Earth]**
(*sopra – sotto* [above – below])

Genesis 1: In the beginning God created the heavens and the earth.

Il 'sopra' determina il 'sotto' [The 'above' determines the 'below'], this has relevance for the essence of the Church too.

Coelum – Angeli – invisibilia – mundus invisibilis creatus [Heaven – angels – invisible things – the created invisible world].

Sanctus [Holy] – always sung in unity with heaven, with the angels.

If the contemporary rationalist mindset has broken free from the 'invisible world', this world returns in various ways: angels and demons.

Newman ⟶ On the angel (creation) that comforts the Son of God in Gethsemane.

Pascal
Scholem
St Thomas

Communio [Communion] with the world of angels.

Sext; None; Concluding meditation; The Way of the Cross; Reading; Adoration of the Blessed Sacrament; Penitential psalms; Rosary (I); Vespers; Rosary

Meditation 4: ***Hexaemeron* [The six days of creation]**
Catechesis on the creation 'out of nothing'.

St Catherine of Siena

I am He who IS. You – she who is not.[1]

Every creature has its own goodness (value).

The Creator wanted a diversity of creatures and their mutual belonging. *Per analogiam* [By analogy]: the Church – body (organism).

Einstein

The beauty of creatures: cosmos. The hierarchy of creatures. Analogy: the hierarchical order in the Church.

Sigismund's Chapel in Wawel Cathedral

The anthropocentrism of the work of creation.

Human being – the only creature that God wanted for its own sake (*G[audium et] S[pes]*).

Spaemann
Pius XII

Opposition: man as auto-creator – versus the createdness of man (*creaturalità dell'uomo*). Man 'does not create himself', but is created.

1 See n. 3, p. 23 [1 September 1964].

Einstein | analogiam: Kościół – Lit. (organizm)
Piękno stworzeń: Kosmos. Hierarchia stworzeń // Analogie: ład hierarchiczny w Kościele.

Antropocentryzm dzieła stworzenia człowiek – jedyne stworzenie, którego Bóg chciał dla niego samego (GS [illegible])

kopot [illegible] in tracta | Szczególnie: człowiek jako auto-kreator – i stwórczość człowieka (creatività dell'uomo). Nie „stwarza samego siebie" ale jest stworzony

Spaemann

Pius XII

Solidarność wszystkich stworzeń skierowanych do chwały Stwórcy

Hexa-emeron: 4 środki – Szabat
Creazione fatta in vista del Sabat (gloria di Dio)

16. Lit. SS. Nom. Jesu / BMV / S. Joseph

17 [Divina Provvidenza]
Medit. V
~~[illegible]~~ Tutto ordinato alla salvezza dell'uomo
Causa Prima – causae secundae

dr. Tarn. cd. Słowo Jan | Bóg nie potrzebuje niczego ani nikogo, a równocześnie Jego najlepszym zamiarem w Wszechrzeczy „przyczynowość" stworzeń – a ~~[illegible]~~ w szczególności stworzeń rozumnych i wolnych.

do Tom. 11.

Ostatecznie [illegible] Stwórcy
„Proście Pana żniwa, aby posłał żniwiarzy"

The solidarity of all creatures oriented towards the glory of the Creator.

Hexa-emeron – Six days – Sabbath.

Creazione fatta in vista dello Shabbat [Creation in view of the Sabbath].

(*Gloria di Dio* [Glory of God].)

Litany of the Holy Name of Jesus, Blessed Virgin Mary, St Joseph

Meditation 5: ***Divina Providenza*** **[Divine providence]**

Tutto ordinato alla salvezza dell'uomo [All is oriented towards the salvation of man].

St Thérèse of the Child Jesus

Causa Prima – causae secundae [The primary cause – the secondary causes].

God does not need anything or anyone, yet at the same time His reign over the world 'brings about' the causality of creatures, in particular the rational and free creatures.

St Thomas Aquinas

Man – works together with the Creator

'Pray therefore to the Lord of the harvest to send out labourers into his harvest'.[1]

We participate in the salvation of the world.

Synod of 1985
Card. Tomašek
Danielou

This is the order of the divine providence, to work for the kingdom of God – to pray – to suffer.

Lavorare – pregare – soffrire [To work – to pray – to suffer].

Rosary (I); Adoration of the Blessed Sacrament; Meditation continued; Compline

27 February

Intentions; Prayers; Adoration; Matins

Meditation: *Creator – coeli et terrae – hexaemeron – Providentia* [The Creator – heaven and earth – the six days of creation – providence].

Holy Mass; Thanksgiving; Prayers; Litany for the Homeland; Prayer for the seven gifts of the Holy Spirit; Act of Consecration to Our Lady; Lauds

Meditation 6: Topic for the day:

Ecclesia – in foedere antique mirabiliter praeparata [Church – prepared in a remarkable way by means of the old covenant].[2]

1 See Matthew 9:38.
2 See *Lumen gentium* 2.

Unde malum? [Where does evil come from?] From the creation to the redemption.

Adamo – Cristo; Cristo – Adamo [Adam – Christ; Christ – Adam].

In uno solo omnes peccaverunt [In one man all men sinned].[1]

Quomodo possibile? [How is it possible?]

Solidarietà peccati [Solidarity of sin] *exsules filii Evae* [the banished sons of Eve].

– *solidarietà salutis* [solidarity of salvation].

Recapitulatio omnium in Christo [The union of all things in Christ].[2]

St Bernard ⟶ *Destinatio omnium dipende da uno ('fiat' Mariae)* [The fate of all depends on one thing (Mary's 'let it be')].

Centesimus annus ⟶ *Peccato originale – doct. soc. della Chiesa* [Original sin – the social teaching of the Church].

Spaemann ⟶ *Peccato originale* [Original sin] is the lack of original grace.

There has not been enough of St Paul here: for if one man's trespass led to condemnation for all men, so one Man's act of righteousness leads to acquittal for all men.[3]

Unde malum? Ex malo usu libertatis [Where does evil come from? From a faulty exercise of freedom].

Terce

Meditation 7: ***Protoevangelium* [Proto-gospel]**

Eucharistic Prayer IV

The Book of Genesis, going against the rationalist mindset, gives a convincing answer to the question: *unde malum* [where does evil come from]?

The consequences of original sin:

(a) In the domain of human work: 'in the sweat of your face you shall eat bread'.[4]

Paul VI *L[aborem] E[xercens]*

(b) In the domain of civilisation and culture: with great achievements – so much suffering. How many ethical problems? How much injustice?

(c) In the domain of the man–woman relationship (cf. what

1 See Romans 5:12.
2 See Ephesians 1:10.
3 See Romans 5:18.
4 See Genesis 3:19.

has been analysed in relation to 'male and female He created them').[1] Especially the hardships of motherhood.

Augustine: *matrimonium – remedium concupisc.* [marriage – remedy for concupiscence].

Protoevangelium [Proto-gospel]: The first promise of the Messiah–Redeemer.

G[audium et] S[pes] ⟶ 'The struggle between good and evil over the ages'.

Sext; None; The Way of the Cross; Adoration of the Blessed Sacrament; Reading; Litany of the Saints; (Rosary); Vespers; (Rosary)

Meditation 8: ***Foedus cum Noe*** **[The covenant with Noah]**
God heals the wounds of sin through penance.

Noah the just is the symbol of *Ecclesia delle genti* [the Church of nations].

(Noah – '*pagano giusto*' ['the just pagan']), to some extent, a representative of natural religions. Likewise Melchizedek, Job. *'Le nazioni' (battezzate tutte 'le nazioni'): cultura, lingua, storia* ['Nations' (baptise all 'nations'):[2] culture, language, history].

Opposition: the tower of Babel – Noah's ark.

Paul's words in the Areopagus.[3]

Nazioni [hanno] anche i loro demoni [Nations also [have] their own demons], as has become evident in this century. Nationalisms. Statolatry.[4]

Saints are excellent representatives of their nations, but none of them is solely 'national'.

Foedus cum Noe [The covenant with Noah] is something permanent.

It precedes the covenant with Abraham, the father of our faith.

1 See Genesis 1:27.

2 See Matthew 28:19.

3 See Acts 17:22–32.

4 Statolatry is an idolatry of the state. Pope Pius XI accused Italian fascists of promoting it among young people in his 1931 encyclical *Non abbiamo bisogno* (We Do Not Need): 'We find ourselves confronted by a mass of authentic affirmations and no less authentic facts which reveal beyond the slightest possibility of doubt the resolve (already in great measure actually put into effect) to monopolize completely the young, from their tenderest years up to manhood and womanhood, for the exclusive advantage of a party and of a regime based on an ideology which clearly resolves itself into a true, a real pagan worship of the State – the "Statolatry" which is no less in contrast with the natural rights of the family than it is in contradiction with the supernatural rights of the Church.'

Litany of the Sacred Heart of Jesus, Blessed Virgin Mary, St Joseph; *Veni, Sancte Spiritus* [Come, Holy Spirit]

Meditation 9: ***Antiquum Testamentum*** **[The Old Testament]**
Israel. The people of the covenant. *Terra Sancta* [The Holy Land].

The Hebrew community in Rome – since the times of the apostles, Peter and Paul, to our times. The contribution of Pius XII during World War II.

God has chosen Abraham: By you all the nations of the earth shall be blessed.[1]

After the period of the patriarchs, God forms His people – the exodus from Egypt – Moses – the covenant of Sinai.

Catechism

Israel in an ethnic sense. Israel in a theological sense: the offspring of Abraham in the spiritual sense.

(Shoah – hatred of the God of Israel: the God of the old and new covenant.)

Ratzinger

(The meaning of epiphany – pagans, finding Christ, enter the inheritance of Israel.)

Antico Test. è la Storia dell'amore di Dio [The Old Testament is the Story of God's love]. (In liturgy – the Old Testament is irreplaceable.)

The Church can never break away from the Old Testament.

Law (Torah) is a preparation for Christ (*paedagogus* [teacher]): *Ecclesia mirabiliter praeparata in Vetere Testamento* [The Church was prepared in a remarkable way in the Old Testament].

Rosary (II); Eucharistic Adoration; Meditation continued; Compline

28 February Intentions; Prayers; Matins

Meditation: (*Unde malum? – Protoevangelium – Foedus cum Noe – Antiquum Testamentum* [Where does evil come from? – the Proto-gospel – the covenant with Noah – the Old Testament].

Ecclesia in Foedere antiquo mirabiliter praeparata [The Church was prepared in a remarkable way by means of the old covenant].

1 See Genesis 12:3.

Holy Mass; Thanksgiving; Prayer for the seven gifts of the Holy Spirit; Act of Consecration to Our Lady; Lauds

Meditation 10: ***Ecclesia in novissimis temporibus constituta* [The Church constituted in the present era]**[1]

Et incarnatus est [And was incarnate].

(*Ad Gal.* [Letter to the Galatians].) '*Quando venit plenitudo temporum, misit Deus Filium suum, natum de muliere*' ['When the fullness of time had come, God sent His Son, born of a woman'][2] – *et Incarnatus est* [and was Incarnate]: we fall to our knees.

The Great Jubilee of 2000 (to introduce anew).

To fall to our knees before the Bethlehem manger – reality – not a myth – faith – the mystery of the incarnation, which is one with the faith in one God (monotheism).

The Church is simultaneously the body of Christ and a true community.

Christ: God–Man. Humanity – *instrumentum animatum Divinitatis* [the living instrument of Divinity]. The Church partakes in this unity.

Incarnatus est de Spiritu S. ex Maria Virgine et homo factus est [And by the Holy Spirit was incarnate of the Virgin Mary and became man].

Passion of Our Lord Jesus Christ according to Luke

Meditation 11: ***Mysteria vitae Gesù* [The mysteries of Jesus' life]**

Il Verbo si è fato uomo, perché l'uomo diventasse figlio di Dio: divinizzazione: il nostro modo di essere uomini è rinnovato [The Word became man so that man might become a son of God: divinisation: our humanity is renewed].[3]

Catechism

Man partakes in the divine filiation of the Son–Word: He in us, we in Him:

Church – a community of the adopted sons of God.

Mysteria vitae Gesù [The mysteries of Jesus' life] from the birth to the passion, death and resurrection – the redemp-

1 See *Lumen gentium* 2.

2 See Galatians 4:4.

3 See the *Catechism of the Catholic Church*, 460.

tive mysteries of God–Man. He who has seen Me has seen the Father.[1]

Ignatian meditation.

Redemptor hominis

Redemption – *mysterium tremendum* [overwhelming mystery] – everything in Christ's life has redemptive power.

Vita Christi [The life of Christ]:

- *per noi* [for us]
- *davanti noi (di fronte a noi)* [before us (in front of us)]
- *in noi* [in us].

St John of the Cross
St John Eudes

Pro-existentia Christi [Christ's pro-existence] (Schürmann).

Therefore *'sequela Xristi' appartiene alla vita della Chiesa* [the 'imitation of Christ' belongs to the life of the Church].

'*Mia cosa sola*' ['Only my thing'].

Liturgia, sacramenti – vita Cristi [Liturgy, sacraments – the life of Christ].

Our life completely with Christ and in Christ, from Christ. He wants to use our life for the glory of the Father.

Meditation continued; The Way of the Cross; Adoration of the Blessed Sacrament; Reading; Sext; None; (Rosary); Litany of the Saints; (Rosary); Vespers

Meditation 12: ***Et super hanc petram*** **[And on this rock]**[2]

Christ gave His Church a structure which is to last for ages.

Mulieris dignitatem

The choice of the Twelve.

A structure that is *ordinata alla santità* [oriented towards sanctity] – *Maria prende la struttura gerarchica, l'ordine ministeriale* [Mary accepts the hierarchical structure, the order of ministry].

The sending out of the apostles: 'I am with you always, to the end of the age'.[3]

The apostles in the school of Christ.

Different moments; those moments can be the basis for an examination of conscience for those who are the apostles' successors.

The woman of Cana; Jesus and children.

1 See John 14:9.
2 See Matthew 16:18.
3 See Matthew 28:20.

The apostles' ambitions at the time when Jesus announces His suffering – in the last moment of the supper.

Lord, you know everything; you know that I love you.[1]

Litany of the Holy Name of Jesus, Blessed Virgin Mary, St Joseph

Meditation 13: ***Ecclesia ex latere Christi* [The Church from the side of Christ]**

O Crux, ave spes unica [Hail to the Cross, our only hope].

'*Tu, che sei uomo, Ti fai Dio*' ['You, being a man, make yourself God'][2] – for the Sanhedrin this was the reason to sentence Christ to death on the cross.

The issue of identity. They thought that by sentencing Jesus to death they did God a favour.

Jesus' lament over Jerusalem.

'Father, forgive them, for they know not what they do . . .'[3]

'Hardness of heart' – for they saw the miracles that Jesus performed.

How often would I have gathered your children together, Jerusalem.[4]

The responsibility for Christ's cross falls on the whole inheritance of original sin and the whole history of sin, which has always meant 'no' to God.

(St Paul: The Son of God loved me and gave Himself for me.)[5]

Gethsemane – the cross – complete surrender to the Father for the sins of the whole world. Humanity's 'no' to God was nailed to the cross.

Rosary (III); Eucharistic Adoration; Meditation continued; Compline

29 February Intentions; Adoration; Prayers; Matins

Meditation: (*Incarnatio – Mysteria Christi – Super hanc petram – Ecclesia ex latere Christi* [Incarnation – the mystery of Christ – on this rock – the Church from the side of Christ]).

1 See John 21:17.
2 See John 10:33.
3 See Luke 23:34.
4 See Matthew 23:37.
5 See Galatians 2:20.

Holy Mass; Thanksgiving; Prayer for the Homeland; Prayer for the seven gifts of the Holy Spirit; Act of Consecration to Our Lady (Grignion);[1] Lauds

Hugo Rahner

Meditation 14: ***Ecclesia – effuse Spiritu manifestata* [Church – made manifest by the outpouring of the Spirit]**[2]

Patri [to the Father]

Tradidit spiritum [He gave up His spirit].[3]

Spiritus S. – Dio nascosto [the Holy Spirit – the hidden God].

'If any one thirst, let him come to Me and drink . . . this He said about the Spirit, which those who believed in Him were to receive'.[4]

the word '*tradere*' [to return, to give up]: the meaning + → the encyclical *D[omnium] et V[ivificantem]*

Pentecoste – viene dato lo Spirito Santo, viene manifestata la Chiesa [Pentecost – the Holy Spirit is given, the Church is made manifest].

This is the Church that was born on the cross '*ex latere Christi*' ['from the side of Christ'].

'*Tradidit spiritum*' ['He gave up His spirit'].

Cf. *Dominum et vivificantem.*[5]

St Thomas

Thomas Aquinas: *Verbum spirans amorem* [The Word breathing love].

Father, into Thy hands I commit my Spirit![6]

The Father – the Son – the Holy Spirit are revealed on the cross.

The Holy Spirit is the first gift of the resurrection: Receive the Holy Spirit.[7]

new age
St Hippolytus
St Irenaeus

Pentecost – the 'time of the Church' begins: *effuso Spiritu Ecclesia manifestata* [the Church made manifest by the outpouring of the Spirit].

Terce; Passion of Our Lord Jesus Christ according to John

Meditation 15: ***Respice fidem Ecclesiae* [Look on the faith of the Church]**

Manifestatio Spiritus S. consistit in 'vita theologali': fides, spes, caritas [The manifestation of the Holy Spirit consists in 'theological life': faith, hope, charity].

1 See n. 1, p. 66.
2 See *Lumen gentium* 2.
3 See John 19:30.
4 See John 7:37, 39.
5 See n. 2, p. 382 [21 February 1994].
6 See Luke 23:46.
7 See John 20:22.

St John of the Cross, Justinus, Carmel, Father Marie-Eugene of the Child Jesus, Newman, B. M., Cardinal Kung Pin-Mei

Fides: assenso ad revelata participatio vitae Divinae: attinge ad Divina [Faith: assent to a revealed participation in divine life: reach for divine things].

(St John of the Cross: *Dios por participación* [God through participation]).

Faith is certain – it has a greater certainty than human cognition because it is based on the divine Word (revelation).

Our Lady's 'night of faith' (cf. the encyclical *Redemptoris Mater*).[1]

Lord, look not on our sins, but on the faith of Your Church . . .

colonna della Verità [the pillar of the truth].[2]

Meditation continued; Sext; None; Rosary; The Way of the Cross; Rosary; Adoration of the Blessed Sacrament
Reading: (Solovyov);[3] B. Forte[4]
Penitential psalms; Vespers

Meditation 16: ***Oratio – spei interpres* [Prayer – the mediator of hope]**

Edith Stein
Vienna
St Stephen

Nessun processo di secolarizzazione può soffocare in noi il soffio dello Spirito S. [No process of secularisation can quench the breath of the Holy Spirit in us].

Chi prega, spera [He who prays, hopes].

St Thomas

Preghiera è interprete del nostro desiderio verso Dio [Prayer is the means by which our desire is made known to God]: Thy kingdom come. Thy will be done . . .

Deliver us from evil . . .

Ratzinger

La preghiera è la lingua della nostra speranza [Prayer is the language of our hope]. What is hope?

Catechism

J. Pieper → *Spes sperat Deum a Deo* [Hope hopes for God from God].

Caietano → *Spes non deludit* [Hope does not delude].

Bruckner

In Te, Domine, speravi, non confundar in aeternum [In you, O Lord, I put my trust, do not let me ever be put to shame].[5]

1 The encyclical *Redemptoris Mater* (Mother of the Redeemer) was promulgated by Pope John Paul II on 25 March 1987.

2 See 1 Timothy 3:15.

3 See n. 4, p. 304 [14 February 1989].

4 Bruno Forte (b. 1949) is an Italian theologian and Archbishop of Chieti-Vasto.

5 See Psalm 30:2 (31:1.).

6. Laudes

7. Medit. XVII — Ecclesia – effuso Spiritu manifestata

tradidit spiritum

Spiritum ! – Ord nascente

„[illegible] ... „[illegible] ... [illegible]

Pentecoste – viene dato lo Spirito Santo, viene manifestata la Chiesa

[illegible] ... „ex latere Christi"

„tradidit spiritum" !

Cf. Dominum et Vivificantem

[illegible] : Verbum Spirans Amorem

[illegible] ... [illegible] ... Ojca – Syna – Duch Ś.

[illegible] ... Duch Ś. : [illegible] Ducha Ś.

[illegible] ... : effuso Spiritu Ecclesia manifestata

8. Tertia — Primo Ott. [illegible] ... [illegible]

Medit. XVI

9. [illegible] ... Ecclesia

10. Meditazione XVI

Hugo Rahner
Thomas
Hippolit
Ireneus

8
9
10
11
12
13
14
15
17
18
19

Deviazioni della speranza [Deviations from hope]:
acedia
(*demonio/del mezzogiorno*) – *torpore spirituale* [the demon/of noonday – spiritual torpor]
Medicina: perseveranza [Remedy: perseverance].

St Thérèse of the Child Jesus →
Amore della propria povertà [Love of one's own poverty].
Beati i poveri di spirito [Blessed are the poor in spirit].

Litany of Our Lord Jesus Christ, Priest and Victim, Blessed Virgin Mary, St Joseph

Meditation 17: Love is the greatest.[1]

Caritas – amor amicitiae [Charity – friendly love]

'No longer do I call you servants, but friends' (J).[2]

St Thomas →
Amicitia: benevolentia [Friendship: benevolence].
Communicatio mutua [Mutual communication].

How can there be *communicatio* [communication] between the Infinite and the finite?

St Thomas →
But Jesus says: 'I have called you friends.'

Lombard → John of the Cross
Communicatio [Communication] is possible through grace (*participatio Div. naturae* [participation in the divine nature]) – P. Lombard:[3] the Holy Spirit Himself animates the human spirit.

St Thomas: *instinctus Spiritus S.* [The instinct of the Holy Spirit].

If we become friends to God, we should also become friends to each other.

Friendship and spousal love. A purification of senses, feelings and will is necessary.

St Thomas →
'We cannot live without love.'
'*Gusto della vita*' ['The enjoyment of life'].

Rosary (I); Eucharistic Adoration; Holy Hour; Compline

1 See 1 Corinthians 13:13.
2 See John 15:15.
3 Peter Lombard (c.1096–1160) was an acclaimed scholastic theologian and Bishop of Paris.

1 March Intentions; Prayers; Matins

Morning meditation: *Ecclesia Spiritu effuso manifestata: tradidit spiritum – Respice fidem Ecclesiae. Oratio: spei interpres – Caritas – amor amicitiae* [The Church made manifest by the outpouring of the Spirit: He gave up His spirit – Look on the faith of the Church. Prayer: the mediator of hope – charity – friendly love].

Holy Mass; Thanksgiving; Prayers; Litany of the Polish Nation; Prayer for the seven gifts of the Holy Spirit; Act of Consecration to Our Lady; Lauds

Meditation 18: ***Ecclesia – in fine saeculorum gloriose consummabitur* [The Church – at the end of time will gloriously achieve completion]**[1]

Ecclesia peregrinans [The pilgrim Church].

Peregrinans [on pilgrimage] on the way to the homeland.

La Chiesa è promessa della Patria [The Church is a promise of the Homeland]: (*Concittadini dei Santi* [Fellow citizens of the Saints]).

Hope for heaven is at the same time a stimulus to become engaged with the earthly life.

Deviazioni [Deviations]: horizontalism, utilitarianism.

von Balthasar The Church: *Chiesa è nella storia, ma simultaneamente la Trascende!* [The Church is in history, but simultaneously transcends it!]

This is expressed by: the sacraments: the signs.

(*humilitas Sacramentorum* [the humility of the sacraments].)

Terce; (Good Friday)

Meditation 19: ***Sanctorum Communio* [The communion of saints]**

(*Sancta Sanctis* [Holy things for a holy people].)[2]

Comunione alle cose sante [Communion in holy things].

Vatican II *Comunione alle persone sante* [Communion among holy people].

'*noi tutti siamo Chiesa*' ['we all are the Church'].

1 See *Lumen gentium* 2.

2 See the *Catechism of the Catholic Church*, 948.

Nostra debolezza aiutata dalla loro sollecitudine [Our weakness is helped by their solicitude].

Thérèse of the Child Jesus

The Apocalypse: the city – heavenly Jerusalem – coming down out of heaven.[1]

What do we expect from saints?

Union with God, grace, eternal salvation, all support on this path.

'*Comunicantes*' . . . ['United' . . .] in the Eucharist.

Merton
Leon Blois

Only in heaven will we see how much we owe to the communion of saints.

Sext; None; Meditation continued; The Way of the Cross; Reading; Adoration of the Blessed Sacrament; Litany of the Saints; Vespers

Meditation 20: ***Tertio millennio adveniente***[2]

L[umen] G[entium]

Novissima [The last things]: *L[umen] G[entium]*, chapter VII.

G[audium et] S[pes]

The West – the East (secularisation – persecution).

Threats to faith and the Church are on the rise; sects.

Augustine

The Church is on a pilgrimage amid persecution from the world and consolation from God.

Those whose lives were oriented towards the heavenly kingdom simultaneously promoted civilisation and culture.

'My yoke is sweet'.[3]

We are pilgrims on earth, but pilgrims are not vandals.

Tertio Millennio does not blot out the things that Christians are guilty of.

Desiderio dell'unità dei cristiani [the desire for the unity of Christians].

Coptic-Orthodox monks ⟶

(But the spirit of this world may also have an influence here.)

Gertrud von Le Fort ⟶

Maria non vince con la spada in mano, ma con la spada nel cuore [Mary does not triumph with a sword in Her hand, but with a sword in Her heart].

Litany of the Sacred Heart of Jesus, Blessed Virgin Mary, St Joseph; Chaplet of the Five Wounds of Christ; *Veni Sancte Spiritus* [Come, Holy Spirit]

1 See Revelation 21:2.

2 The apostolic letter *Tertio millennio adveniente* (As the Third Millennium Draws Near) was issued by John Paul II on 10 November 1994.

3 See Matthew 11:30.

Meditation 21: ***Obviam Sponso*** **[To meet the Bridegroom]**[1]
Tre aspetti [Three aspects]:

St Augustine *duomo di* [cathedral of]

(1) Liturgy. *Maranatha* [Our Lord, come].[2] Behold, I shall come soon. The Church expresses this '*Maranatha*' by celebrating the Eucharist.

The prayer '*versus Orientem*' ['towards the East']: *Oriens ex alto* [the Rising Sun from on high]:[3] the cosmic symbolism.

anticipazione della nuova venuta di Cristo [anticipation of the new coming of Christ]: *Obviam Sponso* [To meet the Bridegroom].

Augustine

(2) *Obviam Sponso: desiderio di essere conformati a Cristo* [To meet the Bridegroom: the desire to resemble Christ].

con le lampade ardenti [with burning lamps].[4]

Carità pastorale per la Chiesa [Pastoral love for the Church].

(3) '*Obviam Sponso*': *Sponsa semper magis conformis allo Sposo* ['To meet the Bridegroom': The Bride resembles the Bridegroom more and more]. The martyrs of the twentieth century.

Origen

(a) '*Tempo della Chiesa*' – *tempo dell'attesa. Anche i Santi del cielo attendono con noi* ['The time of the Church' – the time of waiting. The saints in heaven wait with us too].

Catechism

(b) *Tempo della prova della Chiesa* [The time of trial for the Church]. *Tempo di svegliarsi* [Time to wake up].[5]

(c) *Venuta dello Sposo – tempo sarà la sua sovrana decisione* [The coming of the Bridegroom – the time of His coming will be His sovereign decision] so that God may be everything to everyone.[6]

Rosary (II); Eucharistic Adoration; Meditation continued; Compline

2 March

Intentions; Morning prayers; Matins
Morning meditation: (*Reassumptio omnium dierum* [The conclusion of all days])

1 See Matthew 25:6.
2 See 1 Corinthians 16:22.
3 See Luke 1:78.
4 See Matthew 25:1–13.
5 See Romans 13:11.
6 See 1 Corinthians 15:28.

Holy Mass; Thanksgiving; [Litany] for the Homeland; Prayers

Meditation 22:

Au coeur de l'Église je serai l'amour [I will be love in the heart of the Church] (*s. Ther. ab Jesu Inf* [St Thérèse of the Child Jesus]).

Chiesa santa [the holy Church].

The widow's penny: 'she has put in everything she had', the conclusion of the whole gospel, 'do not let your left hand know what your right hand is doing'.[1]

The disciples have to learn who is truly great in the heavenly kingdom.

Catechism
Folio
the full text
Fr Bali

The widow – *figura della Chiesa* [the figure of the Church].

We bless the Father for the holiness that He gives to the Church: the words of St Thérèse of the Child Jesus: '*Au coeur de l'Église je serai l'amour*' ['I will be love in the heart of the Church']. Holiness is possible for everyone.

Conclusion; Final words; *Pater Noster* [Our Father]
UIOGD
AMDG[2]

1 See Mark 12:44 and Matthew 6:3.

2 See p. xxi.

16–22 February 1997
Exercitia Spiritualia
[Spiritual Exercises]
Led by Cardinal R[oger] Etchegaray[1]

~

16 February Lenten Lamentations;[2] Litanies; 6.00 p.m.: Exposition of the Blessed Sacrament; Vespers

Introductory meditation 1:

Tertio millennio adveniente:[3] year 1: Christ.

The Fifth Gospel – written by Christians with their lives.

The experience of the Roman Curia goes well beyond the Curia (Card. Confalonieri)[4] – a community of dicasteries:[5] to pray together – 'Pray also for us, that we may proclaim the mystery of Christ.[6]

The Word became flesh – Jesus Christ.

Memoriale di Pascal: 'fuoco' [Pascal's *Memorial*: 'fire']⁷ (like Moses and the burning bush); without Christ we do not know Who God is nor who we are.

Adoration of the Blessed Sacrament; Meditation continued; Compline

17 February Intentions; Prayers; Adoration
Morning meditation: Moses *ad montem Horeb* [on Mount Horeb]
Holy Mass; Thanksgiving; Act of Consecration to the Blessed Virgin Mary; Lauds

---

1 Roger Etchegaray (b. 1922) is a French cardinal who served as Archbishop of Marseille (1970–85), President of the Pontifical Council for Justice and Peace (1984–98) and President of the Pontifical Council *Cor Unum* for Human and Christian Development (1984–95).

2 See n. 6, p. 221 [11 March 1984].

3 See n. 2, p. 416 [1 March 1996].

4 Carlo Confalonieri (1893–1986) was an Italian cardinal who served as Prefect of the Congregation for Bishops (1967–73) and Dean of the College of Cardinals from 1977 until his death.

5 Dicasteries are administrative subdivisions of the Roman Curia.

6 See Ephesians 6:18–19.

7 Pascal's *Memorial* records a religious vision he had on 23 November 1654. It begins with the words: 'Fire. God of Abraham, God of Isaac, God of Jacob, not of the philosophers and the scholars . . .'

Meditation 2: The names of Jesus Christ:

the Son of God

↓

'This is my beloved Son, with whom I am well pleased.'[1]

↑

in relation to the Father.

'He who has seen Me, has seen the Father.'[2]

St John of the Cross, St Theresa

Abbá [Father].

'We shall see Him as He Is.'[3]

'Our Father': sons in the Son.

Prayer for the gifts of the Holy Spirit; Passion of Our Lord Jesus Christ according to Matthew; Terce

Meditation 3:

Father – Fatherhood.

Opposition to contemporary thought (*societas represiva* [repressive society]).

Simultaneously, there is a growing nostalgia for the Father.

'*Nemo tam pater quam mater*' ['No one can be both father and mother'].

Perdono [forgiveness] – (cf. Rembrandt's painting).

Dives in Misericordia

(Ali Ağca)[4]

St Thérèse of the Child Jesus

The Church carries out the service of divine mercy.

(Pascal)

Joy of forgiveness

'There will be more joy in heaven . . .'[5]

(Urs von Balthasar)

'*Misericordia a generatione in generationem*' ['Mercy from generation to generation'].[6]

Sext; None; Meditation continued; The Way of the Cross; Adoration of the Blessed Sacrament; Litany of the Holy Name of Jesus; Litany of the Saints; Litany of the Blessed Virgin Mary; Litany of St Joseph; Reading; Vespers

---

1 See Matthew 3:17.

2 See John 14:9.

3 See 1 John 3:2.

4 Mehmet Ali Ağca (b. 1958) shot and wounded Pope John Paul II on 13 May 1981 in St Peter's Square. John Paul II forgave Ağca and visited him in prison in 1983. The Pope maintained contact with Ağca's family over the years and met his mother in 1987. Ağca was pardoned by the Italian president Carlo Azeglio Ciampi at John Paul II's request and deported to Turkey in June 2000.

5 See Luke 15:7.

6 See Luke 1:50.

giovedì **8** agosto

s. Gaetano

Thursday Donnerstag Jeudi
ЧЕТВЕРТ Jueves خميس

August August Août
АВГУСТ Agosto

17. II

Feria II

1 Int. Pres. i Ador.

2 Medit. Mat.

I. Mojżesz od matki [illegible]

3. Sacram. Grat. actio
Akt. [illegible]

8

4. Laudes

9

5. Medit II

10

Imiona Jezusa Chrystusa:

11

Syn Boży

„Ten jest Syn mój [illegible] w którym mam upodobanie" [illegible]

12

w relacji do Ojca

13

„[illegible] Abba, Ojcze"

14

[illegible] Józef

15

„Ojcze nasz" [illegible]

16

[illegible] Passio DNJ [illegible]

18

7. Tertia

19

8. Medit. III

G	V	S	D	L	M	M	G	V	S	D	L	M	M	G
1	2	3	4	5	6	7	8	9	10	11	12	13	14	15

32 s.w. 220-145

[illegible]

Meditation 4:

Spirito S. (Spirito di Cristo) [The Holy Spirit (the Spirit of Christ)].

= teaches what Christ taught.

Credo [in] Spiritum Sanctum [I believe [in] the Holy Spirit].

Dominum et vivificantem [the Lord and the giver of life].

The encyclical (part III) part II 'will convince the world' . . .

Pentecost: the Holy Spirit gives proper meaning to every word of the Gospel and power to evangelisation: the breath of life.

Anticipated Matins (Tuesday); *Veni Creator* [Come, Creator (Spirit)]

Meditation 5:

'Go therefore and make disciples of all nations . . .'[1]

Evangelisation.

Paul VI *Evangelii nuntiandi.*[2]

Encounter of religions: Assisi 1986.[3]

Judaism = pre-Christian religion.

Nostra aetate.[4]

Common heritage with Israel.

Incontro/scontro delle religioni una sfida maggiore del nostro tempo [Meeting/confrontation of religions is the biggest challenge of our times]; one cannot speak of '*vie parallele*' ['parallel ways'] to salvation.

Christ – the only way to salvation.

Rosary (I); Adoration of the Blessed Sacrament; Meditation resumed; Compline

18 February Intentions; Prayers; Adoration

Meditation: ('*Pater noster*' – *de textis Feriae III* ['Our Father' – from Tuesday readings])

Holy Mass; Thanksgiving; Prayers; Act of Consecration (Grignion); Prayer for the gifts of the Holy Spirit; Lauds

1 See Matthew 28:19.

2 The apostolic exhortation *Evangelii nuntiandi* (Evangelisation in the Modern World) was issued by Pope Paul VI on 8 December 1975.

3 Pope John Paul II organised the first World Day of Prayer for Peace, which brought together 160 religious leaders representing 32 Christian Churches and 11 non-Christian religions, in Assisi on 27 October 1986.

4 *Nostra aetate* (In Our Time) is the Declaration on the Relation of the Church with Non-Christian Religions of the Second Vatican Council. It was promulgated by Pope Paul VI on 28 October 1965.

Meditation 6: Prayer.

To a certain extent, we know Christ's prayer. He prayed, above all, alone (in the room of His heart).[1] He certainly prayed with the Psalms.

The prayer in Gethsemane.
The prayer on the cross. – this is the highest ideal
Christ's prayers.

The agony of Christ is simultaneously the culmination of His mystery (all words, all actions – all this is the fullness of prayer and mystery).

Christ's prayer has to become our prayer. We are called to partake in it.

The things which Christ teaches us about prayer are very simple and deep at the same time. *'Pater' noster . . .* [Our 'Father' . . .]: 'we dare to say': my Father and our Father.

Terce; Passion of Our Lord Jesus Christ according to Mark

Meditation 7:

Lectio Divina [Divine reading]. Prayer needs to be grounded in the word of God.

St Ignatius of Antioch

The Gospel – Prayer – Preaching.

Christianity is a religion of the Book (the word of God).

Lectio divina – studium [Divine reading – studies] (Constitution *Dei verbum*) – *'lumina'* ['lights'].

(Botticelli): *'Madonna del Libro'* ['Madonna of the Book'] – texts by the Church Fathers (Patristics) – the contemplative dimension (Carmel).

Claudel

Lectio divina has to be embedded in the Church: (liturgy).

Sext; None; Meditation continued; The Way of the Cross; Adoration of the Blessed Sacrament; Penitential psalms; Vespers

Meditation 8: 'The Crucified' [illegible].

Coming into the world, He already says: 'I have come to do Your will, Father'.[2] From the moment when He comes into the world, He prepares for the 'hour', therefore – not only these three hours on Calvary, but a long preparation to fulfil what Isaiah prophesied in the song of Yahweh's Servant.

Cullmann
Claudel

1 See Matthew 6:6.
2 See Hebrews 10:5, 7.

Suffering: a problem without answer in the human dimension. Christ has given the answer: He took our cross by Himself – He truly carried our sorrows (Is.).[1]

Dostoyevsky
Scheler

After Christ, suffering is no longer '*scandalum*' ['a scandal'], but '*mysterium*' ['a mystery'].

Bulgakov
Journet

The folly of the cross – *follia crucis*.

Stabat Mater [The (Sorrowful) Mother Stood]:[2] O You, who suffered with Him.

Anticipated Matins

Meditation 9: *Ave, Verum Corpus* [Hail, True Body].[3]

Guitton

'If we have died with Christ, we shall also live with Him.'[4]

'For this reason the Father loves me, because I lay down my life. No one takes it from me, but I lay it down of my own accord' . . . I have power . . .[5]

'He descended into hell': as if it was the final consequence of the incarnation: 'He descended to the dead'.

Rilke

'Death': if we have died with Christ, we shall also live with Christ.

Von Balthasar
Study on St
Thérèse of the
Child Jesus

St Thérèse of Lisieux: the last eighteen months of her life: 'night': 'to die of love'.

'I am not dying, I am entering Love'.

The 'diary' of dying.

The 'Good Thief' – '*ha rubato il Cielo*' ['he has stolen Heaven'].

Rosary (II); Adoration of the Blessed Sacrament; Meditation continued; Compline

19 February

Intentions; Prayers; Eucharistic Adoration
Meditation: (Nineveh – Jonah)
Holy Mass; Thanksgiving; Act of Consecration (Grignion de Montfort); Prayer for the gifts of the Holy Spirit; Lauds

Meditation 10:

'*Volto di Cristo, volto dei fratelli*' ['The face of Christ, the face of our brothers'].

---

1 See Isaiah 53:4.
2 See n. 1, p. 29 [3 September 1964].
3 *Ave Verum Corpus* (Hail, True Body) is a short Eucharistic hymn dating from the fourteenth century. It has been attributed to Pope Innocent VI.
4 See Romans 6:8.
5 See John 10:17–18.

(Icon – it is more than a portrait, image): the East.

Who is my neighbour? The parable of the Good Samaritan.

The diversity of human faces is an expression of the richness of Christ's face.

The Church – *fondatrice della fraternità* [the founder of brotherhood]; *promotrice* [promoter].

Burundi

'You shall love your neighbour as yourself'.[1]

NB (Actually, the entire topic is contained in the title.)

Terce; Passion of Our Lord Jesus Christ according to Luke

Meditation 11:

'*Volto di Cristo, volto dei sacerdoti*' ['The face of Christ, the face of priests'].

'*Sacerdos – alter Christus*' ['Priest – another Christ'].

The situation in the diocese – the situation in the Roman Curia, also in the Curia – *verum ministerium sacerdotale, pastorale* [true priestly, pastoral ministry]: *ad limina* visits![2]

↑

Observations

Suggestion!

↓

Bishops in the Curia

Sext; None; Meditation continued; The Way of the Cross; Adoration of the Blessed Sacrament; Litany of the Saints; Reading; Litany of the Holy Name of Jesus, Blessed Virgin Mary, St Joseph; Vespers

Meditation 12:

Bernanos

The Church – *mysterium* [mystery].

The same *mysterium* as the *mysterium* of Christ. (Paul VI, *Ecclesiam suam.*)[3]

The images of the Church (*L[umen] G[entium]*); the Council chose the image of the 'people of God'.

Renan

The faith in the Church is organically connected with the faith in Christ. The Church – the kingdom of God.

To believe in the Church means to take responsibility for

1 See Mark 12:31.

2 Diocesan bishops are obliged to make a visit *ad limina apostolorum* (to the doorstep of the apostles) to pay their respects at the tombs of Ss Peter and Paul and to provide the Holy See with a report on the state of their dioceses every five years.

3 The encyclical *Ecclesiam suam* (His Church) was promulgated by Pope Paul VI on 6 August 1964.

Guitton, H. Rahner

the whole world from the perspective of the kingdom of God.

The history and geography of the Church:

The Holy Church

The Church of wilderness (in wilderness)

I fall down to my knees before the mystery of the Church.

Anticipated Matins; *Veni Sancte Spiritus* [Come, Holy Spirit]

Claudel

Meditation 13: The Church – Mother.

A mother who gives birth to us in the sacrament of baptism.

'He can no longer have God for his Father, who has not the Church for his mother' (St Cyprian).[1]

(Catechumens.)

(De Lubac)

Mary – the Mother in the Church – the Mother of the Church (the encyclical *Redemptoris hominis*).[2]

Do we love the Church?

Teilhard de Chardin

There can be no reform without love.

To love the Church – means to look at the Church with Christ's eyes.

The Church – the only place of human salvation.

Rosary (III); Adoration of the Blessed Sacrament; Meditation continued; Compline

20 February

Intentions; Prayers; Eucharistic Adoration
Morning meditation: (Reading – Esther – 'whatever you ask for . . .')[3]
Holy Mass; Thanksgiving; Prayers; Act of Consecration to the Blessed Virgin Mary; Prayer for the gifts of the Holy Spirit; Lauds

Meditation 14:

Riconosci nell'offerta della Tua Chiesa la Vittima immolata per la nostra Redenzione [Look upon the oblation of Your Church, recognising the sacrificial Victim by whose death You willed to reconcile us to Yourself].[4]

'*Eucharistia facit Ecclesiam – Ecclesia facit Eucharistiam*' ['The Eucharist makes the Church – the Church makes the Eucharist'].

---

1 St Cyprian (*c.*200–258) was Bishop of Carthage and an important early Christian writer.

2 The encyclical *Redemptor hominis* (The Redeemer of Man) was Pope John Paul II's first encyclical. It was promulgated on 4 March 1979.

3 See Esther 7:2.

4 See Eucharistic Prayer III.

Padri del deserto [The Desert Fathers]

The way in which you celebrate the Eucharist shows what kind of priest you are.

The Liturgy of the Word – The liturgy of the sacrifice.

The joy of communion (*communio*) in Christ.

The Eucharist and the mission.

China; Rome.

The liturgical reform of Vatican II.

Terce; Passion of Our Lord Jesus Christ according to John

Meditation 15: *Cristo casto* [The chaste Christ].

Tre segni del Regno: castità – povertà – obbedienza [Three signs of the Kingdom: chastity – poverty – obedience].

Cristo casto [The chaste Christ] – celibate for the heavenly kingdom.

'Did you not know that I must be about my Father's business?'[1]

'Whoever does the will of God is my brother, and sister, and mother . . .'[2]

Do not hold Me, for I have not yet ascended to the Father.[3]

Paul VI, *Sacerdotalis caelibatus*:[4] Christological motivation.

Celibacy has an anthropological meaning.

The 144,000 in the Book of the Apocalypse.[5]

Sext; None; Meditation continued; (The Way of the Cross); Adoration of the Blessed Sacrament; Penitential psalms; Vespers

Meditation 16: *Cristo povero* [The poor Christ].

St Francis of Assisi
Mother Teresa of Calcutta
St Martin of Tours

'*Dio è Colui che non possiede e non può essere posseduto*' ['God is the One who does not possess and cannot be possessed'].

Cristo – icona di Dio povero [Christ – the icon of the poor God]; 'though He was rich, yet for your sake He became poor, so that by His poverty you might become rich.'[6]

---

1 See Luke 2:49.
2 See Mark 3:35.
3 See John 20:17.
4 The encyclical *Sacerdotalis caelibatus* (Of Priestly Celibacy) was promulgated by Pope Paul VI on 24 June 1967.
5 See Revelation 7:4.
6 See 2 Corinthians 8:9.

All the achievements of the Church throughout the ages have grown out of poverty.

Pascal (Pascal's death).

(*Poveri di Jahvè* [The poor of Yahweh].)

Jesus of Nazareth: poverty.

The First Sunday of Lent – the Gospel of Christ's temptation.

Anticipated Matins

'*Ubi caritas est vera*' ['Where true charity is'].

Meditation 17: *Cristo obbediente* [The obedient Christ].

'*Vengo per fare, o Dio, la Tua volontà*' ['I have come to do Thy will, O God'].[1]

The twelve-year-old Jesus.

Gethsemane.

'Obedient unto death, even death on a cross.'[2]

Adam – Christ.

per inobedientiam unius [by one man's disobedience].

per obedientiam Unius [by one Man's obedience].[3]

My food is to do the will of the Father.[4]

Fr Bidogar SJ, Fr de Lubac, St John of the Cross

'My hour' – the hour predicted and set by the Father.

For a Christian, obedience is also the way to the Father (it is more difficult to give orders than to listen).

Obedience comes from 'listening' (to the Word).

To love obedience.

Sinai – the Mount of Eight Beatitudes.

Rosary (I); Adoration of the Blessed Sacrament; Holy Hour; Compline

21 February

Intentions; Prayers; Eucharistic Adoration; Litany of the Polish Nation
Morning meditation: (Ezekiel – the Sermon on the Mount)
Holy Mass; Thanksgiving; Prayers; Act of Consecration to Our Lady (Grignion); Prayer for the gifts of the Holy Spirit; Lauds

Meditation 18:

Christ – the new Adam.

1 See Hebrews 10:7.
2 See Philippians 2:8.
3 See Romans 5:19.
4 See John 4:34.

(St Paul: the first Adam – the last Adam.)[1]

Disobedience – obedience [illegible].

In God's thought the last (second) Adam is before the first, even though *in ordine executionis* [in the order of execution] the second Adam comes after the first.

(The union of all things *in Christo* [in Christ]:[2] the leading thread of all history.)

Born before all creation.

The firstborn of the entire creation.

Adam – Christ.

Eve – Mary: the Mother of all living.

Christus – nostrum 'Amen' [Christ – our 'Amen'], 'Yes'.

Terce; Prayer for Good Friday

Meditation 19: '*Testimone fedele*' ['The faithful witness'].

(Revelation) The faithful witness.[3]

Revelation – the letter to the Churches – a Christological
Claudel book – Christ – the faithful Witness (Martyr).

Martirio dei Cristiani dei primi secoli e in tutti i secoli [The
D. Rops martyrdom of Christians of the early centuries and in all centuries].

martirio e battesimo [martyrdom and baptism].

martirio ed Eucaristia [martyrdom and the Eucharist].

Seven letters of St Ignatius of Antioch:

Then, St Anthony the Hermit, a special form of '*martyrium*' ['bearing witness'].

For all Christians are called to bear witness (*Martiri giapponesi* [Martyrs of Japan]).[4]

!!(*martiri del nostro secolo* [the martyrs of our age])

(*Tertio millennio adveniente*)[5]

martyrologium [martyrology]

Eastern Orthodox – Catholic – Anglican (Uganda) – Evangelicals

1 See 1 Corinthians 15:45.

2 See Ephesians 1:10.

3 See Revelation 1:5.

4 The Martyrs of Japan were a group of Christians who were executed by crucifixion on 5 February 1597 in Nagasaki. They were canonised by Pope Pius IX on 8 June 1862.

5 See n. 2, p. 416 [1 March 1996].

Alexander Men[1]
The Church is strong when it is crucified.
Jerzy Popiełuszko[2]
China
Albania (Cardinal Koliqi)[3]

Sext; None; Meditation continued; The Way of the Cross; Adoration of the Blessed Sacrament; Litany of the Saints; (Reading); Litany of the Sacred Heart of Jesus, Blessed Virgin Mary, St Joseph; Vespers

Meditation 20: '*Nostro Signore*' ['Our Lord'].

Paul

Dominus Noster [Our Lord].

'. . . God has bestowed on Him the name which is above every name'.

. . . Jesus Christ is Lord.[4]

Paul VI

ΚΥΡΙΟΣ [LORD].

La Signoria di Cristo si estende a tutte le cose visibili e invisibili [The reign of Christ extends to all things visible and invisible] – *è 'cosmica'* [it is 'cosmic'].

'*Pantokrator*' ['Almighty'].

(St Paul) '*pleroma*' ['fullness'].

The world knew Him not . . . He came to His own home, and His own people received Him not.[5]

Between 'already' . . . 'not yet' – constant tension.

Parousia: 'He who comes'.

The Feast of Christ the King is the culmination of the whole liturgical year of the Church.

Anticipated Matins (The Chair of St Peter)

---

1 Alexander Vladimirovich Men (1935–90) was an influential Russian Orthodox priest and theologian. He was the founder of the Open Orthodox University and one of the founders of the Russian Bible Society and *The World of the Bible* journal. He was murdered on 9 September 1990 by an axe-wielding assailant in his home town, Semkhoz.

2 Bl. Jerzy Popiełuszko (1947–84) was a Polish priest associated with the Solidarity movement in communist Poland. He was murdered in 1984 by the agents of the Security Service of the Polish Ministry of Internal Affairs. He was beatified on 6 June 2010 by Cardinal Angelo Amato on behalf of Pope Benedict XVI.

3 Mikel Koliqi (1902–97) was an Albanian priest and cardinal, and the founder of Catholic Action in Albania. He was arrested in February 1945 as the communist dictatorship began persecuting religious organisations. He spent five years in prison.

4 See Philippians 2:9, 11.

5 See John 1:10–11.

Meditation 21: *Veni Domine Jesu* [Come, Lord Jesus].

The world lives with an obsession of its destruction, its end.

The life of the Church is oriented towards '*Maranatha*' ['Our Lord, come'], towards the second coming.

'*Donec veniat*' ['Until He comes'].

Eternity has already 'entered' time.

'The time was fulfilled' with Christ's crucifixion and resurrection.[1]

We have already entered the fullness of time with the risen Christ.

What are we doing to advance His coming?

!*Eucharistia: parusia anticipata* [Eucharist: anticipated Parousia].

The ideal of Christian hope: the acclamation after the substantiation! The Lord's Day.

(The Final Judgement according to Mt. 25.)

Eternal life: And this is eternal life, that they know Thee, Father, and Jesus Christ whom Thou hast sent.[2]

The Parousia of Christ is the beginning of 'new creation'.

That God may be 'Everything to every one'.[3]

Rosary (II); Eucharistic Adoration; Meditation continued; Compline

22 February Intentions; Prayers; Adoration of the Blessed Sacrament
Morning meditation: (*cathedra S. Petri* [the Chair of St Peter])
Holy Mass; Thanksgiving; Prayers; Act of Consecration, Grignion de Montfort; Prayer for the gifts of the Holy Spirit; Lauds

Meditation 22: Mary:

Causa nostrae laetitiae;

The cause of our joy.

At the Annunciation.

Salvatore – Precursore [Saviour – Precursor].

Akathistos [the Akathist hymn]: rejoice!

AMDG.[4] JPII ☧

1 See Mark 1:15.
2 See John 17:3.
3 See 1 Corinthians 15:28.
4 See p. xxi.

'Blessed is the womb that bore You, and the breasts that You sucked . . .'[1]

Mary: ten days in the Upper Room, awaiting the coming of the Holy Spirit.

This is where '*devozione Mariana*' ['Marian devotion'] was born.

St Anselm

Claudel

[1966: (Piekary)![2]
Deus Pater omnium rerum creatarum
Maria Mater re-creatarum.
[God is the Father of all created things,
Mary is the Mother of re-created things].]

Cath. S. Petri [The Chair of St Peter].

Beatus es Simon Petre [Blessed are you, Simon Peter].[3]

Conclusion; Final words; Magnificat
UIOGD[4]

---

1 See Luke 11:27.

2 Piekary Śląskie is a city and pilgrimage site in the region of Silesia in southern Poland. Karol Wojtyła visited the Marian shrine in Piekary on numerous occassions between 1965 and 1978. In 1966, he took part in the millennial celebrations of the Christianisation of Poland in Piekary.

3 See Matthew 16:17.

4 See p. xxi.

1–7 March 1998
Exercitia Spiritualia [Spiritual Exercises] Led by Cardinal J[án] Ch[ryzostom] Korec SJ (Nitra)[1]

1 March

6.00 p.m.: Lenten Lamentations;[2] Exposition of the Blessed Sacrament; Vespers II: First Sunday of Lent

Introductory meditation (1):

The witness of the Church of catacombs in the twentieth century!

He came to bear witness.

Tertio millennio adveniente.[3]

Year of the Holy Spirit.

Twentieth century: two attempts (*experientiae* [experiments]) to live without God – perhaps they have become yet another discovery of the truth about God.

Curia Romana [The Roman Curia] – '*cenacolo permanente*' ['permanent Upper Room'].

Paul VI.

Silence and focus on God's presence.

Forza della Chiesa [the power of the Church].

Jesus Christus heri et hodie et in saecula [Jesus Christ is the same yesterday and today and for ever].[4]

Adoration of the Blessed Sacrament; Meditation continued; Anticipated Matins; Compline

2 March

Preparation for Holy Mass; Adoration of the Blessed Sacrament; Prayer for the gifts of the Holy Spirit; Litany of Polish Saints

---

1 Ján Chryzostom Korec SJ (1924–2015) was a Slovak priest, Bishop of Nitra and a cardinal. Because of the communist government's suppression of the Catholic Church, he spent many years working as a priest without governmental authorisation. He was imprisoned in 1960–68 and after his release from prison, he had to support himself as a labourer and factory worker.

2 See n. 6, p. 221 [11 March 1984].

3 See n. 2, p. 416 [1 March 1996].

4 See Hebrews 13:8.

Morning meditation: (*de die!* [for the day!])
Holy Mass; Thanksgiving; Prayers; Lauds

Meditation 2:

Da Dio o dal nulla? [Out of God or out of nothing?]

Creation!

Monod

No rational structure comes into being '*per casum*' ['by accident'].

The Book of Genesis: *contra* [in contrast]: various materialisms, evolutionism.

There is one God. The maker of heaven and earth:

God entrusted this truth to Israel.

The Creator of man: in the image and likeness of God '*dal nulla*' ['out of nothing']: The world could not have come into being by itself. It must have been created.

The Church – the new Israel – is to preach this fundamental truth about creation. It has to do it against the background of all the challenges of our age.

Passion of Our Lord Jesus Christ according to Matthew; Terce

Meditation 3: *Verità sull'uomo* [The truth about man].

Human being – *mysterium* [mystery].

Shakespeare

profunditas est homo et cor eius abyssus [man is profound and his heart is deep].[1]

Psalm 8.

Outer man – inner man.

What is man that God gave His Son?[2]

Chesterton

God – Man.

Man and the animate world.

Man – a being that prays. Human traces lead to God.

Michelangelo

(From the primitive traces to the Sistine Chapel.)

Pascal
Weizsäcker
Malraux

Christ: *perfetta immagine di Dio* [the perfect image of God].

[*Adamo – Cristo* [Adam – Christ]
primo – secondo Adamo [first – second Adam]]

How to protect the future of man!
The negation of God → the negation of man

1 See Psalm 63:7 (64:6).
2 See Psalm 8:5(4) and John 3:16.

Dio, abbi pietà di noi! [God, have mercy on us!]

Sext; None; Reflection on meditations II and III; Adoration of the Blessed Sacrament; Litany of the Saints; Reading; Litany of the Holy Name of Jesus, Blessed Virgin Mary, St Joseph; Vespers

Meditation 4:

'*Mysterium iniquitatis*' ['The mystery of evil']

Genesis 3. The sin of the human beginning.

The inheritance of the original sin – so visible in our century.

The experience of one's homeland and life.

Man opposed his 'own' plan for life to God's plan.

L'uomo presenta la fine della Creazione [Man represents the end of the creation].

Arriva a vantarsi del suo peccato [He goes so far as to take pride in his sin].

The consequence of sin is death.

'*Mors aeterna*' ['Eternal death'] is more dangerous than death.

The only Saviour – Jesus Christ.

Meditation 5: *Super praedicato* [On the statement]:

('*profunditas est homo et cor eius abyssus*' ['man is profound and his heart is deep']).[1]

Meditation [6]:

'*Salvatore promesso*' ['The promised Saviour'].

The history of Israel has its beginning in Abraham.

Isaiah's prophecy about Emmanuel born of a virgin.[2]

Jeremiah, Daniel, Micah.

'*Servo di Dio*' ['the Servant of God'] (Isaiah).

A man of sorrows.[3]

All this in the Proto-gospel.

Messia promesso e aspettato! [Promised and awaited Messiah!]

The promise speaks of a 'young woman' *promessa e aspettata* [promised and expected] (Mary).

1 See Psalm 63:7 (64:6).

2 See Isaiah 7:14.

3 See Isaiah 53:3.

John the Baptist – his vocation was to point to the Messiah who was present. In Him, the entire history of humankind reaches its culmination: 'The Word became flesh' (John 1).

Rosary (I); Eucharistic Benediction; Anticipated Matins; Meditation continued; Compline

3 March

Preparation for Holy Mass; Adoration of the Blessed Sacrament; Prayer for the gifts of the Holy Spirit; Litany of the Polish Nation
Morning meditation: (on the Word, on the Lord's Prayer)
Holy Mass; Thanksgiving; Prayers; Lauds

Meditation [7]:

Mysteria vitae Christi [Mysteries of Christ's Life].

Il Vangelo è una forza! [The Gospel is power!]

Jesus Christ – the only Mediator between God and man.

Only through Him can we come closer to the Father.

Every Mass includes all the *mysteria* [mysteries] of Christ's life.

The Gospel [is not] only a biography, but the '*annunzio di salvezza*' ['proclamation of salvation']. *Verità rivelata* [Revealed truth].

Life, cross, resurrection.

Everything is ongoing.

Christ works in the Church: the word and the sacraments.

Messaggio continuo [Continuous message].

How many people participate in this *Mysterium* [Mystery]!

The Mother of Christ integrally belongs to this *Mysterium.*

Christus heri hodie et in saecula [Christ is the same yesterday and today and for ever].[1]

We live His life, His salvific *Mysterium.*

Terce

Meditation [8]:

Primi discepoli [First disciples]: Andrew, Peter, Zebedee's sons, until then John the Baptist's disciples.

'Follow Me'.[2]

1 See Hebrews 13:8.
2 See Mark 1:17.

This is the beginning of a series of callings which belongs to the history of the Church:

Rabbi, where are you staying?

Come and see[1] – (the motto of Paris).[2]

They went, they saw, they stayed with Him.

Andrew brings Simon, his brother.

Christ to Simon: 'you shall be called Cephas, which means *Petrus/Pietro* [Peter, rock]'.[3]

Nomen – munus [Name – office].

'We have found the Messiah'.[4]

Munus Petri [The office of St Peter] for the Church.

Amore – Autorità [Love – Authority] – without which there could be no Church.

Peter's calling as a paradigm of all vocations in the Church.

Concluding meditation: 'Christ lives in me'.[5]
The Way of the Cross; Adoration of the Blessed Sacrament; Reading; Penitential psalms; Vespers; Litany of the Sacred Heart of Jesus, Blessed Virgin Mary, St Joseph

Meditation [9]:

'*Cristo parla anche a noi*' ['Christ speaks to us too'].

'*Spersonalizzazione*'. *Numeri* ['Depersonalisation'. Numbers]. Mass – not people.

The Holy Scriptures name and call by name. Jesus – person – the Good Shepherd calls everyone by their name; 'I have been with you so long, and yet you do not know Me'.[6]

'Martha, Martha' . . . etc.

'Mary' (after the resurrection).

'*Saulo, Saulo*' ['Saul, Saul'].

'Christ loved me and gave Himself up for me'.[7]

'He Himself knew what was in man';[8] He knew it from the inside.

The Samaritan woman, Nathanael, Zacchaeus. Christ

1 See John 1:38–39.
2 The theme of the Twelfth World Youth Day held in Paris in 1997 was: 'Teacher, where are you staying? Come and see'.
3 See John 1:42.
4 See John 1:41.
5 See Galatians 2:20.
6 See John 14:9.
7 See Ephesians 5:2.
8 See John 2:25.

knows and loves each of us in the same way. 'To whom shall we go?'[1]

'O Lord,
it is You who have set Your eyes on me
Today Your lips
have spoken my name.'[2]
'*Totus Tuus*' ['Entirely Yours']

Reflection continued.

Meditation [10]:
'*Segregatus in Evangelium*' ['Set apart for the Gospel'].[3]

Priestly vocations – *segregatus in Evangelium.*

Presbyterorum ordinis.[4]

'*Ut labia sacerdotum scientiam custodiant*' ['for the lips of a priest should guard knowledge'],[5] above all '*scientiam spiritualem*' ['spiritual knowledge']; *scientiae sacrae* [sacred knowledge].

Therefore a priest has to pray a lot and read a lot (*scientia sacra* [sacred knowledge]).

(Saints Cyril and Methodius.)

'*Segregatus in Evangelium*' ['Set apart for the Gospel'] by the power of the Holy Spirit, who creates authentic priestly identity in us.

People entrust their problems and secrets to the priest.

'*Donum et mysterium*' ['Gift and mystery'].

Holy priests.

Sacerdos – alter Christus [Priest – another Christ].

Holy priests,
whom God gave to Slovakia
in the time of persecutions.

Rosary (II); Eucharistic Benediction; Anticipated Matins; Reflection; Compline

1 See John 6:68.

2 This quotation is a refrain of John Paul II's favourite Polish song '*Barka*' ('My Boat'). It was written in 1974 by Father Stanisław Szmidt and is based on the Spanish song '*Pescador de hombres*' ('Fisher of men').

3 See Romans 1:1.

4 See n. 1, p. 160 [28 February 1980].

5 See Malachi 2:7.

4 March: Feast of St Casimir

Preparation for Holy Mass; Adoration of the Blessed Sacrament; Lauds of St Casimir; Prayer for the gifts of the Holy Spirit; Litany of the Polish Nation
Morning meditation: (liturgical texts – St Casimir)
Holy Mass; Thanksgiving; Prayers; Lauds

Meditation [11]: *Sacerdote immerso nei misteri* [Priest immersed in the mysteries].

Immersus in mysteriis!! [Immersed in the mysteries!!]

Life of faith, supernatural life.

To be a good shepherd, a priest has to be good to others!

The life of a priest 'exceeds' (goes beyond!) human life.

He remained alone to be for all.

s. Gregorius: ars artium regimen animarum [St Gregory: the government of souls is the art of all arts].

Don Bosco.

The priest has to preach difficult truths too (*de novissimis!* [on the last things!]).

Like Christ – the priest has to be '*immersus*' ['immersed'] in the mysteries of creation and redemption.

(Reflection after the meditation); Passion of Our Lord Jesus Christ according to Luke; Terce

Meditation [12]:

'*La parola viva di fede*' ['The living word of faith'].

Hegel

A priest '*immersus in Mysteriis*' ['immersed in the Mysteries'] is able to preach such a living word of faith. This word, at the same time, ought to be 'contemporary' to respond to the needs of people today.

The uses of literature and art.

The word of faith has to sound authentic in the context of many words of contemporary 'mass' culture. It has to be a word of faith, not only a word of human knowledge and technology.

'Sin' – an unavoidable topic.

The word of faith always points to the way to eternal life.

Topic: '*eternità*' ['eternity']!

[Example:
Mikojan and his mother.]

Sotto la guida dello Spirito Santo [Under the guidance of the Holy Spirit].[1]

Meditation continued; Sext; None; The Way of the Cross; Adoration of the Blessed Sacrament; Litany of the Saints; Litany of the Holy Name of Jesus, Blessed Virgin Mary, St Joseph; Vespers; Reading

Meditation [13]:

'*Vivificati dall'amore*' ['Made alive by love'].

Christ calls different people to different tasks (*munus – munera* [office – offices]).

There is no shortage of people, Christians, who follow the Lord Christ, opposing the 'world', in any given age.

There is no shortage of difficulties on their way.

The 'world' has its own ways. One has to lead a deep spiritual life not to give in.

They have to be meek.

They have to use methods that have been tried out before.

Witness of the 89-year old priest from Nitra:	*animato dall'amore di Cristo* [made alive by Christ's love]
	– and many others

Anticipated Matins

Meditation [14]:

'*Dalla preghiera alla missione*' ['From prayer to mission'].

How can you serve others without prayer? without Christ?

'Apart from Me you can do nothing'.[2]

Our priesthood grows together with prayer.

Prayer – the source of creativity – to pray means to meet God who comes.

If there is a 'crisis' in the Church, it is always a crisis of our prayer.

'Apostolate, activity, is already prayer' – this view needs to be corrected.

To speak of Christ means to speak from His abundance.

This is the experience of Christ's apostles of all times.

The contribution of Vatican II.

1 See Galatians 5:18.

2 See John 15:5.

Rosary (III); Eucharistic Benediction; Evening reflection; Compline

5 March

Preparation for Holy Mass; Adoration of the Blessed Sacrament; Prayer for the gifts of the Holy Spirit; Litany of the Polish Nation
Morning meditation: (*sec. textus liturgicos* [according to liturgical texts])
Holy Mass; Thanksgiving; Prayers; Lauds

Meditation [15]:

È Dio che fa crescere [It is God who makes one grow].[1]

The Church has made an effort to evangelise after Vatican II, but only God makes the seed grow despite the indifference, even hostility and hatred, of many.

'Have trust, I have overcome the world'.[2]

The twentieth century has confirmed this; many conversions!

Prayer to the Holy Spirit.

Terce; Passion of Our Lord Jesus Christ according to John

Meditation [16]:

(*Mistero della persona di Gesù* [Mystery of the person of Jesus]).

The cosmonaut's words about the earth that has become the homeland for the Son of God.[3]

(A huge number of publications on Christ).

Jesus Christ is the Son of Man if He is also the Son of God.

The witness borne by St Stephen.

Christ had to prepare the disciples gradually to receive this truth.

Prophet – and more than a prophet.

(Peter's declaration!!! (Matthew 16).)

Before Caiaphas: Christ's words: 'I and the Father are one'.[4]

Christ – present here: *Adoro Te devote* [I devoutly adore You].

Sext; None; Meditation continued; Adoration of the Blessed Sacrament; Reading; Penitential psalms; Litanies as usual; Vespers

1 See 1 Corinthians 3:7.
2 See John 16:33.
3 This may be a reference to James Benson Irwin (1930–91), an American astronaut and aeronautical engineer, who was the eighth person to walk on the Moon. He famously remarked that 'Jesus walking on the earth is more important than man walking on the moon'.
4 See John 10:30.

venerdì **6** settembre

s. Petronio vescovo

Friday Freitag Vendredi Пятница Viernes

September September Septembre Сентябрь Septiembre

13. Medit. XV

„Vivificati dal amore" ~~[illegible]~~

[Chrystus prowadzi różnych do nowych zadań uczniów]

~~nie brakuje~~ w każdej epoce ludzi, chcących którzy idą za Chrystusem Panem, przeciwstawiając się „światu"

Trudności na tej drodze nie brakuje.

„Świat" ma swoje sposoby. Trzeba głębokiego życia wewn., aby nie ulec.

muszą być pokorni
muszą stosować wypróbowane środki

świadectwo ~~[illegible]~~ kapłana z [illegible]

i animato dal amore di Cristo

i [illegible] innych.

14. Matut. anticipatum

15. Medit. XIII

„Dalla preghiera alla missione"

Jakże można bez modlitwy służyć wszystkim? bez Chrystusa?

„Beze Mnie nic uczynić nie możecie"

Kapłaństwo [illegible] rośnie [illegible] z modlitwy

Modlitwa – źródło [illegible]

modlitwa ~~[illegible]~~ Boga, który przychodzi.

L M M G V S D L M M G V S D L
16 17 18 19 20 21 22 23 24 25 26 27 28 29 30

Meditation [17]:
'*Ultima cena*' ['Last supper'].

Credo quidquid dixit Dei Filius nil hoc verbo Veritatis verius. [I believe all that the Son of God has spoken, there is nothing truer than this word of truth.]	From the retreat leader's own experience of adolescence under communism.

The events of the Last Supper (Eucharistic Canon IV) and, at the same time, *Mysterium* [Mystery].

Dostoyevsky

Mysterium fidei! [The mystery of faith!].

The sacrifice of the new and eternal covenant.

Adoro Te devote [I devoutly adore You].

Anticipated Matins

Meditation [18]:
(*La Croce, il giudizio della grazia* [The Cross, the judgement of grace].)

Evening prayer, in a way 'vespers of redemption'.

The final words of Christ: 'Father, forgive . . .'[1]

(Witness borne by an atheist.)

The agony of the Son of God.

'*Per riunire insieme i dispersi figli di Dio*' ['To gather into one the children of God who are scattered abroad'.][2]

The sacrifice of love.

Cross, the judgement of grace.

Redemptor mundi salva nos! [Redeemer of the world, save us!].

Fulget Crucis mysterium [The mystery of the Cross gleams].

Rosary (I); Eucharistic Benediction; (Holy Hour); Compline

6 March

Preparation for Holy Mass; Adoration of the Blessed Sacrament; Prayer for the seven gifts of the Holy Spirit; Litany of the Polish Nation
Morning meditation: (*sec. liturgiam diei* [according to the liturgy for the day])
Holy Mass; Thanksgiving; Prayers; Lauds

1 See Luke 23:34.
2 See John 11:52.

Meditation [19]:

Alla risurrezione attraverso la morte [Through death to resurrection].

'The Son of Man must be lifted up (on the cross), so that the risen one is revealed'.[1]

Esaltazione [lifting up] (crucifixion) – *glorificazione* [glorification].

There is a deep connection between the two.

Death and resurrection constitute one *mysterium* [mystery]. In this mystery and through this mystery Christ fulfilled the redemptive mission for which He came into the world. This is an absolute '*novità*' ['novelty']!

['the empty tomb'
'*apparizioni del Risorto*'
['the appearances of the Risen (Christ)']]

Senza la Risurrezione non ci sarebbe un Vangelo [Without the Resurrection there would be no Gospel]: if Christ has not been raised, then our faith is in vain.[2] The Church, mission, everything, have drawn their primary justification from Christ's resurrection.

Through His resurrection, Christ has drawn all to Himself! By the power of the Holy Spirit: *abisso del mistero* [the depth of the mystery].

Reflection; (Prayers for Good Friday); Terce

Meditation [20]:

(*Gesù nell'Eucaristia – il dono dei doni* [Jesus in the Eucharist – the gift of gifts].)

La Morte di Cristo nella Croce era un Sacrificio salvifico [Christ's Death on the Cross was a salvific Sacrifice].

The sacrifice made was accepted by the Father: *Morte e Risurrezione* [Death and Resurrection].

The Eucharist: the sacrament of death and resurrection.

Vittima glorificata [The glorified Victim] (Apocalypse).

1 See John 3:14.
2 See 1 Corinthians 15:14.

Signore glorificato: mistero dell'eternità sacramentalmente presente nell'Eucaristia [The glorified Lord: the mystery of eternity sacramentally present in the Eucharist].

This is also the *culmen* [highest point] of God's love – it is not possible to go further than that.

This is expressed, made real, in every Eucharist, every day around the world.

Corpo spiritualizzato [Spiritual body],[1] 'The Lord is the Spirit'.[2]

Nell'Eucaristia il Cristianesimo è insuperabile
[In the Eucharist, Christianity is insuperable].

Reflection; Sext; None; The Way of the Cross; Adoration of the Blessed Sacrament; Reading; Vespers

Meditation [21]:

'*La Chiesa del Signore*' ['The Church of the Lord'].

Lumen gentium [Light of the nations].

Chiesa – sua efficienza dipende da Dio [The Church – its efficacy depends on God].

Successo invisibile [invisible success]; difficult to 'measure' and to 'count'.

On criticism in the Church.

Evangelical 'revolution' without bloodshed.

On the contribution of the Church to social transformations and cultural development.

(Slovak experience.)

Attachment to the Church. Respect and love for the Apostolic See.

Cristo e Chiesa vanno insieme [Christ and the Church walk together].

Simon, do you love me?[3]

Gratitudine per la Chiesa, 'Madre e Maestra' [Gratitude to the Church, 'Mother and Teacher'].

Reflection

1 See 1 Corinthians 15:44.
2 See 2 Corinthians 3:17.
3 See John 21:15–17.

Meditation [22]:

'*Madre della Chiesa*' ['The Mother of the Church'].

(*L[umen] G[entium]* VIII), *R[edemptoris] M[ater].*

The Mother of the Church in the Church of the Apostles (Jerusalem): '*assidui nella preghiera*' ['they devoted themselves to the prayers'].[1]

Preghiera di Maria
[Mary's prayer].
'*Conservava nel suo Cuore*'
['kept in her Heart'].[2]

{ The Upper Room
Pentecost

Maria 'immersa' nella meditazione dei Misteri [Mary 'immersed' in meditation on the mysteries].

Marian devotion – personal, but also communal. *Ausiliatrice dei cristiani* [Help of Christians].

Rosary (II); Eucharistic Benediction; Concluding meditation; Compline

7 March: Feast of Ss Perpetua and Felicity

Preparation for Holy Mass; Adoration of the Blessed Sacrament; Prayer for the gifts of the Holy Spirit
Morning meditation: (*sec. textus liturg.* [according to liturgical texts])
Holy Mass; Thanksgiving; Prayers; Lauds

Meditation [23]:

'*Spirito S. nella Chiesa*' ['The Holy Spirit in the Church'].

Pentecoste [Pentecost] that continues in the Church: *la discesa dello Spirito S. continua* [the descent of the Holy Spirit continues] in our age, to no smaller degree than at any other point.

God is greater than our hearts.[3]

[the experience
of the atheistic system
has confirmed the work
of the Holy Spirit – also now!]

1 See Acts 2:42.
2 See Luke 2:19.
3 See 1 John 3:20.

The Roman Curia: '*permanente cenacolo*' ['permanent Upper Room']: *flatus Spiritus S.* [the breath of the Holy Spirit]. (*De V.* [On V.]).

Conclusion; Final words; Magnificat
UIOGD[1]

1 See p. xxi.

21–27 February 1999
Exercitia Spiritualia [Spiritual Exercises] Led by Bishop A[ndré-Joseph] M[utien] Léonard of Namur[1]

21 February 6.00 p.m.: Lenten Lamentations;[2] Exposition of the Blessed Sacrament; Vespers II (for the First Sunday of Lent)

[*L'eterna Trinità. Viatico dell'uomo*
sul cammino del terzo millennio.
[The Eternal Trinity. Human viaticum
on the way into the third millennium.]]

Introductory meditation (1): *Convertirsi all'Unico Necessario* [To convert to the one thing that is necessary].[3]

The beginning of Lent.
Christ calls us to convert.
Christ, who loves us.
Apocalypse: to the Seven Churches — Christ – the beginning of the final times.
The Church in waiting.
Do you love me?[4]
He knocks at our door.[5]

Adoration of the Blessed Sacrament; Meditation continued; Compline

22 February Preparation for Holy Mass; Adoration of the Blessed Sacrament; Prayer for the gifts of the Holy Spirit; Litany of the Polish Nation
Meditation: *Cath. S. Petri* [The Chair of St Peter]
Holy Mass; Thanksgiving; Prayers; Lauds

---

1 André-Joseph Léonard (b. 1940) is a Belgian priest who has served as Bishop of Namur, Archbishop of Mechelen-Brussels and Primate of Belgium.
2 See n. 6, p. 221 [11 March 1984].
3 See Luke 10:42.
4 See John 21:15–17.
5 See Revelation 3:20.

Meditation 2:

Il Figlio Unico di Dio [The Only Son of God].

I and the Father are one[1] etc.

Passion of Our Lord Jesus Christ according to Matthew; Terce

Meditation 3: *Giovedì Santo* [Maundy Thursday].*

'He loved them to the end'.[2]

* The talks are very rich in content. It is difficult to note down everything. We trust that the full text will be published.

Sext; None; Adoration of the Blessed Sacrament; The Way of the Cross; (Reflection after meditations II and III); Litany of the Saints; Litany of the Holy Name of Jesus, Blessed Virgin Mary, St Joseph; Reading; Vespers

Meditation 4: *Venerdì S.* [Good Friday].

'My God, my God, why hast Thou forsaken me?'[3]

Reflection on the meditation

Meditation 5: *Sabato S.* [Holy Saturday].

'*E in spirito andò ad annunziare la salvezza agli spiriti che attendevano in prigione*' ['In the Spirit he went and preached salvation to the spirits in prison'] (1 Peter 3:19).

Rosary (I); Adoration of the Blessed Sacrament; Anticipated Matins; Concluding meditation of the day; Compline

23 February Preparation for Holy Mass; Adoration of the Blessed Sacrament; Prayer for the gifts of the Holy Spirit; Litany of the Polish Nations
Meditation of the day: (St Polycarp)
Holy Mass; Thanksgiving; Prayers; Lauds

Meditation 6:

Il Figlio abbandonato e glorificato [The abandoned and glorified Son].

'God has made Him both Lord and Christ, this Jesus whom you crucified'.[4]

Resurrection; glorification.

Passion of Our Lord Jesus Christ according to Mark; Terce

1 See John 10:30.
2 See John 13:1.
3 See Matthew 27:46.
4 See Acts 2:36.

Meditation 7:

'*Gesù, unico Salvatore del mondo*' ['Jesus, the only Saviour of the world'].

'There is no other name under heaven given among men by which they could be saved'.[1]

(The certainty of salvation in Christ.)

Sext; None; Adoration of the Blessed Sacrament; The Way of the Cross; (Reflection after talks VI and VII); Penitential psalms; Litany of the Sacred Heart of Jesus, Blessed Virgin Mary, St Joseph; Reading; Vespers

Meditation 8:

'*Credi tu questo*? Do you believe this? Yes, Lord, I believe that you are the Christ, the Son of the living God'.[2]

Reflection after the meditation: (Solovyov: Anti-Christ)![3]

Meditation 9:

'*Gesù Cristo, dimora e sorgente dello Spirito*' ['Jesus Christ, the dwelling and source of the Spirit'].

'He on whom you see the Spirit descend and remain . . . this is He who baptises with the Holy Spirit' (John 1:33).

Rosary (III); Adoration of the Blessed Sacrament; Anticipated Matins; Final (concluding) meditation of the day; Compline

24 February Preparation for Holy Mass; Adoration of the Blessed Sacrament; Prayer for the gifts of the Holy Spirit; Litany of the Polish Nation
Morning meditation: (Jonah – Nineveh)
Holy Mass; Thanksgiving; Prayers; Lauds

Meditation 10:

Lo Spirito del Padre e del Figlio [The Spirit of the Father and the Son].

God has sent the Spirit of His Son into our hearts, crying, 'Abba, Father'.[4]

The Trinitarian mystery.

Rublev's icon.[5]

'*Filioque*' ['and from the Son'].

---

1 See Acts 4:12.

2 See John 11:26–27.

3 Possibly a reference to Vladimir Solovyov, *War, Progress, and the End of History: Three Conversations, Including a Short Tale of the Antichrist*, trans. Alexander Bakshy (Great Barrington, MA, 1990).

4 See Galatians 4:6.

5 The most famous icon by Andrei Rublev, a fifteenth-century Russian painter, is *The Trinity* (Russian: *Troitsa*).

Terce

Meditation 11:

'*Dulcis hospes animae*' ['Sweet guest of the soul'].

'God's love has been poured into our hearts through the Holy Spirit who has been given to us' (Romans 5:5).

(St John of the Cross.)

Sext; None; Adoration of the Blessed Sacrament; The Way of the Cross; (Reflection after the morning talks); Litany of the Saints; Litany of the Holy Name of Jesus, Blessed Virgin Mary, St Joseph; Reading; Vespers

Meditation 12:

'*La speranza di una vita nuova*' ['The hope of a new life'].

'The Spirit helps us in our weakness' (Romans 8:2).

(Romans 8 – '*speranza cronica*' ['persistent hope'].)

We need the full text very much!

Meditation 13:

'*Il Padre del Signore nostro Gesù Cristo*' ['The Father of our Lord Jesus Christ'].[1]

No one knows the Father except the Son.[2]

Rosary (III); Adoration of the Blessed Sacrament; Anticipated Matins; Concluding meditation; Compline

25 February Preparation for Holy Mass; Adoration of the Blessed Sacrament; Prayer for the gifts of the Holy Spirit; Litany of the Polish Nation
Morning meditation: (*textus diei* [texts for the day]): Esther, a school of prayer
Holy Mass; Thanksgiving; Prayers; Lauds

Meditation 14:

L'eterna paternità di Dio [The eternal fatherhood of God].

'He is the image of the invisible God, the firstborn of all creation (Col.)'.[3]

Terce

Meditation 15:

Il 'Padre nostro' [The 'Our Father'].

'Pray then like this:

Our Father who art in heaven'.[4]

1 See e.g. Ephesians 1:3, 1 Peter 1:3, 2 Corinthians 1:3.
2 See Matthew 11:27.
3 See Colossians 1:15.
4 See Matthew 6:9.

Passion according to John; Sext; None; Adoration of the Blessed Sacrament; Reflection after the meditation; Penitential psalms; Litanies: Sacred Heart of Jesus, Blessed Virgin Mary, St Joseph; Reading; Vespers

Meditation 16:

La 'confessione di Cristo' [The 'confession of Christ'].

'For our sake God "made" Him to be sin who knew no sin, so that in Him we might become the righteousness of God' (2 Cor. 5:21).

Anticipated Matins

Meditation 17:

The sacrament of reconciliation.

We beseech you on behalf of Christ, be reconciled to God (2 Cor. 5:20).

[*Assumendo le nostre parole confessionali nella sua grande Confessione.*
[Taking the words of our confessions into his great Confession.]] !

Adoration of the Blessed Sacrament; Rosary (I); Holy Hour; Compline

26 February Preparation for Holy Mass; Adoration of the Blessed Sacrament; Prayer for the gifts of the Holy Spirit; Litany of the Polish Nation; Morning meditation; Holy Mass; Thanksgiving; Prayers; Lauds

Meditation 18:

At the evening of life, we shall be judged on our love.[1]

As you did it to one of the least of these my brethren, you did it to Me.[2]

Terce

Meditation 19:

Trinità, Eucaristia – sacerdozio [Trinity, Eucharist – priesthood].

(The multiplication of bread, Mt. 25.)

Sext; None; Eucharistic Adoration; The Way of the Cross; (Reflection); Litany of the Saints; Litanies; Reading; Vespers

1 See the *Catechism of the Catholic Church*, 1022.

2 See Matthew 25:40.

Meditation 20:

Maria, Madre della nostra fede e del nostro amore [Mary, Mother of our faith and our love]. '*Maria . . . serbava tutte queste cose meditandole nel suo cuore*' ['Mary . . . kept all these things, pondering them in her heart'] (Lk.).[1]

Meditation 21:

Spes nostra salve! [Hail our hope!][2]

'The Spirit and the Bride say, "Come"'.[3]

Rosary (II); Adoration of the Blessed Sacrament; Anticipated Matins; Reflection on the whole retreat; Compline

27 February Preparation for Holy Mass; Adoration of the Blessed Sacrament; Prayer for the gifts of the Holy Spirit; Litany of the Polish Nation; Morning meditation; Holy Mass; Thanksgiving; Prayers; Lauds

Meditation 22:

Desiderare molto, desiderare tutto [To wish for much, to wish for all].

'If any one thirst, let him come . . .'[4] Amen. Come, Lord Jesus.

Conclusion; Final words; Magnificat
UIOGD[5]

1 See Luke 2:19.
2 See the hymn *Salve Regina* (Hail Holy Queen).
3 See Revelation 22:17.
4 See John 7:37.
5 See p. xxi.

12–18 March 2000
Exercitia Spiritualia [Spiritual Exercises] Topic: '*Testimoni della Speranza*' ['Witnesses to Hope'] Led by Monsignore [François Xavier Nguyễn] Văn Thuận[1]

~

12 March

6.00 p.m.: Lenten Lamentations;[2] Exposition of the Blessed Sacrament; Vespers II (First Sunday of Lent)

Introductory meditation (1):

'*Genealogia di Gesù Cristo*' ['The genealogy of Jesus Christ'].[3]

- patriarchs; (Matthew/Luke)
- kings; the family of David
- kings.

  Virtue – and sin
  Faithfulness – and unfaithfulness
  Promise
  Grace – mercy.

Adoration of the Blessed Sacrament; Meditation continued; Anticipated Matins; Compline

13 March

Prayers; Adoration of the Blessed Sacrament; Prayer for the gifts of the Holy Spirit; Litany of the Polish Nation; Morning meditation; Holy Mass; Thanksgiving; Prayers; Lauds
(*Spera in Deum* [Trust in God])

Talk/Meditation 2:

'*Simon, quid dicis de meipso?*' ['Simon, what do you say about me?'][4]

---

1 François-Xavier Nguyễn Văn Thuận (1928–2002), Servant of God, was Bishop of Nha Trang and Coadjutor Archbishop of Saigon. In 1975, he was imprisoned and sent to a 're-education camp' by the communist government of Vietnam. He was released 1988 and forced to go into exile. He served as the President of the Pontifical Council for Justice and Peace in Rome, and in 2001 he was made a cardinal.

2 See n. 6, p. 221 [11 March 1984].

3 See Matthew 1:1–17 and Luke 3:23–38.

4 See Matthew 16:15.

(Jesus does not remember sins.)
(Parables.)
(Gospel paradoxes.)
He does not measure.
He is love.
He is mercy (Sister Faustyna).[1]
(*Gesù Salvatore* [Jesus, Saviour],
mia speranza [my hope].)
Mater misericordiae [Mother of mercy].
Mater spei [Mother of hope].

Terce; Sext; None; Passion of Our Lord Jesus Christ according to Matthew

Talk/Meditation 3:
'*Redde rationem villicationis tuae*' ['Turn in the account of your stewardship'].[2]

Un bilancio all'inizio XXI secol. [A recapitulation at the beginning of the twenty-first century].

(*Jubil. della Curia* [Jubilee of the Curia].)
The Apocalypse: to the Seven Churches.[3]
(*Adsumus Domine* [We have come, Lord].)

The Way of the Cross (short); Angelus; Reading; Litany of the Saints and the usual litanies; Vespers

Talk/Meditation 4:
'*Sic Deus dilexit mundum*' ['God so loved the world'].[4]
(*Il mondo dell'oggi!* [The world of today!])
G[audium et] S[pes] (The Church in the present world).
The Testament of Paul VI, Servant of God.

'Statistical' data speak of multidimensional progress, at the same time, there are negative indicators, including – the crisis of moral values.

In this context:
Anno Sancto iubilare [to rejoice in the Holy Year].

1 St Faustyna Kowalska OLM (1905–38) was a Polish nun and mystic. Her visions inspired the Catholic devotion to the Divine Mercy. She was canonised by Pope John Paul II on 30 April 2000.
2 See Luke 16:2.
3 See Revelation 1:11.
4 See John 3:16.

The Church – hope of the world – Christ, crucified and

(Pascal) risen from the dead.

Maria – spes nostra [Mary – our hope].

Talk/Meditation 5:

?'*porro unum*' ['hence one thing'].[1]

?*Dio e non la opera di Dio* [God and not the works of God]

– the calling of Abraham; unconditional trust in God, who calls a '*nube dei testimoni*' ['cloud of witnesses'].[2]

Văn Thuận's personal experience.

work that we do as the 'work of God'.

(*ad Hebr.* [Letter to the Hebrews].)

Porro unum est necessarium [One thing is needful].[3]

'*Se seguite Gesù, la gente vi seguirà*' ['If you follow Jesus, people will follow you'].

Martirio di S. Cypriano [The martyrdom of St Cyprian].

Rosary (I); Adoration of the Blessed Sacrament; Anticipated Matins; Concluding meditation; Compline

14 March Morning prayers; Adoration; Prayer for the gifts of the Holy Spirit; Litany of the Polish Nation; Lauds

Morning meditation: (*de die* [for the day])

Holy Mass; Thanksgiving; Litanies of the Sacred Heart of Jesus, Blessed Virgin Mary, St Joseph; Terce; Sext; None; Daily prayers; Lauds celebrated in the chapel

Evdokimov ⟶ Talk/Meditation 6:

L'avventura della speranza [The adventure of hope].

('*Sive manducatis, sive bibitis*' ['Whether you eat or drink'].)[4]

(*Il momento presente* [The present moment]).

(*Vivere il momento presente* [To live in the present moment].)

Christus heri et hodie

[Christ yesterday and today] (!)[5]

!(the experience of imprisonment – !)

(Hour, minute, second)

in Cristo [in Christ].

---

1 See Luke 10:42.

2 See Hebrews 12:1.

3 See Luke 10:42.

4 See 1 Corinthians 10:31.

5 See Hebrews 13:8.

in Dio/immersi in Dio [in God/immersed in God].

Sacramenti del momento presente [sacraments of the present moment].

(Paul VI's Testament)

The experience of the prisoner-bishop.

(Concern for the diocese.)

If I follow Christ in every 'now' of my whole life, He will lead us through . . .

(Sr Faustyna.)

Passion of Our Lord Jesus Christ according to Mark; (Terce celebrated in the chapel)

Talk/Meditation (7):

'*Verba mea Spiritus et vita sunt*' ['My words are Spirit and life'].[1]

Essere Parola [To be Word].

Parole di Gesù [Jesus' words] cannot be compared to anything.

(To whom shall we go? You have the words of eternal life.)[2]

(Dei Verbum)

(St Jerome)

The experience of a prisoner '*Vademecum*' ['Go with me'].

– *Verbo che prende dimora in noi* [The Word that dwells in us].[3]

– *verba in Verbo* [the words in the Word].

Annunciare [To preach].

Vivere [To live].

Servire il Vangelo della speranza [To serve the Gospel of hope].

The Way of the Cross; Penitential psalms; Reading; Vespers

Talk/Meditation 8:

Vinculum perfectionis [The bond of perfect unity].[4]

L'atto d'amore [The act of love]:

↓

non basta teoria [theory is not enough].

(Mother Teresa.)

John XXIII.

1 See John 6:63.

2 See John 6:68.

3 See Colossians 3:16.

4 See Colossians 3:14.

Per amare la persona; bisogna accostarla [to love a person, one has to get close to them].

(*persona, non* [illegible] [person, not . . .])

!!! experience from prison: '*lei ci ama?*' ['do you love us?'].

↓ . . . '*gli amò fino alla fine*' ['he loved them to the end'].[1]

about the pectoral cross(!) that comes from prison.

Talk/Meditation (9):

Extra muros – omnia omnibus [Outside the walls – all things to all men].[2]

Il popolo di Dio a noi affidato [The people of God entrusted to us].

The memories of the bishop-prisoner: the deportation '*extra muros*' ['outside the walls'].

Christ – *mortuus extra muros* [died outside the city walls], numbered with the transgressors.[3]

Just like the apostles, we are called to go 'into all the world'[4] – *extra muros di Gerusalemme* [outside the walls of Jerusalem].

'*Consummatum est*' ['It is finished'].[5]

Missions!

St Paul.

Rosary (II); Adoration of the Blessed Sacrament; Anticipated Matins; Concluding meditation; Compline

15 March

Morning prayers; Adoration of the Blessed Sacrament; Prayer for the gifts of the Holy Spirit; Litany of the Polish Nation; Lauds
Morning meditation: *de die* [for the day]
Holy Mass: *Speranza contro ogni speranza* [Hope against all hope]; Terce; Sext; None

↙↗

Lauds, Terce [celebrated] in the chapel

Talk/Meditation (10):

Eloi, Eloi, lama sabachthani [My God, My God, why hast Thou forsaken Me?][6]

1 See John 13:1.
2 See 1 Corinthians 9:22.
3 See Isaiah 53:12.
4 See Mark 16:15.
5 See John 19:30.
6 See Mark 15:34.

(*Abbandonato dal Padre* [Abandoned by the Father].)
↓ (the experience of imprisonment.)
kenosis [self-emptying].
↓ impoverishment.
the perfection of redemptive love.
In my flesh I complete what is lacking
in Christ's afflictions
for the sake of His Body – the Church.[1]

Passion of Our Lord Jesus Christ according to Luke; Litanies as usual

Talk/Meditation (11):

Nunc corpus dividi potest? [Can the body be divided now?].
Affinché il mondo creda [So that the world may believe].[2]
(Ecumenism)

- 13 January. St Paul
- document on justification

[illegible]

- the case of Hus[3]
- the Egyptian Patriarch Schenouda[4]
- *Domenica del perdono* [Forgiveness Sunday].[5]

Litany of the Saints; *Angelus*; Reading; Vespers

Talk/Meditation (12):

ad Hebr. [Letter to the Hebrews]

Semen Christianorum [The seed of Christianity]. cf. *T[ertio] M[illennio] A[dveniente].*
Martiri oggi [Martyrs today].
(*Martiri vietnamiti* [The Vietnamese Martyrs].)[6]

---

1 See Colossians 1:24.

2 See John 17:21.

3 Jan Hus (*c.*1372–1415) was a Czech priest, philosopher and early Christian reformer. He was a key predecessor to Protestantism and was burned at the stake for heresy against the doctrines of the Catholic Church.

4 See n. 3, p. 243 [28 February 1985].

5 Forgiveness Sunday is celebrated by the Eastern Orthodox Christians in the last week before Lent (the eighth week before Eastern Orthodox Easter).

6 The Vietnamese Martyrs fall into several groupings: from those of the Dominican and Jesuit missionary era of the seventeenth century to those killed in the politically inspired persecutions of the nineteenth century. The Vatican estimates the number of Vietnamese martyrs at between 130,000 and 300,000. John Paul II decided to canonise those whose names are known and unknown on 19 June 1988, giving them a single feast day (24 November).

vidi turbam magnam quam dinumerare nemo potest [I saw a great multitude which no man could number]

(Solovki Islands)[1] ⟷ ecumenical meaning of *Martyria* [martyrdom].

Lager.

St Maksymilian M. Kolbe.

Martiri dell'odio etnico in Burundi/Ruanda [Martyrs of ethnic hatred in Burundi/Rwanda].

Martiri della purezza (mgr Romero) [Martyrs of purity (Mgr Romero)].[2]

O Crux ave, spes unica [Hail to the cross, our only hope].

Anticipated Matins

Talk/Meditation (13):

'*In oratione Dei*' ['In prayer to God'].[3]

(*Il testimonio di Gesù* [The testimony of Jesus].)

(Prayer – union with God.)

Many examples (to be prayer).

'*Pregare sempre*' ['To pray constantly'].[4]

(Patriarch Athenagoras)

Difficulties in prayer.

(The experience of imprisonment.)

(*Pregare con il testamento di Gesù* [To pray with Jesus' testament].)

Rosary (III); Adoration of the Blessed Sacrament; Concluding meditation; Compline

16 March

Morning prayers; Adoration of the Blessed Sacrament; Prayer for the gifts of the Holy Spirit; Litany of Polish Saints; Lauds; Morning meditation; Holy Mass; Thanksgiving; Prayers

Meditation/Talk (14):

'*Caro mea pro mundi vita*' ['My flesh for the life of the world'].[5]

Concorporei et consanguinei in Cristo [Partaking in the body and blood of Christ].

---

1 The Solovetsky Islands, or Solovki, are an archipelago located in the Onega Bay of the White Sea, Russia. After the October Revolution, the islands attained notoriety as the site of the first Soviet prison camp (gulag), opened in 1921.

2 Bl. Óscar Arnulfo Romero y Galdámez (1917–80) was a priest and the Archbishop of San Salvador. He spoke out against poverty and social injustice. He was assassinated while offering Mass in the chapel of the Hospital of Divine Providence in 1980. He was declared a martyr by Pope Francis on 3 February 2015 and was beatified on 23 May 2015.

3 See Luke 6:12.

4 See 1 Thessalonians 5:17.

5 See John 6:51.

Hoc facite in meam memoriam [Do this in memory of me].[1]

(Memories from prison.)

The Eucharist among prisoners.

'*Assidui in fractione panis*' ['They devoted themselves to the breaking of bread'].[2]

dottrina soc. della Chiesa [the social teaching of the Church].

Passion of Our Lord Jesus Christ according to John; Litanies as usual (Sacred Heart of Jesus, Blessed Virgin Mary, St Joseph); Terce; Sext; None

Talk/Meditation (15):

Jesus vivens in Ecclesia sua [Jesus living in his Church].

Con voi tutti i giorni [I am with you all days].[3]

Synodi continentales: Christus in Ecclesia [Continental synods: Christ in the Church].

Witness borne by Christians.

'if you have love for one another'.[4]

Curia Rom., Xristus [the Roman Curia, Christ] among us.

Grace of the Jubilee!

Penitential psalms; *Angelus*; (Reading); Vespers

Talk/Meditation (16):

Imago Trinitatis [Image of the Trinity].

La mia speranza è la Chiesa [The Church is my hope].

La Chiesa è comunione perché partecipa alla vita della Santissima Trinità [The Church is communion because it participates in the life of the Most Holy Trinity]. Vatican II

dimensione spirituale/personale [spiritual/personal dimension].

e anche sociale/materiale [and also social/material].

servizio (diaconia) della Curia [service (diaconia) of the Curia].

visita 'ad limina' ['*ad limina*' visit].[5]

↗↙

students of Rome

('prison'.)

1 See Luke 22:19.

2 See Acts 2:42.

3 See Matthew 28:20.

4 See John 13:35.

5 See n. 2, p.425 [19 February 1997].

Anticipated Matins

Talk/Meditation (17):

Sicut Tu in Me et Ego in Te [As Thou art in Me, and I in Thee].[1]

(*Vivere la comunione* [Living out the communion].)

Nuova Pentecoste della Chiesa [New Pentecost of the Church].

Spinga lo Spirito S. [May the Holy Spirit prompt].

fratello – via alla santificazione [brother – the way to sanctification].

prossimo – accogliere l'altro [neighbour – to receive the other].

'Prison.'

'*Prima va a riconciliarti con tuo fratello*' ['First go and be reconciled to your brother'].[2]

'*Comunicazione*' ['Communication'].

St Teresa: '*Castello interiore*' ['The Interior Castle'].

Rosary (I); Adoration of the Blessed Sacrament; Concluding meditation; Holy Hour; Compline

17 March: Commemoration of St Patrick

Morning prayers; Adoration of the Blessed Sacrament; Prayer for the seven gifts of the Holy Spirit; Litany of the Polish Nation; Lauds; Morning meditation; Holy Mass; Thanksgiving; Prayers

Talk/Meditation (18):

Pusillus grex [Little flock].

'*Non abbiate paura*' ['Fear not'].[3]

(The situation of minority.)

(The story of Gideon.)

minoranza qualitativa [qualitative minority].

(David/Goliath.)

(*Chiesa ha le sue armi per combattere* [The Church has weapons for the battle]).

The kingdom of God is like a grain of mustard seed, the smallest of all the seeds.[4]

1 See John 17:21.
2 See Matthew 5:24.
3 See Luke 12:32.
4 See Mark 4:31.

La Chiesa è chiamata a vivere di questo stile ('minoritario') [The Church is called to live in this way ('minority')], which is confirmed by the figures of the saints (for example, St Francis).

Procedamus in Nomine Domini
[Let us go in the Name of the Lord]
'le mura della nuova Gerico cadranno'
['the walls of the new Jericho will fall'].

Terce; Sext; None; Litanies as usual: Sacred Heart of Jesus, Blessed Virgin Mary, St Joseph; Prayers for Good Friday

Talk/Meditation 19:

(*Accipite Spiritum Sanctum* [Receive the Holy Spirit].)[1]

(*Per rinnovare la faccia della terra* [To renew the face of the earth].)[2]

Opera dello Spirito S. nei primi secoli della Chiesa e nelle epoche successive [The work of the Holy Spirit in the first centuries of the Church and in subsequent times].

(*XIII – povertà di S. Francisco* [the thirteenth century – poverty of St Francis].)

Until our times.

(Examples: the world youth days and others.)

The Holy Spirit *cambia la storia* [changes history]?

Yes. Through Vatican II.

To renew the face of the earth, the Church makes an examination of conscience.

The entire process of renewal was begun by John XXIII, who called for a Council.

(Vietnam.)

Paul VI
La Chiesa ha bisogno della sempre nuova Pentecoste
[The Church needs an always renewed Pentecost].

The Way of the Cross; (Angelus); Litany of the Saints; Reading and writing texts; Vespers

1 See John 20:22.
2 See Psalm 103 (104):30.

Talk/Meditation 20:

Ecce Mater tua [Behold, your Mother].[1]

Il modello della Chiesa [The model for the Church].

(*'Notte oscura' della nostra epoca* [the 'dark night' of our times].)

Card. Ratzinger, von Balthasar

(1) Annunciation (incarnation).
Maria – Chiesa [Mary – Church] (*L[umen] G[entium]* VIII).

(2) *Beata es, quia credidisti* [Blessed is she who believed].[2]
Chiesa – comunità dei credenti [Church – community of the faithful].

(3) *Stabat Mater iuxta Crucem* [The Mother stood by the Cross].[3]
(Experience).
Servire (Stella dell'evangelizzazione) [to serve (the Star of evangelisation)].
(Cana of Galilee.)

'*Ecce filius Tuus*' ['Behold, Your son'].[4]

Accepit Eam in sua [Took Her to his own].[5]

('*Maria mi ha liberato*' ['Mary has liberated me'].)

Experiences.

(R[edemptoris] M[ater])

Anticipated Matins

Talk/Meditation (21):

Nunc et in hora mortis nostrae [Now and at the hour of our death].

Anzianità, infermità, morte [Old age, illness, death].

(*Anzianità nella Scrittura* [Old age in Scripture].)

s. Paulus: 'reposita est mihi corona iustitiae' [St Paul: 'there is laid up for me the crown of righteousness'][6] [illegible].

(the meaning of diseases) human body.

Strong in Christ's cross.

1 See John 19:27.
2 See Luke 1:45.
3 See John 19:25.
4 See John 19:26.
5 See John 19:27.
6 See 2 Timothy 4:8.

giovedì **10** ottobre

s. Daniele martire

Thursday Donnerstag Jeudi October Oktober Octobre

ЧЕТВЕРТ Jueves الخميس ОКТЯЪРЬ Octubre أكتوبر

aby zachować oblicze ziemi, Kościół stoi
[illegible] sumień

a cały proces odnowy zapoczątkowany przez Jana XXIII zwołaniem Soboru
[Wietnam]

Paolo VI
[La Chiesa ha bisogno della sempre nuova Pentecoste]

10. Via Crucis

11 (Angelus) Lot 55-[illegible]

12 [Loquuntur et scribuntur testo]

13 Vesp.

14 Conf. Medit. XX

Ecce Mater tua
Il modello della Chiesa

[J. Ratzinger
v. Balthasar]

[il 'notte oscuro' della nostra epoca]

1) Zwiastowanie (Ant. [illegible])
Maria – Chiesa (LG, VIII)

2) Beata es, quia credidisti
Chiesa –
[comunità dei credenti]

3) Stabat Mater iuxta Crucem

[doświadczenie]
servire – (stella della evangelizzazione)
[Cana Gal.]

M	G	V	S	D	L	M	M	G	V	S	D	L	M	M	G
16	17	18	19	20	21	22	23	24	25	26	27	28	29	30	31

Ave Crux [Hail to the Cross] on which the redemption of the world was achieved.

ai Tuoi fedeli 'vita mutatur non tollitur' [to Your faithful: 'life is changed but not taken away'].

Christus vivebat [Christ lived] *per la 'sua ora'* [for 'his hour'].

(P. J. Lagrange: *Gerusalemme, Gerusalemme* [Jerusalem, Jerusalem].)

Paul VI's Testament.

Rosary (II); Chaplet of the Five Wounds of Christ; Adoration of the Blessed Sacrament; Concluding meditation; Compline

18 March

Morning prayers; Adoration of the Blessed Sacrament; Prayer for the gifts of the Holy Spirit; Litany of the Polish Nation; Lauds; Morning meditation; Holy Mass; Thanksgiving; Prayers; Terce; Sext; None

Concluding talk (Meditation 22):

La Gioia della speranza [The joy of hope].

Sul cammino di Emmaus [On the road to Emmaus].

'*La pace sia con voi*' ['Peace be with you'].[1]

Sadness will change into joy.

Dalla genealogia di Gesù [From the genealogy of Jesus].

fino all'Apocalisse [to the Apocalypse].

'*coelum novum et terra nova*' ['a new heaven and a new earth'].[2]

(Conclusion) (*Apostoli con Maria Madre di Gesù* [Apostles with Mary, Mother of Jesus])

Eschatology.

Jesus will come for the Judgement.

Hope of eternal life.

'*Confirmata est super nos misericordia Tua*' ['For great is Your steadfast mercy towards us'].[3]

AMDG
UIOGD[4]

1 See Luke 24:36.
2 See Revelation 21:1.
3 See Psalm 116 (117):2.
4 See p. xxi.

4–10 March 2001
Exercitia Spiritualia [Spiritual Exercises] Led by Cardinal [Francis Eugene] George [OMI][1]

~

4 March Lenten Lamentations;[2] Exposition of the Blessed Sacrament; Vespers

Talk 1. Introductory meditation: '*Venite seorsum*' ['Come away by yourselves'].[3]

Adoration of the Blessed Sacrament; Morning meditation; Compline

5 March Prayers; Adoration of the Blessed Sacrament; Prayer to the Holy Spirit; Litany of the Polish Nation; Morning meditation; Holy Mass; Thanksgiving; Lauds

Talk 2: '*Conversione e distacco*' ['Conversion and separation'].
('We have left all we had . . .'[4]
reflection.)

Passion of Our Lord Jesus Christ according to Matthew; Terce

Talk 3: '*Conversione e perdono di Dio*' ['Conversion and God's forgiveness'].
('Your sins are forgiven . . .
go, and do not sin again.')[5]

Reflection after the talk; Sext; None; The Way of the Cross; Litany of the Saints; Reading; (Daily) [prayers]; Vespers

Talk 4: *Il pentimento e il santo realismo* [Penance and holy realism].
Lk. 14
↓
we are redeemed

---

1 Francis Eugene George OMI (1937–2015) was an American priest and cardinal. He served as Bishop of Yakima (1990–96), Archbishop of Portland, Oregon (1996–97) and Archbishop of Chicago (1997–2014).
2 See n. 6, p. 221 [11 March 1984].
3 See Mark 6:31.
4 See Luke 18:28.
5 See Luke 7:48 and John 8:11.

and all that is related to this –

Africa, Asia (*status naturae lapsae et redemptae* [the state of lapsed and redeemed nature].)

salvezza universale [universal salvation].

Anticipated Matins; Rosary (I)

Talk 5: *Perdono reciproco e solidarietà* [Mutual forgiveness and solidarity].

Lk. 15 (the Prodigal Son).

(*Peccato – separazione* [sin – separation]) – (*perdono – solidarietà* [forgiveness – solidarity]).

The experience of the World Youth Day: *giovani – anziani* [the young – the old].

Adoration of the Blessed Sacrament; Concluding meditation; Compline

6 March

Morning prayers; Adoration of the Blessed Sacrament; Prayer for the seven gifts of the Holy Spirit; Litany of the Polish Nation; Holy Mass; Thanksgiving; Lauds; Daily prayers; Litanies

Talk [6]: *Libertà* [Freedom].

Libertà che viene dal pentimento [Freedom that comes from penance].

(Lk. 19) Zacchaeus!

Passion of Our Lord Jesus Christ according to Mark; Terce

Talk 7:

Libertà di perdonare anche i nemici [Freedom to forgive even one's enemies].

(American experiences) (Lk. 6:27–36).

Sext; None; Reflection; The Way of the Cross; Prayers; Reading; Vespers

Talk 8:

'*Videbit omnis caro salutare Dei*' ['All flesh shall see the salvation of God'].[1]

(Lk. 13:29–30.)

Rahner and Vatican II: The Church is becoming a global Church.

1 See Luke 3:6.

(*Mondiale – non solo universale* [worldwide – not only universal].)

(Cardinal Suhard): '*humanismo planetario*' ['planetary humanism'].

'*Sacramento universale*' ['Universal sacrament'].

'*Recapitulari omnia in Christo*' ['To unite all things in Christ'].[1]

(de Lubac.)

(The process of globalisation.)

Anticipated Matins

Talk 9:

'*Omnis caro*' ['All flesh'][2] (Lk. 1) *Myst. Incarnationis* [The mystery of incarnation].

tocca tutto quello che è umano [it touches on everything that is human].

affinché uomo diventi Dio [so that man might become God].

'*ut in invisibilium amorem rapiamur*' ['that we are drawn to the love of things invisible'].[3]

Rosary (II); Adoration of the Blessed Sacrament; Concluding meditation; Compline

7 March Morning prayers; Adoration of the Blessed Sacrament; Prayer for the gifts of the Holy Spirit; Litany of the Polish Nation; Holy Mass; Thanksgiving; Daily prayers; Litanies; Lauds

Talk 10: *Potere liberatorio di Dio* [Liberating power of God].

Mysterium quae supera expectationi [Mystery that exceeds expectations] [illegible].

'*Nunc dimittis . . .*' ['Now let your servant depart . . .'][4]

. . . *L'eccesso di grazia* [The excess of grace].

Passion of Our Lord Jesus Christ according to Luke; Terce

Talk 11:

Il potere salvifico di Dio ci libera affinché possiamo essere noi Figli di Dio [God's power of salvation liberates us so that we may be Sons of God]:

1 See Ephesians 1:10.

2 See Luke 3:6.

3 See the Roman Missal, Preface I of the Nativity of the Lord.

4 See Luke 2:29.

– *nella propria identità personale* [in one's personal identity].
– *nella propria identità in Cristo* [in one's identity in Christ].

attraverso il dono dello Spirito S. [through the gift of the Holy Spirit],

'*nuova creazione*' ['new creation'].

Sext; None; The Way of the Cross; Reflection; Reading; (Daily) [prayers]; Vespers

Talk 12:

Il potere salvifico di Dio ci dona la libertà di ricevere e di dare [God's power of salvation gives us the freedom to receive and to give].

(The washing of feet.)

(Like children); the conversation with a young man, others.

Esperienza dei Santi [Experience of Saints].

Anticipated Matins

Talk 13:

'*La libertà di soffrire*' ['The freedom of suffering'] (Acts 21).

'for the name of Jesus . . .' (Continental synods).

Abbracciare la sofferenza [To accept suffering]: Mary/*Stabat Mater* [The (Sorrowful) Mother stood].[1]

Rosary (III); Concluding meditation; Compline

8 March Morning prayers; Adoration of the Blessed Sacrament; Prayer for the seven gifts of the Holy Spirit; Litany of the Polish Nation; Holy Mass; Thanksgiving; Daily prayers; Litanies; Lauds

Talk 14:

Comunione nella Parola di Dio. Ascolto di Cristo. Lc. . . . [Communion in the Word of God. Listening to Christ. Luke . . .]

(*Maria e Marta* [Mary and Martha].)

Guardini *Experientia Ecclesiale nostra* [Our Church experience].

una crisi della meditazione [a crisis of meditation].

incapacità dell'ascolto [inability to listen].

in quel senso siamo chiamati [in this sense, we are called].

Passion of Our Lord Jesus Christ according to John; Terce

1 See n. 1, p. 29 [3 September 1964].

Talk 15:

La comunione sacramentale [The sacramental communion].

Agire in Cristo [To act in Christ] (Lk. 22).

The words instituting the Eucharist.

Cons. pastorale [Pastoral consequences].

Sext; None; Reflection; Daily prayers; Reading; Vespers

Talk 16:

La comunione dinamica. La Chiesa pellegrina [The dynamic communion. The pilgrim Church] (Lk. 24).

(Emmaus.)

(*Popolo in cammino* [The people on the way].)

Anticipated Matins

Talk 17:

Gerusalemme celeste: la pace [Heavenly Jerusalem: peace].

Pregate per la pace di Gerusalemme [Pray for the peace of Jerusalem].[1]

(*Eterna comunione con Dio* [Eternal communion with God].)

La Chiesa dei Santi [The Church of Saints].

Rosary (I); Eucharistic Adoration; (Concluding reflection); Holy Hour; Compline

9 March: Feast of St Frances of Rome

Morning prayers; Eucharistic Adoration; Prayer for the gifts of the Holy Spirit; Litany of the Polish Nation
Holy Mass; Thanksgiving; Daily prayers; Litanies; Lauds

Talk 18: *Missione* [Missions].

La missione nella povertà e con potere [The mission in poverty and with power] (Lk. 9 . . .).

(*Sinodo per Africa* [Synod for Africa].)

(Charles Foucauld.)[2]

(*Movimento dei lavoratori cat. in America* [The Catholic Worker Movement in America].)

---

1 See Psalm 121 (122):6.

2 Bl. Charles de Foucauld (1858–1916) was a French priest living among the Tuareg in the Sahara in Algeria. He was assassinated outside the door of the fort he built for the protection of the Tuareg people, and is considered to be a martyr.

Potere della communio Sanctorum [The power of the communion of Saints].

BMV, della preghiera etc. . . . [Blessed Virgin Mary, of prayer, etc.].

Terce; Prayers for Good Friday

Talk 19:

La missione alle pecore perdute [The mission to all lost sheep] (Lk. . . .).

'*Ho ritrovato la pecora che si è perduta*' ['I have found the sheep which was lost'].[1]

'*Pecora perduta*' *(Lc.): trovare e salvare* . . . ['Lost sheep' (Lk.): to find and to save . . .].

(The experience from Chicago: homosexuality.)

(The bad and good thief.)

Synods: Africa.

Rosary; Chaplet of the Five Wounds of Christ; Sext; None; The Way of the Cross; (Reading); Vespers

Talk 20:

'*Confirma fratres*' ['Strengthen your brothers'] (Lk. 22 . . .).

(*Synodi continentales* [Continental synods]: America, Asia).

Peter– *ministero petrino* [the Petrine ministry].

– *successori di Pietro* [Peter's successors].

Transfiguration of Jesus – Gethsemane.

Confirma – con la sua fede [Strengthen – with his faith].

Vatican II.

Anticipated Matins

Talk 21:

'*La missione nello Spirito S.*' ['The mission in the Holy Spirit'] (Lk. 24).

Synodi continentales [Continental synods].

(The Acts of the Apostles.)

allo Spir. S. [in the Holy Spirit].

Fedeltà: 'lasciarsi guidare' [Faithfulness: 'to let oneself be guided'].

1 See Luke 15:6.

domenica **20** ottobre

s. Irene

Sunday Sonntag Dimanche
Воскресенье Domingo الأحد

October Oktober Octobre
Октябрь Octubre أكتوبر

8. Sexta Hora
9. Refl. Preces consuetae.
Lectura
10. Vesp.
11 Conf. XIV
La comunione dynamica. La chiesa pellegrina. (Lk 24)
(Emmaus!
Popolo in cammino)
12. Matut. anticipatum
13. Conf. XV:
Jerusalemme celeste: la pace
(Pregate per la pace di Gerusalemme
eterna
communione con Dio)
La Chiesa dei Santi
14. Con Ros. [illegible]
15 Ador. Euch.
Verbal. meditat.)
16. Sessione [illegible]
17 Compl.

M	G	V	S	D	L	M	M	G	V	S	D	L	M	M	G
16	17	18	19	20	21	22	23	24	25	26	27	28	29	30	31

'Pater pauperum – Dator munerum – Lumen cordium . . .' ['Father of the poor – Giver of gifts – Light of the hearts . . .'].[1]

Vita sec. Spiritum [Life according to the Spirit].

Eucharistic Adoration; Rosary (II); Concluding meditation; Compline

10 March

Morning prayers; Eucharistic Adoration; Prayer for the gifts of the Holy Spirit; Litany of the Polish Nation; Holy Mass; Thanksgiving; Daily prayers; Litanies; Lauds

Talk 22:

'Magnificat': *Sacra Conversazione* [Sacred Conversation] (Lk. 1).

'Magnalia Dei' ['The mighty works of God'].[2]

– *gioire in Dio suo Salvatore* [to rejoice in God, her Saviour].

–*canto della Chiesa* [the song of the Church].

L[umen] G[entium]

Ringraziamento [Thanksgiving]
AMDG[3]
UIOGD: *ut in omnibus glorificetur Deus* [that in all things God may be glorified]

1 See the hymn *Veni Sancte Spiritus* (Come, Holy Spirit).
2 See Acts 2:11.
3 See p. xxi.

17–23 February 2002
Exercitia [Exercises]
Led by Cardinal [Cláudio] Hummes OFM[1]

17 February 6.00 p.m.: Lenten Lamentations;[2] Exposition of the Blessed Sacrament; Vespers II: Vespers for the First Sunday of Lent
Introductory meditation (1):
'*Convertirsi all'unico necessario*' ['To convert to the one thing that is necessary'].[3]
Adoration of the Blessed Sacrament; Meditation continued; Anticipated Matins; Compline

18 March Prayers; Angelus; Adoration of the Blessed Sacrament; Litany of the Polish Nation; Holy Mass; Thanksgiving; Daily prayers; Lauds
Talk–Meditation 2
(Passion of our Lord Jesus Christ according to Matthew); Terce; Sext; None; Reading; The Way of the Cross; Litanies as usual: Holy Name of Jesus, Blessed Virgin Mary, St Joseph; Litany of the Saints
Talk–Meditation 3
Vespers
Talk–Meditation 4
Anticipated Matins
Talk–Meditation 5
Adoration of the Blessed Sacrament; Rosary (I); Concluding meditation; Compline

19 February Prayers; Angelus; Adoration of the Blessed Sacrament; Litany of the Polish Nation; Holy Mass; Thanksgiving; Daily prayers; Lauds
Talk–Meditation (6) (handout)
Passion of Christ according to Mark; Terce
Talk–Meditation 7
Sext; None; The Way of the Cross; Litany of the Sacred Heart of Jesus, Blessed Virgin Mary, St Joseph
Reading: (Testament)
Penitential psalms; Vespers
Talk–Meditation (8)
Anticipated Matins
Talk–Meditation (9)
Rosary; Adoration of the Blessed Sacrament; Concluding meditation; Compline

---

1 Cláudio Hummes OFM (b. 1934) is a Brazilian cardinal. He served as Archbishop of Fortaleza (1996–98), Archbishop of São Paulo (1998–2006) and Prefect of the Congregation for the Clergy in the Roman Curia (2006–10).

2 See n. 6, p. 221 [11 March 1984].

3 See Luke 10:42.

venerdì **25** ottobre

s. Crispino

Friday Freitag Vendredi
пятница Viernes الجمعة

October Oktober Octo
октябрь Octubre

Exercitia r. 2002 17.–23. II
Card. Hummes OFM

17. II. h. 18

1. Gorzkie żale
8 2. Expositio SS-mi
9 3. Vesp. I: Nieszpory I. niedz. W. Postu
10 4. Medit. introductiva „Convertirsi all'unico necessario"
11 5. Ador. SS-mi
6. Medit. [illegible]
12 7. Matut. anticipatum
13 8. Compl.

14

15 18. II.

1. Preces. Angelus. Ador. SS-mi.
16 Lit. [illegible]
17 2. Sacrum. Grat-actio. Preces [illegible]
18 3. Laudes
19 4. Cont. I Medit. / Passio DNJChr sec. Matth.
5. Tertia
6. Sexta [illegible]
7. Lectura !

43 s.w. | M M G V S D L M M G V S D L M | 4 5 6 7 8 9 10 11 12 13 14 15 | 298-6

20 February

Prayers; Angelus; Adoration of the Blessed Sacrament; Litany of the Polish Nation; Holy Mass; Thanksgiving; Daily prayers; Lauds
Talk–Meditation (10) (handout)
Passion according to Luke; Terce
Talk–Meditation (11) (handout); Talk–Meditation (handout)
Sext; None; The Way of the Cross (Paul VI); Litanies: Holy Name of Jesus, Blessed Virgin Mary, St Joseph
Reading in relation to the Testament
Litany of the Saints; Vespers
Talk–Meditation 12 (handout)
Anticipated Matins
Talk–Meditation 13
Rosary; Adoration of the Blessed Sacrament; Concluding meditation; Compline

21 February: Feast of St Peter Damian

Prayers; Angelus; Adoration of the Blessed Sacrament; Litany of the Polish Nation; Holy Mass; Thanksgiving; Daily prayers; Lauds
Talk–Meditation 14 (handout)
Terce
Talk–Meditation (15) (handout)
Passion according to John; Sext; None; Litanies (Thursday); Penitential psalms; Reading
The president of Syria[1]
Vespers
Talk–Meditation (16)
Anticipated Matins
Talk–Meditation (17)
Rosary (I); Adoration of the Blessed Sacrament; Holy Hour; Compline

22 February: Feast of the Chair of St Peter

Prayers; (Angelus); Adoration of the Blessed Sacrament; Litany of the Polish Nation; Holy Mass; Thanksgiving; Daily prayers; Lauds
Talk–Meditation (18)
Terce
Talk–Meditation (19)
Sext; None; The Way of the Cross; (Litany of the Saints); Litanies: Sacred Heart of Jesus, Blessed Virgin Mary, St Joseph; Rosary (II); Daily prayers
Reading; Putting things in order
Litany of the Saints; Vespers
Talk–Meditation (20)
Anticipated Matins
Talk–Meditation (21)
Rosary (I); Adoration of the Blessed Sacrament; (Concluding meditation?); Compline

23 February: Feast of St Polycarp

Prayers; Angelus; Adoration of the Blessed Sacrament; Litany of the Polish Nation; Holy Mass; Thanksgiving; Prayers; Lauds

---

1 John Paul II met the President of Syria, Bashar al-Assad, in Damascus in May 2001, during his pilgrimage in the footsteps of St Paul, and Assad returned the visit to the Vatican in February 2002.

Talk–Meditation (22)
AMDG
UIOGD[1]

1 See p. xxi.

9–15 March 2003
Exercitia Spiritualia [Spiritual Exercises] [Led by Bishop Angelo Comastri][1]

9 March 6.00 p.m. Lenten Lamentations;[2] Exposition of the Blessed Sacrament; Vespers II for the First Sunday of Lent

Introduzione [Introduction] (1):

'*Il tempo è compiuto*' ['The time is fulfilled'].[3]

Adoration of the Blessed Sacrament; Meditation continued; Anticipated Matins; Compline

10 March Morning prayers; Angelus; Litany of the Polish Nation; Holy Mass; Daily prayers; Lauds
Talk 2
Passion of our Lord Jesus Christ according to Matthew; Terce; Sext; None; Reading; Litany of the Holy Name of Jesus, Blessed Virgin Mary, St Joseph
Talk 3
The Way of the Cross; Reading; Litany of the Saints; Vespers
Talk 4
Anticipated Matins; Compline

11 March Morning prayers; Angelus; Litany of the Polish Nation; Holy Mass; Daily prayers; Lauds

Talk 5. Meditation:

(*Dio lentamente scopre il suo volto. Egli è misericordia* [God slowly reveals his face. He is mercy].)

Passion of Our Lord Jesus Christ according to Mark; Terce

Talk 6:

(*Ma l'uomo è infedele e Dio si riveste misericordioso e fedele* [But man is unfaithful, and God is clothed in mercy and faithfulness].)

---

1 Angelo Comastri (b. 1943) is an Italian priest and cardinal. He is the current President of the Fabric of Saint Peter, Archpriest of St. Peter's Basilica and Vicar General for the Vatican City State. He served as Bishop of Massa Marittima-Piombino (1990–94) and Territorial Prelate of Loreto (1996–2005).

2 See n. 6, p.221 [11 March 1984].

3 See Mark 1:15.

Sext; None; The Way of the Cross; Reading; Penitential psalms; Vespers

Meditation. Talk 7:
('*Dio si specchia nell'infelice matrimonio di Osea*' ['God is reflected in the unhappy marriage of Hosea'].)

Anticipated Matins

Talk (8). Meditation:
'*Fedeltà e infedeltà fino a quando?*' '*Geremia annuncia una sorprendente decisione di Dio*' ['Faithfulness and unfaithfulness until when?' 'Jeremiah announces God's surprising decision'].[1]

12 March Morning prayers; *Angelus*; Litanies: Holy Name of Jesus, Blessed Virgin Mary, St Joseph; Litany of the Polish Nation; Holy Mass; Daily prayers; Lauds

Talk (9). Meditation:
('*Ezechiele spinge lontano lo sguardo: Vi darò il mio Spirito*' ['Ezekiel looks far: I will give you my Spirit'].)[2]

Passion of our Lord Jesus Christ according to Luke; Terce

Talk (10). Meditation:
('*Gesù è l'ultima Parola di Dio, perché è la prima Parola di Dio*' ['Jesus is the last Word of God because He is the first Word of God'].)

Sext; None; The Way of the Cross; Reading; Litany of the Saints; Vespers

Meditation 11:
Gesù: tre meravigliose parabole [Jesus: three wonderful parables].

Meditation 12:
The parable of the prodigal son.

Anticipated Matins; Adoration of the Blessed Sacrament; Rosary; Concluding meditation; Compline

13 March Morning prayers; Angelus; Litany of the Sacred Heart of Jesus, Blessed Virgin Mary, St Joseph; Holy Mass; Litany of the Polish Nation; Daily prayers; Lauds

Talk 13. Meditation:
('*Andiamo a Betlemme per seguire i passi del Figlio di Dio fatto*

1 See Jeremiah 31:31–34.
2 See Ezekiel 36:26.

Uomo' ['Let us go to Bethlehem to follow in the steps of the Son of God who became Man'].)

Terce

Talk 14. Meditation:
'*Che cosa è il Natale? Quale volto di Dio si rivela?*' ['What is Christmas? What face of God does it reveal?']

Sext; None; Passion of Our Lord Jesus Christ according to John; Reading; Vespers; Penitential psalms

Talk 15. Meditation:
('*È giunta l'ora! Che cosa è l'ora di Cristo?*' ['The hour has come! What is the hour of Christ?'].)[1]

Anticipated Matins; (Holy Hour)

Talk 16. Meditation:

Holy Hour, Compline

('*L'ora di Gesù – la risposta ai pellegrini greci – e lavanda dei piedi*' ['The Hour of Jesus – the response to the Greek pilgrims – and the washing of feet'].)[2]

14 March

Morning prayers; Litany of the Sacred Heart of Jesus, Blessed Virgin Mary, St Joseph; Adoration; Litany of the Polish Nation; Holy Mass; Thanksgiving; Lauds

Talk (17). Meditation:
'*L'ora di Gesù nelle vite dei Santi . . . S. Stef., Paolo, Francesco, Teresa de Lisieux, Maria Goretti, Massimilian Kolbe, Teresa Benedetta della Croce (Edith Stein)*' ['The hour of Jesus in the lives of Saints . . . Ss Stephen, Paul, Francis, Thérèse of Lisieux, Maria Goretti, Maksymilian Kolbe, Teresa Benedicta of the Cross (Edith Stein)'].

Sext; None; Angelus; The Way of the Cross; Reading; Vespers

Talk (18)/Meditation:
'*Il Sacramento dell'amore e il comando dell'amore*' ['The sacrament of love and the commandment of love'].

Anticipated Matins

1 See Mark 14:41.
2 See John 12:20–23 and John 13:3–20.

Talk (19). Meditation:

'*Maria ai piedi della Croce*' ['Mary at the foot of the Cross'].

Concluding meditation; Compline

15 March

Morning prayers; Litany of the Holy Name of Jesus, Blessed Virgin Mary, St Joseph; Litany of the Polish Nation
Holy Mass; Thanksgiving; Daily prayers; Lauds

Talk (20). Concluding meditation:

'*Giona, ossia la paura di annunciare l'amore di Dio*' ['Jonah, or the fear of preaching the love of God'].

Predicator. singol. [Great preacher].

Terce; Sext; None

(The retreat ends here.)
AMDG
UIOGD[1]
Deo Gratias [Thanks be to God].

1 See p. xxi.

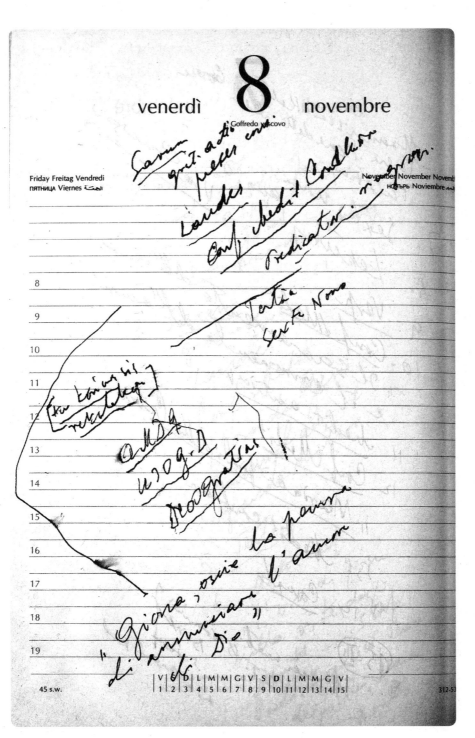

venerdì **8** novembre

Goffredo vescovo

Friday Freitag Vendredi
пятница Viernes الجمعة

November November November
ноябрь Noviembre

Laudes

Predicatori

Tertia
Sexta Nona

8

9

10

11

12

13

14

15

16

17

18

19

"Giona, ossia la paura
di annunciare l'amore
di Dio"

V	S	D	L	M	M	G	V	S	D	L	M	M	G	V
1	2	3	4	5	6	7	8	9	10	11	12	13	14	15